LAND AND LEGAL TEXTS IN THE EARLY MODERN OTTOMAN EMPIRE

The Ottoman Empire and the World

Published in association with the British Institute at Ankara

BIAA | BRITISH INSTITUTE AT ANKARA

Understanding Turkey and the Black Sea

The Ottoman Empire sat at the crux between Asia, Africa and Europe and connected systems of trade, politics and culture across continents. It also contained diverse worlds within it through the many peoples, languages and religions its imperial frame encompassed. These worlds of the Ottoman Empire informed the expanding horizons of the early modern period through both its internal dynamics and far-flung interactions.

This series situates the Ottoman Empire in this early modern world it inhabited by publishing books that take a fresh look at the interactions between politics, society and culture within the empire and beyond, between its establishment in the fourteenth century and the first decades of the nineteenth. During these centuries of immense change, the Ottomans expanded, consolidated and transformed an empire of great human and ecological diversity which occupied a central role in global history, the effects of which can still be felt today. The series welcomes work which transcends the traditional boundaries between approaches, including those between political history, gender studies, social history, Islamic studies, environmental history and literary studies to understand how the empire worked and how it fit in a wider world.

The series is published by I.B. Tauris in conjunction with the British Institute at Ankara (BIAA). The BIAA is internationally renowned for its support of new independent academic research in the region across various fields, including archaeology, ancient and modern history, heritage management, social sciences and contemporary issues in public policy and political sciences.

Series editor
Christopher Markiewicz, University of Birmingham, UK

Advisors
Amila Buturović, York University, Canada
Emine Fetvacı, Boston College, USA
Joshua M. White, University of Virginia, USA
Stefan Winter, The Université du Québec à Montréal, Canada and Koç University, Turkey

LAND AND LEGAL TEXTS IN THE EARLY MODERN OTTOMAN EMPIRE

Harmonization, Property Rights and Sovereignty

Malissa Taylor

I.B.TAURIS
LONDON • NEW YORK • OXFORD • NEW DELHI • SYDNEY

I.B. TAURIS
Bloomsbury Publishing Plc, 50 Bedford Square, London, WC1B 3DP, UK
Bloomsbury Publishing Inc, 1385 Broadway, New York, NY 10018, USA
Bloomsbury Publishing Ireland, 29 Earlsfort Terrace, Dublin 2, D02 AY28, Ireland

BLOOMSBURY, I.B. TAURIS and the I.B. Tauris logo
are trademarks of Bloomsbury Publishing Plc

First published in Great Britain 2023
This paperback edition published in 2025

Cover design: Adriana Brioso
Cover image: The Great Abu Sa'ud Teaching Law, folio from a
Divan of Mahmud 'Abd-al Baqi. The Metropolitan Museum of Art (25.83.9.)

A catalogue record for this book is available from the British Library.

A catalog record for this book is available from the Library of Congress.

ISBN: HB: 978-0-7556-4768-2
PB: 978-0-7556-4772-9
ePDF: 978-0-7556-4769-9
eBook: 978-0-7556-4770-5

Series: The Ottoman Empire and the World

Typeset by Newgen KnowledgeWorks Pvt. Ltd., Chennai, India

For product safety related questions contact productsafety@bloomsbury.com.

To find out more about our authors and books visit www.bloomsbury.com
and sign up for our newsletters.

CONTENTS

Acknowledgements vii
Note on Transliteration ix
List of Abbreviations x

INTRODUCTION 1
Sources 5
Harmonization and sovereignty 7
Property: Bundles and layers 9

Chapter 1
LIFELONG *TASARRUF*, LAND TENURE PRACTICES, AND LAW OVER THE *LONGUE DURÉE* 11
Ottoman territories and varieties of tenure for the military class 13
Cultivator tenure and its legal systemization 16
Military fiscal change and land tenure 21
Land tenure rights trickle up 23
The old and the new 28

Chapter 2
CONQUERING A NEW TERRAIN: ESTABLISHING THE SULTAN'S LEGISLATIVE AUTHORITY 31
Texts and contexts 33
'Preserved in the *bayt al-mal*': Acquiring land for the treasury 34
'Neither tithe nor *kharaji*': The status of the land for transaction and tax 38
Building a coherent law 43
Conclusion 47

Chapter 3
CANONICAL VOICES: DISCRETION AND ANALOGY IN THE FORMATION OF THE HARMONY TRADITION OF LAND TENURE 49
Contexts of the text 51
Pir Mehmed and sultanic latitude 54
The formation of a tradition: Deferential and not so deferential interpretation 60
Conclusion 66

Chapter 4
'THE BOOKS OF *FIQH*': THE *KANUNNAME OF CANDIA* AND THE CONSOLIDATION OF A NEW DOCTRINE IN HANAFI ACADEMIC TEXTS 69
Harmony at a crossroads 71
The *Kanunname of Candia* as critique: Reinstituting the Hanafism of the 'books' 74
The sultan as legislator: Texts, commentaries and fatwas 78
The change in doctrine: The sultan has a choice 81
Conclusion 85

Chapter 5
THE AGE OF THE *MUTASARRIFS*: DIFFUSION, RIGHTS AND DISCRETION IN THE EIGHTEENTH CENTURY 87
Background 89
Convergence 91
Expansive transactions: Permission and analogism 97
Conclusion 101

Chapter 6
FROM HARMONY TO UNIFORMITY: DEFENSIVE SOVEREIGNTY AND THE OTTOMAN NINETEENTH-CENTURY REFORMS 103
Miri Tasarruf: Stability in a sea of change 107
Creating a normal subject 111
Codifying Islamic law 113
Defending Islam: From 'built on the *kanun*' to 'built on the *fiqh*' 118
Conclusion 121

CONCLUSION 123

Notes 129
Selected Bibliography 181
Index 197

ACKNOWLEDGEMENTS

This book grew out of a fascination with a particular text and my curiosity about its story: why was it produced, for whom and how did it impact legal practice in the Ottoman Empire? I could hardly have asked this question, much less familiarized myself with the text, if not for the support of a variety of mentors, colleagues, friends and institutions. I have been fortunate to have studied with inspirational teachers throughout my long career as a student, beginning with my instructors at St Francis. It was there that Michael Radow first instilled in me a love of history and encouraged my curiosity about the Middle East, for which I warmly thank him. At Princeton University, the American University in Cairo and later at NYU, I had the opportunity to learn from faculty who had not only mastered their respective subjects, but were also generous with their time and infectious in their enthusiasm. I owe them – Jerry Clinton, Haleh Esfandiari, Margaret Larkin, Andras Hamori, Shaun Marmon, Molly Greene, Heath Lowry, Elizabeth Sartain, Ariel Salzmann, Zachary Lockman, Khalid Fahmy and Shiva Balaghi – a tremendous debt of gratitude. Finally, it was at the University of California Berkeley that I received the training that helped me find my way to this book from Beshara Doumani, Leslie Peirce, Saba Mahmood, Carla Hesse, Thomas Dandelet and Thomas R. Brady, Jr.

I received funding from a Fulbright Hayes DDRA grant and Council of American Overseas Research Center multi-country research grant to pursue my dissertation research. The Massachusetts Society of Professors provided me with additional support to make two short research trips to Turkey while I was writing the manuscript. As a general matter, I am extremely grateful for the public assistance I have received to pursue my language training and research; it is the taxpayer-supported programmes like FLAS, Fulbright and the Center for Arabic Study Abroad that made it possible for someone like me – impecunious and lacking in any Middle Eastern background – to enter this field. I also thank the many private institutions that provided for my education and training. Studying at Princeton University did much to set me on this path, and I could never have attended that remarkable school if not for its commitment to geographical diversity and needs-blind admission. Without such extensive financial support, people like me could never hope to write books like this one.

In Turkey, I would particularly like to thank the staff of the Süleymaniye Library, who provided me with any help I required and also with hot tea on cold days. I am also indebted to the American Research Institute in Turkey for providing a home base to my studies in Turkey and giving me so many opportunities to meet with and learn from accomplished scholars. Foremost among the colleagues I befriended there was Linda Darling, to whom I am eternally grateful for her incredible generosity and sharp intellect. She supported the writing of this book at every step and the manuscript benefited immensely from her insightful comments. Other colleagues I met in Turkey influenced and energized me, in particular Lale Can, Fariba Zarinebaf, Victoria Holbrook, Denwood Holmes, Deniz Gürgen, Mostafa Minawi and Radha Dalal. They made my years of research a rich and stimulating experience, and I am grateful for the hours and conversations we shared.

Additionally, there are many other people to thank for their contributions to this book. I am especially indebted to Hasan Karataş, who repeatedly provided logistical support that was crucial for bringing this project to fruition. I can never thank him enough. I would also like to thank a number of other scholars and friends for reading and commenting on parts of the manuscript at various stages: Baki Tezcan, Boğaç Ergene, Amy Singer, Amir Toft, Lale Can, Amos Nadan and Faiz Ahmed. I profited greatly from their comments, and thank them for taking the time to share their expertise with me. This is not to say that they bear responsibility for any faults found in this book; these are, of course, mine alone.

Finally, I would like to thank my family and friends for their support in what has been a very long and arduous journey. Those who have sacrificed most so that this book could be written are Andrew, Jackie, Emmy and Paul Ralston. I thank them for their patience while I poured so much of my time and attention into this project. They have enriched my life beyond words and deserve far more gratitude than I could express in these few lines of text. The constant encouragement of Bathabile Mthombeni, Sarah and Kristen Reifsteck, Silvia Ruzanka and Rebecca Starks was an invaluable source of support for me. Finally, to my parents and sister: you have seen me through, again. Thank you.

NOTE ON TRANSLITERATION

Arabic names, terms and titles of works in the body of the text and footnotes are translated according to a modified version of IJMES rules: no macrons or diacritics are included except for *'ayn* (') and medial and final *hamza* ('). Ottoman Turkish transliteration will follow modern Turkish orthography, but will also denote *'ayn* (') and medial and final *hamza* ('). When transliterating a specific passage in its entirety, Arabic is fully transliterated according to the IJMES rules for Arabic transliteration, and Ottoman Turkish is transliterated according to the IJMES rules for Ottoman Turkish. In the bibliography and footnotes, citations of names and titles of works in Arabic or Ottoman Turkish are also fully transliterated according to IJMES style. When I am discussing a transaction or concept without reference to a specific passage, and the word is shared between Ottoman Turkish and Arabic, I typically use the Arabic style of transliteration if the term is of Arabic origin. In particular, terms that are commonly used in Islamic jurisprudence and are broadly shared in both the Arabic and Ottoman Turkish texts will be transliterated according to the IJMES rules for Arabic. That is, *kharaj*, rather than *harac*, and Zayd rather than Zeyd.

There are some exceptions for words with Arabic origins but which are primarily associated with Ottoman administrative practice. These words will be translated in the form familiar to Ottomanists, such as *avarız*, *hüccet*, *me'mur* and *kanun*. There are a few words that are arguably more 'Islamic legal' than 'Ottoman administrative' that I nevertheless chose to render according to the transliteration rules for Turkish, like *mu'accele* and *mü'eccele*. The motive for this was practical: their spelling in Arabic transliteration is so similar that it risks confusing the non-specialist reader. Terms familiar to a general readership are not italicized, hence sharia and fatwa will not appear in italics, but *kanun* will. Place names will be given as they are commonly known and spelled in English rather than transliterated, unless there is no commonly used English name. Hence, the Ottoman capital is Istanbul rather than İstanbul.

ABBREVIATIONS

AH	Hijri
BOA	Başbakanlık Osmanlı Arşivi
BSOAS	*Bulletin of the School of Oriental and African Studies*
EI²	*Encyclopaedia of Islam. New Edition.*
ICAS	Islamic College Press London
IJMES	*International Journal of Middle East Studies*
IREMAM	The Institute of Research and Study on the Arab and Muslim Worlds
IU	İstanbul Üniversitesi Nadir Eserler Kütüphanesi
JESHO	*Journal of the Economic and Social History of the Orient*
JOTSA	*Journal of the Ottoman and Turkish Studies Association*
MAD	Maliye'den Müdevver Defterler
MTM	'Osmanlı kanunnameleri', Milli Tetebbular Mecmuası i/I-2, Istanbul, Matba'a-i 'Amire, 1331/1903
PDL	Princeton University Digital Library
PUSC	Princeton University Special Collections
SYK	Süleymaniye Yazma Eserler Kütüphanesi
TDVİA	*Türkiye Diyanet Vakfı İslām Ansiklopedisi*
TT	Tapu Tahrir Defterleri
ZAL	al-Maktaba al-Waṭaniyya al-Sūriya Asadiyya, Ẓāhiriyya collection

INTRODUCTION

In the early twentieth century, the renowned Ottoman historian M. Fuad Köprülü created a new journal dedicated to printing important historical documents relating to the empire's history.[1] The first issue of this journal, *Milli Tettebular Mecmuası*, published a land law text known as the *Kanun-ı Cedid-i Osmani*. This text had been assembled sometime between 1084 H/1673 CE and 1129 H/1717 CE and is composed entirely of pieces of earlier texts, most of which date between 1540 CE and 1655 CE.[2] The editors of *Milli Tettebular Mecmuası* selected one among the dozens of extant copies of this text for publication in 1913.[3] It was no accident that this text appeared in the journal's original issue, for its historical significance was indisputable. As a text that had been assembled in the late seventeenth or early eighteenth century, it was a step towards answering a question, perhaps *the* question, hanging over Ottoman historians throughout the twentieth century: how had the relationship between land, law and sovereignty evolved from the sixteenth century to their own time? How had the empire passed from the nearly mythic age of the sixteenth century to the self-consciously modernizing age of the nineteenth century? In this book, I will argue that the text of the *Kanun-ı Cedid-i Osmani* does indeed provide some answers to this question – still the central question of Ottoman history – and that these answers challenge what we think we know about the empire's passage into the modern age.

Historians have long viewed land tenure and the law governing it as the core of Ottoman history. Many of the most famous twentieth-century Ottoman historians, such as Halil Inalcik and Ömer Lütfi Barkan, wrote copiously about land tenure law.[4] The Ottomans, their foreign contemporaries in Europe and later generations of historians have all viewed the land tenure system and its law as key to understanding the successes of the Ottoman polity and the nature of the empire itself. As an agrarian empire, usage of land and its revenues became a staple topic in the political literature produced by the Ottoman elite, for the rules of land tenure touched everything: the livelihood of the vast majority of subjects, the provisioning of the army and the solvency of the treasury. Even in towns, reliance on the hinterland for provisioning meant that the fate of the urban population was inextricably intertwined with that of the rural. Although the circumstances of the empire changed considerably over the course of the early modern period, its agrarian nature did not; codifying land tenure law was a key element of the modernizing reform programme known as the Tanzimat in the mid-nineteenth century. Even at the time of the empire's dissolution in the twentieth century, the population was overwhelmingly rural, and the economy remained tied to agriculture.

Despite this acknowledged centrality, studies squarely focused on the land tenure law for the seventeenth and eighteenth centuries are few in number. Most scholarly attention has been reserved for the two well-known 'bookends' of land tenure law: the reign of Süleyman I (r. 1520–66) and the 1858 Land Code; in both periods, the characterization of the land law has been treated as a microcosm for the political order as a whole. The first period was long considered the peak of a 'classical' age. The sixteenth-century land tenure system and its associated political and economic relations are the basis for most of the heuristic models that scholars have used to describe the Ottoman Empire, all of which emphasize the immense power of the sultan and the tenuous position of his subjects.[5] Through law enacted on the sultan's authority and known as *kanun*, the land tenure law ensured the sultan's control over land and its revenues. The sultan's subjects enjoyed access to these at his pleasure, property rights were regarded as weak or even non-existent. Further cementing terms favourable to the sultan's legal control, *Şeyhülislam* (chief mufti) Ebu's-Su'ud Efendi (d. 1574) reconciled or harmonized *kanun* with the law of Islam, the sharia, by issuing fatwas defining the *kanun*'s practices according to the jurisprudence of the Hanafi *madhhab*, the empire's official school of Islamic law.[6] At the other temporal bookend, scholarship examining the 1858 Land Code has largely viewed this code as an attempt to cope with the existence of, or the modern need for, private property. The vast majority of these studies agree that privatization of the land – whether to the land itself or to the revenues – had considerably altered tenure relations by the eighteenth century.[7] For some, the code displayed legal continuity with the sixteenth-century *kanun* and represented an attempt of the state to either regain lost control over the land or to force de facto 'owners' of land towards a compromise by recognizing their control but specifying limits to these rights and new processes to enforce the limits.[8] For others, the code was a novel embrace of private property and represented either the influence of Western legal thought or a de jure capitulation to de facto realities.[9] However, given the small number of studies examining land law in the two centuries preceding the code, it can be difficult to judge either of these two claims of either continuity or rupture.

Taken together, these bookends present a problem: how do we understand the transition from a property-less sixteenth century to a nineteenth century where property in land was, apparently, ubiquitous? Until the late twentieth century, historians explained this transition through the imperial 'decline' narrative: the quality of the sultans declined and their excessive power could not be sustained; the institutions that had supported their power decayed and the *kanun* fell into abeyance while the ulema (Islamic scholars, particularly those who studied law) claimed legal authority for themselves and for *fiqh* (Islamic jurisprudence) as the law of the realm.[10] As a result, powerful individuals were able to seize control of land through corruption. However, this decline narrative no longer dominates the field. Instead, revisionist histories now maintain that the passing of the 'classical' regime was an ultimately salubrious transformation that created a new, more accommodating relationship between the Ottoman state and its subjects.[11] The breakdown of excessive state power, the marginalization of *kanun* and the land tenure system associated with it and the transition from property-less to propertied subjects were adaptations that contributed to the empire's longevity and dynamism in the early modern period.

The handful of recent studies on seventeenth- and eighteenth-century land tenure law do generally corroborate the revisionist narrative. These studies tend to conclude that land tenure law in these centuries increasingly embraced the idioms of property provided by *fiqh* and abandoned the more restricted usage rights that characterized the sixteenth-century *kanun*.[12] The most influential version of this story is the case made in the outstanding monograph of Martha Mundy and Richard Saumarez Smith, *Governing Property, Making the Modern State*.[13] Although the bulk of this work examines Greater Syria in the late nineteenth and early twentieth centuries, there is a brief but profoundly influential retelling of the broader narrative of Ottoman land law from the sixteenth to the nineteenth century. Positing a transition from a property regime defined primarily by 'office' in the sixteenth century to one later defined by right over property, or 'estate' by the eighteenth century, Mundy and Smith present nineteenth-century reforms as a product of an incremental and organic evolution towards stronger property rights. Whether proponents of decline or revisionism, most historians have stuck to a fairly stable storyline of property's role in early modern Ottoman transition: due to the demise of an old order where the sultan, aided by *kanun*, held the only meaningful property rights, a new regime of property for subjects arose, where *fiqh* rather than *kanun* was the dominant legal element.

Examining the evolution of the land tenure law from 1540 to 1858, this book will demonstrate how the history of the law tells a different story of the empire's passage from the sixteenth to the nineteenth century than the one sketched earlier in the text. Instead of a breakdown in 'classical' institutions and sovereign power following the age of Süleyman and the rise of a substantially new order thereafter, the land law presents a legal order birthed in the sixteenth century that became increasingly widespread, deeply rooted and influential to the empire over the next three centuries. In other words, it presents the reign of Süleyman not as the height of an old order, but the beginning of a new one. Oddly, given that the mid-sixteenth-century harmonization of the land law has long been identified as extremely significant, there has been little inquiry into its long-term impact on later centuries.

This work argues that the sixteenth-century 'harmonization' was not a finite resolution of a legal problem, but rather the beginning of a process initiating legal trends that would deeply impact both notions of property and legislative sovereignty. As has been long known, harmonization efforts in the age of Süleyman led to a systematic legal articulation of the property rights that belonged to the peasants farming lands claimed by the imperial treasury; but what were the consequences? First, the fashioning of these rights into a fairly standard entity – a bundle – was significant because it was part of a broader development in the expansion of property rights for a variety of Ottoman subjects. Chapter 1 demonstrates that two of the property-right bundles that historians have deemed so crucial for the empire's political economy in the eighteenth century – *ijaratayn* and *malikane* – directly mirrored the terms of the peasant bundle. While it has long been noted that these contracts provided greater security over land, buildings and revenues to an economically and socially privileged group of Ottoman subjects, what has not been realized is that they appear to have had a common prototype in the peasant's rights of lifelong possession. In the Ottoman Empire, property rights did not trickle down from a commercial or landed elite to subjects of more modest circumstances; they trickled *up* from the peasant cultivators to the more politically powerful classes. Tracing a widening trend of stronger property rights to the sixteenth century may seem counterintuitive to some, but it is what this book argues.

Second, harmonization mandated a standard definition of the rights granted to cultivators and military grant holders to be used across Ottoman legal and administrative texts. Eventually, these definitions would be integrated into scholastic texts of Hanafism as well. This diffusion took time; it would ultimately lead a larger number of Ottoman subjects to become recipients of the cultivator's rights bundle and to become legally subject to the law built to govern the bundle, but it took until the eighteenth and even the nineteenth century for a fairly uniform understanding of the law to be incorporated into legal texts from Bosnia to eastern Anatolia to Syria. Focusing on this dissemination, Chapters 3, 4 and 5 revise the notion that the changed military-fiscal circumstances of the seventeenth and eighteenth centuries must have meant either that the law enacted for the empire's treasury-owned land slid into irrelevance or was utterly transformed. On the contrary, it seems to have only settled firmly into Hanafi practice in this later period. Furthermore, these chapters also provide a counterpoint to the frequent depiction of this era as one of growing decentralization: in legal texts across the imperial domains, there was a rising cohesion in the approach of Hanafi muftis and scholars to questions of land tenure.

While the bundle awarded to the cultivator would evolve over time, its establishment in a wider variety of legal texts and its diffusion across the empire's provinces was, I argue, more transformational than any changes that accrued to the bundle itself. Chapters 3, 5 and 6 follow debates among muftis about how to discern the contours of the peasants' rights from the seventeenth to nineteenth centuries. These chapters show that although there were lasting disagreements among the muftis over the cultivator's capacity to transfer (some were more liberal than others in the range of transaction they allowed), the scope of these differences remained fairly stable throughout the seventeenth and eighteenth centuries. To the extent that there was an adaptation of the peasant's bundle to the more commercialized economy of the eighteenth century, it was simply that there were a greater number of muftis in that century who settled on the more liberal end of that spectrum; there was little evidence that the bundle was transforming into something more like private property. It was the more liberally transferable version of the rights bundle, well-suited to commercial exchange, that the 1858 Land Code confirmed as the single definition of secure, lifelong possession on the treasury's lands; its concept of property rights owes nothing to Western law. Thus, even in the mid-nineteenth century, reformers did not abandon the rights bundle that the peasants had long enjoyed, but rather found that its limits as well as its guarantees were well suited to a host of new priorities; perhaps chief among these was designating a tax-paying population.

Third and finally, the story of Ottoman land tenure law is often told as one where the dynasty demanded adherence to the *kanun* in the sixteenth century, but that in later centuries, both the status of the sultan as a legislator and veneration for the *kanun* were diminished.[14] A more accurate narrative is nearly the inverse of this familiar one: it is only in the late seventeenth to early nineteenth centuries that all the legal genres of the empire, including all the textual genres associated with Hanafism, fully embraced the vast claims of legal authority that Ebu's-Suʿud had made on behalf of Süleyman in the mid-sixteenth century and affirmed that the sultans' orders and *kanunname*s were the bases of the law. There is a widespread notion among scholars that the ulema have for centuries regarded land law as an arena where the sultan was free to enact legislation on behalf of the land's owner, the treasury; Chapter 2 contends that this notion is highly inaccurate. In fact, Ebu's-Suʿud heavily revised Hanafi doctrine of treasury-owned land in order to transfer legal authority over the land from scholastic texts to the sultan's administrative texts. As Chapters 3 and 4 explain, the integration of his extraordinary claims into Hanafi fatwas, juridical manuals and treatises was accompanied by some amount of resistance and controversy. Ultimately, however, the jurists did accept these innovations. Their acceptance shows that not only can the ulema not be described as usurping or undermining the sultan's legislative authority, but also that the ulema assisted the dynasty in building the scaffolding for the legal sovereignty that the modernizing Ottoman state and its successors would claim over the land.

Sources

Where does one find the land tenure law of the Ottoman Empire? Before the nineteenth century, it was spread across a wide variety of texts, not all of them produced by employees of the state. Of late, scholarly discussion of the role of genres and textual forms in shaping law has provided helpful insights to the way that power and sovereignty are produced and executed.[15] Such insights are helpful for conceptualizing the workings of a law constructed from legal texts belonging to a multitude of genres and embodied in different forms. This study traces the dialogue between texts created by members of the chancellery, appointees of the 'learned' branch of the bureaucracy known as the *ilmiye*, and independent scholars, jurists and statecraft writers. A number of sources in this study were created by ulema, that is, scholars trained in Islamic jurisprudence. Of these, fatwas are the most crucial source material for this study, not only because they are a plentiful source produced in this period, but also because they allow us to follow the arc of a theoretical conversation across time. Fatwas are legal opinions written by a jurist (a scholar of Islamic law) serving as a mufti. In a break with previous Islamic practice, Ottoman muftis were appointed by the dynasty; in the Arab provinces however, some scholars who held no appointment gave fatwas simply because they were regarded as erudite enough to do so, in conformity with pre-Ottoman practice.[16] Nearly all of the fatwas examined in this study were issued by officially appointed muftis, and as such, they have a character that is both scholarly and administrative; while addressing theoretical questions of the sharia's meaning, the mufti was also performing an administrative function on behalf of the state. Texts of academic jurisprudence, that is, comprehensive manuals of *fiqh*, commentaries on these manuals as well as treatises on specific topics make up a category of source material that was primarily scholastic in nature. In addition, this book relies upon legal source compilations assembled by the Ottoman judges of this era as guidebooks or academic references; these were often a mix of fatwas and excerpts of academic jurisprudence.

As will be clear from this group of sources, I am dealing primarily with texts that Brinkley Messick terms the 'library' sources of the Islamic legal tradition. Messick argues that different textual forms associated with Islamic law 'script' the sharia in two ways: as archive and as library.[17] The former includes documents like *hüccet*s (rulings of the Islamic judge, the *qadi*) that are 'context rich' and deal in the specificities of persons, times and place. The library scripts are theoretical and doctrinal works and include juridical manuals and treatises. Fatwas, Messick has noted, have a foot in each world in that they are given in response to particularities; yet once 'stripped' of specificities they too can become library references.[18] Clearly, a study like this one that focuses on library sources is not the only way to study land tenure law. Looking at the context-rich sources of the archive, such as land transactions on the ground through court records or direct responses to petitions, is also a valuable way to study it, though it is not the only useful way. The library sources are not divorced from facts on the ground; in particular, the ambiguous position of the fatwa between the archive and the library connected local realities to theoretical frameworks. Understanding the library sources will be helpful to future studies focusing on the court, and help us understand where the court and its documentation fit within a wider textual tradition. Library sources are worthy of study in part because they allow us to see the 'macro' picture of Hanafi discourse about land, and also because of their influence; the council drafting the 1858 Land Code would state quite explicitly that it was indebted to them, and the text the council produced corroborates this statement.

Given that this study is examining law in the Ottoman context, it deals not only with the library sources that Messick identifies but also with texts compiling orders issued by the sultans known as *kanunname*s, which, although not genres typically regarded as sharia scripts, were also 'library' sources for legal writers and imperial office holders. Some of these were issued directly by the dynasty's chancellery, but others were compiled in an unofficial capacity by persons who collected together *kanun*s on the topic of land law. Throughout this book, I often refer to texts whose content originated in the chancellery as conveying the sultan's orders, or 'order-giving'; while fatwas and *hüccet*s also conveyed the sultan's orders, this was the primary function of texts such as *kanunnames*, *firmans* (imperial edicts) and cadastral registers. This is not to say that the content all came directly from the sultan, but rather that the texts contained practices that the dynasty committed to enforcing. For this study, I consulted *kanunname*s issued by the chancellery that Inalcik calls 'general' *kanunnames* that recorded broadly prevailing rules within the empire.[19] Additionally, the more archive-like *kanunname*s made to govern particular provinces were also consulted. The most central source of this book, the *Kanun-ı Cedid*, is an unofficial compilation and is only one of many land tenure *kanun* compendia that referred to their contents as '*kanun-ı cedid*', a phrase that could suggest 'revised' or 'up-to-date' *kanun* as much as 'new law or new *kanun*' in this period.[20] This text is perhaps the library source par excellence: it draws from numerous archival texts produced by different administrative personnel for more than a century, strips them of their temporal and spatial specificities and presents them as a reference for personnel across the empire. The diversity of the textual forms it incorporates – *firman*s responding to petitions, *kanunname*s issued for provinces, discrete *kanun*s, fatwas – is a perfect illustration of the way that land law can only be understood as an edifice of different textual forms arranged to 'fit' together, or harmonize, in a specific way. To understand why a particular writer embraced a particular view of property rights, it is essential to understand which texts he was responding to and which kinds of texts and authors he was addressing.

Harmonization and sovereignty

As the preceding section on sources makes clear, this study adds to a current of scholarship that has revised the long dominant view in the field that Islamic law was a jurists' law which remained exclusively under the control of the ulema, with rulers or administrators having little to no role in its evolution.[21] Scholars studying the law of the Ottoman Empire have substantially challenged such views; they have noted the ability of the dynasty to designate its preferred interpretations within the Hanafi school for enforcement; to create a canon of approved texts for educating its ulema personnel; to broadly control how the law was adjudicated at court and to issue orders about all of the above that the academic texts of *fiqh* affirmed as valid and binding.[22] This book too argues that the sultan and his administration made significant changes to the Hanafi practice of law. In fact, I will argue that these changes were of more profound nature than many of the other interventions that scholars have already identified. The impact of the harmonization efforts aimed at the land law in the sixteenth century have often been deemed very consequential for the practice of the *kanun*, which Inalcik saw as undergoing Islamization.[23] While the impact on *kanun* was indeed momentous, harmonization also had profound effects upon Hanafism.

Both the stories that this book narrates – the increasing institutionalization of the peasant's bundle and the increasing acceptance of the sultan's legislative authority over *miri* land along with its incorporation into textual production – were consequences of harmonization. To be clear, I do not mean to endorse either the view that *kanun* and sharia were actually harmonized by any particular mufti or the view that they were irreconcilable. Rather, I wish to show that the question of how the sultan's orders were to be dealt with as a source of the law was a question that the muftis continually theorized for three centuries, and that their reconciliations had consequences for their understanding of property rights. Harmonization has long been understood as attempts by Ottoman jurists – most notably the famous *şeyhülislam* Ebu's-Su'ud Efendi – to explain the provisions of *kanun* in such a way that they did not conflict with Hanafi understanding of the sharia. Reflecting the secular and nationalist spirit of their era, prominent Ottoman historians like Halil Inalcik, Ömer L. Barkan, Uriel Heyd, Richard Repp and Colin Imber saw sharia as a religious law, *kanun* as a worldly and secular law and concluded that the two were at odds with each other.[24]

As the field has moved away from the secular/religious dichotomy, harmonization has fallen out of favour with some historians – particularly Turkish scholars – many of whom insist that there was no need for harmonization in the sixteenth century because Ottoman procedure in the *kanun* had always developed in a complementary fashion with the sharia: in this view, Ebu's-Su'ud did not reconcile; he simply systemized.[25] The utility of the standard conceptualization of harmonization has also been called into question by Guy Burak, who has argued that any account of how the Ottomans reconciled *kanun* and sharia must reckon with the dynasty's enactment of a specific version of Hanafism through adoption of the Hanafi school of law as its official *madhhab* and the emergence of officially appointed muftis to designate the opinions within the Hanafi school that would be enforced.[26] He maintains that through its control of schools, offices and authorized texts, the Ottomans created a practice of sharia authorized by the *kanun*.

This book argues that for the land law, the discursive question of harmonization (is practice x enacted in the *kanun* valid because the *fiqh* allows practice y?) is intimately related to Burak's harmonization via dynastic selection and enforcement. On the one hand, the questions of whether *tapu* was to be understood as a Hanafi sale or an advance on rent and whether peasant tenure should ultimately be conceptualized as a Hanafi loan or as a lease were persistent issues; one simply cannot write about the land law in any meaningful way without addressing how the muftis understood harmonization in this sense. However, *kanun* as a set of practices structuring the hierarchy of the *ilmiye* played an important role in why conversations about reconciliation adopted the parameters they did. Ebu's-Su'ud's vision of how to settle these discursive questions was influential not only for its elegance but also because his position at the pinnacle of the *ilmiye* allowed him to impose this vision on the *ilmiye* as a whole, and to preclude judges from ruling differently. In this first phase of reconciliation, Ebu's-Su'ud pioneered a way for the state to harmonize its documentation by creating terminology and a conceptual apparatus that could be incorporated in all administrative output – fatwas, *hüccet*s, cadastral registers, *firman*s and *kanunname*s. What effects followed from this? This book argues that it opened new avenues for the sultan to create law, that it initiated a new dialogue between the different textual genres that together constituted the law and that it meant a proliferation of property-right bundles that replicated the terms of the peasant's bundle. The ongoing reconciliation efforts in fatwas and juridical texts of the following centuries rescripted the property rights of treasury lands, the sultan's legal powers over these lands and the method of land tax classification, profoundly altering Hanafi teaching.

Property: Bundles and layers

Does it make sense to speak of property rights in the Ottoman Empire prior to the nineteenth century? Or is the idea of a 'property right' simply an anachronism?[27] In this study I have chosen to speak of property rights, but it is important to clarify what this terminology means. A property right need not be connected to a theory of property, nor does it necessarily imply a distinct legal separation between persons and things.[28] For the purposes of this study, a property right is any discrete right to usage, exclusion, transaction or revenue derived from land: a right to farm the land is deemed a property right, as is the right to forbid the building of sheds. The aggregate of the rights held by individuals or particular classes of people is referred to as a 'bundle' of rights.[29] The bundle is a useful concept because it allows different arrangements that involve multiple property rights – such as rent, usufruct, ownership – to be broken into their constituent rights and compared. A fairly standard definition of contemporary private property, for example, defines it as a bundle consisting of eleven discrete property rights.[30] As a result, this study frequently defines the terms appearing in the Ottoman sources as particular bundles of property rights, including in the sixteenth century. As it happens, the idea of possessing a bundle fits well with the articulation of property relations in Hanafi jurisprudence: typically, muftis discussed a person's rights over land by pairing the word for possessing or using (*tasarruf*), with the name of a bundle that specified the particular property rights the person enjoyed. Hence, the concept of the bundle is a good fit for the source material.

My chief contention is that the bundle of rights that was legally systematized for the peasants in the sixteenth century was relatively strong; it was difficult to strip the peasant of possession if the land was worked, even if the possessor was not the person actually performing the labour.[31] Although Martha Mundy and Richard Saumarez Smith have skilfully made the case that the sixteenth-century bundle is office-like and only becomes more property-like in later centuries,[32] in my view this characterization exaggerates the difference between conceptions of the bundle in the sixteenth versus the eighteenth century. It also has the unintended effect of reinforcing the narrative that property rights were essentially non-existent in the sixteenth century, whereas in the eighteenth, they had appeared. The sixteenth-century bundle had property-like as well as office-like features that should not, in my opinion, be downplayed: for instance, the ability of family members to pre-emptively claim the land after the cultivator's death, even if they were unable to cultivate the land personally. Likewise, the eighteenth- and nineteenth-century bundle retained important office-like features, including the circumstances in which it could be revoked. My point is that the cultivator's bundle was a property configuration that the muftis treated as peculiar throughout this period and its definition was contested within fairly consistent parameters: I will argue that instead of a gradual segue from office to estate, there was disagreement between Ebu's-Su'ud and his immediate successors about the extent of property rights that the possessor enjoyed, and that the resulting tension continued to characterize the muftis' positions on property rights into the nineteenth century.

Drawing on contemporary scholarship on Islamic law, I sometimes employ the terminology of 'layers' to discuss the property rights that belong to different individuals or groups over the same object.[33] Such terminology rightly captures that in the Ottoman Empire, property rights over land, buildings and derived revenues tended to be vested in multiple persons rather than concentrated into a single person. Contrary to popular perception, this aspect of the law is an area of overlap rather than divergence with early modern Europe. In early modern Anglo-America and Great Britain, where the most 'absolute' theories of private property gained ground in the discourse of political theory and taxation, such theories made little headway in real property law itself until the nineteenth century.[34] In legal practice, property regimes of partial and collective rights prevailed while national and local leaders declared that land was unsuited to exclusive control and unfettered commodification; they articulated support for property regimes that promoted distributive justice throughout the early modern period.[35] The nineteenth-century shift towards a property law that concentrated property rights into single persons was a phenomenon visible at roughly the same time in both the 'West' and the Ottoman Empire.

Ultimately, I am arguing that the cultivator's bundle was the first iteration of a property formation that was deeply institutionalized in Ottoman legal and administrative practice by the nineteenth century. For centuries, it embodied multiple ideals of harmony that were cherished by the Ottoman elite. The literature of statecraft and *kanunnames* argued that this bundle successfully balanced the interests of individual cultivators, families and village communities with those of revenue-collecting soldiers and the treasury. Other statesmen and jurists would see it as demonstrating the compatibility between *kanun* and sharia. Even as these ideals of harmony began to recede in the nineteenth century and new political values were adopted, this property configuration showed remarkable resilience. It was perhaps the most enduring legacy of the sixteenth century.

Chapter 1

LIFELONG *TASARRUF*, LAND TENURE PRACTICES, AND LAW OVER THE *LONGUE DURÉE*

The title page of the original edition of Thomas Hobbes's *Leviathan* (1651) presents an engraving which is an apt visual metaphor for the concept of sovereignty that Hobbes expounds. It presents a picture of a crowned king, whose body is composed of a multitude of other men. The engraving has become iconic, but its origin is not as well known. The figure of the crowned king made of many bodies was inspired by the anamorphic drawings of Jean-François Niceron (1613–46), and in particular by a drawing of fifteen Ottoman sultans, which, when observed through a lens designed by Niceron, morphed into a single image of the French King Louis XIII.[1] First drawn in 1635 or 1636, the picture was meant to convey the august grandeur of the king of France by portraying him as subsuming in his one person the entirety of the Ottoman dynastic line. Niceron's image was a testament to the way that the princes of early modern Europe enviously regarded the Ottoman sultans as the epitome of imperial might. It is also clear from the derived image on the frontispiece of *Leviathan* that the Ottomans haunted the theorization of sovereign power in Europe, providing an example that inspired both admiration and denunciation.

In the mid-sixteenth century, the Ottoman Empire was among the world's largest and mightiest polities, spanning thousands of miles of territory in Europe and Asia. Another Frenchman concerned with the image of the king of France, the political theorist Jean Bodin (1530–96), described the Ottomans in ways that reflected both his fascination and his distaste for the immense wealth and power of empires that excelled at territorial conquest. In Bodin's writings as in those of his early modern peers, the emerging theory of the state was saturated with concern for property. Through an engagement with property, theorists began to articulate the proper contours of an increasingly powerful sovereign authority by distinguishing between public versus private and governance versus ownership.[2] For many such theorists, the problem with overmighty sovereigns was that they failed to limit themselves to their rightful mastery of the public realm and extended their reach to things that should be in the care and private mastery of their subjects. In Bodin's view, the Ottoman sultan possessed an unlimited mastery over his subjects' bodies and possessions, and it was this worrying lack of boundaries between public power and private right that set the Ottoman Empire apart from the other realms of Europe, where 'every subject hath the true proprietie of his own things'.[3] While in theory, he conceded, all peoples held their 'goods of their sovereign prince', the reality of unbridled sovereign authority in the Ottoman Empire meant that no subject had secure possession of anything, least of all a landed estate. Bodin's understanding of the sixteenth-century Ottoman Empire as a polity built on the denial of property rights for its subjects has had remarkable staying power.

This chapter provides an introduction to the history of the land tenure system and land tenure law in the Ottoman Empire that places these subjects within a broader narrative of evolving property rights in the Ottoman Empire. While summary information on Ottoman land tenure can be found in many works, this chapter will acquaint the reader with the standard fare of *timar*s and tax farms, soldiers and peasants, by telling an unconventional story about this familiar cast of people and institutions. In most versions of this story, the key transition concerns the rights of the military elite. Scholars have long agreed with Bodin that over the course of the fifteenth and sixteenth centuries, Ottoman administrators were increasingly unwilling to extend secure tenure over land or its revenues to the men of the sword who collected land tax.[4] Unlike the hereditary aristocracy of Western Europe where an estate in land was granted in perpetuity and passed from one generation to the next, the Ottoman military elite were the sultan's servants, remaining dependent on his favour.[5] This system, where agricultural revenues were tightly controlled by the central administration, became increasingly defunct over the course of the seventeenth century, leading to the emergence in the eighteenth century of a group of Ottoman elites who were less dependent on the sultan's largesse and better able to secure long-term access to agricultural revenues, primarily through the lifelong tax farm known as a *malikane*. This group was more the sultan's partners than his servants; as the sultan relied upon them for services that were secured by negotiation and collaboration rather than by directive.[6] The narrative is therefore one of contrast between an old order where subjects' claims to the land were extremely contingent to one where they were more robust.

This chapter argues for a different understanding of the transition from the sixteenth to eighteenth century. It argues that the sturdier property rights enjoyed by elite subjects in the eighteenth century were replications of the rights awarded to the peasantry in the sixteenth century. Hence, this 'enfranchising' of the elites is not purely the story of an old order passing away, but also the story of how some institutions of the old order took root and became even more central to defining the character of the empire in its final centuries than they had been in the sixteenth century. The institution of which I speak is the peasantry's bundle of rights to the land that was systematized and legally enshrined in the mid-sixteenth century. Compared with the military elite, Ottoman administrators granted the peasants a far greater security to utilize, alienate and inherit the land in order to pay their taxes and support their families. This contrast has often been noted and ascribed to the general Ottoman commitment to justice and to preventing powerful classes from abusing the peasantry.[7] However, the narrative of justice does not adequately capture the resulting consequences for the evolution of property rights in the empire, for after its definitive legal articulation, the peasants' bundle of property rights 'trickled up' to other classes of higher politico-social status. One of these bundles, known as *ijaratayn*, was present on land but would primarily secure urban real estate under the same terms that the peasantry held its land; the other, as indicated earlier in the text, was the lifelong tax farm known as the *malikane*. Both of these conveyed the same bundle of rights to their possessors as peasant cultivators possessed to land; all three constituted a uniquely Ottoman set of property rights. Additionally, they were all key to shaping the contours of Ottoman fiscal, economic and political realities in the eighteenth century.

Previous scholarship has demonstrated how the wider diffusion of this property-right bundle was prompted by major shifts in the political economy and resulting fiscal pressure. Briefly surveying these shifts, this chapter will focus on the increasing allure of stability in the eyes of administrative officials and their willingness to give up a certain amount of control over revenues in return for stability. Historians have long noted this trend, but not always realized that it is the thread connecting the peasants' property-right bundle to *ijaratayn* and *malikane*. Where this chapter differs from prior accounts is in identifying the systemization of the peasants' bundle as heralding the emergence of these stronger property-right bundles for the more powerful social classes. In other words, I will argue that it was not only social, economic and political forces that played a role in producing *ijaratayn* and *malikane*, but also the existence of a prototype – namely, the peasant's bundle – that was well known to legal and administrative personnel by the late seventeenth century. The existence of the peasant's bundle as a well-defined legal entity was the result of what the sixteenth- and seventeenth-century Ottoman elites referred to as 'harmonization' or 'reconciliation' (*tevfik* or *tatbik*) of *kanun* and sharia. Among other things, this 'harmonized' articulation of the land law specified the contours of the peasants' bundle so that it conformed to the dynasty's notion of a correct balance of right between the land's cultivators, the treasury and the military grant holder. Allowing a uniform implementation of this correct balance of rights across all legal and administrative genres, the 'harmonized' land law specified land usage rights, transactions and taxes in the vocabulary and conceptual mapping of Hanafism; it would inaugurate the production of the intricately coordinated legal and administrative texts that would govern the land for the next three centuries. It was through this process that the defining feature of *ijaratayn*, *malikane* and the peasant bundle – an advance (*mu'accele*) that was not a conventional advance – was defined, validated and disseminated throughout Ottoman legal and administrative practices. As a result, this chapter will argue that the age of Süleyman was the origin point of both Ottoman land tenure law and a new trend in property rights that would shape Ottoman fortunes in the seventeenth and eighteenth centuries. Legions of Ottoman muftis and other legal writers, including the compiler of the *Kanun-ı Cedid*, have shared this view.

Ottoman territories and varieties of tenure for the military class

When Ottoman legal writers formulated their views on land, they drew upon a long history of legal thought pertaining to the specific lands which constituted the empire. Soon after the death of the prophet Muhammad in 632, Muslim armies flowed out of the Arabian Peninsula and conquered the adjacent territories, much of which had previously belonged to the Byzantine or Sasanian Empires. The areas that today comprise Iraq, Syria and Egypt quickly fell to the Muslim invaders, but the Byzantines were able to successfully defend Anatolia from the various attempts of Muslim armies to invade it for more than four hundred years. From the year 1071, the defeat of the Byzantine emperor Romanus Diogenes in the Battle of Manzikert opened Anatolia to settlement by Muslim Turkish pastoralists, and a major demographic shift commenced as Turks began to settle there in ever larger numbers. In the wake of the Mongol invasions of the thirteenth and fourteenth centuries, a fragmented political environment emerged in Anatolia. Confederations of Turkish tribes led by chiefs known as *beys* founded small autonomous states; styling themselves *gazis*,[8] they raided neighbouring territories held by other *beys* or by local Christian princes. The Ottoman Empire was born around the year 1300 as one of these small, frontier states of Anatolia. The eponymous Ottoman founder, Osman Bey, attracted a diverse variety of followers in the tumultuous border regions, including numerous Christian fighters as well as Muslims.[9] Embarking on more than three hundred years of expansion, the Ottomans first absorbed the other small *beyliks* of Western Anatolia and their territories. By the middle of the sixteenth century, the Ottomans had united the entirety of Anatolia, southern Europe as far as Hungary and Ukraine and the Arabic-speaking lands from Tunis to Iraq. This vast expanse contained not only a diversity of peoples but also a variety of land tenure patterns, which were part and parcel of the socio-economic relations prevailing in each region.

As in nearly every agrarian state in Eurasia in the fourteenth and fifteenth centuries, the land tenure regime of the Ottomans was tied to supporting its military. Over the course of the fourteenth century, the Ottoman military made a transition from a confederation of tribal volunteers to a more specialized and centrally controlled fighting force. The land tenure system that was developing in tandem with the growth and specialization of the army would, in these first centuries of Ottoman rule, largely support the members of the cavalry, known as *sipahis*. Unlike the janissaries – their better-known infantry counterpart – *sipahis* were a group to which those who had distinguished themselves in battle could be elevated, but they also constituted a hereditary class.[10] Quite frequently, they were the former elite of conquered areas who submitted to Ottoman rule and were confirmed in their positions.[11] In exchange for his military service, a *sipahi* received a grant of revenues derived from land known as a *timar*.[12] It was not a grant in perpetuity, and could be taken away. The *sipahi* could lay claim to a new *timar* only if he was still regularly performing the required military service.

The so-called *timar* system is often referred to as the basis of a 'classical' Ottoman land order. From the middle of the fifteenth century, Ottoman administrative records show an increasingly regularized system of allocating the agricultural taxes of much of Rumelia and Anatolia to *sipahis* as *timars*.[13] The lands whose revenues were granted as *timars* were often designated as *miri*, or royal. The Ottoman administration held that *miri* lands were those that belonged to the

Ottoman treasury (*bayt al-mal*) and would be administered by the sultan for the welfare of the Muslim community. Although it is not clear exactly when this claim that the treasury owned the land first appeared, it has been linked to the growth of the *timar* system and the desire of the sultan's fiscal bureaucrats to maximize the treasury's share of land revenues.[14] The doctrine of treasury ownership was not an Ottoman innovation: many, perhaps most, Islamic dynasties had espoused some form of it, including the Ottoman dynasty's predecessors in Anatolia, the Saljuks.[15] Its usefulness for fiscal administration is easy to grasp: through treasury ownership, fiscal administrators had complete control – in theory – over allocating the resources of land and revenues derived from it.

Not all the Ottoman lands were divided into revenue grants for the military. There were other lands, known as *salyane*, that collected revenues differently due to the exigencies of terrain, distance or local politics: these provinces included Egypt, with its dependence on the Nile and long-standing indigenous system of tax collection, and the mountainous region of Kurdistan where the tribal chiefs organized production and collection.[16] There were also lands whose revenues were collected by tax farmers under contract from the treasury. While this method of collection is largely associated with the post-sixteenth-century order of the empire, there were quite a few great families in Syria that were integrated into the Ottoman order as tax farmers from the time of the Ottoman conquest in 1516.[17] The sultan could also award a fighter with a *temlik*, often referred to as 'freehold' (*milk*) property, as the revenues generated by the land belonged permanently to the assignee and could not be taken away.[18] *Temlik* had been more common before the *timar* system became more institutionalized in the fifteenth century, but it was not entirely eradicated in later centuries.[19] Cultivators too might claim that the land they tended was their own *milk*, particularly if it was irrigated land with vines or trees on it. The Ottoman *kanunname*s opposed these claims, but some muftis – especially those in Syria – supported them.[20]

Perhaps the most important of all of the non-*timar* landholding categories was that of *waqf*. A *waqf* was akin to an endowment, an important institution in Muslim lands long before the founding of the Ottoman Empire. If a person owned an orchard, a field or some other revenue-generating property like a mill or rental property, he could set aside the revenues of that property in perpetuity for a designated beneficiary by creating a *waqf*. Classical Hanafi doctrine held that a *waqf* could be created only from *milk* property, yet by the founding of the Ottoman Empire, the ulema accepted that a sultan could make a charitable *waqf* from taxes owed to the treasury on *miri* land. In provinces like Egypt, anyone could make this kind of *waqf*.[21] The founder of the *waqf* designated the beneficiaries in its founding charter: *waqf*s supported charitable activities, institutions of learning and libraries, hospitals, urban drinking fountains, lodges for travellers and even funds for the care of stray cats and dogs. However, most *waqf*s simply generated revenue for family members designated as beneficiaries by the founder. It was the responsibility of the *waqf*'s superintendent, known as a *mutawalli*, to see that resources of the *waqf* were maintained and that the revenues were disbursed according to the charter created by the founder. Once a *waqf* had been made, it could not be rescinded, and Muslim rulers were expected to respect the status of *waqf* lands, though many did not.[22]

As Ottoman military and fiscal practice shaped over the fifteenth and into the sixteenth centuries, Ottoman administrators worked to tighten the sultan's control over land revenues and to constrain the access of the military class to these revenues.[23] More land fell under direct Ottoman rule rather than rule through conquered vassals, grants of *temlik* had become less common and *waqfs* came under increased scrutiny from the fiscal administration looking to maximize tax receipts.[24] The *timar* system too was reshaped by these trends. In its earliest phase, the *timar* system seems to have not been quite so different from the landholding patterns of hereditary aristocracy, for it was often accompanied by gestures of accommodation with the local elite. These included the recognition of a heritable *timar* in Bosnia called *baştina*, and a practice in central and eastern Anatolia called *malikane-divani* wherein the local elite preserved its former fiscal demands upon the peasants.[25] But as the empire became a more heavily bureaucratized state centralizing the collection and allocation of revenues, the relatively tenuous position of the *sipahi* became more discernable. While the *sipahi* status and the claim to a *timar* passed from father to son, the sons had no claim to the specific *timar* that their fathers had possessed. Indeed, as the system matured in the fifteenth century, it was the policy of the sultans to assign *timars* to *sipahi*s that were outside their native regions to discourage them from developing strong local ties.[26] The *timar*s were also periodically rotated for the same purpose; sixteenth-century *sipahi*s were expected to regularly spend periods without *timar*s and would have to apply for another *timar* while still being expected to perform the requisite military service.[27] By the seventeenth century, *timar*s were more often awarded for service on the battlefield than through a hereditary claim.[28] The timar system, then, became a system that offered but did not guarantee revenue and status to military elites that they could maintain for themselves and pass to their sons.

Cultivator tenure and its legal systemization

If the military and administrative elite's tenures were unstable, the same cannot be said for the peasants. The same trends of increasing fiscal centralization that made the *sipahi*'s situation tenuous favoured security for the cultivators. While the sultan was wary of guaranteeing a *sipahi*'s access to the land's revenues, he saw only benefit in guaranteeing peasant access to the land: the latter ensured a steady flow of tax revenue. Halil Inalcik long maintained that peasant rights on the land were fairly secure and evidence of Ottoman justice towards the peasant.[29] While Inalcik's characterization has been influential, some assessments have been less rosy and emphasized that peasant rights were also largely contingent on the sultan's favour.[30] This study maintains that Inalcik was correct to emphasize security of the peasant's rights as a legal matter, for even though the peasants were vulnerable to abuses, the bundle itself was strong. Nevertheless, Inalcik examined peasant tenure primarily as an element of Ottoman fiscal organization, and this caused him to overlook the impact of the legal institutionalization of the peasant's bundle over the long term.

By the middle of the sixteenth century, the cultivators were able to legally secure a bundle of property rights that guaranteed lifelong tenure and heritability. The chief features of the bundle already existed, but its systematic articulation in the terminology and conceptual framework of Hanafism was new in the sixteenth century. The formulation of land-usage rights and obligations as a Hanafi construct meant that the peasant's bundle could be treated coherently and uniformly by all Ottoman officials – whether governors, accountants or judges, and so on – and documented as such across all genres of Ottoman legal and administrative texts. Although these different genres of legal texts had never existed in isolation and had previously informed one another in content and formal characteristics, their dialogue would become far more pronounced from Süleyman's era. This systematic formulation was significant for several reasons; among other things, it scripted a land law that was sharia practice, but it also brought the land law firmly under Ottoman administrative control, a subject that we will visit at greater length in Chapter 2. Here, we will focus on the property-right bundle that emerged from this systematic formulation of the land's law and its transformative role in the empire's history.

The reign of Süleyman I from 1520 to 1566 saw a marked effort to create a rational administration of law, to exercise sovereign power through law and to build institutions promoting social and political harmony.[31] Bureaucratic efforts to create a systematic approach to land tenure law was simply one piece of this broader programme. Administrative efforts were focused largely on how information recorded in the cadastral registers and *kanunname*s was to inform the work of the judges in their courtrooms and be properly recorded in the court's registers. Ottoman subjects would come to the judge's court desiring to buy, sell or endow the land. For the judges, however, it was questionable whether these transactions were valid or prohibited: if the land was *miri*, as fiscal administrative documents either stated or implied, then neither the peasants nor the *sipahi* were landowners with the right to sell or endow it. How then could either cultivators or *sipahi*s transact the land? If the treasury owned the land, what exactly was the relationship between the cultivator and the land? If cultivators were not owners, what was bought and sold in the many court records of *miri* land's exchange that had the appearance of sales contracts?[32]

In the first two decades of Süleyman's long reign, several administrators made efforts to produce a systematic and coherent legal approach to land tenure practice, although they did not all arrive at the same solutions.[33] It was to be Ebu's-Su'ud Efendi that Ottoman biographers and commentators most often credited with bringing a comprehensive coherence to land law and establishing how the practices authorized under the rubric of *kanun* fit or 'harmonized' with the sharia practices described in Hanafi *fiqh*.[34] First as the *kazasker* (chief judge) of Rumelia from 1533 to 1545 and then as *şeyhülislam* (chief mufti) from 1545 to 1574, Ebu's-Su'ud issued a number of detailed statements on the rules of land tenure defining most of the lands of Ottoman Europe and Anatolia as treasury-owned, or *miri* land, with a special regime of law governing it. The biographer 'Ata'i says of both Ebu's-Su'ud and his predecessor Kemalpaşazade: 'It is true that the effect of their *ijtihad* (jurisprudential reasoning) was the reconciling (*tatbik*) of the Ottoman *kanun*s with the noble sharia and the ordering of religious and administrative affairs on the best possible basis.'[35] This is not to say that prior to Ebu's-Su'ud, the Ottomans were convinced that the two were entirely separate from one another and substantially in conflict, but rather that Ebu's-Su'ud's vision of *how* all the components fit together would be found both impressive and definitive by most of his administrative colleagues and their successors. It was also, uncoincidentally, a vision that enhanced administrative authority over taxation and legislating property rights. What was clear from both Ebu's-Su'ud's efforts and those of his predecessors was that Süleyman's administrators were not content to have individual judges in the provinces making their own decisions about how practices described in the provincial registers were related to transactions in the Hanafi manuals of jurisprudence; it was for officials at the pinnacle of the administration to make these decisions and then to command the ranks to follow their guidance on the meaning of harmonization.

If discussing the imposition of a newly sultan-empowering legal order as 'harmonization' obscured that it was in fact an imposition, there are reasons why conceptualizing it as harmonization or reconciliation was satisfying to many within the cadres of the elite. *Kanun* had long been an important part of the imperial idiom for asserting the legitimacy of the dynasty.[36] For many of Ebu's-Su'ud's contemporaries (though by no means all of them), the Ottoman *kanun* was synonymous with an ideal practice of statecraft singular to the Ottomans, and it explained their success.[37] The claim of harmony between this unique Ottoman tradition and the divine order of the sharia was another argument for the singularity of the Ottoman state, which was a perfect synthesis of the best that God and man could construct. As we will see, not all Ottomans shared 'Ata'i's conviction about a harmonious fit; some critics charged that specific practices validated in the *kanun* could not be reconciled with the sharia. Nevertheless, such skepticism seems to have had little impact on state policy until the latter half of the seventeenth century; prior to that time Ebu's-Su'ud's formulation appears to have been increasingly integrated into the administrative practices of land tenure, finding its way into *kanunname*s, fatwas, *hüccet*s and *firmans*.[38]

In Ebu's-Su'ud's legal treatment of land, each class of persons had a specific bundle of rights to land and its produce, with the result that control of the land was spread across layers of class rather than wielded by a single owner. This attempt at balance – between the rights of the peasantry to use the land and those of the *sipahi* to sustain himself from the revenues – also fit with the ideals of harmony and justice elaborated in the literature of statecraft and the implementation of these ideals through increasingly formalized bureaucratic procedures in the sixteenth century.[39] Land was a resource upon which many interests – both competing interests of subjects and dynastic interests – converged and had to be reconciled in order to maintain the social and political order. With this order in mind, Ebu's-Su'ud wrote that the cultivators did not own the land, but rather possessed (*tasarruf*) it on loan or through rent from the treasury. The term *tasarruf* was a commonly used juridical term for something that a person had the right to dispose of and which he had the right to use. In the *fiqh*, the specific bundle of rights through which a person possesses (*tasarruf*) something is often spelt out explicitly: that is, if one owns something in freehold, a jurist might describe it as 'possession (*tasarruf*) by way of freehold (*milk*)'.[40] Increasingly, when discussing peasant tenure in the abstract, the muftis discussed the bundle of rights held by the peasants under the rubric of *tasarruf*; so much so that the term *tasarruf* came to serve as the most common term for the rights bundle itself.[41] Similarly, the muftis frequently referred to the cultivator of a land as the land's *mutasarrif*, or possessor.

The most consequential feature of the cultivators' *tasarruf* was that it bestowed possession for life so long as they kept the land continually under cultivation: unlike the military elite, their tenure was not to be revoked unless they failed to cultivate.[42] This term was adopted from practices long extant in situ in a number of Ottoman core provinces, where the dominant tenure for cultivators was referred to as hold by *tapu* or *tapulu*.[43] On *tapulu* lands, the flipside of the cultivators' strong claim to the land they farmed was the *sipahi*'s claim to their labour on the land: they were not free to leave their villages and settle elsewhere. If they did, the *sipahi* could force them to return.[44] A cultivator acquired *tasarruf* of the land by paying a fee – itself called *tapu* – to the *sipahi* to obtain this lifelong tenure on the land.[45] If *tapu* was a burden, it was nevertheless the fee that purchased security: once it was paid, neither the *sipahi* nor another cultivator could challenge the *mutasarrif*'s possession, and he could expect to retain his farm for life.

On *miri* land, the peasants owned as freehold the crops, trees, houses and livestock that provided their livelihood and they could sell and inherit these according to the standard transaction rules of the *fiqh*. However, the cultivators could not sell the land itself, or inherit it or endow it, because the land was not their freehold; it belonged to the treasury. Despite this, a cultivator could cede his rights to another cultivator in exchange for money and with the *sipahi*'s permission, a transaction that Ebu's-Su'ud designated a 'release' (*tafarrugh*/ *faragh*) or delegation (*tafwid*) – hereafter both referred to as a 'transfer' – since Hanafi *fiqh* insisted that only tangible objects, not intangible rights, constituted property that could be sold.[46] Additionally, Ebu's-Su'ud's earliest and most influential statement on land tenure, the *Kanunname of Budin*, included a limited inheritance right that had long characterized tenure on *tapulu* land: sons, but no other family members, could inherit their father's *tasarruf*.[47] However, this succession was called transmission (*intiqal*) to distinguish it from the Hanafi law of inheritance (*irth*) that governed *milk* property. By allowing the peasants to transfer the bundle of rights and transmit it to sons through transactions that specifically devised for *miri* land, Ebu's-Su'ud ensured that documentation of such transfers in court judgements (*hüccets*) and fatwas would clearly distinguish that the land being exchanged was *miri* and not freehold. Maintaining this distinction was important for taxation rates, for control of *timar* revenues and for keeping *miri* land from becoming *waqf*; hence, judges were exhorted to ensure that transactions were properly recorded.[48]

As for the *sipahis*, they represented the treasury's interests and were authorized to collect the taxes and to exercise a general oversight over the land's productivity.[49] In Ebu's-Su'ud's writings and those of the jurists that followed him, a more generic term for the person with such authority, *sahib al-ard* (hereafter 'deputy'; that is, the person deputized by the treasury to exercise some of its rights on the land) began to be used. Like the category of *miri*, this latter term was adapted from the *fiqh*, and indicated that a specifically legal order, distinct from the military-fiscal administration of the *timar* system, was developing in this period. The standardized legal person known as the deputy was not always a *sipahi*; other kinds of administrative personnel could be awarded a *timar*, or one of the larger grants of *miri* land known as *zeamet* and *has*.[50] As the treasury's deputy, his permission was necessary for a number of cultivator actions. In order for a transfer of *tasarruf* to be valid, the *sahib al-ard* had to permit it and receive the *tapu* fee. Additionally, peasants had to seek the *sahib al-ard*'s permission to make such changes as erecting new buildings or planting new trees or gardens. Among the deputy's rights was his entitlement to the payments from the cultivators who resided on the lands of the *timar*. He collected the agricultural taxes, the miscellaneous taxes on sheep and beehives and other 'traditional imposts' (*tekalif-i 'örfi*). There were also punitive fees: if the peasants left the land fallow instead of planting it, they had to pay a fine. While the deputy had a number of powers over the peasants and claims upon their labour, *kanunnames* typically stressed that these powers had limits: he could not turn the peasant off the land nor meddle in succession to the land if a son or a legally recognized claimant to *tapu* survived nor demand payments beyond those specified in the imperial registers.[51]

One of the greatest conundrums that Ebu's-Su'ud faced was how to understand the deputy's claim to the *tapu* fee – a long-established, *kanun*-regulated practice – within the framework of Hanafi transactions. The most obvious interpretation of it, that it purchased the deputy's recognition of the new cultivator as the lifelong *mutasarrif*, ran into the problem that for Hanafis only freehold property could be bought and sold.[52] Since Ebu's-Su'ud sometimes described the relationship between the treasury and the peasants as one where the peasants rented land that belonged to the treasury, he would justify *tapu* as an advance on rent (*mu'accele*) that was due to the treasury.[53] Other muftis would sometimes describe *tapu* as a fee for registering a new possessor, but neither of these made for a very neat analogy.[54] The problem that *tapu* posed to a Hanafi understanding of transactions was best described by the famous sixteenth-century scholar Mehmed Birgevi (d. 1573), who was at times a sharp critic of Ebu's-Su'ud. As previous scholarship has demonstrated, Birgevi argued that whether or not one accepted treasury ownership of the land, there could be no juridical justification for the *tapu* fee.[55] Birgevi first noted that if *tapu* was a tax and the peasant was merely a renter, then the peasant was not responsible for the tax because the Hanafis made taxes the responsibility of the owner. If *tapu* was truly an advance on rent then it must correspond to a specific amount of the overall rent. This meant, among other things, that if a cultivator died before the contract period terminated, the deputy should return the payment to the cultivator's heirs because the cultivator had overpaid his rent. In reality, there was no end to the 'rental' period, and once paid, *tapu* was never returned. As a result, Birgevi concluded, Hanafism had no framework to accommodate the *tapu* fee; it was an illegal extortion. There is no doubt that the incorporation of the *tapu* fee into a legally coherent scheme of Hanafi transactions was theoretically challenging. However, its inclusion into the increasingly standardized land tenure regime emerging in the sixteenth century was to be met more often with acceptance than rejection by the ulema, and because the *tapu* payment was key to securing the lifelong tenure of the cultivator, the legal institutionalizing of the fee was extremely consequential.

In conclusion, the balance, or harmony, associated with Ebu's-Su'ud was twofold. First, he posited a balance of rights between deputy and cultivator that apportioned rights to the land based on what the state needed most from each. Cultivators received lifelong, robust property rights because it made fiscal sense to protect their ability to produce. At the heart of the process for obtaining the lifelong *tasarruf* was payment of *tapu*. The controversy over the *tapu* fee highlights the other harmony; namely, that Ebu's-Su'ud pronounced practices such as these – sanctioned in the *kanunname*s and essential to maintaining the ideal balance of *sipahi* and cultivator rights that would support the state – to be reconciled with the procedure of the courtroom and the conventions of the fatwa. Establishing exactly how this 'fit' was to work, he used his position at the top of the *ilmiye* and his partnership with the other high-ranking officials in Süleyman's administration to see his particular vision increasingly implemented across the legal texts and administrative records produced by state personnel. What I want to emphasize here is the foundational aspect of Ebu's-Su'ud's intervention. Ebu's-Su'ud was a dominant voice in a centuries-long discussion about how different textual forms intersected and 'fit' with one another. In the many texts composed in the seventeenth and eighteenth centuries addressing the land tenure law, it is rare to find any references to fatwas or *kanun*s that predate the reign of Süleyman. In the texts of these later centuries, it was as though the land tenure law had only sprung into being in the mid-sixteenth century, primarily in the writings of Ebu's-Su'ud.[56]

Military fiscal change and land tenure

Over the course of the late sixteenth century and most of the seventeenth, the stability of the peasant's rights on the land – lifelong hold, the ability to pass the land to children if they had them and the ability to transact with permission – contrasted ever more starkly with the position of the administrative and military elite classes. During this period, the Ottoman Empire experienced tremendous upheaval that resulted in a more varied and complex system of land-revenue holding options for the elite. Freezing weather associated with the Little Ice Age stalled military efforts; provincial rebellions, peasant flight and regicide created strains that had not been seen since Timur the Lame shattered the empire in 1402.[57] Simultaneously, the empire was faced with the same evolving fiscal-military pressures that confronted its contemporaries across Eurasia. These combined pressures changed the configurations of revenue-collecting tenures in the empire and offered new options to the elites, but none of these options immediately offered a stronger guarantee of control over land or its revenues.

In particular, the expansion of tax farming and the reduction of military benefices is considered one of the most significant transformations in the history of the empire. In response to the refinement and proliferation of firearms on the battlefield, the size of the Ottoman army had been growing. The number of infantry troops, both janissary and irregular, increased sharply in the sixteenth and seventeenth centuries: the former grew from 13,000 in the 1550s to 38,000 in the 1600s.[58] Corresponding to the same trend, the demand for cavalry officers diminished; this, combined with the need for cash to pay the salaries of the infantry, led to some *timar*s and *zeamet*s being converted to tax farms. In this new fiscal arrangement, the right to collect taxes was auctioned off for a period of typically three years, although the treasury could (and did) revoke the contract before the term was up.[59] For the tax farmer, it was therefore a risky and insecure investment. The contract to collect was awarded to the highest bidder who agreed to pay the treasury a particular cash amount for the duration of the contract, whether (or not) he was able to obtain that amount from the peasant taxpayers. In 1670, a certain Isma'il Efendi was awarded a contract to collect the taxes for two villages – Dayr al-Qanun and Kafr al-Zayt – in the province of Damascus. Isma'il Efendi pledged to remit 330.25 kuruş for these villages annually.[60] Although this arrangement, known as *iltizam*, helped bring in much-needed cash, most contemporary seventeenth-century Ottoman observers saw the reduction in military *timar*s and the rise in tax farming as synonymous with military and fiscal decline. They believed that the reduction in *timar*s weakened Ottoman military forces by reducing the number of fighting men and further complained that the few *timar*s remaining no longer went to the 'deserving' combatants but to palace favourites and peasants who had attained them through corruption.[61] Generations of historians accepted these observations, and the 'decline' of the *timar* system became a central feature in narratives of a more comprehensive 'Ottoman decline' after the reign of Süleyman.[62] However, revisionist studies of the last forty years have seen the transition to tax farming as both ensuring the empire's survival and modernizing the fisc.[63] For revisionists, scaling back the *timar* system to expand an infantry paid in cash allowed the military to reshape itself according to the needs of the time, and was both rational (in the Weberian sense) and progressive (in the Marxist sense).

Although Linda Darling has recently argued that the scale of the *timar* to tax-farming transition has been exaggerated, it still seems reasonable to hold that there was a more diverse set of revenue collecting tenures that had emerged by the middle of the seventeenth century.[64] In addition to *timar*s, *waqf*s and the spread of tax farms, there appeared large private holdings called *çiftlik*s or *falaha*s which became an important feature of land tenure and fiscal practice in some areas of the empire.[65] As a subject of great scholarly scrutiny, *çiftlik*s have been intensely studied to see if they heralded the emergence of market-oriented estates which wealthy individuals held as de facto or de jure private property.[66] The consensus that has emerged is that they were neither; rather, they remained *miri* land and thus subject to all its constraints.[67] The result, therefore, of evolving fiscal-military practice was that a broader variety of tenure and tax collecting options became available to the administrative elite. However, none of these options offered more security to the possessor, for they were all subject to regular confiscation.

The growing diversity of tax-collecting arrangements also meant a growing complexity in determining the legal rights held by the tax-collecting class. The land tenure *kanuns* adopted in the sixteenth and seventeenth centuries had been directed at the *timar* system and assumed that the deputy was in most cases a *sipahi*. Were tax farmers and treasury agents – personnel whose titles varied depending on the type of collection grant but which included *voyvodas*, *mukataacıs* and *mültezims* – able to claim the deputy's legal powers over the land and the cultivators? On this important question, *kanuns* and fatwas provide surprisingly little insight.[68] Occasionally, fatwas do explicitly state that a specific *voyvoda* or *mukataacı* was authorized to exercise such prerogatives as 'giving the land by *tapu*'.[69] Likewise, the seventeenth-century *Şeyhülislam* Çatalcalı 'Ali Efendi (d. 1692) ruled that a *mukataacı*'s permission was necessary to erect a building on *miri* land.[70] These fatwas suggest that some of these revenue collectors did have legal authorization to assume the powers of the legal person known as the deputy (*sahib al-ard* or *sahib-ı arz*) although it is not clear whether they possessed such authority as a general matter or only in a limited number of cases.[71] Unlike the situation of the *sipahis*, whose legal rights were spelled out very clearly in *kanunnames* and fatwas, the standing of other kinds of tax-collecting personnel within the legal framework of land tenure was never articulated with the same precision.

Land tenure rights trickle up

In the long run, it was the need for fiscal stability, as well as a greater need for payments in cash, that ultimately drove a broader dissemination of the relatively strong property rights enjoyed by the peasants. Ottoman political thought and administrative policy had consistently emphasized the need to keep peasants settled in their villages and engaged in production.[72] By contrast, the Ottomans had demanded the mobility of their elite class through both military campaign and the rotating of posts. It is not surprising therefore that in the sixteenth and seventeenth centuries, the class of Ottoman subjects with the strongest legally enforceable property rights on land was the peasantry rather than the elite. However, the legal 'harmonization' of the peasant's bundle, that is, its systematic articulation and dissemination in Ottoman legal administration, was likely one factor allowing this situation to change at the end of the seventeenth century and the beginning of the eighteenth. At that time, circumstances were ripe for the bundle of rights held by the peasantry to 'trickle up' the social ladder to other Ottoman subjects, including the elites. Several historians have posited the eighteenth century as a time with a new emphasis on settlement: the empire's borders began to stabilize, tribes were encouraged to settle down and mobility that had been long accommodated or even mandated was discouraged.[73] Additionally, expansion in tax farming and trade in an increasingly monetarized economy meant that new opportunities for accumulating riches beckoned to those with money to invest.[74] Consistent with these trends, the eighteenth century was a time when a number of new paths to lifelong tenure on land or to space in commercial and residential buildings emerged – only a few of which will be dealt with here.[75] As we will see, Ottoman officials, including muftis, appeared generally inclined to see these innovations as beneficial for institutional stability and overall prosperity.[76]

Two new property-rights bundles that took root in the late seventeenth century – *ijaratayn* and *malikane* – were both bundles which secured lifelong *tasarruf* for the holder in terms that legally mirrored the peasant's bundle. While it is impossible to prove that Ottoman jurists and administrators consciously modelled *ijaratayn* and *malikane* on peasant *tasarruf*, it seems more likely than not that they did. The key component in the formulation of both of these new rights bundles would be the transition from a limited-time contract or rental to one that was lifelong, and a transition from an advance (*muʿaccele*) that was a fixed portion of the rent to one that was a payment for the lifelong hold, as was *tapu*. What can be stated with confidence is that the basic structure of the cultivator's bundle was legally replicated in *ijaratayn* and *malikane* and extended to other, more privileged groups in the Ottoman social hierarchy: those classes to benefit from these new bundles were tradesmen, moneyed urban investors and powerful families of the military class. The proliferation of these bundles securing lifelong *tasarruf* was one of the most consequential developments of the eighteenth and nineteenth centuries, profoundly impacting economic life, fiscal policy and political order.

The bundle of rights known as *ijaratayn* could be held by renters on *waqf* properties, whether land or buildings, and became widespread in the *waqf*-owned properties of Istanbul in the eighteenth century.[77] The term literally means 'the two rents', and refers to the structure of payments of the tenancy: the renter, also known as a *mutasarrif*, paid a large up-front 'rent' (*muʿaccele*) that was more like a purchase price and thereafter paid a regular rent calculated on a daily or monthly basis (*müʾeccele*) that was fixed for the duration of the contract and could not be raised. So long as he paid the yearly or monthly rent, the *mutasarrif* was entitled to remain renter for life. With the permission of the *mutawalli*, he could transfer (the same term, *faragh*, was used) possession of the *ijaratayn* to another. When the *mutasarrif* died, his children, but no other heirs, would receive equal shares to the right to renew the *ijaratayn* lease, which they did by paying a new up-front rent and contracting a new yearly cost.[78] The advent of *ijaratayn* has intrigued historians because it required Hanafi personnel to set aside at least two normative rules in the rental of *waqf* property. First, Hanafi jurisprudence did not usually allow rental property held in *waqf* to be rented longer than three years.[79] Second, some ulema held that structuring rent payments as *muʿaccele* and *müʾeccele* was only permissible if the *muʿaccele* met Mehmet Birgevi's definitional rigour outlined previously: it must be a specified amount of the totality of the rent incurred over the duration of the contract.[80] The *muʿaccele* of *ijaratayn* did not meet this standard, for like *tapu*, it allowed the renter to take up a lifelong tenancy so long as he continued to pay the rent. What is clear is that from a legal standpoint, the acceptance of this *muʿaccele* that was not 'technically' a *muʿaccele* but rather a compensation in return for lifelong tenure lay at the heart of *ijaratayn*'s increasingly widespread usage.

Given the similarities in structure, a number of historians have seen *ijaratayn* as an extension of the *miri* land tenure system to *waqf*.[81] Perhaps a better way to conceive it is that both the peasant's bundle on *miri* land and the renter's *ijaratayn* bundle were grounded in the terms of *tapu* and were given their systematic shape in the sixteenth and seventeenth centuries. Long before *ijaratayn* was a regular feature of renting urban *waqf* properties in Istanbul, an identical arrangement existed routinely on agricultural land held by rural *waqf*s.[82] On these lands, cultivators held the land by *tapu*, farming under terms similar to those that had been systematized for *miri* land. Instead of paying the *tapu* fee and yearly taxes to a *sahib al-ard* in return for lifelong tenure, they made these payments to the *waqf*s *mutawalli*.[83] A fatwa issued by the seventeenth-century *Şeyhülislam* Zekeriyazade Yahya Efendi states that when a cultivator died childless, the land he farmed that belonged to a *waqf* was 'liable for *tapu*' and that the *mutawalli* could give the land to a new cultivator after collecting the *tapu* fee.[84] The muftis' fatwas appear unfazed by peasants holding *waqf* land for a lifetime tenure by *tapu*, despite its irregularity in length of tenure, structure of payments, heritability and so on. Given that the terms of *tapu* pre-dated the Ottomans, one may hazard a guess that many lands were farmed by *tapu* before they were endowed, that the arrangement continued thereafter and that the muftis were not eager to tamper with terms that had long been acceptable to all.[85]

The question is how this bundle came to be established as valid for renters on any *waqf* property – that is, buildings in addition to land. As early as 1624 or 1625, a *firman* indicated that all such properties were to be treated as similar:

> On the sultan's *waqf*s, those who are *mutasarrif*s through *muʿaccele* and *müʾeccele* of land, residential houses, or commercial spaces, if they transfer to others or their parents die and for three months with no excuse they neglect to acquire permission and inscribe (the transfer of the rights) in the *waqf*s register, then the *mutawalli* can delegate it to someone else and rent it to whomever he wants.[86]

What this *firman* indicates is that the sultan already regarded the terms of *ijaratayn*, including the rights of children to inherit them, to apply to commercial and residential buildings as well as land. While some historians believe that *ijaratayn* could be found on urban *waqf* property as early as the sixteenth century, Süleyman Kaya maintains that while sixteenth- and seventeenth-century Ottoman muftis found lifelong *tasarruf* secured by *muʿaccele* to be acceptable for agricultural land held in *waqf*, they refused to accept similar terms for a *waqf*s buildings or orchards.[87] It was only in the late seventeenth century, he maintains, that such resistance abated. Whenever *ijaratayn* began to be applied to buildings, many historians associate its proliferation in urban areas with the eighteenth century.[88] They conclude that due to the frequency of urban fires and earthquakes that destroyed *waqf* properties in Istanbul starting in the late seventeenth century, muftis and other Ottoman administrators began to allow and even encourage *waqf* administrators to offer lifelong tenure to prospective tenants in a bid to rehabilitate properties that would otherwise sit in ruins. Some fatwas lend support to the role of these disasters in legitimating the *mu'accele*, stating that the *waqf* needed this upfront 'rent' for a repair without which the property would be worthless.[89] However, it is clear that a *waqf* did not need to be in distress to rent by *ijaratayn*: in the eighteenth century, lease of *waqf* property by *ijaratayn* became so widespread in Istanbul that Barnes speculates it may have become more common than the traditional single rent.[90]

The extension of this bundle of rights to residential and commercial renters on *waqf* properties became a widespread and normative arrangement in the city of Istanbul in the eighteenth century. Because of the role of the fires, the history of *ijaratayn* can be written as the story of a compelling social need that pushed judges, muftis and other Ottoman authorities to reshape the law. However, as the *firman* cited earlier demonstrates, there was a legal infrastructure already in place for these judges, muftis and other administrative personnel to turn to when compelling social need arose. It is true that the fires likely popularized the arrangement and made officials more likely to see a benefit for the *waqf* in bestowing this bundle upon the renter.[91] However, the bundle that *ijaratayn* offered to these renters was not an innovation, but one already widespread on both *miri* and *waqf* agricultural land and regulated by *kanun* on both land and buildings held by *waqf*s by the early seventeenth century. The muftis' broader acceptance of it across different property types and social classes appears to be less of a leap, therefore, when we recall that they already accepted that the exchange of *mu'accele* for lifelong tenure was beneficial on agricultural land, whether *miri* or *waqf*.

Perhaps the best-known bundle of rights that replicated the terms of the cultivators' *tasarruf* was the tax farm known as the *malikane*. It was to be the *malikane* that would finally secure for the military elite class of the Ottoman Empire the same terms of access to *miri* revenues that peasants had possessed on *miri* land since the sixteenth century. The *malikane* debuted at the end of the seventeenth century when the treasury was under extraordinary pressure. After more than a decade, the Ottoman military in 1695 was still mired in an unsuccessful struggle against an alliance of the Habsburgs, Venetians, Poles and Russians in the War of the Holy League. Desperate to tap into the resources of the empire's mightiest and wealthiest subjects, administrators in Istanbul saw a need to come to new terms with its provincial magnates. The administration was willing to give more security to these elites if it was able to demand more in return.

The *malikane* was a tax farm that allowed its *mutasarrif* to hold the right to collect taxes from a village for as long as he lived. The *malikane* evolved in a context where it was becoming more common for the treasury to demand a specified advance from the tax farmers who held collection rights through *iltizam*, and these payments were playing an increasingly important role in fiscal planning.[92] For the *iltizam* holder, the advance he paid was a 'real' *mu'accele:* it was a large percentage of the totality of the revenue that the tax farmer would owe on the contract, and both the period of contract and the total sum it was to bring to the treasury were specified. As with *ijaratayn*, the key innovation of the *malikane* was to make this *mu'accele* into a payment that was no longer a 'real' advance on a specified sum, but rather a payment that secured lifelong possession, like the *tapu* fee. The *mutasarrif* of a *malikane* paid *mu'accele* and thereafter remitted smaller annual payments to the treasury for the rest of his life: in 1695, Ahmad Ağa and Husayn Ağa received a *malikane* contract to collect taxes for the same villages – Dayr al-Qanun and Kafr al-Zayt – that Isma'il Efendi had contracted twenty-five years previously. The yearly amount they pledged was nearly identical: 330 kuruş; what was different was that they paid a *mu'accele* of 1,430 kuruş to secure their right to collect in these villages and a third one as well.[93]

There were other familiar features in the transmission of the *malikane* from one holder to another. The *malikane* was awarded by auction – it was bestowed upon the highest bidder on the *mu'accele*. When the *malikane* was initially offered across the imperial domains in 1695, anyone with the money to pay was allowed to bid for one, but after 1714, bidding was confined to the military class.[94] Through this restriction, access to a *malikane* became a perquisite of those who served the state as warriors or administrators. Although it went back to the auction block upon the possessor's death, the *mutasarrif*'s son could pre-empt the sale to an outsider by agreeing to pay the highest bid for the *mu'accele* that the treasury had received.[95] Post-mortem transmission of the *malikane* was more restricted than that of either *miri tasarruf* or *ijaratayn*, but its strict limitation on partibility and its recognition of the *mutasarrif*'s child or children as having a special claim upon the father's patrimony was in keeping with the general pattern of transmission for the other two.[96] The *malikane*'s *tasarruf* could also be transferred during the possessor's lifetime (again, the same vocabulary, *faragh*, was used in the documents) as long as the judge serving in the province where the revenue source was located – as well as the chief judges of Rumelia and Anatolia – agreed that the transaction was appropriate and gave their permission.[97] Here again, the *malikane*'s transaction with supervisory permission confirmed the resemblance between this bundle and that of the peasant.

Offering this bundle to its elites was a profound reversal of earlier trends in Ottoman administration. As we have seen, in the sixteenth and most of the seventeenth centuries, both administrative policies and fiscal realities had left most members of the military class with no secure long-term claims to *miri* land or its revenues. However, the Ottoman administration of the late seventeenth century decided that circumstances had changed, and it would be in the treasury's interest to offer stability to its powerful subjects as well as its humble ones. Prior to the *malikane*, the normal three-year term of tax farming had encouraged the tax farmer to extract as much revenue as possible during the short duration of the contract without any concern for the long-term viability of the village and its cultivators.[98] This led to considerable hardship for the villagers, who sometimes simply abandoned their villages. The firman accompanying the introduction of the *malikane* noted that if the tax farmer had a permanent interest in the village's ability to produce, this would lead to a better outcome for all concerned:

> the [*malikane*] *mutasarrif* knows that so long as he lives, the village he has contracted will not be given to another for protection or mastery, so he concerns

> himself with its improvement so that the harvest tithe that he takes for himself will increase. Because he assists the poor cultivators with their seeds and the rest of the things they need and preserves them from the outstretched hand of oppressors as well as injustice and enmity, their [the peasants'] circumstances are placed in order.[99]

By positing a link between the stability of the tax collectors and the ability of the cultivator to produce, treasury officials now had reason to want the tax farmers to stay in place, just as they had previously wanted the cultivators to stay in place. With stability in mind, the treasury offered to the elite class the same bundle of rights that had been enshrined for the peasantry since the reign of Süleyman: lifelong *tasarruf*, *faragh* (transfer) with permission and *intiqal* (the ability to pass the bundle) to a male child after death.

The 'harmonization' of the cultivator's bundle within a Hanafi framework opened the door for a specific constellation of property rights to take root in Ottoman legal and administrative practices. This bundle was to be the first of three – including *ijaratayn* and *malikane* – that bestowed lifelong possession by (1) paying a *muʿaccele* that was not a 'real' muʿaccele according to Hanafi transactional law and (2) remitting regular rent or tax payments thereafter. When political and economic forces drove Ottoman officials to bestow more robust property rights upon a broader number of subjects, it seems unlikely that the officials recreated the terms of peasant *tasarruf* by pure coincidence; it is more likely that their familiarity with the peasant's bundle moulded those devised for the elites and urban investors. However, even if there was no direct influence, the fact remains that in the eighteenth century, Ottoman elites acquired property-rights bundles that were uncannily similar to those of the peasants. However it came about, lifelong property rights had finally 'trickled up' to urban investors and military elites. If the awkwardness of the *tapu* fee had made the cultivator's *tasarruf* difficult to reconcile with Hanafi jurisprudence in the sixteenth century, both the payment and the lifelong tenure became deeply established within the empire's legal practice by the eighteenth.

The old and the new

In 1739 the Ottomans won a decisive victory over Austria and Russia, ending what was to be their last successful campaign in Europe. The city of Belgrade returned to Ottoman rule, having been ceded to Austria in the 1699 Treaty of Karlowitz that had concluded the War of the Holy League. By the early eighteenth century, the Ottomans were evolving from a state that sought territorial expansion to one that sought reconquest; after two disastrous wars with Catherine the Great of Russia in the second part of the century, they were sought to maintain territorial integrity. The various bundles conveying lifelong *tasarruf* played a vital role in the Ottoman ability to survive, adapt and navigate the challenges of the eighteenth and nineteenth centuries. Of these bundles, the *malikane* was perhaps the most momentous in shaping Ottoman fortunes. The revenue raised from this new fiscal device is seen as crucial to the continuing ability of the empire to fund its military operations – often heavily delegated to provincial administrators – until the second half of the eighteenth century.[100] The portfolio of assets that brought in the largest amount of yearly income was controlled by the head accountancy (*Baş Muhasebe*). In 1697 only 5.3 per cent of its income came from revenues related to *malikane*, but by 1774 it was 43 per cent and the amount of income had increased from 10,752,920 *kuruş* to 161, 619,480 *kuruş*.[101] For a time, the treasury not only raised more revenue but, by collecting three regular payments per annum from the *malikane mutasarrifs*, it also received a predictable and more regularized stream of income that facilitated planning for expenses and how to meet them.

While its fiscal benefits were of great importance, the *malikane* was also the catalyst of a political transformation that unfolded during the eighteenth century. Previous Ottoman elites had at regular intervals lost access to the *timar*s and tax farms that were the source of their wealth, but the *malikane* allowed a newly stable class of elites, known as *ayan*, to secure their wealth and status and to pass both to their offspring and clients. A number of families rose to prominence this way within the bureaucracy and in the provinces; both military administrative and *ilmiye* positions tended to be dominated by a new class of such powerful families and their clients.[102] Across the Ottoman domains, local dynasties emerged who dominated the provinces through the 'intendent' position that oversaw the local tax farms.[103] Frequently combining tax farming with political office, families like the 'Azms of Damascus and the Karaosmanoğlus of Manisa became the power brokers outside of Istanbul.

The strengthening of such families through lifelong *tasarruf* of tax revenues supported the emergence of a politics that was both more pluralistic and more accountable. Across Anatolia and Rumelia, the position of *ayan* evolved into an elected office, in which numerous stakeholders had a vote.[104] This trend towards pluralism was not confined to the provinces but would ultimately erupt on a larger stage. The *ayan* and the central bureaucracy often had shared goals and found ways to come to terms with each other through negotiations rather than fiats and defiance. For example, an *ayan* family like the Jalilis of Mosul obtained lucrative contracts to supply provisions to Ottoman troops fighting the Persians, and in return the administration received a reliable stream of supplies.[105] While the relationship had its tensions, the *ayan* had greater incentive to support a government that upheld its prerogatives and which would continue to abide by the greater accommodation extended to them. Additionally, the *ayan* no longer looked at one another solely as competition to be neutralized but also as peers with similar interests, which could be better protected if they acted in unison. Hence, in 1808, it was the *ayan* who ended the janissary coup that had removed Sultan Selim III and who collectively agreed to protect the sultanate in the Deed of Alliance, the empire's first Magna-Carta-like document.[106] On behalf of the newly enthroned reformist sultan, Mahmud II (r. 1808–1839), the grand vizier Mustafa Bayraktar signed this document that limited the sultan's 'authority to revoke statuses, offices, and contracts and order confiscations and executions'.[107] In other words, the privileges which the *ayan* had first experienced through lifelong *tasarruf* of their tax farms served as the basis for the first limitation on the sultan's power explicitly stated in a political document.

For roughly half a century, the *malikane* provided enough income to keep the empire in good fiscal health. However, this was due in part to a long peace with Europe from 1739 to 1768 where there was little demand for military expenditure, but also a lack of investment in strategic military renewal to prepare for future wars.[108] The result was two humiliating losses to Catherine the Great's Russia at the century's end. By the time that ambitious military reform began in 1798, the Ottomans were decisively outmatched by their rivals in the European theatre. Reform was costly, and early in the administration of Mahmud II new streams of revenue were sought through *ijaratayn* contracts granted on imperial *waqf*s; *ijaratayn* was to have an important role in the government's fund-raising efforts as the administration considered how it might draw more revenue from *waqf* property.[109] In other words, the innovative forms of lifelong *tasarruf* that had arisen on the model of peasant tenure continued to supply a financial lifeline to the empire well into the era of reform.

By the mid-nineteenth century, the question of how to meet the empire's expenses had become critical. Surveying the stakeholders of the rural economy, administrators pondered how to effectively manage the empire's most important productive asset: its agricultural land. Tasked with discerning what laws had come to govern the land in their own time, a council of scholars and bureaucrats assembled to draft a single text, a land code, that would meet the reforming empire's needs. As they would state when they presented their finished code in 1858, to find the extant land law they had consulted a massive corpus of interlocking texts that had come to govern the land law, in particular *kanunname*s and collections of fatwas, although it is clear they also included manuals of jurisprudence. The resulting code affirmed the continuing centrality of the bundle granted to the cultivators as lifelong *tasarruf* in the empire's political and economic life; just as it had been key to establishing a well-funded and well-ordered polity in the past, the reformers saw it as key to creating a well-funded and well-ordered polity in the present. In the following chapters, we will turn our attention to the forging of this textual tradition where this committee had located the land law, and how it had, over three centuries, largely coalesced around what the land law was, how it was made and where it applied.

Chapter 2

CONQUERING A NEW TERRAIN: ESTABLISHING THE SULTAN'S LEGISLATIVE AUTHORITY

If Ottoman ulema accepted that the sultan made the land law, what in their view authorized him to do so? There is a widespread belief that in the Ottoman period and even before it, Muslim jurists had concluded that land law was an arena where the sultan (or the imam, as he was called in many texts) possessed the ability to make the law.[1] This view is questionable. According to many such ulema – the famous Syrian scholar Ibn Taymiyya (1263–1328), for example – overseeing treasury assets like land revenues and allocating them for state expenses did fall under the sultan's jurisdiction. As long as he followed general guidelines set by sharia, then his decisions about these matters could be considered governance that was compliant with sharia (*al-siyasa al-shar'iyya*).[2] However, Ibn Taymiyya was equally adamant that such governing, though licit, was not law-like in character.[3] In his view, rulers issued specific orders in response to specific circumstances, and these should not be treated as general rules that created binding precedent. Guy Burak has argued that the authority of a sovereign-made 'dynastic' law was a key intervention of the Mongols, and that prior to the Mongol invasions – and afterwards in places like the Mamluk domains that had never experienced Mongol rule – the validity of a ruler issuing a 'law' remained suspect to the ulema.[4] Other scholars tend to agree that in the pre-Ottoman and pre-Mongol Muslim states, 'the domain of *siyasa* was (at least in the eyes of religious theorists) one of ad hoc pragmatic action rather than of law'.[5] The ulema had long expected the sultan to make war and keep order, but a sultan creating law that was to be observed consistently and in perpetuity was a novel development.

To this we may add yet another caveat: although the awarding of agricultural revenues as grants to soldiers and administrators was the sultan's purview, jurists did not see matters of peasant tenure as equally subject to the sultan's discretion.[6] Burgeoning with treatment of the cultivator's relationship to the land and distinctions between owners, renters and sharecroppers, the *fiqh* explained how to transact land, how to classify it for taxation and how much tax could be extracted from cultivators; Ottoman *şeyhülislam*s like Kemalpaşazade and Ebu's-Su'ud saw the jurisprudence on these matters as a constraint that could not be ignored. It would therefore be inaccurate to say that by the sixteenth century it had been established that jurists regarded the sultan as widely free to legislate matters pertaining to land, especially when it came to issues of cultivator tenure and transactions. Given that many *kanunnames* nevertheless contained land tenure provisions that dealt with these issues, there was a question of what status these directives held within the practice of the jurists.

The *Kanun-ı Cedid* opens by telling the reader that the sultan is empowered to make the law of land tenure because the lands of Rumelia and Anatolia are in the possession of the *bayt al-mal* (public treasury). Most of the first section of the text is composed of fatwas issued by Ebu's-Su'ud or *kanunnames* that he authored, marking him as the designated architect of the sultan's legal authority. If the *Kanun-ı Cedid* asserts that the sharia ultimately authorizes the practices in the land tenure *kanun*, it avoids highlighting the ways in which Ebu's-Su'ud's understanding of a sultan's powers over treasury lands is far more vast than any of the previous Hanafi jurists had imagined. Not surprisingly, a number of scholars have viewed Ebu's-Su'ud's use of the *bayt al-mal* paradigm as an 'Islamic' sanctioning of pre-existing practice and sultanic control over land tenure law.[7] However, thinking of it this way obscures that it was a dramatic and consequential intervention into Hanafi teaching. Ebu's-Su'ud and his successors substantially redefined the Hanafi understanding of the sultan's powers over land in the *bayt al-mal* by rescripting the treasury as a specifically Ottoman institution. Far from giving the sultan unfettered control of the land, previous Hanafi juridical texts gave the sultan no role in bringing land into the treasury's custody and explicitly bestowed upon the sultan only two or three narrowly conceived powers that were based on his claim to the *kharaj* tax. Ebu's-Su'ud's rethinking of the *bayt al-mal* paradigm in light of Ottoman administrative priorities – such as preventing arbitrary dispossession of the cultivator – led him to argue that treasury control of the land was secured immediately by the sultan's conquest of it. This was a profound break with previous Hanafi teaching. Furthermore, the sultan did not just set the land's tax rates and organize *kharaj* collection, he had sole control over legislating the property rights. It is an irony that earlier generations of Ottomanists viewed the adoption of the *fiqh*'s terminology for land law as a move that would diminish the sultan's capacity to legislate; in fact, the reformulation of the relationship between the sultan and the *bayt al-mal* was a doctrinal justification of far greater legal authority.

As a text that set out to comprehensively define Ottoman land law at the end of the seventeenth century, the *Kanun-ı Cedid* presented Ebu's-Su'ud's theoretical mission not as religious window dressing for raw temporal power, but as the scaffolding upon which the current law had been constructed. The text presented the land law existing at the end of the seventeenth century as a coherent body of law built by Süleyman, his administrators and their successors. For the text's compiler, the age of Süleyman was not a golden age but rather a foundational one: it marked the beginning of an era where the sultan or his appointed officers exercised sovereign legal control of the land law and could alter, amend and abrogate the law as needed with the expectation that every branch of the bureaucracy and every document produced by it would shift accordingly. The compiler then catalogued exactly how successive sultanic administrations had wielded this power. It detailed the laws governing usage rights for cultivators and how they were acquired or transferred; the burgeoning post-mortem transmission laws, which were enacted in the post-Süleyman era; the taxes due on cultivators and other licit demands of the *sipahi* or deputy; the procedural issues regarding the times of harvest and payments; jurisdictions of administrative personnel and dispute resolution between cultivators and officials. Thus, the *Kanun-ı Cedid* credits Ebu's-Su'ud with creating a framework that allowed the sultans' officials to make and remake the existing land law through *kanunname*s, *firman*s, registers, fatwas and petitions all grounded in the same terminology and conceptual universe. For the compiler, the land law was dynamic and evolving not in the centuries before Süleyman but in the centuries that followed.

Texts and contexts

One could argue that Ebu's-Su'ud was engaged in an Ottoman conquest of his own. He seized a particular space – one that was both physical (the empire's lands) and textual (Hanafi jurisprudence on the issue of treasury-owned land) – and redefined it in ways that gave the sultan a singular claim to legislatively control it. This move was not only consistent with a broad range of strategies that the sixteenth-century Ottomans were using to amplify the sultan's power and the larger project of building and organizing the sultan's regime, but it also had relevant correlates in other parts of the early modern world. As was the case in many early modern empires, it highlighted the connection between legal and geographic imaginaries in conceptualizing sovereignty.[8] Historians have long noted that bids by European monarchs to expand their territory and concentrate their legal and bureaucratic might were accompanied by new 'political theologies' wherein rulers acted as delegates of God and claimed God-like demands of obedience.[9] Similarly, historians of the Islamic world have also paid increased attention to the blossoming of a new fifteenth- and sixteenth-century politico-theological vocabulary of universal sovereignty – featuring World Conquerors, Lords of Conjunction, Vicegerents of God, and so on – that was addressing the universalist claims of rivals in Europe as well as Muslim audiences of potential allies and foes.[10] There were any number of monarchs in early modern Eurasia looking for theorists and administrators who would assist them in making absolutist claims or finding mechanisms to consolidate their legal power. In Christian Europe, many relied on what Perry Anderson calls a 'skilled stratum of legists' trained in Roman law and hence able to provide such services.[11] Not a few of these legists were men of the church, which was at the centre of reviving Roman law and pioneering a new concept of a prince as the sole legal authority in the papacy.[12] The Ottomans too made use of a highly skilled set of bureaucratic personnel that, increasingly in the sixteenth century, had received formal training in Islamic jurisprudence.[13] As a member of such a cadre, Ebu's-Su'ud certainly seemed like the kind of theorist that any early modern monarch would have been glad to have in their employ, and his mission would have been infinitely recognizable to his scholar–statesmen peers.

The evolution of the Ottoman ruling institution in the sixteenth and seventeenth centuries is also pertinent to the transformation of lawmaking that the *Kanun-ı Cedid* is illustrating. Eurasian empires not only made claims to greater power, they also developed large bureaucratic institutions, formal administrative processes and produced copious documentation to realize these claims. As such, the greater number and organization of Ottoman administrative personnel in this period was key to expanding the might of the Ottoman state on the battlefield and within the Ottoman domains. Recent studies have examined the tension between the rhetoric of the sultanate that designated all power as concentrated in the person of the sultan while in practice his authority was delegated and enacted by a sprawling bureaucracy. According to Hüseyin Yılmaz, the different sections of the administration functioned by design as checks on one another and on the sultan, which meant that actions taken in the name of the sultan reflected a process of consensus among various administrative officials rather than the single will of a sultan or a grand vizier.[14] Heather Ferguson has observed that the cadre of officials who composed the political works known as 'advice literature' in the sixteenth and early seventeenth centuries no longer saw the sultan as the embodiment of statecraft but rather idealized 'an abstracted and bureaucratized vision of governance'.[15] This tension will be apparent in this chapter as well as those that follow. While the *Kanun-ı Cedid* records laws enacted on the sultan's authority, its component pieces are rarely attributed to a sultan; far more often, they are attributed to specific members of the sultan's regime and call attention to the role of multiple bureaucrats and bureaucratic processes in constructing the law.

The bureaucrat that most concerns us in this chapter is the *şeyhülislam*, the head of the learned section of the bureaucracy known as the *ilmiye*. From the fifteenth century, the *ilmiye* had become an increasingly hierarchically organized entity with defined paths of entry, ranks and promotions, and its membership had increasingly come to think of themselves not only as scholars, but as scholar-bureaucrats who formed a part of the Ottoman administrative elite.[16] There is some question as to when the *şeyhülislam* emerged as the head of this branch of the bureaucracy, but general agreement that Ebu's-Su'ud's appointment in 1545 cemented its importance.[17] Perhaps it should come as no surprise that a bureaucrat of such high rank would take a foundational role in articulating the practice of land tenure law.[18] Although he is said to have 'Islamized' the *kanun* and opened a path for the *ilmiye* to take a more assertive role in making and administering the land law, he in fact opened a path for officials working in different parts of the bureaucracy to make continuing interventions in the land law in a complementary and coherent way.

'Preserved in the bayt al-mal*': Acquiring land for the treasury*

The concept of ownerless treasury lands – typically referred to as *aradi al-mamlaka* or *aradi al-hawz* in the *fiqh* – was certainly present in the influential Hanafi works of jurisprudence that were widely studied in the Ottoman Empire.

The eminent Hanafi scholars Fakhr al-Din Qadikhan (d. 592 AH/1196 CE), Ibn al-Bazzaz al-Kardari (d. 827 h/1424 CE) and Farid al-Din 'Alim ibn 'Ala' al-Ansari (d. 786 AH/1384 or 1385 CE) all conceived of it in relatively similar ways. It was a place where land escheated if there were no heirs when its proprietor died, or that came under the supervision of the imam because there was no one able to produce the *kharaj* owed on it. Ebu's-Su'ud's innovation would be to redefine the *bayt al-mal* as an institution that did not acquire land haphazardly over time, but rather which took control of all newly conquered land from the moment of conquest. A profound break with earlier Hanafi teaching, it gave the sultan an immediate claim to control over the land that previous Hanafi teaching had not bestowed.

The early Hanafis concluded that a Muslim sovereign had two options for how to treat a land newly conquered by the Muslims: one option was to divide the land among the victorious soldiers and let them rent it to the cultivators; this land was *'ushri* and paid a tax amounting to a tithe (*'ushr*) of its produce.[19] The other was to allow its previous owners to retain the land, with the provision that they pay an agricultural tax called *kharaj* and the poll tax on non-Muslims called the *jizya*. The rate of *kharaj* varied according to what the land could bear, but it could be high – as much as 50 per cent of the produce – and could be levied as either a fixed sum (*kharaj muwazzaf*) or a designated portion of the harvest (*kharaj muqasama*).[20] The dominant view of the school over time came to be that if the land was later acquired by a Muslim, it did not become tithe-land, but rather remained subject to *kharaj* since it was the status of the land at the time of conquest that was the basis for the classification.

Whether the land was given to the conquering soldiers or to the previous owners, the Hanafi school was unanimous that the land became the *milk* property of either the conquerors or the conquered.[21] The Hanafi doctrine designating *kharaji* land as *milk* was unique among the Sunni schools. While the three other schools held that *kharaji* land was land that the imam had designated as a *waqf* for the benefit of the Muslim community or property of the treasury for the same purpose, the Hanafis did not.[22] This is the reason that early in the development of the Hanafi legal tradition, simply naming a land as *kharaji* came to mean that it was held in freehold ownership, in other words: *milk*.[23] Designating the land *kharaji* rather than tithe after conquest was the favoured position of the Hanafi school: according to Abu Yusuf (d. 798) – an early Hanafi authority on land classification and tax – the caliph 'Umar ibn al-Khattab had favoured confirming the possession of the conquered inhabitants and imposing *kharaj*.[24] 'Umar declared that this choice was better because the money collected from the cultivators would be held in perpetuity for the Muslims and would support the community for generations. Some scholars find it highly unlikely that 'Umar in fact recognized peasants as proprietors, but the question of whether the early Hanafis were correct or incorrect in their interpretation of 'Umar's actions is beside the point.[25] Whatever historical reality transpired, the position of the school was that newly conquered land became *milk*, usually *milk* belonging to the previous possessors out of respect for the precedent that Hanafis attributed to 'Umar.

As a consequence, Hanafi jurisprudence since the ninth century treated land as *milk* and treated it extensively as a subject of taxation, rental, pre-emption, inheritance and sale while the subject of land possessed in the *bayt al-mal* remained a marginal topic.[26] Qadikhan, Ibn al-Bazzaz and al-Ansari treated these lands, which they called the *aradi al-mamlaka* or *aradi al-hawz*, as *kharaji* lands that had come to the custody of the treasury or the imam primarily through abandonment by those who had tended them.[27] The scholar al-Ansari, who compiled the work *al-Fatawa al-Tatarkhaniyya*, cited various other scholars who collectively asserted that the imam took responsibility for *kharaji* lands with no owner, or whose owner 'was incapable [of farming] or left it untilled or abandoned it'.[28] As a result, there was some attempt to set guidelines for how the lands' owners might be able to reclaim them, or how much of the produce was still the owner's property. Only lands that escheated to the treasury because a cultivator died with no heirs was unambiguously in the permanent custody of the treasury.

Baber Johansen has demonstrated that a major innovation in Hanafi doctrine arrived in the writings of a prominent fifteenth-century Hanafi scholar living in Mamluk Egypt, al-Kamal ibn al-Humam (d. 1457).[29] Ibn al-Humam argued that the land of Egypt in its entirety had come into the possession of the treasury because its cultivator-owners had died without heirs, and thus the land had reverted to the treasury.[30] The context for this claim was one similar to the situation of Ottoman Rumelia and Anatolia: in Mamluk Egypt, patterns of cultivation and tax collecting did not easily accommodate a claim of proprietorship by either the grant-holding military men or the peasant cultivators, with a resulting disagreement over who had the right to sell or endow such lands.[31] Given these circumstances, Ibn al-Humām's innovation can be understood much in the same vein as Ebu's-Su'ud's: that is, as a legal theory that could create administrative coherence. The embrace of Ibn al-Humam's theory by the very influential Egyptian Hanafi scholar Zayn al-Din b. Ibrahim Ibn Nujaym (d. 1563) ultimately led to its adoption as the dominant position among the Arab Hanafis.[32]

Ebu's-Su'ud's intervention was to be far more radical than Ibn al-Humam's. It is unclear that he was familiar with Ibn al-Humam's work, for he never mentions the theory of the 'death of the cultivators' as a justification for treating land as *miri*.[33] Ibn al-Humām adhered to the standard Hanafi teaching that after conquest the land had been someone's *milk*, and the imam or the treasury took custody of it only after a lengthy, piecemeal historical process of its owners dying without heirs. However forced it appeared, the theory conformed to pre-existing Hanafi doctrine. It is worth noting that *Şeyhülislam* Kemalpaşazade, Ebu's-Su'ud's highly respected predecessor, had also stuck close to the conventional Hanafi explanation of how the lands had entered the treasury: no one knows any longer who the owners were at the time of conquest, he wrote, or the owners died out.[34] This was an explanation with limited use for the sixteenth-century Ottoman state. The 'death of the cultivators' was formulated to deal with lands that had been under the governance of Muslim sovereigns for centuries, where the idea of successive generations of cultivator-proprietors dying and leaving lands to the treasury was at least plausible. By contrast, Süleyman's administration needed a theory that could explain why land conquered in his own lifetime, or more importantly, land that would be conquered in the future, could be regarded as treasury land immediately.

With regard to the question of how the treasury had acquired the land in the Ottoman case, Ebu's-Su'ud squarely adopted the position of the other Sunni schools that was foreign to Hanafism: he declared that newly conquered lands became property of the treasury upon conquest. In one of his fatwa-like statements that was made for the *Kanunname of Thessaloniki and Skopje* dating to 1568 or 1569, he wrote:

> What is called *arz-ı memleket* is *kharaji* in origin. However, if it had been given as *milk* to its owners, it would have been divided among many heirs at their deaths, with each heir receiving a meager portion. Assigning *kharaj* to each share would have caused great problems, or in fact been impossible. Because of this, the *raqaba* of the land was kept for the *bayt al-mal*.[35]

Ebu's-Su'ud laid out here a new doctrinal position for the Hanafis based on Ottoman state practice.[36] In this reconfiguration, the treasury was not where land was placed after individual claims to it expired, it embodied the first claim to the land after conquest. In this same statement, the way that Ebu's-Su'ud defined tithe and *kharaji* land – as land that the sultan granted as *milk* – implied that Hanafi teaching allowed the sultan to either give the land as *milk* or not to do so; at the time, this was not the position of the school. Beyond this insinuation, he made no explicit claim that taking newly conquered land for the treasury was consistent with prevailing Hanafi teaching in the *fiqh*. However, he did frame it as the only course of action that would allow the sultan to exercise a right that no Hanafi jurist would deny him: the right to assign and collect *kharaj* from treasury lands.[37] The consensus in the Hanafi juridical literature that land owed *kharaj* to the imam and it was licit for him to take a variety of actions to ensure that he received it was left unstated in the text but would have been familiar to learned readers.[38] Hence, his statement presents not as a swapping of the Hanafi doctrine for the Shafite one, but as an expansion of the Hanafi position to include the Ottoman administrative procedure for assigning *kharaj*. Using the Ottoman procedure was justifiable, his statement maintains, when the procedure familiar from the juridical literature would obstruct rather than facilitate the collection of the tax. As such, this statement is not simply a justification for Ottoman practice, it rescripted Hanafi practice of the sharia itself.

Ebu's-Su'ud's redefinition of the *bayt al-mal*'s lands has not produced a great deal of scholarly appreciation for how radical it was. In all likelihood, it is because this shift has been seen as an Islamic varnish on pre-existing administrative practice.[39] Hence it is not reckoned to have substantially impacted either administrative practice or Hanafi teaching. As we will see later and in subsequent chapters, however, the vision of the sultan and the treasury–land relationship enacted in the *kanunnames* and fatwas written by Ebu's-Su'ud would ultimately redefine the Hanafi understanding of this relationship across all Ottoman legal genres, including those that were scholastic rather than administrative.

'Neither tithe nor kharaji*': The status of the land for transaction and tax*

We have seen that Ebu's-Su'ud rescripted the functioning of the Hanafi *bayt al-mal* and created a doctrine positing *miri* as the primary category of land in Rumelia and Anatolia; what powers did he assign to the sultan over these lands? Unlike the texts of jurisprudence that were a formative influence on his thought, Ebu's-Su'ud would claim a recognizably legal authority for the sultan over the land; decisions made by the sultan, once propounded in registers and *kanunnames*, were binding as a set of rules in perpetuity unless later replaced through the same process. The most innovative way that Ebu's-Su 'ud would make this claim would be in selectively stripping *miri* land of its *kharaji* character. Ottoman historians often find it difficult to understand whether Ebu's-Su'ud essentially understood *miri* land as *kharaji* or as something different.[40] This is because Ebu's-Su'ud shows some inconsistency on the question: when he wrote about taxation issues, he tended to emphasize that the 'origin' or 'essence' of *miri* land was *kharaji*, but when he responded to questions about transactions and property rights, he stressed that *miri* was not *kharaji* because it was not *milk*. Ebu's-Su'ud's formulation of agrarian taxes have received a good deal of perceptive scholarly treatment; hence I will touch on taxation matters only briefly at the end of this section. The more interesting and less examined issue is how Ebu's-Su'ud understood the sultan's power to legislate the property rights of *miri* land, primarily tenure and transactions. On this subject too, his work would reshape both the process for making land law and Hanafi teaching of property right and tax.

According to the texts of Hanafi jurisprudence, what powers over treasury land did the sultan possess? In the Arabic-speaking lands, a number of texts on treasury land cited the fourteenth-century Somali scholar al-Zayla'i, who wrote with regard to the *aradi al-mamlaka*: 'The imam has *wilaya 'amma* (general governance), and it is for him to make managerial choices in the interests of the Muslims.'[41] While this sounded like a robust kind of authority, its elaboration typically made clear that the jurists conceived of this power as the kind of 'ad hoc pragmatic action', which Marion Katz has described. Al-Zayla'i himself made this remark preceding his conclusion that the imam had the power to sell the *aradi al-mamlaka* if he deemed it beneficial to the interests of the Muslims. Like other Hanafi jurists, al-Zayla'i saw the sultan's power as a mandate for taking specific actions that maintained production and the flow of *kharaj* revenue. Discussion of the sultan's role was typically limited to how the sultan – not the cultivators – could transact the land. The jurists explicitly and unanimously condoned the sultan's leasing such lands to 'capable' cultivators or arranging for their sharecropping in order to collect the *kharaj* due from the land.[42] There was some disagreement about whether the sultan could sell these lands, although from the sixteenth century a number of prominent Hanafis agreed with al-Zayla'i that if the finances of the state required it, it was permissible.[43] That these lands were classified as *kharaji* and actually paid *kharaj* was indisputable.

Ebu's-Su'ud had reservations about conceptualizing treasury land as *kharaji*: as we have seen, the dominant doctrine in the Hanafi school was that *kharaji* land was *milk*. Likewise, paying the *kharaj* on a piece of land was proof of freehold ownership.[44] Ebu's-Su'ud desired no confusion on that score, especially if it meant the issuing of court records that documented transactions of sale or *waqf* that supported a claim that the land was *milk*. He therefore took the radical position that *miri* land formed a separate and distinct third category of land not extensively dealt with in the books of Hanafi *fiqh* and which was therefore a blank slate for the sultan's legal authority. Ebu's-Su'ud faced a number of queries where he was asked to explain whether the land was tithe or *kharaji*. It was in response to such questions that he advanced the position that *miri* land was not only land that belonged to the treasury but land that could not be either *kharaji* or tithe *because* it belonged to the treasury. In one fatwa, he explained the difference between tithe and *kharaji* land, adding 'both of these two types of land are the *milk* of their possessors. But most of the lands in these greatly blessed domains are not like these. They are neither tithe nor *kharaji*, but rather *aradi al-mamlaka* because [their owner] is the treasury.'[45] Another fatwa makes it even clearer that when property rights are the issue, *miri* land is not *kharaji*.

> Question: Is *miri* land what the books call tithe land or *kharaji* land?
>
> Response: What the books call tithe land and *kharaji* land is the *milk* of its possessors. For both of them the rules (*ahkam*) that apply to *milk* are valid in their entirety. On *miri* land, not one of these rules is valid. Its origin is *kharaji*, but it has not been given as *milk* to anyone and assigned to the *bayt al-mal*.[46]

This statement went well beyond the declaration that *miri* land is not *milk*; rather it declared the rules of the *fiqh* for the category of *milk* in its entirety – transactions, usage rights and so on – to be null and void on *miri* land. In yet another statement, after explaining tithe and *kharaji* land at length, he writes that 'the land that is expounded in the books of sharia is of these two types. But there is another type of land that is neither tithe nor *kharaji* in the way described: this is called *arz-ı memleket*.'[47] In other words, the 'books of the sharia', do not explain the order of treasury land, they only deal with tithe land and *kharaji* land. Taken together, these statements relayed the message that the rules of land tenure and transaction in the Hanafi texts of jurisprudence did not apply to *miri* land; one should not look to these texts to find such rules.

Hanafi jurisprudence was not quite as silent on tenure and transactions relevant to *miri* land as Ebu's-Su'ud claimed. The position of the cultivator had received some attention – albeit fleeting – in the juridical texts. In these texts, there was a general understanding that the cultivator's lack of ownership meant that transactions that were normal for *milk* could not be valid. Ibn al-Bazzaz wrote that since the cultivators of these lands did not own them, they could not sell them.[48] This lack of transactability was not a problem, at least theoretically. Because the Hanafis treated *aradi al-mamlaka* as *kharaji* lands that were delegated, rented or given to sharecropping by the ruler, the cultivators' rights and powers over the land were like those of tenants rather than owners.

> If the sultan gives land which has no owner – and this is called royal lands (*aradi al-mamlaka*) – to a people in order for them to pay *kharaj*, it is permitted. It is permitted that he do so in one of two ways: they take the place of the owners by cultivating it and paying *kharaj*, or by paying rent in the amount of the *kharaj*.[49]

Legally, the cultivators were conceived as tenants rather than proprietors, but this did not mean that they could be easily turned off the land. Hanafi rental law had changed in the late medieval period, reflecting new realities on the ground where cultivators no longer exercised powers of ownership over the land, if indeed they ever had. Jurists like Qadikhan ruled that peasant communities did not need a lease in order to be legally regarded as renters, and that cultivators who had lived on such lands for ten years could not be evicted because, at that point, they possessed lifelong tenure: *haqq al-qarar*.[50] By the thirteenth century, if not before, many Hanafis concluded that if peasants owned trees or buildings on land they rented, the landlord could not demand that they destroy these properties at the end of the rental period, as had previously been the case.[51] Instead, the landlord must continue renting the land to the cultivator (unless it caused some harm) so that he would not be separated from his *milk* property. Cultivators who built houses, planted trees or who had made improvements to their rented land possessed a right that was called *kirdar*: this meant that they had the right to stay on the land as long as they cultivated, and the Hanafis allowed the sale of *kirdar* as well.[52] Hence, even before the Ottoman land tenure system began to take shape, the Hanafi law of rental was developing mechanisms for coping with non-proprietary cultivators and their need for stable access to the land and to its transaction.

Ebu's-Su'ud was fully aware of these developments and incorporated some elements – like *haqq al-qarar* for the lifelong tenure of the cultivator – into his fatwas. Although his Turkish-language fatwas did not typically allude to the great Hanafi authorities in these matters, his Arabic-language fatwas acknowledged some indebtedness to jurists such as Ibn al-Bazzaz and Qadikhan on issues of peasant usage and transaction.[53] On the whole, however, the Hanafi jurists' nascent solutions to peasant security and transaction through rights bundles like *kirdar* – which owed much to local custom in their own lands – were not suitable for his purposes. It is clear that the jurists did not connect rights like *kirdar* or *haqq al-qarar* to the powers of the sultan.[54] Rather, the cultivators established these rights through their own acts of cultivation and continuous use. In the texts of *fiqh* then, peasant security and alienation of their land rights remained independent of the sultan's ultimate authority over treasury-owned land. The lack of sultanic control over these matters ran against the grain of Ottoman administrative order. By the 1530s and 1540s there were already a number of *kanunname*s – some general in scope and others crafted for specific provinces – that regulated some aspects of tenure and transaction as well as tax.[55] *Tapu* certificates had been issued in accordance with these, and judgements issued in court were based on these *tapu* documents.[56] In effect, the textual genres produced by the chancellery were already functioning in place as the law of the land on tenure and transactions. The question was, from the perspective of what the sharia required, what was the status of these texts?

By stripping Hanafi juridical texts of authority over the category of *miri* land, Ebu's-Su'ud laid the groundwork for accepting the sultan's written orders as the only legal texts governing the category of land that encompassed the vast majority of plowlands in Rumelia and Anatolia; in voiding the 'rules' of the *fiqh*, he cleared a space for the sultan's laws to fill. In Turkish, his fatwas are typically oblique, simply explaining the terms of tenure and the proper terminology for transactions: the *tafwid/tafarrugh* transaction instead of sale and transmission (*intiqal*) instead of inheritance. How Ebu's-Su'ud had discerned this order to be the valid order for *miri* land was left unstated. For instance, why could land be left fallow for up to three years before it could be confiscated? Was this a precedent laid down in the Hanafi texts? An order of the sultan? An adoption of a widespread custom among the people? The *Kanunname of Thessaloniki and Skopje* once again offers an answer. Ebu's-Su'ud begins by enumerating the ways in which 'the efficacious registers of the sultan and the up-to-date imperial writs' have secured the prosperity of the sultan's subjects of all kinds.[57] He then adds, 'but in the old venerable registers, there is no detailed account of the situation of land of the protected domains'. As a result, it continued, questions had arisen of whether the land was *kharaji* or tithe; was it *milk*? What was the rate of taxation? Could it be endowed? Because the sultan ordered him to clarify these matters, he wrote, he would present at length an explanation of the different categories of land, and particularly, that of *miri* land.

It is here that we find an answer to the question of where one locates the rules of *miri* land and how they are made. This *kanunname*, speaking with Ebu's-Su'ud's voice, presented the law of *miri* land as having long existed in the old registers drawn up for the provinces. Ebu's-Su'ud's own explanation is merely an elaboration of the rules contained in these registers and an account of their shar'i basis. In Ebu's-Su'ud's 'kanunized' voice, it is the sultan's registers – not the texts of *fiqh* – where one finds the law of *miri* land: indeed, the fact that his response to an order from the sultan to expound upon the *miri* order became itself the basis of this *kanunname* (and subsequently, other *kanunnames* as well) only serves to illustrate this point more clearly. On *miri* land, there is no order other than the one enacted by the sultan's *firmans*, *kanunnames* and registers, that is, the texts issued at the sultan's directive. It was the sultan's orders and registers which proclaimed that *tasarruf* legally passed from one person to another with the *sipahi*'s permission and the payment of *tapu*. It was, again, texts enacting the sultan's orders that set the rules for alterations to the land and their tax consequences, and it was, yet again, the sultan's orders that designated who was eligible to claim the cultivation right when a cultivator died. Ebu's-Su'ud accepted that there were some restrictions on what the sultan could rule in regard to all of these matters but, more to the point, he had largely eliminated any source of law for *miri* land outside of the sultan's orders in the transaction and tenure of *miri* land.

As adamant as Ebu's-Su'ud could be that *miri* was 'neither tithe nor *kharaji*' with regard to property rights, he was equally adamant that the land still owed the *kharaj* tax. Repeatedly, Ebu's-Su'ud stated that what the peasants paid was in fact *kharaj muqasama* and *kharaj muwazzaf* even though these taxes were known by their customary names of tithe and *çift akçesi* or *ispence.*[58] It was this seeming contradiction that would prove to be a heavily debated (and condemned) aspect of Ottoman administration in the Arab provinces.[59] Like Ebu's-Su'ud, the eminent Egyptian jurist Ibn Nujaym also concluded that once the land became property of the treasury, it ceased to be *kharaji.*[60] However, he applied this conclusion to very different ends: he found it to be an effective, if cynical, way to argue that Egyptian *waqf*s – and many Egyptian individuals – should not have to pay any agricultural taxes. This position, that the peasants were tenants on treasury land and hence owed rent, not tax, to the treasury, was one that Ebu's-Su'ud rejected. Keeping the cultivator's payments under the rubric of tax rather than rent was favourable to the treasury. Without a rental contract, rent fell due only if the land was worked: if the payment was understood as rent rather than as tax, it would not be obligatory for the cultivator to pay it in a year if he chose to leave the land fallow. On the other hand, we have seen that the *kharaj* tax was due from any *kharaji* land whether or not it was cultivated, so long as planting was feasible. While a tax was clearly preferable to rent from a fiscal standpoint, Ebu's-Su'ud's resistance to conceptualizing the peasants' payments as rent was complicated by the fact that he not infrequently described the relationship between the treasury and the peasant as one of rent by defective lease (*ijara fasida*), although he also employed an analogy of loan (*'ariya*) rather than rent.[61] Insisting that these taxes were *kharaj* by another name also allowed the rates of taxation to be adjusted according to what the land could support, and that even rates such as one-half of the produce could be justified, though it seems that very high rates were not common.[62] This insistence was yet another example of the way that Ebu's-Su'ud rescripted sharia practice to conform to the Ottoman administrative practice laid out for *miri* land in the sultan's registers, as Heather Ferguson has perceptively observed.[63] Unlike transactions, Ebu's-Su'ud affirmed that the taxes described in the texts of *fiqh* were applicable to *miri* land; nevertheless, he insisted that the definition of *kharaj* in the sultan's domains resided in the sultan's registers, as did the rules pertaining to *miri* land generally.

In conclusion, the Ottoman position that the sultan was the undisputed – and in some visions, exclusive – source for the law of property rights and transactions on treasury lands was more a break than continuity with past Hanafi juridical understanding. The great Hanafi jurists of the twelfth through fourteenth centuries whose scholarly texts were well known in the Ottoman Empire had no such conception of the sultan's power over treasury land. By claiming that Hanafi juridical texts offered guidance for the tenure and transactions for tithe and *kharaji* land – but not for *miri* – Ebu's-Su'ud defined *miri* land as a terrain, both physical and juridical, where the texts enacting the sultan's authority were the only pertinent law. This was an innovation that bestowed a far more potent legislative authority on the sultan, while simultaneously scripting the order of *miri* land as sharia practice.

Building a coherent law

How did Ottoman administrations put into practice the legal power over the land articulated in the fatwas and fatwa-like *kanunname*s of Ebu's-Su'ud? Arguably, the sultan did not need a juridical theory to justify law making, it was a power that could be – and was – argued to rest on the sultan's mandate to bring order and justice to the world. Nevertheless, it could only help the sultan's cause to say that there was no way for the sultan's law to clash with the sharia on *miri* land because the *fiqh* had no law for *miri* land. It is also clear that in the wake of Ebu's-Su'ud's theoretical endeavours, the way that Süleyman and his successors made the law for *miri* land changed rather abruptly. In these changes, we can see plainly the sultan (or, more accurately, his administration) assuming the wider legislative power that theory bestowed. It is widely known that Ebu's-Su'ud claimed for Süleyman the right to intervene in debates among the Hanafi jurists and to choose to elevate one position to an enforceable status while disposing with competing interpretations in the Ottoman courts.[64] Süleyman had the same ability to adopt and pledge to enforce some parts of pre-existing *kanun* and to dispense with others.[65] The *kanunnames* meant for empire-wide observation contained numerous discrete provisions and some of these were inconsistent with one another or created administrative difficulties. There was also variation in the provisions of *kanun* from one province to another, or variation in local custom that may have been considered part of the *kanun* by the provincial population. Putting the sultan above custom and earlier iterations of *kanun* gave him an option of rooting out such discrepancies and creating a more uniform land law, which could be applied across the imperial domains.

A prime example of this issue is seen in the conflicting *kanun*s about the circumstances in which the peasant could be dispossessed of his *tasarruf*. It was the sixteenth-century Ottoman administration that shored up the cultivator's protection from confiscation: earlier precedents had not always been as favourable to the cultivator. One *kanun* in the *Kanunname of Bayezid II* (r. 1481–1512) states: 'If a peasant abandons his farm or leaves it untilled either from sickness or poverty or old age, let the *sipahi* take *bennak resmi* from him, and take the land from his possession and give it to another.'[66] The power of confiscation that this *kanun* granted to the deputy was extremely broad: if any peasant failed to produce in a given year, the *sipahi* could confiscate the land in his possession even if the cultivator had a valid (or temporary) reason for failing to cultivate. A seventeenth-century jurisprudence guide composed by a judge, Mustafa b. Süleyman Balizade (d. 1662), suggested that the amount of time before confiscation differed according to what was customary in each community: it referred to confiscation of unattended land happening after a 'known' or 'customarily defined' (*ma'rufa*) period.[67] As we have seen, this broadly defined power of confiscation had some basis in Hanafi *fiqh*, where even *kharaji* land held as *milk* could be taken from its owner and given to another to tend if the owner was unable to work it and pay *kharaj*. While the jurists agreed that the imam should return the land to its owner if he became capable of working it, cultivators on treasury lands were not the owners and therefore had no claim to restoration if they were removed. However, in the same *Kanunname of Bayezid II* there is another *kanun*, which is more restrictive about the *sipahi*'s power to dispossess the cultivator: 'It does harm to the *sipahi* for a peasant to leave his land fallow for three years if that land will support cultivation. In order to redress the harm, *örf*[68] permits that a land that has remained unplanted three years will be taken from its possessor and given to someone else who pays the *tapu* fee.'[69] It was this latter rule that was consistently embraced in the fatwas of Ebu's-Su'ud and which became a regularized feature of the cultivator's property-rights bundle. With one important exception, the other tradition that gave more leeway to confiscate simply disappeared from later *kanunnames*.[70]

There was as yet another step for the dynasty to take in order to fully embrace the power that Ebu's-Su'ud had claimed for it. Ebu's-Su'ud's earlier work does not give the impression that he was formulating a justification for the sultan to intervene in ongoing practices and change them. He seemed more concerned with systematizing the available traditions of *kanun* and choosing which to enforce and which to discard, just as he did in limiting the power of the deputy to confiscate the cultivator's holding. At some point, though, it seems to have occurred to Süleyman's administrators that if the sultan had the power to make the rules of tenure on *miri* land, then he was not necessarily obligated to choose among pre-existing *kanuns*, customs or precedents in the *fiqh*; he could in fact make new rules. The sultan's role here was shifting from one that was more of a designator of applicable law to one where making the law was a more prominent component.[71] This was a shift in emphasis more than a complete break with precedent, but its emergence seems to have been an unforeseen or indeed a not-altogether-thought-out consequence of Ebu's-Su'ud's insistence on Süleyman's legal stature. The phenomenon that best illustrates this gradual assumption of a more properly legislative sort of power – a power that did not align with the prevailing understanding of the sultan's powers over lands in the treasury as the jurists understood them – was the issue of allowing females to hold and transact *tasarruf*.

When a cultivator of *miri* land died, who would be allowed to take his place on that land? When Süleyman came to the throne, the answer varied somewhat from province to province, but was largely consistent in one respect: females did not succeed to the land of a male relative. The *Kanunname of Budin* declared that since *miri* land was not *milk*, it could not be inherited. Rather, the right of *tasarruf* could be transmitted to his son who could then take his father's place upon his death. The *kanunname* specifies that sons only have this right. If no sons remained, then the *sipahi* was to appoint someone from 'outsiders capable of making [the lands] flourish (*ḫāric'den ta'mīre ḳādir kimesneler*)' to take the *tasarruf*.[72] The son received the land from his father without paying any fees, but the outsider appointee became the legally recognized cultivator only upon paying *tapu*. Although in Budin the *kanun* recognized the son as the sole family member with a right to take the place of a deceased cultivator, the provincial *kanunnames* of Karaman and Izvornik (dating to 1528 and 1548 respectively) specified some circumstances where the deceased's brother could become heir to the *tasarruf* if no son survived him.[73] Whether it was only sons or both sons and brothers that were designated heirs, there was a general unanimity that daughters, and women in general, were excluded. It is worth noting that the *Kanun-ı Al-i Osman* issued during the reign of Süleyman specifically prohibited daughters from taking the *tasarruf* of their fathers, stating: 'If a cultivator dies without a son, but a daughter remains and claims "this land was my father's, and therefore I have come [to claim it]", the *sipahi* is forbidden to give the land to the daughter.'[74] This succession policy was entirely in keeping with the jurists' writings about the sultan's powers over lands that belonged in the treasury. By excluding daughters, Sultan Süleyman was aligned with the jurists: as a general rule, the ulema did not regard females as 'capable' cultivators able to pay agricultural tax and hence eligible for possessing treasury land.[75] Notable is that the language used by a number of the jurists to describe the kind of tenant the sultan should seek out: 'capable of making the land flourish' is a phrase that was directly incorporated into the *Kanunname of Budin*.[76] The jurists, the sultan and prevailing custom all appeared to be aligned on this point.

No later than 1568, however, the law had changed. In that year, Sultan Selim II ordered, and Ebu's-Su'ud issued a concurring fatwa, that a cultivator's daughter could pre-empt others from taking the *tasarruf* when he died, provided that he had no sons and that she would pay the *tapu* fee.[77] A similar order granting the opportunity to take the land by *tapu* first to a daughter and then to a brother in the absence of a son appears in the text known as the *Ma'ruzat*, a work which recorded the position that would be enforced in the Ottoman courts on points of law that were controversial in the Hanafi school.[78] There were likely multiple reasons for this decision. One may have been related to justice and equity: brotherless Muslim women expected to be the chief heir of their father.[79] As early as 1550, a petition from daughters asking for their father's lands had led to a conditional legal change where Ebu's-Su'ud acknowledged that if a cultivator had brought waste land under cultivation and died without a son, his daughter was entitled to the land's *tasarruf* as long as she paid *tapu*.[80] Another reason may be related to what Alan Duben believes to be the dominant model of household in the Turkish-speaking Ottoman lands. Duben writes that male siblings usually divided households upon their father's death, meaning that joint households with two brothers co-habiting with their respective wives and children were rare.[81] If a cultivator died with a daughter but no son, then there was likely no other 'capable' male cultivator – the deceased's brother or his sons – already living on the farm to contest her claim and present himself as the natural heir.

The decision to allow transmission to daughters was yet another break with the preceding Hanafi *fiqh*'s conception of the sultan's authority over treasury land. While Ebu's-Su'ud's vision of the sultan's powers had been more expansive than the *fiqh*'s since early in his career, the tenure laws that Süleyman enacted had nevertheless been consistent with the few priorities articulated by the earlier Hanafis. The policy of excluding daughters was ideologically consistent with the jurists' understanding of the sultan's responsibility to keep the land in productive, masculine hands. Nonetheless, it was abandoned by the reign of Selim II. The sultan was not simply in the business of creating his own transaction law; he no longer found it necessary to hew to one of the few responsibilities that the jurists had explicitly enjoined upon him; that is, ensuring that the land remained under the care of capable (male) cultivators. The redefinition of treasury land as a domain where the sultan had a free hand to enact his own law that reversed precedent was even more firmly established.[82]

With the sultan's administrators empowered to create novel legislation for *miri* land, the exercise of the sultan's legal power took a new turn from the 1560s. Over the next five decades, successive sultanic administrations would issue new *kanuns* that built a regularized post-mortem transmission law dedicated primarily to keeping viable farms intact rather than splitting them among multiple heirs, almost as though it was creating a dynastic policy for peasant households. The process by which the law was created showed both a greater coordination among administrative offices and a rise in shared coherence across documentation. Administrators began to examine *firmans* issued in response to petitions that cultivators presented to the sultan and adopting some of these as *kanun* made the law generally applicable to *miri* land.[83] The transmission (*intiqal*) law spelled out in these *kanuns* eventually comprised six or seven blood relatives if the deceased cultivator was male: first sons, then daughters, then brothers, then sisters, then the father and finally the mother.[84] An agnatic grandson could pay *tapu* and claim the land of his grandfather so long as the latter left no living sons; such a grandson's claim preceded that of the daughter.[85] By declaring that no relatives outside of this group had a claim to the land on the basis of kinship, the Ottoman state created something like a 'family charter' for the empire's cultivators.[86] After these family members came a host of others with shared property rights who could expect to lay claim to *tasarruf* before it was offered to an outsider: anyone who owned *milk* property such as trees or buildings on the land would have priority, followed by cultivators who held joint possession of the land through a partnership, followed by any cultivator resident in the village who desired more land to work. These regulations gave those with pre-existing property interests priority and militated against fragmentation of the farm by ensuring that heirs who inherited the trees or the farmhouse according to the rules of *irth* would have priority in taking the land with their inheritance and hence would be able to reconstitute the farm.

The construction of this transmission law brightly illuminates the difference between the older Hanafi conception of the sultan's power over the land of the treasury, and that prevailing in the Ottoman Empire from the mid-sixteenth century and afterward. The transmission law originated in the 'ad hoc pragmatic action' of responding to cultivator petitions. However, when the responding order or *firman* was 'stripped' of its particulars and presented as *kanun* governing all such situations in the future, it was enacting a sovereign legal power.[87] By the time this law started to emerge, Ebu's-Su'ud had been writing for over twenty years that such *kanuns* were actionable in the mufti's fatwa and the judge's *hüccet* and that they presented no conflict with other sharia practices in the texts of *fiqh*. Although his fatwas did not typically attribute transaction law directly to the sultan, he was not coy about the origin of the post-mortem transmission law: 'An order has been given that if a daughter remains, and no son, she is given [the land] by paying *tapu*. It has been ordered that it is not to be rented to anyone else.'[88] There was no question of how this part of the law had come into being: the sultan had created it. The legal enactment of the daughter's place in transmission – its passage from petition to *firman* to *kanun* and then to fatwa – highlights the practical side of Ebu's-Su'ud's achievement. The sultan could create new substantive law for *miri* land, and those laws could be administered by judges and muftis without concern that their enactment conflicted with the law existing in the texts of *fiqh*. These transmission laws were not the only new laws instituted in this period; a number of other responses to petitions made the transition to *kanun*. These new *kanuns* addressed matters like the ability of the cultivator to maintain his holding while he was absent from the village or if outsiders could acquire village lands. The *Kanun-ı Cedid* would present this land law that had grown heavy with such provisions as valid because the land was held by the treasury, thus eliding how this understanding of the treasury departed from previous Hanafi teaching.

Conclusion

Jean Bodin was not wrong to identify territorial conquest as a key element in the way the Ottomans understood the legal powers of their sultan. Rapid expansion and the challenge of organizing a newly sprawling empire had inspired new visions of legal order in the mid-sixteenth century. Perhaps it comes as no surprise that legal historians have identified the conquest of the Americas and the questions of land ownership that arose there as the basis for ascendant theories of sovereignty and property in Western law.[89] Tamar Herzog writes of the process of appropriating land from indigenous people and granting it to Spanish subjects: 'The king could intervene in the existing legal order and both relinquish and create rights. This, it was argued, was the meaning of sovereignty: the king's superior and eminent domain over all the land allowed him to distribute it according to public need, denying certain (existing) privileges and creating others anew.'[90] This was the power that Bodin identified as belonging to the Ottoman sultan in the mid-sixteenth century, and one that he sought to claim for the king of France as well. Seeking a more defined control over land and the wealth it produced, a number of Süleyman's contemporaries claimed greater power to make the laws, in addition to executing them or judging them.

The very different context of the late seventeenth and early eighteenth centuries that produced the *Kanun-ı Cedid* was also an age defined by the Ottoman governing elite's desire for success in territorial expansion. Although the *Kanun-ı Cedid* highlights the consistency between the powers assumed by the Ottoman sultan and those that the ulema understood as arising from guardianship of the lands in the *bayt al-mal*, there were important ruptures between the two. The preceding jurists understood the sultan's powers in more limited terms directly related to raising and distributing revenue; they did not envision the sultan as a legislator crafting a new system of tenure and transactions. This expansion of sovereign legal power through redefinition of the *bayt al-mal* was not the only method the Ottomans implemented to gain greater control over the law. The elevating of the Hanafi school to official *madhhab*, the bureaucratization of the ulema into a hierarchy headed by the *şeyhülislam* and the designation of particular positions within the school for enforcement had made the Ottoman sharia a more state-vetted and state-enacted sharia. In addition, sultans began to issue more positive law, which was obligatory upon judges; although these interventions were often related to procedure of the court, they sometimes were truly substantive law-making.[91] Prior to the sixteenth century, Hanafi jurists did not conceive of the lands of the *bayt al-mal* as a place where the sultan could establish order as he saw fit; it was the sixteenth century, and primarily Ebu's-Su'ud who rescripted this juridical concept to fit the new realities of a more powerful and more organized sultanate and bureaucracy. The result would be seen not only in fatwas and *hüccet*s of *ilmiye* scholar bureaucrats, but eventually in the scholarship of the *fiqh* as well.

Chapter 3

CANONICAL VOICES: DISCRETION AND ANALOGY IN THE FORMATION OF THE HARMONY TRADITION OF LAND TENURE

In the seventeenth century, what laws governed land tenure in the Ottoman Empire? What were the texts in which these laws could be found? How were these laws to be administered by *ilmiye* personnel? For the historians who have viewed the *Kanun-ı Cedid* as a comprehensive compendium that simply states the existing law, this text was evidence that the muftis recognized the pre-eminent role of the *kanun* in the governance of land and that their views mirrored those of Ebu's-Su'ud Efendi.[1] To be sure, the selection and arrangement of the fatwas and *kanuns* in the text give the impression that the compiler is merely imparting an interpretive tradition that had already attained both consistency and a broad consensus. However, this is hardly an accurate representation of the state of the ulema's understanding of the land tenure law during this century: there was far more complexity and disagreement on questions of how to discern and implement the land law than we would know from reading the *Kanun-ı Cedid*, which embraced some jurists and strands of thought while ignoring or discarding others. Rather than reflecting the coalescing of an authoritative juridical tradition, the *Kanun-ı Cedid* took an active role in attempting to forge one.

When one examines more broadly the fatwas of the seventeenth-century ulema, one has the impression that what the biographer 'Ata'i had called 'the harmonization of *kanun* and sharia' was not a quick temporal event that ended with Ebu's-Su'ud, but rather that it was an ongoing process that stretched across centuries, in both theoretical and practical terms. The land law could be located in fatwas, scholarly treatises, *fiqh* manuals, *firmans*, *kanunnames* and registers: some of these textual forms were familiar to the ulema but others had not been part of the ulema's training. More so than the ulema of previous centuries, the seventeenth-century ulema were expected to access the content of these less familiar textual forms like registers and *firmans* and to determine how such content 'fit' together with the more familiar genres of jurisprudence to determine the law. The lack of consensus among them about how to determine this fit should not surprise us. As the previous chapter demonstrated, Ebu's-Su'ud's position on the radically different nature of *miri* land and the laws governing it were a profound break with preceding Hanafi thought, and it stands to reason that his successors might reject some of his views or move them in new directions. This is not to say that the seventeenth-century *ilmiye* was divided between those who believed that '*kanun* and sharia' were in harmony and those who did not; as this chapter shows, most muftis can be placed within a 'harmony tradition' of jurisprudence that generally presumed that the sultan's orders were compatible with the practice of Hanafi jurisprudence.[2] However, their work exhibited competing approaches to the question of how such compatibility was to be understood.

When the early-nineteenth-century Damascene scholar Muhammad Amin ibn 'Abidin (d. 1836) encountered the land tenure fatwas of the *şeyhülislams*, he described them as 'curiosities' (*ghara'ib*) that were 'built upon orders of the sultan'.[3] Such a statement is helpful; rather than asking whether the muftis did or did not rule in conformity with the sultan's orders, we might ask how the muftis working within the harmony tradition 'built' their fatwas from the various texts containing the sultan's orders. That Ottoman fatwas were issued on the basis of *kanunnames* and other chancellery texts has long been recognized, but the question of their interpretive stance towards these texts has received less attention.[4] Were the sultan's orders *a* source of the law, or the *only* source of law on *miri* land? Was *miri* land sui generis or could the mufti derive the law governing it through analogy with the categories of land and landholding treated in the Hanafi juridical sources? As these questions indicate, a mufti might 'build' a fatwa in at least two distinct ways. These two approaches were more like the ends of a spectrum rather than mutually exclusive orientations – as we will see, a single mufti could be pulled in either direction depending on the question at hand. One approach can be described as 'autonomist' in nature. It emphasized discretion of the sultan and the deputy in enforcement and further advanced Ebu Su'ud's claim that *miri* land and the legal order prevailing on it were substantially different from the regime of Hanafi laws that governed other kinds of land. It regarded the sultan's orders, registers and officials as the only source of law on *miri* land and was deferential to the plain meaning of these orders and documents. By contrast, the other approach relied more on analogy with provisions of the *fiqh* governing tenancy, transactions and *waqf*. These 'analogist' fatwas tended to assimilate *miri* land's transactions and the rights of its beneficiaries with those that existed in the *fiqh* – particularly those relating to *waqf*. These fatwas were more likely to qualify or amend processes and rights delineated in sultanic orders and *kanunnames*.

This chapter explains how an approach to land law combining aspects of the autonomist approach and the analogist approach began to slowly emerge in the seventeenth century. Because the *Kanun-ı Cedid* presented an unwaveringly autonomist view of the land law, it obscured the importance of analogist contributions to the shaping of this evolution and failed to include fatwas and precedents that would come to dominate the views of the eighteenth-century muftis. For much of the seventeenth century, there was a wide range of opinions among the muftis about what kinds of textual sources composed the land law and the role of the sultan as legislator. An examination of fatwas and scholarly commentary from the early to mid-seventeenth century composed by two provincial muftis and a judge will illustrate the breadth of disagreement that existed about what the land law was and in which texts it could be located. By the middle of the seventeenth century, the *şeyhülislam*s were starting to navigate a middle course that combined a general deference to the sultan's orders while allowing themselves some leeway to qualify or expand rights granted in the *kanun*. Their position tended to confirm the sultan's orders as the ultimate source of the land law, but in some issues they would use analogical reasoning to 'build upon' these orders in ways that were quite significant. Over time, fatwas on the law of intervivos transactions proved the most likely to be influenced by analogist reasoning, while usage rights and post-mortem transmission would adhere more to autonomism.

Contexts of the text

Why would someone compose a text canonizing the autonomist views of the ulema as the embodiment of the harmony tradition, while excluding more analogist voices? The answer to this question is related to the general upheaval of the late sixteenth and early seventeenth centuries described in Chapter 1. In response to the various crises of the period, numerous members of the administrative elite class (though by no means all) admonished the sultan to unswervingly adhere to the *kanun* and restore order.[5] As the next chapter explores, a 'return to *kanun*' was not the only solution proposed to the empire's woes in the seventeenth century, but it was a sentiment with a strong following among a certain Ottoman elite cadre who blamed an influx of outsiders into the privileged military class for the empire's problems and the 'corruption' of the *timar* system. A number of works appeared during the seventeenth century that articulated the 'proper' Ottoman institutional order that should be observed or restored according to the authoritative *kanun*s, and a fair few of these addressed the *timar* system, the status of the land and the law governing it.[6] The *Kanun-ı Cedid*'s seemingly exhaustive approach to the topic of land transaction and tax, and its highly organized assembling of its various authoritative sources were features that linked it to other *kanun*-reliant texts seeking to comprehensively map the 'rightful' Ottoman imperial order.

The compiler of the *Kanun-ı Cedid* was likely a person with ties to the *timar*-holding administrative elite, for the autonomist fatwas he selected for the text staunchly defended the prerogatives of the deputy (*sahib al-ard*); fatwas frequently identified the deputy as a *sipahi*. Those muftis who qualified the plain meaning of the *kanun* in favour of analogy with land law in the *fiqh* – usually *waqf* – often curtailed the deputy's latitude. The fatwas selected for the *Kanun-ı Cedid* consistently ruled that acquiring *tasarruf* of *miri* land could not circumvent the deputy; any path to earning *tasarruf* rather than paying *tapu* to the deputy was rejected. Although the text defended a largely unrestricted reading of the deputy's powers, the *Kanun-ı Cedid* incidentally documents an emerging transformation of the deputy's scope of action. In the late sixteenth and early seventeenth centuries, the new *kanun*s governing post-mortem transmission (*intiqal*), statutory limits on challenges to possession, *tapu* amounts and other issues were enacted, and these increased the dynasty's direct reach into the organization of rural production.

The result was a narrowing of the deputy's latitude in controlling which cultivator possessed the land or how possession could be terminated. In all probability, the *Kanun-ı Cedid* was a product of a compiler seeking to put forward the most advantageous interpretation of the deputy's position within a legal landscape where the *kanun* increasingly regulated the deputy's actions, and the deputy was less often called on to exercise discretion.

Keeping up with the new *kanuns* seems to have required some effort on the part of Ottoman personnel who were responsible for enforcing it. There are a number of documented attempts of judges to keep abreast of newly issued *kanuns*, accompanied by statements that knowing and adjudicating the *kanun* was the judge's duty.[7] Through the first quarter of the seventeenth century, the sultan's seal-bearer, known as the *nişancı*, was the most likely official to whom judges and muftis as well as other administrators might turn for guidance on applying the *kanun* pertaining to *timars* and land tenure.[8] As the official responsible for registering *kanuns* and seeing that they did not contradict each other, it was the *nişancı* who was regarded as the administrator with the primary oversight over the *kanun*, and the historian and eminent man-of-letters Mustafa ʿAli famously referred to this official as the 'mufti of *kanun*'.[9] Officials serving in this position were sometimes responsible for compiling the compendia of land tenure *kanuns* that were in circulation before the compiling of the *Kanun-ı Cedid*.[10] Of these compendia, the most frequently referenced was a text usually dated to 1609 that was the last to bear the name of a sultan, the *Kanunname of Ahmed Khan* (r. 1603–17).[11] Some compendia attached the name of a well-known *nişancı* presumably in a bid for authority, even though they were clearly composed after the death of *nişancı* in question.[12]

What the compiler of the *Kanun-ı Cedid* clearly understood was that, by the late seventeenth century or early eighteenth century, he could not create a text of land tenure law safeguarding the prerogatives of deputies by compiling a *kanunname* made solely of *kanuns* and *firmans*. Over the course of the seventeenth century, the muftis' fatwas had created another source of the land law that had become a key component of the law, and without them, a detailed elaboration of the law was not possible. Although Barkan regarded the fatwas of the *Kanun-ı Cedid* as 'illustrating and providing examples' of issues settled in *kanun*, many of the fatwas are not simply illustrating, they are extrapolating.[13] Choosing only fatwas deferential to the *kanun*, the compiler presented these fatwas – and not the analogist fatwas – as co-constitutive of the land law. Their appearance in a text that was recognizably of the *kanunname* genre imbued these fatwas – like those of Ebu's-Suʿud – with a sense of scripting sharia and the sultan's orders at the same time, and becoming themselves *kanun*-like. While the Damascene Ibn ʿAbidin marvelled at the discovery of fatwas built on the *kanun*, these fatwas were to be an authoritative source of the law for the Turkish-speaking ulema who populated the upper echelons of the *ilmiye* throughout the eighteenth century and would be incorporated into the 1858 Land Code.

We have already seen that Ottoman *şeyhülislams* had taken an active role in ruling on land taxes, tenure and transactions governed by *kanun* no later than the sixteenth century. The *şeyhülislam* did not make rulings on all matters related to the land tenure issues: questions such as who had the proper qualifications for receiving a *timar* were issues out of the *ilmiye*'s jurisdiction.[14] However, matters like tenure rights and their transaction or inheritance frequently came before *ilmiye* officials like judges and muftis; as the head of the *ilmiye*, the *şeyhülislam* acted as an authority who articulated the legal position to which the *ilmiye* membership should adhere. He was empowered to resolve conflicts between other members of the *ilmiye*, to canonize jurisprudential texts and to resolve arguments of the past.[15] In addition, the *nişancı*'s office evolved in the seventeenth century to have less of a legal character, leaving the *şeyhülislam*s increasingly as the primary authority overseeing the *ilmiye*'s implementation of land law from approximately the 1620s.[16]

The increasing jurisdictional control over land law was understood by earlier scholars as 'religious' personnel overtaking the previously 'secular' control of the law.[17] In light of recent scholarship on muftis emphasizing their character as office holders and dynastic appointees, perhaps a better understanding of this transition is one of administrative evolution: legal authority began to be concentrated in one branch of Ottoman administrators, the *ilmiye*.[18] As the head of this branch, the *şeyhülislam* may well have seen it as within his purview to intervene in land transactions and tax disputes to resolve them as he saw fit, even if it broke with precedent set by one of his predecessors in that office or set forth in a *kanun*.[19] Hüseyin Yılmaz has argued that it was part of the *şeyhülislam*'s duties to act as a check on initiatives of the sultan or others in his administration that they deemed contrary to the sharia or public interest, and hence we might speculate that some saw prohibition of any flawed practice – whether it be *kanun* or anything else – as part of the mandate of the office.[20] However, the *şeyhülislam*s may have seen this not as requiring 'secular' legislation to submit to 'religious' doctrine so much as a head administrator exercising one of the powers granted his office; that is, resolving a conflict between authoritative precedents.

The compiler of the *Kanun-ı Cedid* would incorporate fatwas, but would do so in a way that made it clear the compiler did not see them as a source of law parallel to the *kanun*, but as a source derived from *kanun* and ultimately subordinate to it. They are arranged to give this impression by first giving the sultan's order on an issue and then providing fatwas that deal with the same issue. I reiterate that we should not take this configuration of the proper 'fit' between *kanun*s and fatwas to universally represent the views of Ottoman personnel on the subject; as we will see, it was not the only view.[21] Prominently featured in the *Kanun-ı Cedid* are three eminent muftis whose reputation as authorities on the land tenure law was likely established before the compiler created the text. Two of these muftis, Zekeriyazade Yahya Efendi (d. 1644) and Baha'i Mehmed Efendi (d. 1654), were *şeyhülislams*. The third, Pir Mehmed Üsküpi (d. 1611), was a provincial mufti whose scholarly reputation had given him a status of authority beyond his rank. The *Kanun-ı Cedid* presented the fatwas of these three muftis, along with those of Ebu's-Su'ud, as the *ilmiye*'s relevant contribution to the complex textual edifice that governed the land in the late seventeenth or early eighteenth century. With their credentials that lent them weight, these were the voices which would provide guidance to the muftis and judges of later centuries, not only supplementing but largely effacing those of the great Hanafi authorities in the past.

Pir Mehmed and sultanic latitude

If much of the *Kanun-ı Cedid* paid homage to a trio of great *şeyhülislams* (Ebu's-Su'ud, Yahya and Baha'i Mehmed), the single most prominent voice in the text is one that emanated from the provinces: Pir Mehmed Üsküpi. For a sterling example of autonomism, we need look no further. In character, his oeuvre can be seen as a logical extension of Ebu's-Su'ud's, for he too understood *miri* land as operating under a radically different regime of law largely incomparable to the rules of *fiqh* that applied to other lands. He likewise shared Ebu's-Su'ud's view that the sultan was the singular source of law on *miri* land, and more so than the other principal contributors to the *Kanun-ı Cedid*, he sought to establish normative terminology that captured the sui generis status of *miri* land and the law governing it. As we will see, the later seventeenth-century muftis appear to have generally been more in alignment with Pir Mehmed than with the ulema serving as *şeyhülislam* in his own time. Given his impact on the practice of Ottoman land law, he seems to defy the downward flow of authority that we have come to expect from the *ilmiye*. Indeed, the diffusion of the harmony tradition across the empire's provinces challenges the notion that the fatwas of *şeyhülislams* always set the most important trends for the provincial muftis, as the discussion later in the text will demonstrate.

According to biographers, Pir Mehmed had a colourful life, starting his career as a *devşirme* recruit and suffering dismissal from a post as teacher at the Maktul Ibrahim Pasha Madrasa in Razgrad (located in contemporary Bulgaria) after evidence emerged of sexual impropriety in 1582.[22] Shortly thereafter he was appointed mufti of Skopje, and he remained in that position until his death in 1611. Although his career never advanced beyond the status of provincial mufti, the quality of his fatwas gained him a formidable reputation. His son is believed to have assembled his fatwas posthumously to produce two texts that were intended to be, and which became, classic guides to legal questions for Ottoman muftis and judges.[23] One of these guides, *Zahirü'l-Kudat* (The Judges' Assistant), was particularly concerned with land law questions and also preserved land law fatwas issued by Yahya Efendi and Baha'i Efendi.[24] It may be that this text was the main source of fatwas for the compiler of the *Kanun-ı Cedid*, for there is considerable overlap between them.

Pir Mehmed's fatwas sharply differentiated the order of *miri* land from that which governed *milk* or *waqf*. As a provincial mufti, he was bound to explain his rulings and their precedent, an obligation not required of the *şeyhülislams*.[25] Consequently, he incorporated long and thorough explanations into his fatwas, and these explanations document where he locates authority over land law far more explicitly than the terse responses from the *şeyhülislams*. His fatwas in *Zahirü'l-Kudat* often convey that the land law was still developing in his lifetime and that he frequently faced questions where he had no precedent to guide him. Most of these fatwas showcasing Pir Mehmed's confusion were omitted from the

Kanun-ı Cedid, although one manuscript copy has preserved a wider number of them.[26] It is often when the mufti faces indecision that his thoughts about how to discover what the law is become most clear.

Question: When Zayd[27] dies, he leaves his pregnant wife, Hind. After his uncle 'Amr takes his lands' *tasarruf*, Hind gives birth to a daughter, Zaynab. Is the mother able to claim possession for Zaynab?

Response: It's clear that there is an order from the sultan to give it to the daughter, but an order has not appeared specifying if she can take it when she makes the claim after it [the land] has been already given away to someone else … in this case, it's necessary to request a response from the temporal authorities (*ulu'l-amr*).[28]

This passage makes clear that it is the sultan's orders governing this situation, but the problem is that two of the sultan's directives appeared to be at odds with each other. Once a land was given to a cultivator by *tapu*, it was not supposed to be revoked; this was a bedrock principle of the land law. On the other hand, the daughter was to have a right of refusal to pay *tapu* and take her father's land before an outsider. Hence, the mufti requires clarification.

To receive clarification, Pir Mehmed states that he needs guidance from 'those in authority'. This latter term comes from the Quranic verse 'O those who believe! Obey God, obey the prophet and those in authority among you!'[29] The term was used not infrequently to refer to the temporal authorities in general and the sultan in particular. While it is not clear which specific official he intended to turn to, it is clear that he expected someone deputized with the sultan's authority to resolve the issue. In response to queries about *miri* land, Pir Mehmed repeatedly conjures up a space that is exclusively governed by the sultan's written orders and records: his answers are peppered with phrases like, 'a *firman* has been issued to give it to her' or 'the sultan's order (*emr-i sultani*) bestows *tasarruf* on him'.[30] When asked if some villagers could make an in-kind payment in lieu of a tithe, he referred the questioners to the sultan's cadastral register.[31] Drawing a sharp distinction between *miri* land and *milk*, nowhere in Pir Mehmed's fatwas on *miri* land does there appear any citation of the great pre-Ottoman Hanafi jurists and their authoritative works. The one exception, a citation of the jurist Qadikhan, which cites the jurist's admonition to obey the sultan, only serves to drive the point home.[32] Ottoman *şeyhülislams* such as Ebu's-Su'ud and his predecessor Çivizade are the only juridical authorities he cites, and these were Ottoman officials no less than those in the chancery.[33] In short, Pir Mehmed's fatwas treated the sultan not as the most authoritative source of law on *miri* land, but as the *only* source of law.

If Pir Mehmed's views seem extreme in their emphasis on the land as a domain ruled by the sultan alone, it should be remembered that the opposite extreme was also present in the seventeenth century. Vani Mehmed Efendi (d. 1685), who would become the preceptor of Sultan Mehmed IV and a close advisor of the grand vizier Köprülü Ahmed Pasha, served as mufti of Erzurum from 1657 to 1661.[34] In the questions brought before him, he uniformly regarded the land as *kharaji* rather than *miri*, and even included a response stating that sale of land is permitted, because it is *milk*.[35] This despite the fact that a *kanunname* issued for the province of Erzurum in 1540 mandated a tenure and taxation regime that included all the features of a standard *miri* regime for that time: *resmi çift*, *tapu*, post-mortem transmission to male heirs, although there was a move to rename the *ispence* – the *resmi çift* paid by non-Muslims – as *kharaj*.[36] One of the more curious aspects of Vani's fatwas are the units of measure and currency that he uses. Instead of using the conventional unit for farmland, the *dönüm*, or that for currency, the *akçe*, he gave responses full of terminology that was only present in academic works of *fiqh*. When asked about the taxes owed on *kharaji* land for a vineyard, an orchard or wheat, he replied,

> On every patch of arable land (*jarib*) with a length and width of 60 cubits (*dhara'*), if there are grapes or trees then ten *dirhams* are to be taken. If there's wheat or barley sown, then one *dirham* is taken from each *jarib* with one measure (*sa'*) of wheat … just as 'Umar [the caliph 'Umar ibn al-Khattab] imposed [thus] on every *jarib* of sixty cubits.[37]

Here, he supplies an answer that is more theoretical than grounded in the practices prevailing in the province; as in a number of his other responses, he refers here to the authoritative precedent set by the second Muslim caliph, 'Umar.[38] If 'Umar's example takes centre stage, the practice of the Ottoman sultans has no role at all: as a general rule Vani's responses to taxation questions mention no *firmans*, no registers, no state-generated documents of any kind; his citations consist exclusively of scholarly works of *fiqh*.[39] He acknowledged the existence of *timars* and *timar*-holders – the latter are described as the rightful recipients of *kharaj* – but there is no mention of *tapu*.[40] In Vani Mehmed's fatwas, the peasants are proprietors of the land and the taxes they pay are assigned in the books of *fiqh*, not the sultan's registers. This vision was the mirror opposite of Pir Mehmed's; while Pir Mehmed saw no law for the land but that enacted by the sultan, Vani regarded the land law as existing exclusively in the books of *fiqh*. As the next chapter will explore, the question of which view would carry more weight over the long term would remain unsettled throughout the seventeenth century.

Like his predecessor Ebu's-Su'ud, Pir Mehmed searched for terminological distinctions that emphasized that *miri* land was fundamentally different from *milk* and its acquisition was not governed by the law described in the *fiqh*. He was asked many questions like the one cited earlier in the text, where he was asked who was the rightful *mutasarrif* of a specified land. In his responses to these queries, Pir Mehmed often made the distinction between *miri* land and *milk* property by invoking the terms *istihqaqiyya* and *'ata'iyya*.

> Question: When Zayd dies childless, his summer pasture requires *tapu*. His mother wants it and upon her request, the *sipahi* takes

1,102 *akçes* from her and gives her a certificate (*tezkere*) marking the transfer. Five years pass, then an outsider named 'Amr comes and says 'I bought [this summer pasture] from the sons of Zayd's uncle.' Is 'Amr able to displace the mother?

Answer: No, *miri* land is not something to which there is entitlement to rightful ownership (*istihkakiye değildir*), it's a grant (*'ata'iye dir*). He (the *sipahi*) gives it to whom he wishes. Having given it to the mother, the uncle's sons should not interfere at all. Their sale has no validity. Pir Mehmed.[41]

In this fatwa, 'Amr makes a claim of *istihqaq*; that is, he requests to have property that is not currently in his possession returned or bestowed to him, the rightful owner. As a legal term of art, *istihqaq* is similar to replevin in English common law.[42] One also sees a more general meaning of *istihqaq* in legal discourse which has the meaning of 'entitled to' or 'deserves.' The word resonated in a number of registers, yet all of them had to do with possessing a claim to ownership of something not in one's grasp that should be honored and should not be denied. Had the field been *milk*, then Zaid's uncle and his uncle's sons would have been the major heirs and could have sold the field, or a majority stake in it, to 'Amr and he could demand it be turned over to him. But Pir Mehmed rules that because the land is *miri*, there is no such right. Just as Ebu's-Su'ud had declared that a host of normal transactions were void on *miri* land – such as sale, *waqf*, inheritance – Pir Mehmed would avow repeatedly that any claim involving *istihqaq* was connected to *milk* property and was void on *miri* land.[43]

Through a blanket rejection of *istihqaq* on *miri* land, Pir Mehmed emphasized two principles, both of which were consistent with the *Kanun-ı Cedid*'s general trend of preserving the power of the deputy. First, he makes a firm distinction between the nature of *miri* land and that of *milk* that emphasized the sultan's latitude on the former. His statement above that, '*miri* land is not something to which there is entitlement to rightful ownership, it's a grant,' is one that he used frequently to describe how a cultivator comes into possession of *miri* land or can lay claim to it. Using the Arabic word for a grant from the ruler (*'ata'*), he maintains that *tasarruf* of *miri* land is, like a *timar*, a grant from the sultan.[44] It was for the sultan alone to choose who would cultivate and on what terms. Second, Pir Mehmed emphasized the unassailable security of the cultivator who has paid *tapu* and had been recognized by the deputy as the holder of *tasarruf*. Since the decision of appointing a cultivator rested solely with the sultan or his deputy, once the chosen cultivator had paid *tapu*, the cultivator took irreversible possession of the *tasarruf*. No one could challenge the cultivator thereafter by bringing an inheritance claim that was valid only for *milk* property, or for any other reason. The role of the deputy, who actually exercised the sultan's power of choosing a cultivator and collecting *tapu*, was deemed essential in the passing of *tasarruf*. The one obvious exception to this understanding, which Pir Mehmed acknowledged, was father-to-son transmission, which did not require *tapu*.[45] Aside from this important exception, it is clear what Pir Mehmed considers the general rule to be: the sultan or his agents had no restraint on choosing who would have the *tasarruf*, and the cultivator had no basis from which to challenge that decision.

The cases in which Pir Mehmed deals with the lack of *istihqaq* concern postmortem transmission, but a different fatwa suggested that he was picking up on a line of thought already developed in a different context by Ebu's-Su'ud. After all, inheritance was but one means by which a person could claim to be legally entitled (*mustahiqq*) to a property. Pir Mehmed was asked if cultivators who had worked a field for fifteen years without authorization could be dispossessed by the deputy, who gave the field to other cultivators who paid *tapu* for it. Ruling that the deputy's action was valid, Pir Mehmed was then asked if the unauthorized cultivators had *istihqaq* because they had been there for fifteen years, and he answered 'no', citing Ebu's-Su'ud.[46] In this circumstance, the mufti was being asked if the unauthorized renters had earned the right to stay because of the long period over which they had invested their labor in the field. Ebu's-Su'ud and Pir Mehmed's rejection of this path to establishing the right to lifetime tenure was instructive: if a cultivator could establish a right to a particular *miri* land solely through long residence and labor and without the sultan's consent, then the sultan's power to choose the cultivator was compromised. Like Ebu's-Su'ud, Pir Mehmed refused to countenance that a cultivator could – through residence, labor or kinship ties – independently establish a right to work the land that the sultan would be forced to respect.

With its compiler favouring autonomist views of the sultan's power, the *Kanun-ı Cedid* does not convey that the Ottoman ulema did not universally agree with Pir Mehmed about the sultan's latitude to choose the cultivator. The question of whether a cultivator could in fact 'earn' the right to cultivate on *miri* land without paying *tapu* or receiving deputy permission remained an issue characterized by divergent opinions in both the seventeenth and eighteenth centuries. An extremely important voice with an opposing point of view on this subject that was that of Sadık Mehmed Sakızi. Sakızi, who was a fairly obscure seventeenth-century Ottoman judge, compiled a reference book of fatwas, selections from well-known books of the Hanafi school, *firmans* issued by the sultan, and his own juridical analysis in 1649.[47] Composed in Arabic, this work known as the *Surrat al-Fatawa* would become highly influential among Ottoman ulema in both the Turkish and Arabic-speaking provinces in the eighteenth and nineteenth centuries.[48] This work is perhaps the first work of Hanafi jurisprudence that integrated *kanuns* related to land tenure law and that described the law prevailing on treasury land in a way that was broadly consistent with the vision of Ebu's-Su'ud. If one judges by the number of citations it received in provincial fatwas, it had a claim to being a far more influential channel of transmitting the law of *miri* land than the *Kanun-i Cedid*. Of the cultivator's bundle of rights, Sakızi wrote that 'Once a man has *tasarruf* of a *miri* land for ten years, the *haqq al-qarar* is established and the land cannot be taken from his hand.'[49] He attributed this position to the eminent jurist Fakhr al-Din Qadikhan (d. 1196), whose influence over the Ottoman ulema was considerable. This explanation opened the door to an interpretation that long-time residence could establish the peasant's right to remain on the land independently of the sultan's appointment. There were at least two eighteenth-century provincial muftis who cited Qadikhan's opinion in ruling that a cultivator's possession of *miri* land could not be challenged after ten years.[50]

Such fatwas indicate that we need to keep two things in mind: first, the importance of specific texts in transmitting specific positions within the harmony tradition. Sakızi's text and its popularity in the eighteenth century was responsible for this interpretation of the 'ten-year rule', which departed not only from Pir Mehmed's understanding but also from the fatwas of the *şeyhülislams* that would qualify its meaning. Second, it was clear that not all muftis saw *miri* land as a space ruled exclusively by the sultan's edicts and laws. The writings of the pre-Ottoman authorities of the Hanafi school continued to have relevance in their eyes, and had not been entirely replaced by the order imposed by the sultan. Moreover, the question around where the ten-year rule 'came from' draws attention to the fact that the muftis could trace the origins of specific provisions of the land law to a variety of different sources and hence endow it with the pedigree of their choice. In the case of the ten-year rule, there were a number of Ottoman *kanun*s that imposed 'statutory limits' on challenging the *tasarruf* of a cultivator who had been peaceably cultivating and paying his taxes in a location for ten years. One iteration of the 'ten-year rule' prohibited deputies from forcing a cultivator to return to a former village after ten years had passed.[51] Likewise, Sultan Süleyman had ruled that after ten years, it was too late for either *sipahi*s or other cultivators to raise a claim that a resident cultivator had not rightfully acquired *tasarruf* of the land.[52] But neither Pir Mehmed nor two *şeyhülislam*s – Hacı Mustafa Sun'ullah (d. 1612) and Menteşzade Abdürrahim (d. 1716) – took these orders to mean that *tasarruf* could be earned by long-time residence. These muftis ruled that when it was a known fact that *tapu* had never been paid rather than a subject of dispute, the cultivator did not have *tasarruf* on the land, no matter how much time had passed.[53] Hence, the autonomist position that saw the sultan as the sole source of a cultivator's right remained the established norm on this issue at the *ilmiye*'s highest level, but was not uniformly observed in the provinces.

While Pir Mehmed often emphasized the power of the sultan alone to make the rules of *miri* land, and the bestowing of *tasarruf* as a grant, his frequent references to specific orders, *kanun*s and registers gave the impression that he expected the sultan's power to be practised through a system of orderly and bureaucratic administration.[54] Pir Mehmed's inclination to see the sultan's law as the only law operating on *miri* land might have had something to do with the turbulent state of the countryside in the late sixteenth and early seventeenth centuries. His tenure as the mufti of Skopje overlapped with the worst years of severe weather and drought, *Celali* revolts and the economic strain caused by these disasters and the fruitless war with the Hapsburgs. In maintaining that the only element of divine order that existed on *miri* land was the power of the sultan to create order, Pir Mehmed placed the responsibility as well as the authority to address the crisis of the Ottoman countryside in the hands of the sultan's officials. It is little wonder that a mufti with these inclinations became such a dominant voice in the *Kanun-ı Cedid*, where the compilation presented fatwas as deferential elaborations upon the sultan's commands.

The formation of a tradition: Deferential and not so deferential interpretation

The *Kanun-ı Cedid*'s principal *şeyhülislam* contributors were neither as reliably autonomist in their fatwas as Pir Mehmed had been, although the fatwas in the *Kanun-ı Cedid* do not capture this. Mehmed Baha'i's fatwas best illustrate how a mufti might be pulled towards an autonomist stance on one issue, only to embrace a more analogical one on something relatively similar. The crux of the issue was the extent to which the mufti viewed principles governing non-*miri* land to be applicable to *miri* land as well, and whether, as *şeyhülislam*, the mufti had the authority to pronounce such similarity as the basis for a legal decision. There is no issue that better highlights the consequential differences arising from the analogical and autonomist approaches than the requirement of the deputy's permission for cultivator transfers or alterations to the land. By omitting analogist fatwas issued by the seventeenth-century *şeyhülislams*, the *Kanun-ı Cedid* distorts both our understanding of how the law governing permission was shaping during the seventeenth century and the continuity between the seventeenth- and eighteenth-century muftis on this issue. Profoundly influential to the shape of *miri* transactions, analogists would have more of a role in sculpting the harmony tradition than the *Kanun-ı Cedid* would indicate. On the question of whether the deputy had the power to stop transfers between cultivators when the cultivators failed to ask his permission, it was the analogist position, not the autonomist one, that would prevail.

Şeyhülislam Zekeriyazade Yahya Efendi is renowned for his devotion to the sultan he served in most of his career, Murad IV, as the latter embarked on aggressive military campaigns and attempted to impose a harsh discipline on his elites and subjects alike.[55] First appointed in 1622, Yahya Efendi would serve as *şeyhülislam* for roughly eighteen of the next twenty-two years and came to be considered one of the most eminent holders of the chief mufti's office.[56] He was also a mufti well versed in the *kanun*: according to the headings in the *Kanun-ı Cedid*, two short *kanunnames* summarizing land tenure ordinances were made expressly for Yahya Efendi, and the first of these was prepared by the *nişancı* Okçuzade Efendi at Yahya Efendi's request.[57] If he did request it, it is evidence that he felt he needed to have command of it, a position that while not unusual was also not a universal one among *ilmiye* personnel, as we will see. He was also something of a mentor to Baha'i Mehmed Efendi, who would eventually rise to the office of *şeyhülislam* himself.[58] Save for a year-long interruption beginning in 1651, Baha'i served in that office continuously from 1649 until his death in 1654.[59] Baha'i is known to have had an interest in geography and cosmography, as well as sharing his mentor's passion for poetry.[60] Serving in the time when Sultan Mehmed IV was a child, it was his fate to be caught up in the political and social intrigue attending all who vied for high office in this period, including clashes with rival factions at court and numerous confrontations with leaders of the activist piety movement known as the Kadızadelis.[61] The latter enjoyed support from members of the sultan's innermost circle, and though Baha'i tried to resist their demands to take harsh measures against those they deemed heretical, he was not always able to do so.[62]

In a very impressive master's thesis, Bünyamin Punar has argued that Yahya Efendi's fatwas give greater weight to the *kanun* and were more consistent with Ebu's-Su'ud's vision of *miri* land than either of his recent predecessors in the office of *şeyhülislam*.[63] These muftis, Hacı Mustafa Sun'ullah Efendi (served four terms between 1599 and 1608) and Hocasa'deddinzade Es'ad Efendi (served 1615–22 and 1623–5), had been less attentive to the *kanun*'s requirements. Punar's analysis is cogent, and illuminating of the way that *şeyhülislam*s could take very different positions and leave conflicting precedents for later generations of *ilmiye* personnel. Noting differences between these *şeyhülislam*s regarding the deputy's permission for transactions or changes to the uses of the land, Punar has particularly focused on the question of whether the muftis enforced the provision in the *kanun* that permission from the deputy be explicit rather than implicit.[64] Yet the issue that best highlights the disparity (and overlap) between the favoured muftis of the *Kanun-ı Cedid* versus those excluded like Sun'ullah and Es'ad is a narrower question. Ultimately, all these muftis agreed that permission was procedurally necessary for a valid transfer; where they differed most was in the action that the deputy was authorized to take when the transaction had not been validated by permission, and under what circumstances permission could be withheld.[65] Comparing the fatwas of Es'ad Efendi with those of Baha'i Mehmed, I will argue that these clashes were the most significant for understanding the differences between autonomists and analogists, and the future trends of legal development for *miri* land.

Cultivator actions that required the deputy's permission was one of the issues more fully fleshed out in the new *kanun*s and *firman*s collected in seventeenth-century compendia. Ebu's-Su'ud had stated explicitly that all transactions required the *sipahi*'s permission, and later *kanun*s specified that the *sipahi*/deputy could abrogate any transactions of *tasarruf* between cultivators where he had not given permission.[66] The *Kanunname of Ahmed Khan* specified that the *sipahi*'s permission on transfers of *tasarruf* between cultivators must be explicit and could not be inferred simply from his lack of protest or accepting fees paid by the new cultivator.[67] With its typical emphasis on the latitude of the deputy, the *Kanun-ı Cedid* presented additional *kanun*s proclaiming that the *sipahi* was allowed to tear down buildings that had been built without his permission, or to uproot trees planted without his permission, so long as he did so before the trees bore fruit or before three years had passed.[68] If the *sipahi* chose to let them remain or missed the deadline for uprooting the trees, then he could demand that a tithe for the produce be added to peasant's tax assessment. Baha'i Mehmed Efendi, one of the favoured contributors to the *Kanun-ı Cedid*, gave an autonomist fatwa on this issue:

> Question: If Zayd plants a vineyard on the field in his *tasarruf* without the *sipahi*'s permission, can the *sipahi* say to Zayd, 'Uproot the vineyard and put the field back the way it was?'
>
> Answer: He can.[69]

This case appeared to be a simple matter: there was an order from the sultan, and the mufti followed it. Similar to Pir Mehmed, both Baha'i and Yahya often included in their rulings a statement like, 'Since there is a sultanic order, it is permitted.'[70] Such rulings typified the interpretation of the land law that the *Kanun-ı Cedid* consistently promoted: it enforced the sultan's orders without qualification, including the severe consequences that ensued when peasants evaded the deputy.

While it may seem natural that the *şeyhülislams* would respond with deference to a fairly clear directive of the sultan, they did not always do so. Let us examine the kind of fatwa that did not appear in the *Kanun-ı Cedid*, issued by Baha'i's predecessor *Şeyhülislam* Hocasa'deddinzade Es'ad Efendi, who gave a fatwa that was the exact opposite of Baha'i's:

> Question: Zayd, a *sipahi*, has from olden times received a tithe from a certain land. 'Amr comes from a different place and without Zayd's permission unrightfully plants a garden and builds a building on this land. Zayd says to 'Amr, 'I was owed a tithe from this land. You have done me harm.' Is Zayd able to remove 'Amr's garden and building from the land?
>
> Answer: If 'Amr has the right of *tasarruf* on this land, he is not. He [Zayd] can still take the garden's tithe from its produce, since gardens in that area pay a tithe.[71]

Examining this fatwa, Punar has demonstrated that Es'ad's conclusion in this fatwa mirrors his understanding of the restraints that a *mutawalli* possesses on *waqf* property.[72] Only if the cultivator's unauthorized buildings or trees caused 'harm', that is, they decreased revenue, could the *mutawalli* remove them. Given that the muftis generally ruled that actions benefiting the *waqf* should be permitted, prominent Hanafis who dealt with this question asserted that if the *mutawalli* tore down or uprooted the tenant's buildings or plants, it was the *mutawalli* who was causing damage to the *waqf* and such destruction should be prohibited.[73] The tendency to see the deputy and the *mutawalli* as parallel office holders was in many ways natural, given that agricultural *waqf* land was held in *tapu* and the *mutawalli* was the person responsible for collecting the *tapu* fee and the agricultural taxes. Es'ad's fatwa therefore treated the *miri* deputy as subject to the same constraints that were usually imposed on a *mutawalli*; that is, if the cultivators were engaged in productive activity that would not decrease the revenue, then the deputy should take the money due to him and not interfere. The *sipahi* had to show harm in order to remove the buildings and trees, and while he claimed harm in the fatwa cited earlier, the mufti ruled his claim was meaningless unless he could show that his payment was reduced.

Here, the analogy with *waqf* played the decisive role in a conclusion that, while not entirely irreconcilable with the *kanun*, established a very different standard for decision-making. It should be said that Es'ad Efendi may have been unfamiliar with the *kanuns* issued on the deputy's prerogatives rather than intentionally cavalier. In the early seventeenth century, *firmans* and *kanuns* about land tenure were not yet integrated into the texts that formed the basis of the mufti's knowledge; the number of texts circulating at the time that would have summarized these *kanuns* for an audience of *ilmiye* personnel was as yet small.[74] To be informed of the *kanun*, as we saw with Yahya Efendi, required initiative on the part of the mufti. Yet it is clear some of Es'ad's colleagues in the *ilmiye* did take such initiative, while he does not appear to have done so.[75] While Es'ad Efendi's fatwas are undeniably 'built on' the sultan's orders through their affirmation of the need for permission to transact, it is clear that for Es'ad, *miri* land was not a place where one looked exclusively to the sultan to discern the prevailing law. On the contrary, Hanafi jurisprudence of *waqf* was quite relevant to understanding the relationship between the *sipahi* and the cultivator, and in this case, proved determining. There are various factors that might explain Es'ad's views; Es'ad is identified by Baki Tezcan as one of the chief protagonists among a group of ulema who saw implementation of the sharia as a path to widening their own leverage as political actors while constraining that of the sultan and other members of his entourage.[76] Some incidents in his career suggest that he saw himself as better placed than the sultan to know what the law permitted and what it did not, and he may have felt justified in ignoring the *kanun* if he thought it erroneous.[77] However, it is also possible that he looked at the disarray in the countryside and concluded that undue military interference in peasant activity was the root of agricultural disruptions and must be stopped. The *kanuns* recently issued on post-mortem transmission and subletting did limit deputy discretionary power, and Es'ad's decision to limit it yet further was not entirely out of step with the regime's legal actions in this period.

Whatever its origins, Es'ad's view on this issue was not to become the dominant one. The deferential position that Baha'i articulated – that the deputy could indeed destroy buildings, gardens or orchards made without his permission – would largely prevail in the eighteenth century, though adherence to it would never be entirely universal.[78] When it came to transactions, however, Baha'i's fatwas are indicative of a very different trend. Like his predecessors Sun'ullah and Es'ad, he too largely embraced an analogist approach to the process for transfers. A *kanun* concerning transfers states,

> It is against the *kanun* to transgressively take the land when the deputy has not given permission and received his fee according to the *kanun* … in this situation, if the deputy wishes, he can take his fee [from the usurper] and give his permission for him to have the *tasarruf*. If he wishes, he can void their transaction, and make the former possessor take *tasarruf*.[79]

As with the *kanun* that allowed him to remove buildings or trees that had not received his permission, this *kanun* did not require the deputy to prove his monetary interests harmed in order to reject and reverse an unauthorized transfer; it was left in his discretion to validate it or refuse it.

Despite what this *kanun* stated, it seems fair to say that a different consensus was emerging among the muftis by the mid-seventeenth century, which is nowhere to be found in the *Kanun-ı Cedid*: if the cultivators involved in the transfer asked for permission (either before or afterwards) and the change in cultivator would not result in monetary reduction for the deputy, the latter *could not* refuse permission for the transfer. Here again, the standard of revenue shortfall that limited a *mutawalli*'s power over a *waqf*'s cultivators was applied to the treasury deputy. While the muftis would by and large not require the deputy to meet this standard when he destroyed unauthorized buildings and trees, they typically did require it for transfers. Although the *kanun* did not require the deputy to give a reason for refusing permission, the muftis nevertheless qualified his ability to withhold permission or to invalidate transfers that had not received it. For instance, in the section following the *kanun* cited earlier, the *Kanun-ı Cedid* does not illustrate the text with any fatwas that show the deputy actually removing a usurping cultivator and coercing the old one to take responsibility for the land. On the other hand, it does transmit a fatwa from Pir Mehmed saying that if the transfer did not receive permission in advance, it could be legitimated after the fact, and the *sipahi* could give his permission then.[80] Pir Mehmed's understanding summed up the dominant approach of the muftis across the interpretive spectrum: despite what the *kanun* stated about the deputy having a choice, there was a fairly uniform expectation among the muftis that the deputy would or could only exercise the first option.[81]

On this issue, as opposed to the question about unauthorized trees and buildings, Baha'i and Es'ad Efendi appeared to be aligned. Not surprisingly, Es'ad Efendi was the more categorical of the two: if the *sipahi* experienced no harm, 'he is *ordered* to allow the transfer', Es'ad maintained.[82] Baha'i's fatwas are more ambiguous, yet they seem to be getting at the same principle that Es'ad stated so clearly: unless the deputy had reason to believe that the transfer would damage his own rights to the revenue, he could not stop the transfer. In two fatwas preserved in *Zahirü'l-Kudat* – fatwas that do not appear in the *Kanun-ı Cedid* – Baha'i was asked if a *sipahi* could refuse permission to transfer if he did so out of 'personal bias' (*garaz-ı nefsi*).[83] The mufti replied 'no' to this question, and in a following fatwa declared that a judge could force the deputy to consent in this situation if he refused to relent.[84] Here, Baha'i agreed with Es'ad that a deputy could be forced to allow the transfer if withholding his permission was whimsical, but the fatwa is vague: when, specifically, would a rejection of the proposed buyer be reasonable as opposed to whimsical? In a different fatwa, Baha'i provides a clue to what separates a reasonable rejection from a whimsical one. Writing of a deputy's refusal to allow a cultivator's transfer to a janissary, Baha'i maintained that if the deputy's resistance was made out of a 'proper bias' (*garaz-ı sahih*), then the refusal for the transfer was valid.[85] In other words, he believed it could be reasonable for a deputy to reject men of the military class who sought to acquire *miri* land, though once again he declined to state precisely why this was so. It is one of Baha'i's successors in office, most likely Menteşzade 'Abdürrahim (served 1715–16), who would spell out explicitly why the bias against a soldier was an instance of correct bias (*garaz-ı sahih*).[86] The latter's explanation made clear that a 'correct bias' was synonymous with 'harm': a soldier could claim exemption from the agricultural taxes and thus fail to make the payments to which the deputy was entitled.[87] As a result, Baha'i's line of reasoning leads to the conclusion that like Es'ad, he believed the *sipahi must* give permission unless his revenue will be diminished. Hence, the muftis ruled that the deputy's leeway to refuse transfers was far narrower than one would know from reading the *kanun* governing the subject, or from reading the *Kanun-ı Cedid*'s presentation of the topic.

This position limiting the ability of the deputy to stop or reverse a transfer would be dominant in both the eighteenth and nineteenth centuries. As we have seen, 'Abdürrahim Efendi adopted Baha'i's language distinguishing between a 'personal bias' and a 'proper bias'. A provincial mufti of Bosnia, Ahmed el-Mostari (d. 1776), would adopt Es'ad Efendi's language and state that the *sipahi* was *ordered* to give permission for the transfer unless there was a valid reason for withholding it.

Question:	Zayd sells his immovable property and transfers the land that he received from his father to 'Amr and Bakr, which is recorded in a judge's *hüccet*. The *sipahi* says 'I will not give a document to 'Amr and Bakr showing my permission according to the *kanun*.' Can he [the *sipahi*] do this?
Answer:	No. He is commanded to give permission (*izne vermeğe me'mūrdur*).
Citation:	The deputy is charged with permission, and he is not permitted to withhold permission nor to bestow it upon another. (*Ṣāḥib al-arḍ ma'mūr bi'l-idhn laysa lahu al-imtinā' 'anhu al-idhn wa lā bi-raf'ihā ilā al-ghayr.*)[88]

This same language, 'The deputy is charged with permission, and he is not permitted to withhold permission nor to bestow it upon another' would appear in the nineteenth-century version of a land law compendium first compiled in the eighteenth, and known as *Cami' ül-Icareteyn*.[89] Its compiler, Meşrebzade Mehmet 'Arif Efendi, would affirm that on both *miri* land and *waqf* property held in *ijaratayn*, transfers were valid only with permission of the deputy or the *mutawalli*, but that neither could refuse permission because of bias or simply to cause trouble (*ta'jiz*).[90] He transmitted a fatwa given by Zekeriyazade Yahya Efendi that allowed the *mutawalli* to prohibit a transfer when his permission had not been given, but he commented that the great ulema of his time did not rule that this kind of prohibition was permissible.[91]

The muftis' substantial qualification of the deputy's ability to refuse or reverse a transfer is an excellent illustration of how analogy between *waqf* and *miri* land played a formative role in the land law. It is also an excellent illustration of the kinds of omissions in the *Kanun-ı Cedid* that obscured the significance of the analogical approach to building fatwas from the sultan's orders. Although Baha'i Efendi was one of the favoured contributors of the *Kanun-ı Cedid*, none of these fatwas limiting the deputy's powers was included in the text, whose compiler selected only his most deferential fatwas, thus giving the impression that Baha'i's oeuvre was more consistently autonomist than it was. While many of the autonomist positions presented as normative in the *Kanun-ı Cedid* would become widely accepted as such – for instance, the ability of the deputy to destroy unauthorized buildings and trees – muftis of the eighteenth century and beyond would follow Baha'i and Es'ad in putting limits on the plain meaning of the *kanun* in fatwas about transactions.

Conclusion

By the first half of the seventeenth century, there was more *kanun* for Ottoman personnel to know and to administer. The muftis examined here were a new generation of harmonizers grappling with this larger corpus of texts, which more closely regulated land management at the village level. Among these muftis were distinct differences about what the law of *miri* land was. Was *miri* land sui generis, with a law determined exclusively by the sultan? Or, was it fairly analogous to other kinds of rented land, particularly land held in *waqf*? The answer to these questions led to fatwas that were 'built' from the sultan's orders in different ways. The diversity of views in the fatwas issued in this period pointed to another area of disagreement: namely, what role did the fatwas play as a legal source? Were they a source subordinate to the sultan's orders, or could they depart from a plain reading of the sultan's orders and move the law in a different direction, as they did in the practice of jurisprudence more generally?

This chapter's examination of land tenure *kanun* and fatwas demonstrates that in the first half of the seventeenth century, there was no widely held consensus among the muftis on how to apply the land tenure *kanun*s or perhaps even whether muftis needed to be well informed about the *kanun*s that had been issued; for that matter, a mufti like Vani Mehmed Efendi could altogether ignore the sultan's orders and registers. It is also unclear that any one member of the bureaucracy was tasked with advocating or disseminating a uniform interpretation of *miri* law. In fact, the *Kanun-ı Cedid* and texts like it may have been put together precisely because there was no strongly enforced imperial project to promote a canonical interpretation of the *kanun* governing land. Instead, interested advocates put forward their own visions of a canonical tradition and created texts claiming that the muftis had in fact coalesced around a consistent interpretation of the land tenure *kanun*, such as that in the *Kanun-ı Cedid*.[92] Such texts suggest that individuals other than the sultan and his current cadre of officials had a hand – and a stake – in crafting what the dynastic law of the land should look like.

Among the *şeyhülislams*, and even among the foundational contributors to the *Kanun-ı Cedid*, there was a variety of opinions about how to understand the law governing *miri* land. This variety is not reflected in the *Kanun-ı Cedid*: fatwas that placed limits on the deputy that were not explicitly condoned in the *kanun* were systematically excluded from its text. It was in these omissions that the *Kanun-ı Cedid* fails to convey some of the most important trends in the law's evolution. Transfers were generally understood to be the right of the cultivator, and the muftis showed a broad consensus that the deputy could not arbitrarily derail these, no matter what the *kanun* said. It is interesting that this important development facilitating exchange of land did not occur in an era associated with increasing market activity, but in an era associated with the breakdown of law and order. Even a generally deferential mufti like Baha'i Mehmed allowed himself the latitude to qualify or substantially reinterpret the sultan's orders on this issue, thus putting his fatwas more on a footing of parity with *kanun* as a legal source.

The compiler of the *Kanun-ı Cedid* was not only providing a reference work for the ulema, he was also advocating a particular approach to the interpretation and application of *kanun*. The right way for muftis to approach the *kanun* was to stay apprised of all the relevant *kanun*s and to rule in conformity with their plain meaning, and the wrong way was to use analogy or discretion to limit the applicability of the *kanun* or to undermine it. This was especially the case when the mufti's analogical reasoning led to his denying the deputy a privilege bestowed by the *kanun*. By selecting only the deferential fatwas of Pir Mehmed, Yahya Efendi and Baha'i Efendi to serve as authoritative models and largely ignoring the fatwas of muftis like Sun'allah Efendi and Es'ad Efendi, the compiler of the *Kanun-ı Cedid* presented a canonical version of the land law that emphasized the unique character of *miri* land, the latitude of the sultan in designating how its use and revenues were governed and the need for the muftis to obey the sultan's rules. This despite the fact that at least one of his favoured contributors, Baha'i Mehmed Efendi, did not always take a strictly autonomist position.

The uncompromising autonomism embodied in the *Kanun-ı Cedid* would remain influential in the eighteenth century and the text's fatwas and favoured mufti contributors would continue to loom large as guides to precedent. However, as consensus consolidated on a number of land-related issues, analogism would sometimes play a more dominant role. As the following chapters show, at the same time that a consensus around the harmony tradition was evolving in imperial fatwas, it was also beginning to gain a wider provincial audience and making its way into the more rarified world of academic texts.[93] Increasingly, muftis and scholars throughout the empire were familiarizing themselves with the sultan's orders about rights and transactions on *miri* land: by the eighteenth century, they would be a regularly integrated part of the practice of law in the Ottoman domains.

Chapter 4

'THE BOOKS OF *FIQH*': THE *KANUNNAME OF CANDIA* AND THE CONSOLIDATION OF A NEW DOCTRINE IN HANAFI ACADEMIC TEXTS

After a siege of nineteen years, the fortress of Candia, on the island of Crete, was conquered in 1669. As was normal, a cadastral survey was created for the newly conquered territory, and at the opening of the survey register was a *kanunname* that historians have regarded with persistent fascination. Since the middle of the sixteenth century, provincial *kanunname*s in the European and Anatolian provinces had generally instituted land law practices that were consistent with Ebu's-Su'ud's prescriptions.[1] The *Kanunname of Candia*, however, famously instituted an entirely different vision of land tenure and taxation:

> In the year 1080 of the prophet's *hijra*, the citadel of Candia on the Mediterranean island of Crete was conquered and the island was enlightened with the emblem of the sharia and Islamic majesty. This new conquest of tracts of land and of people who have accepted *dhimma* requires the imposing of *jizya* and *kharaj* upon them.[2] The monarch whom the world obeys has ordered in an imperial rescript that this matter [of levying *jizya* and *kharaj*] and the registration of the island's people and land will be carried out according to the prescribed *sunna* of the prophet that was previously practiced in the lands conquered in the time of the Rightly Guided Caliphs (may God be satisfied with them). In compliance with the lofty *firman*, the island of Crete shall be registered according to the shar'i basis that is expounded in the books of *fiqh* in the following way: ... the *kharaji* lands are the exclusive *milk* of their owners, and they (the owners) are able to sell and buy [the lands] and engage in other uses. And when they die, like the rest of their *milk*, it (the land) will be divided among their heirs according to the inheritance law (*fara'id*).[3]

In what appears to be a major reversal of Ottoman land policy, this *kanunname* explained that the land of Crete was not *miri* land but *kharaji*, and that it was the *milk*, or freehold property, of its current possessors. Explicitly, it noted that all the transactions that were normal for *milk* property – but forbidden on *miri* land – would apply to Crete. The court records on the island of Crete confirm that the land was transacted in the way that the *kanunname* mandated: it was bought, sold, inherited and endowed.[4] A fatwa attributed to the Şeyhülislam Minkarizade Yahya Efendi (served 1662–74) also appears to defend the land regime implemented on Crete.[5] The *kanunname* asserted that this way of classifying the land was enjoined by the 'books of *fiqh*' and was consistent with the practice of the prophet and the 'rightly guided' caliphs. It would not be the only *kanunname* to adopt a *kharaji* regime rather than a *miri* one: from 1669 to 1711, the Ottomans issued a number of provincial *kanunnames* (primarily for the islands of the Aegean) that deviated from the harmony tradition of land classification, tax and transaction that Ebu's-Su'ud Efendi had expounded in the sixteenth century.[6]

The issuing of these *kanunnames* has long caused Ottoman historians to question if they represent a turning point in the history of Ottoman land tenure law towards stronger property rights or a more 'orthodox' Islamic legal practice.[7] If these *kanunnames* suggested that perhaps a lasting new trend in Ottoman land law was taking root, a different *kanunname*, the *Kanunname of Morea*, calls into question the longevity of the trend and provides evidence of the continuing vitality of the *miri* system. The Ottomans regained the Morea from the possession of Venice in 1715, having ceded it in the 1699 Treaty of Karlowitz that ended the War of the Holy League.[8] Like the *Kanunname of Candia*, the *Kanunname of Morea* preceded a detailed cadastral survey, the result of more than a year of labour for the treasury secretaries in the wake of the reconquest. The compiler of the *Kanunname of Morea* made it quite clear that the Morea would be governed by the conventions of the harmony tradition:

> This greatly blessed province, like Rumelia, is *miri* land. At the time of its conquest, the land that is possessed by the *reaya* is again conferred upon them. The ultimate ownership (*raqaba*) of the land has been retained for the treasury. The cultivator has possession (*tasarruf*) by way of a loan that has no set termination date. The cultivator plants and plows and cultivates gardens and orchards and uses the land for all such purposes. He pays *kharaj muqasama* under the name of tithe and *kharaj muwazzaf* by the name of *çift akçesi*. So long as he does not leave the land unplanted and he pays what is due upon him, no one may interfere with him or challenge [his right to cultivate]. To the time of his death, if he wishes, the *tasarruf* of the land is his. When the *reaya* die, their sons take their places and possess the *tasarruf* according to what has been detailed above … . [The land's] sale, purchase, and bestowing as gift and other such transactions such as bestowing ownership and endowing is forbidden. But when someone wants to be rid of these lands, if the *sipahi* gives his permission, the cultivator may receive payment from another for his right on the land and the *sipahi* gives [the land to the new cultivator] by *tapu*. This is currently the rule in Rumelia.[9]

Most of this language has been taken directly from the writings of Ebu's-Su'ud, and some of this language is present in the *Kanun-ı Cedid*, which was likely in some circulation prior to the composition of the *Kanunname of Morea*.[10] The *kanunname* did not go to great lengths to ideologically justify the tenure regime, although it laconically gestured at the theoretical compatibility of the *fiqh*'s taxation regime with long-standing administrative practice and the ownership of the treasury as its basis. Twice, it asserted that the land was to be governed by the law prevailing in Rumelia, as though acknowledging that a different tenure regime was now dominant among the islands of the Aegean.[11] Like the *Kanun-ı Cedid*, the *Kanunname of Morea* is an indication that the harmony tradition still had advocates, and that these advocates were willing to defend its Islamic credentials.

We are confronted with an enigma: one *kanunname* radically departed from the harmony tradition, and the other conscientiously upheld it. If one of these was an outlier, which was it? Was the harmony tradition receding and being replaced, or was it still relevant and even flourishing?

Harmony at a crossroads

Scholarly attention to the *Kanunname of Candia* has tended to obscure a more significant trend in land tenure law dating to roughly the same era. Namely, it is this period (the mid-seventeenth to early eighteenth centuries) that began to see the harmony tradition's deeper rooting within Hanafi textual forms, which gave it both a more authoritative status and a wider audience across the empire. The most significant manifestation of this – and the focal point of this chapter – is that scholastic works of Hanafi jurisprudence produced from the middle of the seventeenth century to the early nineteenth century increasingly incorporated the texts whose dialogue formed the harmony tradition, be it *kanunnames*, *firmans*, the *Maʿruzat* or fatwas 'built' from these. As a result, the most authoritative scholarly texts of the school enshrined the land tenure regime enacted through administrative texts and adopted it as the teaching of the Hanafis; oftentimes, the scholastic texts incorporated those issued by the chancellery as well as the *ilmiye* directly into their scholarly discussions. This movement not only meant a greater consensus among the ulema about what the law of land tenure *was*, it also increased the quantity and the variety of texts in which a fairly uniform concept of *miri* land could be found. These scholastic texts became an important channel for transmitting the rules of *miri* land: in the Arab lands, such texts would prove to be more influential in building a consensus around the land law than texts like the *Kanun-ı Cedid*.[12] Thus, the Hanafi scholastic community and its texts took a leading role in disseminating the law of *miri* land as promulgated in the sultan's administrative documents.

The movement of the land law from administrative textual forms into the scholastic works of *fiqh* in the seventeenth century was not an isolated phenomenon; in fact, recent studies suggest that it could be regarded as entirely unsurprising. According to Samy Ayoub, the jurists of this era showed an expanded recognition of the sultan's legislative powers. Examining manuals, commentaries and specialized treatises, Ayoub has shown that the muftis began to acknowledge that the sultan had a number of discrete legislative powers, something they had not done previously.[13] They inscribed the sultan's orders and *kanuns* into their texts, acknowledging that it was the sultan who set the rules of hearing cases that came to the empire's courts, who made the rules of appointing personnel and their jurisdictions and who could settle doctrinal debates within the school.[14] A similar observation had appeared earlier in the work of Yavuz Aykan in his study on the law court of the Anatolian town of Amid.[15] Separately, Guy Burak has detailed the growth of what he calls an 'archival consciousness' in the seventeenth and eighteenth centuries, in which ulema increasingly relied on documents generated by the sultan's bureaucracy (and took part in creating such documents) in validating legal claims.[16] Perhaps most extraordinarily, Martha Mundy has not only demonstrated that Ibn 'Abidin used government documentation and registers to establish valid property rights and taxation claims, but also that he regarded this documentation as a kind of 'custom of government'.[17] By the early modern period, practices prevailing in a specific time and place – called *'urf* or *'ada* in Arabic and usually rendered into English (somewhat problematically) as 'custom' – had gained a newly explicit consideration in the legal reasoning of the Hanafis.[18] Ibn 'Abidin's views of *'ada* or *'urf* and the weight that he attached to these concepts in jurisprudence have been much written about, but most scholars have understood his usage of the term *'ada* to refer to 'custom', that is, practices that are common among the people of a place.[19] Mundy's assertion that he considers the established practice of a state to have the same weight as established practice among a people brings an entirely new perspective to the status of the sultan's administrative texts and their legal authority in the eyes of the jurists. What all of these studies suggest is that the sultan's orders – not just in the abstract but specified, and duly incorporated into the jurists' texts – played an increasingly decisive role in the functioning of Islamic legal thought and practice in the seventeenth and eighteenth centuries. It should not surprise us to find that land tenure law was no exception.

In one respect, however, it was exceptional: Hanafi scholastic doctrine on land law and tax changed noticeably when it adopted the formulation of these topics that had been promulgated in the *kanunnames*; by contrast, the interventions that Ayoub describes rarely involved a substantive rethinking of doctrine.[20] Integrating the sultan's orders on land tenure into academic Hanafi texts led the jurists to embrace the doctrinal changes that Ebu's-Su'ud had introduced in his sixteenth-century fatwas and fatwa-like *kanunnames*. The doctrine that *miri* land was neither tithe nor *kharaji* and that conquered land came to the *bayt al-mal* from the moment of conquest were both adopted by the academic texts, though the taxation consequences remained an object of dispute. These changes to the way that property rights and taxation on land were discussed in Hanafi scholarship are another reminder that the Ottoman position about the sultan's authority over treasury land was not a continuity with past practice, but a series of shifts; shifts that, as the *Kanunname of Candia* demonstrates, were not without controversy. In sum, the harmony tradition continued to increase its presence across genres of legal text and bring these genres into greater cohesion, even though it meant modifying the teachings of the school in order to bring Hanafi doctrine into alignment with Ottoman administrative practice.

Ironically then, at precisely the time that the *Kanunname of Candia* alluded to 'the books of *fiqh*' as justification for eschewing the *miri* land regime, those 'books of *fiqh*' composed by Ottoman scholars began to expound this regime as part of the doctrine of the Hanafi school. Rather than a new trend that would have an important impact on tenure in the empire, the *Kanunname of Candia* represents a complex reaction to the increasing legal weight of the sultan's order-giving texts in Hanafi jurisprudence. The willingness among seventeenth-century jurists to ascribe more weight to the sultan's orders and documentation than did earlier Hanafi authorities was part of a broader trend in the school accepting that its legal rulings had changed on a number of issues to reflect different times and circumstances.[21] In this vein, Ibn 'Abidin wrote that 'the mufti should not remain inflexibly with what is transmitted in the books of the manifest transmission without regard for his era and the people of that era lest he cause many a right to be lost and the harm he cause prove greater than the benefit'.[22] Such attitudes may have been congealing as the dominant view in the school during the seventeenth century, but the *Kanunname of Candia* shows us that such views were not universal. On the one hand, this *kanunname* was a show of resistance to the idea that practices of the present era could trump what was transmitted by earlier generations in the books of *fiqh*. That is, we can see this *kanunname* as backlash against a newly crystallizing set of norms within the Hanafi school that gave greater weight to currently prevailing practice. On the other hand, the *Kanunname of Candia*'s resistance to the institutionalization of the *miri* regime in the genre of the *kanunname* may have been an acknowledgement of the very phenomenon that Burak and Mundy have described: knowing that administrative documents were becoming an integral part of legal practice and doctrine may have made it all the more urgent for the *kanunname*'s compilers to have the 'correct' property rights and taxes inscribed in the *Kanunname of Candia*. In the end however, the *Kanunname of Candia* did little to arrest the spread of deference to the sultan's legislative authority in scholarship or the dissemination of the regime of property rights and taxation that the sultan had enacted with this authority.

There are other ways that we can see the growing cohesiveness of the harmony tradition and its expanding presence within the legal texts of the empire. The previous chapter demonstrated that it was from the middle of the seventeenth century that the *şeyhülislams* coalesced around a deferential and informed approach to the land tenure *kanun* in their fatwas. It was also in the late seventeenth or early eighteenth century that the *Kanun-ı Cedid* and several similar compendia of land law were composed as references for judges and other administrators.[23] Beyond these developments percolating at the centre of imperial power, there is also legal thought and scholarly activity in the wider Ottoman domains to consider. While this chapter focuses on the harmony tradition's integration into texts of academic jurisprudence composed by both *ilmiye* officials and provincial scholars, Chapter 5 will examine eighteenth-century fatwas issued in the capital and the provinces to show the wider dissemination of the *miri* regime and the bundle of property rights it conveyed upon the land's *mutasarrifs*.

The Kanunname of Candia *as critique: Reinstituting the Hanafism of the 'books'*

The abrupt departure of the *Kanunname of Candia* from land tenure precedent has been something of a puzzle for scholars. Although the Ottomans would not conquer Candia until 1669, most of the island fell quickly under their control after the onset of hostilities between Venice and the Ottomans in 1645. A *kanunname* for the portions of Crete under Ottoman control was completed by 1651,[24] and this *kanunname* included all the expected features of land tax and tenure according to Ebu's-Su'ud Efendi's prescriptions.[25] The *Kanunname of Candia* superseded this previous *kanunname*, and its deviation from standard Ottoman practice was all the more striking given the normality of its predecessor. Some scholars have taken the view that there is an important ideological element in the *Kanunname of Candia*'s interventions or suggested that the *kanunname* took shape under the influence of sharia-minded activists such as Vani Mehmed Efendi (see Chapter 3).[26] However, most recent analyses have presented the *Kanunname of Candia* primarily as an attempt by the Ottoman administration to find a system of land tenure that better fit the peculiarities of Crete's circumstances.[27] That is, it introduced a system of taxation better suited for a rural economy in which grains played a marginal role and which was dominated primarily by commercialized arboriculture like olive growing; or, it reflected changed fiscal priorities that prioritized raising cash sums. The latter explanations have captured factors that possibly weighed into the significant changes to tenure, taxation and registration of assets in the *kanunname*. However, they cannot explain why this *kanunname* not only adopts a new tenure regime but also presents a blistering critique of the standard Ottoman land taxation. There were likely a multitude of reasons for all the innovations adopted in the *kanunname*, but the text is very clearly making an ideological point.

The compilers were attempting to institute a regime that was, in their minds, compliant with the teachings in the manuals and commentaries of the Hanafi school. The *kanunname*'s text is quite explicit about this: it repeatedly invokes the authority of 'the books of *fiqh*', as in the example cited. Such references were a way of proclaiming the *kanunname*'s adherence to the soundest of Hanafi doctrine. Specifically, the phrase referred to the genre of academic texts known as the *furu'* that contained the most authoritative statements of the school's interpretation of the sharia.[28] It was in these texts that Hanafi substantive law was systematically explored and expounded: they were the reference point for fatwas and for judgements in court, and carried more weight in establishing opinion than either of the former genres.[29] There were levels of authority within the *furu'* as well. At the apex were the manuals (*matn/mutun*), which dealt with a wide variety of legal matters. These could be either short works that sought a concise overview or multivolume works dealing with the same topics but in more detail.[30] Next to the manuals in authoritative weight were the commentaries (*sharh/shuruh*) upon the manuals, and just below the commentaries ranked the commentaries upon the commentaries, a genre known as the super-commentaries (*hashiyya*). The texts of later eras would often reflect evolution in the school's views, as newly composed manuals and commentaries took stock of fatwas that addressed new problems or revised the understanding of older ones.[31] Fatwas widely considered to have established new but sound doctrine were incorporated into commentaries and eventually into manuals. Each *madhhab* had a methodology for sorting through layers of authoritative sources and texts to provide cohesiveness for the doctrine of the school, but the law was composed of discrete opinions on specific questions, and was neither uniform nor static.

As Guy Burak has shown, not all Hanafi manuals carried equal weight; some garnered a greater reputation and were more relied upon than others, and there were regionally distinct traditions within the school determining which manuals were the most respected and most frequently cited.[32] The Ottomans regarded a number of such texts composed in prior centuries (e.g. the manual composed by Qadikhan) as canonical classics.[33] However, the tradition of composing these texts was ongoing and, by the end of the sixteenth century, Ottoman scholars of both Rumi and Arab origin – such as Molla Hüsrev (d. 1480) of Anatolia, Muhammad al-Timurtashi (d. 1595) of Ghaza and Zayn al-Din Ibn Nujaym (d. 1563) of Egypt – had written influential Hanafi manuals or commentaries.[34] These manuals included little if any reference to the sultan's orders on *miri* land and did not differ significantly from their pre-Ottoman predecessors. Ebu's-Su'ud acknowledged as much when he wrote that the *miri* category of land and the rules attached to it were not present in the books of *fiqh*. As we have seen, Ebu's-Su'ud introduced a number of innovations around the concept of treasury land that departed from the teaching in the Hanafi manuals: conquered land, he argued, was immediately the property of the treasury; transactions and usage rights were legislated by the sultan; and the taxation regime, though defined in the sultan's registers, should be seen as an analogue of that in the manuals. Each of these three departures was rejected in the *Kanunname of Candia* in favour of the Hanafi school's manifest doctrine (*zahir al-riwaya*) found in the manuals and commentaries from the sixteenth century and before.

What is fascinating about the *Kanunname of Candia* is that it was itself of a genre that derived its authority from the sultanate. Nevertheless, it was quite clear that, as a *kanunname*, it was to be a vessel for the law found in the books of *fiqh*. For the text's compilers, it was the books of *fiqh* that established the land law, and the duty of the sultan's chancellery documents was to put the weight of the sword behind the books of *fiqh*. While it can be rightfully seen as a kind of protest against the *miri* regime, it was far more critical of taxation practice than of the transactions and property rights associated with *miri* land. Notably, the *kanunname* did not state that the books of *fiqh* prohibited the sultan from claiming the land for the treasury upon conquest, it simply praised Mehmed IV for deciding to follow the example of the Rightly Guided Caliphs and institute the regime of property rights they established. For the Hanafis, as we have seen, that meant designating the land both *kharaji* and *milk*; all the transactions that were specified were those that applied to *milk*, but, as was consistent with prevailing Hanafi doctrine, the *kanunname* stipulates that cultivator had to keep the land under cultivation or risk its confiscation.[35] The protection of the three-year rule did not exist on Crete, perhaps because it was part of the *miri* legal regime that was categorically rejected. Instead, the *kanunname* returned the timing of confiscation to the discretion of the sultan or his agents, leaving peasant proprietors more vulnerable to legally permissible confiscation than their counterparts on *miri* land.[36] Despite its fastidiousness about adherence to the books of *fiqh* in a number of matters, the *kanunname* contained no provision about returning the land to its owner if he became able or willing to farm once again.

The *kanunname* took a severe tone about taxation: it scathingly denounced the conventional Ottoman taxation regime. It named and abolished all of the agricultural taxes recorded in the island's *kanunname* from 1651, including the *tapu* fee. These taxes, which were among the most common in the Ottoman provinces at the time, were described as *bid'a* (innovation), meaning a departure from approved practice of the Muslim community. By designating them as *bid'a*, the kanunname rejected Ebu's-Su'ud's claim that they should be regarded as the taxation prescribed in the *fiqh*, but bearing different names. Of them, the *kanunname* stated,

> Hereafter they will not be resumed and only the shar'i taxes enumerated above that are derived from the books of *fiqh* will be required … . If anyone alters (from what is established in the *kanunname* as the rightful taxes) or modifies or makes excuses or makes substitutions, then upon him are the curses of God, the angels and mankind.[37]

Considering how widespread and ordinary the abolished taxes were, the vitriol directed at them is remarkable. Reminiscent of Vani Efendi's fatwas from his days as mufti of Erzurum, the *kanunname* calculated the rightful rates of *kharaj* in the scholarly units of *dirhem*s and *jarib*s rather than in the units of Ottoman administration for currency and space.

The *Kanunname of Candia* represented a specific idea of the Hanafi textual order and how to implement it. Whether or not Vani Efendi had a personal hand in its composition, the *kanunname* shared a number of the ideological convictions that he had proclaimed in his fatwas: the same unwavering commitment to regarding the land as *kharaji* and *milk*; the invocation of the Rightly Guided Caliphs and the particular emphasis on taxation governed exclusively by the prescriptions of the *fiqh*, down to the units of measure. How prevalent was such a vision and why did it find advocates at the highest level of governance when it meant such stark discontinuity with previous administrative practice?

Once again, the instability and recurring crises of the seventeenth century are crucial for understanding Ottoman debate about what textual order governed the land. The tumult of the early seventeenth century was followed by a period of power struggles at the imperial court, while violent rebellions led by both dissatisfied elites and bands of brigands continued in the provinces.[38] The faction of Köprülü Mehmed Pasha solidified its grasp on the office of grand vizier in 1656 and would mostly retain it until 1711; both Mehmed Pasha and his son Ahmed delivered more victories than defeats on the battlefield, but their method of establishing internal order consisted of ruthlessly suppressing their rivals and cultivating relations of clientage.[39] The sense of living in a troubled time and the question of what path could lead the empire to greatness continued to weigh heavily on those concerned with statecraft throughout the seventeenth century.

The 'return to the *kanun*' reform movement that had arisen in response to these challenges was not the only notion of reform that existed in the empire in these years. A different current, one emphasizing 'sunna-mindedness' as Ekin Tuşalp Atiyas puts it, also garnered a number of adherents from a variety of social backgrounds.[40] Vani Efendi was a leader of one such group, the *Kadızadeli* movement, that was influential in the capital during the seventeenth century.[41] The *Kadızadeli*s diagnosed society's ills as stemming from *bid'a*, or deviation from the example of the early Muslim community known as the *selef*. Concerns raised by the *Kadızadeli*s and other *selefi*-oriented reformers struck a chord with many elites as well as commoners. A new anxiety over whether *kanun* was in fact reconciled with sharia was expressed.[42] Mehmed Birgevi, whose teachings the *Kadızadeli*s much admired, had denounced the *tapu* fee in a work of scholarship, but in 1696 there was a *firman* issued to the *kaymakam* (the chief municipal administrator) of Istanbul stating that public affairs needed to be put in conformity with the sharia and the *kanun* 'purified'.[43] Atiyas has shown that throughout the late seventeenth century, Ottoman administrators took an interest in establishing taxation that was in accord with *selefi* precedent, including land tax.[44] That grand viziers sought in this age to inform themselves of Abu Yusuf's foundational views on land tax provides an interesting parallel to the earlier phenomenon of *şeyhülislam*s who had sought to inform themselves of land-related *kanun*s. However, it is unclear if these grand viziers were unconvinced of the harmony between *kanun* and sharia or simply looking for an ideologically cogent way of introducing new policies from which they expected to personally benefit.[45] Whatever political or material interests may have been served by the tenure regime embraced in the *Kanunname of Candia*, its denunciation of the more conventional Ottoman tax regime as *bid'a*, and its claim to follow the practices enjoined by the pious ancestors as recorded in the books of *fiqh*, were priorities that fit well with the agenda of *sunna*-minded reformers of the time.

Selefi configurations of land tenure made little headway in the *ilmiye*, even when sunna-minded reformers were at the height of their influence in the second half of the seventeenth century. *Şeyhülislam* Çatalcalı 'Ali Efendi (served 1674–86 and again in 1692) gave fatwas squarely compliant with the harmony tradition that were very similar to those of Zekeriyazade Yahya and Baha'i Mehmed; both he and Minkarizade Yahya Efendi were associated with *kanunname*s for *miri* land that were composed for the guidance of fatwas.[46] More strikingly, even *Şeyhülislam* Feyzullah Efendi (served 1688, and 1695–1703), the son-in-law of Vani Mehmed, issued fatwas that were squarely in the harmony tradition, affirming *tapu* and its related tenure rules along with recognizing the sultan's registers as the definitive authority on taxation.[47] The challenge for the *selefi*s, however, was not simply that they were trying to sharply revise institutionalized state practice, they were also at odds with the prevailing juridical preference for accepting contemporary practices that were deemed long-standing and beneficial. Given the strength of this countervailing scholarly current, it is not surprising that the *Kanunname of Candia*'s approach to land tenure remained limited to the Aegean and that Vani's approach to land tenure questions would disappear from eighteenth-century fatwas.

The sultan as legislator: Texts, commentaries and fatwas

Scholars have not always recognized the impact of the sultan's land tenure legislation upon Hanafi scholastic teaching. In his highly regarded study of Ebu's-Su'ud Efendi, Colin Imber wrote that the harmonized Ottoman land tenure law 'did not enter the academic Hanafi tradition'.[48] In fact, it began to do just that starting in the seventeenth century. To see this evolution, it is useful to compare two seventeenth-century commentaries with two later works from the early nineteenth century. The authors of these texts are Şeyhizade 'Abdurrahman Efendi, also known as Damad Efendi (d. 1667); the Damascene mufti 'Ala' al-Din al-Haskafi (d. 1677) and the previously mentioned Ibn 'Abidin. Şeyhizade came from a learned Rumi family and had a successful career in the *ilmiye* culminating in his appointment as Kazasker of Rumelia in 1666.[49] Haskafi was a brilliant and ambitious scholar who showed a keen interest in specifically Ottoman ways of applying the sharia and served as the appointed Hanafi mufti of Damascus.[50] Ibn 'Abidin of Damascus, one of the weightiest late Hanafi authorities, was a scholar who is often considered the last great scholar of Islamic law before the trends of the nineteenth century began to abruptly shift its transmission, institutions and modes of practice.[51]

To see the beginnings of the adoption of the harmony tradition within Hanafi academic texts, we begin with two famous commentaries on a manual (*matn*) titled *Multaqa'l-Abhur* (*Convergence of the Seas*). The author of the *Convergence*, Ibrahim ibn Muhammad al-Halabi (d. 1549), is believed to have produced it in 1517, the same year that the Ottoman Empire absorbed the majority of the eastern Arabic-speaking provinces.[52] Born in Mamluk Aleppo in 1460, Halabi had immigrated to Istanbul and become a preacher in one of the great mosques there. Given his own career and personal history, he was well equipped to write about the convergence of empires and the traditions of Hanafism. The *Convergence* was one of the most influential such texts of the later Hanafi period. Although a number of scholars wrote commentaries of it, two particularly well-known commentaries appeared in the second half of the seventeenth century. Şeyhizade's commentary was known as *Majma' al-Anhur* and Haskafi's was known as *Durr al-Muntaqa*; Haskafi sometimes refers to *Majma' al-Anhur* and so was the later of the two.

Two features stand out in Şeyhizade's commentary: first, he introduces into a scholarly work Ebu's-Su'ud's redefinition of the lands in the *bayt al-mal* that had been adopted in the *kanunnames*; second, we see a transition from the older Hanafi accounts of lands in the *bayt al-mal* to descriptions of a specifically Ottoman form of tenure. He opens his discussion of land classification not by stating that the

Ottoman regime does things differently from what the books of *fiqh* prescribe, but rather he posits that Hanafi doctrine itself has changed from what was recorded in the previous books of *fiqh*. After confirming that both tithe and *kharaji* land are *milk*, he continues,

> This [the *milk* status of *kharaji* and tithe land] is well known in all the books of *fiqh*, but some of the later day scholars have stated the legal opinion that in addition to these two there is a land that is neither tithe nor *kharaji* but which is called *ard al-mamlaka*, and is widely known as 'the royal land' (*al-ard al-amiriyya*). This is the land that was conquered either by the sword or through pact, but its people do not own it. Rather it is preserved for the *bayt al-mal* then leased by defective lease on the condition that they cultivate it and provide *kharaj muqasama* from its produce, which is known among the people as a tithe. This is the order of the lands of our country.[53]

Here, the peculiarly Ottoman-era doctrine that treasury land is neither tithe nor *kharaji* is presented as the teaching of the Hanafi school on the basis of fatwas issued by the 'late' Hanafis. In addition, Şeyhizade affirms that the tax owed is nevertheless still the *kharaj* tax, although this tax is known among the people, confusingly, as a tithe.[54] Şeyhizade's commentary thus reproduced the rescripting of treasury-owned land that had first occurred in the fatwas of Ebu's-Suʿud. While it was normal for Hanafi academic texts to incorporate doctrinal change that had been expounded in fatwas, the journey of this new definition of treasury-owned land was unusual. The newer concept of treasury-owned land had gained the ulema's attention not only because it was expounded in fatwas but because it was the actual basis of administration and had been expounded in *kanunnames* as well as fatwas. Surely, its adoption as the basis of judicial and administrative procedure through its enactment in the *kanunnames* played some role in why it had attained a status of widespread practice and consensus of its soundness that led to its integration within the more authoritative academic genre of a commentary in the seventeenth century. Its incorporation into the doctrine of the school marked a new level of textual convergence across the legal genres of the empire, as all of them shifted to embrace the doctrine forming the basis of the harmony tradition.

Second, Şeyhizade's exposition of *miri* land in his commentary on the *Convergence* is not like the descriptions of *al-ard al-mamlaka* that one finds in classic references circulating at the time like the *Fatawa Tatarkhaniyya*. The latter work, like other manuals and commentaries, compiled the views of the previous Hanafi scholars that the compiler found most authoritative. Şeyhizade's commentary did not provide a selection of authoritative views, rather he summarized the law as it had been expounded in the fatwas of Ebu's-Su'ud and enacted in the *kanunnames*:

> It is not the *milk* of those who hold it, they cannot buy or sell or give it as a gift or endow it unless the sultan grants it as *milk*. If one of them dies, his son takes his place and has possession of it according to the aforementioned terms, and if [there is no son], the lands return to the *bayt al-mal*. If a daughter or a

> brother survives him and requests the land, it's given to them as a rental by way of defective rent. If the possessor fails to cultivate for three years or more, the land is removed from his hand and given to another. If one of them wants to transfer to another, he can only do so with the permission of the sultan.[55]

Even without mention of the *tapu* fee or a complete elaboration of post-mortem transmission, Şeyhizade has given a short but relatively comprehensive overview of the Ottoman land tenure system that had been set out in the *kanunnames* and discussed in the *şeyhülslams*' fatwas. This description of *miri* land is quite different in its understanding of *al-ard al-amiriyya* than the Hanafi manuals that were composed earlier. The focal point in those works had been on how the sultan or imam could obtain *kharaj* payments on land that was abandoned and there had been little discussion of the terms of cultivator tenure. Şeyhizade's account owes far more to Ottoman administrative practice than to the treatment of *al-ard al-amiriyya* in the manuals of Qadikhan or Ibn al-Bazzaz or similar previous Hanafi authorities.

The commentary composed by 'Ala' al-Din al-Haskafi was remarkable for several reasons. First, it marked a greater convergence between the traditions of Hanafism prevailing in the Arab provinces with those prevailing in Rumelia and Anatolia. Haskafi appears to be among the first scholars from the Arab provinces who took an interest in land tenure law throughout the Ottoman domains and not just as it applied in his native Syria. Recent studies have emphasized his role in transmitting currents of Hanafism prevailing in Istanbul to a broader audience in the Arab provinces.[56] He examined the topic of land classification with a panoramic discussion that invoked the Hanafis of Egypt as well as those of Rum, drawing on Şeyhizade and Birgevi as well as older works like the *Fatawa Tatarkhaniyya*. He began with a general definition of treasury land and from there, he delved into the actual practice of land tenure in what he calls the 'lands of Rum' concluding with a translation of parts of the *Kanunname of Ahmed Khan*, and two sultanic orders regarding transmission.[57] These sections discussed which family members had the right to ask for the land by *tapu*, the special position of the son and the rights of minors unable to work the land at the time of transmission and how *tasarruf* of land could be lost. Haskafi's commentary marked a new level of engagement in a *fiqh* manual with both the practices of Ottoman land tenure and the textual forms conveying the sultan's orders. It explicitly acknowledged the sultan's orders and their textual forms – law (*qanun*), order (*amr*), the legal questions that were ostensibly resolved by Sultan Süleyman (*Ma'ruzat*) – as determining the specificities of Ottoman legal practice on treasury land.[58] Şeyhizade had also included a summary of the legal order prevailing on *miri* land, but had not explicitly linked this order to the sultan's legislative authority. Haskafi's direct acknowledgement that the sultan's order-giving texts governed the land (at least the lands of Rum) crossed a new threshold in the way that land tenure was discussed in the books of *fiqh* by presenting the substantive law of the *kanunname* as the doctrine of Hanafism.

Although Haskafi was clear that the manuals of *fiqh* should acknowledge the sultan's orders as governing treasury land, it remained unclear whether he believed that the laws in the *kanunname* were applicable throughout the empire or only in the lands of Rum; though it seems more likely that it was the latter.[59] It was on this issue of where the law was applicable that Muhammad Amin ibn 'Abidin was to break new ground. Ibn 'Abidin (1784–1836) is known to have admired and revered Haskafi.[60] One of Ibn 'Abidin's greatest works was the *Radd al-Muhtār*, a super-commentary on Haskafi's commentary, known as *al-Durr al-Mukhtar*, on Timurtashi's manual (*matn*) *Tanwir al-Absar wa-Jami' al-Bihar*, a manual (*matn*). In this commentary, Haskafi's treatment of land tenure is less detailed and more conventional than his exposition in *Durr al-Muntaqa*. In response, Ibn 'Abidin presented a pithy statement conveying how deeply integrated into Hanafi scholarship the land tenure *kanun* had become in his own time. Unlike Haskafi and most other Arab Hanafis, Ibn 'Abidin opposed Ibn al-Humam's theory that all the cultivators who had been owners of land had died, leading the treasury itself to become the owner of the land.[61] As a result, he did not accept that the land in Syria or Egypt should be presumed to belong to the treasury, although in other sections of this same work he made it clear that he accepted that some land in Syria did belong to the treasury, namely, land that its cultivators acknowledge to be *miri*, or *sultani*.[62] His synopsis of the law prevailing on these lands came almost word for word from Şeyhizade:

> Such lands are not wrested from the cultivators so long as they pay what is due on them. They are not inherited when they die, and they cannot sell them. Rather, the Ottoman state (*al-dawla al-'Uthmaniya*) has ordered (*jara al-rasm*) that if a man dies the land goes to his son without a fee, and if not then to the *bayt al-mal*. But if he has a daughter or a brother then they may take it by way of defective lease.[63] If the *tasarruf* holder leaves the land bare for three years or more it is taken from him and given to another. No one can transfer it to another without the permission of the sultan or his representative.[64]

At the end of this short explanation, he refers the reader desiring further information to consult Haskafi's *Durr al-Muntaqa* or his own previous work commenting on the fatwas of the eighteenth-century Damascene mufti Hamid al-'Imadi, known as *al-'Uqud al-Durriyya*; he thus reminded readers that there already existed a Hanafi textual tradition testifying that the sultan's orders were the law of *miri* land within the Ottoman domains. While it was unclear in the writings of Haskafi and in those of Haskafi's great contemporary 'Abd al-Ghani al-Nabulusi, that the sultan's tenure law for *miri* land actually applied to any lands in Syria, Ibn 'Abidin is far more categorical in concluding that *miri* land as an entity had a particular legal regime attached to it, whether in Syria or elsewhere.[65]

The change in doctrine: The sultan has a choice

The most jarring innovation introduced into the Hanafi books of *fiqh* from the harmony tradition in the seventeenth century was that land could be claimed as property of the treasury upon conquest. This position, as many Hanafi jurists would point out, was historically the position of the Shafiʿi school but not the Hanafi; nevertheless, by the end of the seventeenth century the books of *fiqh* as well as *kanunnames* would affirm it as part of Hanafi doctrine. While Baber Johansen has shown that Hanafi doctrine evolved to regard plowland as property of the treasury through the death of its earlier owners, the extent of doctrinal transformation runs deeper than Johansen demonstrated.[66] The *Kanunname of Candia* did not denounce this new doctrine, but it did protest the taxation consequences that were attached to such a move. In this, the *kanunname* reflected concerns shared by Arab Hanafis, who also demanded that taxation status be consistent with that of ownership. Because the jurists were primarily focused on the taxation issue, the magnitude of the change in the sultan's ability to make decisions about the status of the land – and its reversal of earlier teaching – went largely unremarked by the jurists.

As we have seen, Ebu's-Suʿud's position that the treasury would claim the land from the moment of conquest was a break with his Hanafi predecessors; for his part, he made no attempt to argue that Ottoman practice was consistent with past Hanafi teaching on this point (see Chapter 2). Nevertheless, he was not the only sixteenth-century Hanafi to assert that conquered land could move directly into the treasury: his chief critic in his own lifetime, Mehmed Birgevi, also concluded that such action was licit for the sultan. Given that Birgevi criticized many practices that he believed were deviations from the *fiqh*, it is surprising that he provided one of the earliest examples of scholarly writing that affirmed the imam's power to immediately put conquered land in the *bayt al-mal*. Birgevi's reliance on al-Ansari is instructive: in his own explanation of what was and was not acceptable in the prevailing land tenure practices, he read *al-Fatawa al-Tatarkhaniyya* in a way that subverted the dominant Hanafi understanding of the sultan's powers:

> What our fathers and our ancestors acknowledged is that the sultan, when he conquered a place, did not divide its lands between the conquerors. This is permitted, since the imam has a choice between dividing it thus or retaining it for the Muslims until the day of resurrection and imposing *kharaj* upon it. If we said then that the lands are not owned by their possessors but rather their ultimate ownership belongs to the treasury, as is maintained in our time and previously, then its usage is for those who possess it, by one of two ways. It was said in the *Tatarkhaniya* that it is permitted to bestow ownerless land – those lands called *aradi al-mamlaka* – upon a people so that they will give *kharaj*. This is permitted in one of two ways: either they take the place of the owners in cultivating and giving *kharaj*, or they rent for the price of the *kharaj*. What is taken from them is *kharaj* with regard to the imam and rent with regard to them.[67]

In this passage, Birgevi gives an entirely new interpretation of the 'choice' that the imam, or the sultan, faced after conquest. In Birgevi's reading, it was not a choice between making the land either the *milk* of the conquering soldiers or the *milk* of the cultivators; instead, the sultan could either give the land as *milk* to the soldiers or keep it in the treasury and allow the cultivators its use in return for *kharaj* or for rent. Although he does not draw attention to the fact that his interpretation is a departure from traditional Hanafi understanding, his later readers would do so. In effect, this reading substitutes the Shafiʿi doctrine of conquered land for that of the Hanafi.

Birgevi's account is remarkable in its innovation. Furthermore, he shows himself here to be a less intractable critic of Ottoman administrative policy than is often supposed. Birgevi was an influential thinker and particularly esteemed by the Kadızadelis and those Ottomans with *selefi* leanings.[68] His acceptance of *miri* land's legitimacy from the moment of conquest may be the reason that the *Kanunname of Candia* does not denounce the classification of *miri* land at conquest as *bidʿa*; since Birgevi accepted its validity, other *selefi*-oriented ulema may have grudgingly accepted it also.[69] Birgevi then notes that on treasury land, transactions and inheritance law that apply to *milk* are prohibited. He concludes that the second option he delineated – treating the cultivators as renters rather than as substitutes for the owners – is preferable because it was 'less opposed to the sharia and less harmful to the people'.[70] This conclusion would have resonance with the Arab Hanafis, as we will see shortly.

While the classification of land as treasury-owned immediately after conquest was approved by both Ebu's-Suʿud and Mehmed Birgevi, Hanafi texts produced in the following century show that this change was not immediately absorbed by the ulema, including those serving in the *ilmiye*. In the guidebook known as *Mizan al-Fatawa* that was composed by the Ottoman judge Mustafa b. Süleyman Balizade (d. 1073/1662), an addendum to a fatwa concerning treasury possession states:

> The land, whether tithe or *kharaji* or *muwazzaf* or *muqasama*, and the land of Sawad, is owned (*milk*) for us. But for Shafiʿi it is a *waqf* for the Muslims and it is rented and its people are renters on it. And today, most of the lands of Rum and belonging to the Turks is in possession of the treasury. The land is given to the *gazis* and they give it to the *reaya* with rent that is now called *resim* as you find in *Muʿin* (*Muʿinu'l-Mufti* of Pir Mehmed). However, ʿUmar, may God be pleased with him, consulted with the companions and was not pleased with the renting of Bilal and his companions may God be pleased with them all.[71]

In this text, Balizade notes that although the Hanafi and Shafiʿi schools differ in theory about whether the land is *milk* or effectively held by the state and rented, the practice now in the Ottoman lands of Rumelia and Anatolia is that it is held by the treasury and rented. That this is not consistent with what the caliph ʿUmar had enjoined was then duly noted, and he avoided explaining how exactly the lands of the Turks came to reside in the treasury. His work registers that he saw the teaching of the Hanafi school in tension with contemporary practice, and an agreement in principle with the *Kanunname of Candia* about what Hanafi doctrine maintains. Namely, at the moment of conquest, the land should be accounted *milk*, and to be consistent with ʿUmar it would be the *milk* of its cultivators rather than its conquerors. The innovative position of Ebu's-Su'ud and Birgevi appears to have been an accepted part of Ottoman administrative practice but not a feature of academic jurisprudence.

It was in the commentaries on the *Convergence* of Şeyhizade and Haskafi that the new position was absorbed into academic books of *fiqh*. Şeyhizade's wording echoed that of Balizade, noting that the Hanafis differ from al-Shafi'i in their position that the Sawad was made the *milk* of its holders, but he defined *miri* land as 'the land that was conquered either by the sword or through pact, but its people do not own it. Rather it is preserved for the *bayt al-mal*.'[72] Şeyhizade's language does not specifically say that the land enters the *bayt al-mal* at the time it is conquered by Muslims, but contextually it gives such an impression. If he left room for doubt, al-Haskafi's commentary was less shy in presenting the innovative nature of immediately claiming land for the treasury. Early in his discussion of land classification, he takes the standard position that land conquered by the sword or through voluntary submission (pact) is the *milk* of its inhabitants, although he then added that in his own day, the land of Egypt and Syria did belong to the *bayt al-mal* because all the cultivators who had received the land as *milk* had died out.[73] So far, this was the standard position of the Arab ulema and based squarely on Ibn al-Humam. Later in his narrative, however, he writes that the *aradi al-mamlaka* can come to the treasury either by the death of the cultivators or through 'conquest by the sword, remaining [in the treasury] for the Muslims until the day of resurrection'.[74] Here, he makes it clear that there is more than one way for land to enter the treasury: by the death of the cultivators, as Ibn al-Humam has indicated, *or* directly by conquest. Ibn 'Abidin too would adopt this same definition in *Radd al-Mukhtar*.[75] That land became either *kharaji* or tithe upon conquest was thereby relegated to a historical practice followed by earlier imams rather than a practice incumbent on reigning monarchs.

Unlike Birgevi and Şeyhizade however, Haskafi registered that the latter mode of entry into the *bayt al-mal* was at odds with conventional Hanafi doctrine. After summarizing Birgevi's passage that the imam may choose to either divide the land among the conquerors or to keep the land for the treasury, Haskafi writes, 'And this is controversial, because "the caliph's choice to preserve it for the Muslims until the day of resurrection" only means the favoring of the unbelievers with their lives and lands and the latter becoming their *milk*.'[76] That is, Haskafi made clear that if the imam did not divide the land among the conquerors, the Hanafis had understood his other option to be bestowing the land as *milk* upon its conquered possessors and to take *kharaj* from them. Although he pointed out this key departure in Birgevi's reading from past understanding, what he found objectionable was not the retaining of the land for the *bayt al-mal* after conquest, but rather that it was retained for the *bayt al-mal* and still charged with the *kharaj* payment. Following Ibn Nujaym (and for that matter, Birgevi), he found it incoherent that a land that was not *kharaji* nevertheless had to pay *kharaj*. The result is that he incorporated this new definition of how land can enter the custody of the treasury with no protest directed at the mode of acquisition; only the taxes received criticism.

Haskafi and Ibn ʿAbidin both adopted the position that conquered land could be held in the *bayt al-mal* immediately after conquest, which meant that the difference between the Shafiʾi and the Hanafi teaching on this point had essentially disappeared. Perhaps ironically, we find something of a parallel priority in *Durr al-Muntaqa* and the *Kanunname of Candia* in that both demanded that taxation be consistent with the land's categorization, although they came to divergent conclusions about how to resolve this inconsistency. One advocated the coherence of freehold property and *kharaj* taxation, while Haskafi advocated a full acknowledgement of the new circumstances of treasury ownership and hence a corresponding acknowledgement that cultivators paid rent, not tax. What they both appeared to accept was that – contrary to earlier doctrine – it was the sultan's choice to classify the land as *miri* or *kharaji*.

Conclusion

The *Kanunname of Candia* appeared to mark either a major turning point in Ottoman land law and administrative documentation or else a prominent aberration from normal practice. Even though it was an important protest of prevailing trends in land tenure law, it did not succeed in arresting those trends. While it clearly had an impact on subsequent *kanunname*s issued for the other Aegean islands, and perhaps also for Basra, later cadastral surveys and *kanunname*s such as those of Podolia (1681), Morea (1716) and Tabriz (1727) were thoroughly in line with the *miri* regime.[77] Clearly, the compilers of the *Kanunname of Candia* wanted Ottoman policy to adhere to the academic tradition that had been dominant in the *madhhab*. However, here the ground was shifting even as the *kanunname* was composed. From the late seventeenth century, academic works of *fiqh* incorporated the sultan's *kanunnames*, *firman*s and the *Maʿruzat*, and in some cases specifically drew attention to them as the definitive statements of the law establishing the order of *miri* land. Commentaries by Şeyhizade and Haskafi defined *miri* land as it was defined in the sultan's textual directives rather than the Hanafi manuals and commentaries of earlier centuries. They declared it a third category of land, with the special transactions and conditions of usage defined by the administrative texts of the chancellery and the *ilmiye*. Taking a position that was closer to that of the other Sunni schools than to their Hanafi antecedents, they agreed that when conquering new lands, the Ottoman sultans could and did sequester the lands immediately in the care of the treasury. By the end of the seventeenth century, no Ottoman jurist would be able to claim what Ebu's-Suʿud had stated in the sixteenth: that the third category of land, *miri*, was not included in the books of *fiqh*.

From the late seventeenth century, the law governing *miri* land had achieved a new uniformity and a new ubiquity: a standard definition and treatment of it could be found across every genre of legal text circulating in the Ottoman Empire. Located in both administrative and scholastic texts, its integration across both suggested a legal culture whose practitioners had developed conventions for when and how to integrate material across the boundaries of genre. In that respect, we could view the *Kanun-ı Cedid* and the commentaries of Şeyhizade and Haskafi not only as contemporaries but as complementary texts; the former was a *kanunname* that contained numerous fatwas and the latter were texts of *fiqh* burgeoning with *kanuns* and orders from the sultan. Both were references, or in Brinkley Messick's phrase, 'library' genres. The *Kanun-ı Cedid* was a text cobbled together from pre-existing texts which had addressed specific localities and specific situations at the moments when they were each originally issued. Assembled together as a reference work, they no longer governed a particular province or a unique situation, but rather the *miri* land of the empire as a general category. It was this legal regime, disembedded from the confines of any particular locality and valid on *miri* land categorically, that had become embedded in the texts of *fiqh*. The older Hanafi positions on land classification and taxation championed by the *Kanunname of Candia* were no longer the current doctrine of the school.

Chapter 5

THE AGE OF THE *MUTASARRIFS*: DIFFUSION, RIGHTS AND DISCRETION IN THE EIGHTEENTH CENTURY

Ottoman institutional development in the eighteenth century is often characterized as one of rupture with earlier centuries. One of the most important trends associated with the eighteenth-century Ottoman Empire was the emergence of a more monetized economy along with rising commercialism, consumerism and demand for credit.[1] New configurations of economic and political power, often associated with the rise of the provincial notables known as the *ayan*, are seen as a break with past practice, whether the new institutions are understood as decentralization, or a provincial centralization, or a provincial-imperial partnership.[2] For most of the twentieth century, historians viewed these ruptures with the 'classical' institutions as corruptions, although revisionists have characterized the growth of tax farming and the emergence of the *ayan* and their households as the rise of new institutions better suited to realities of a territorially larger and increasingly monetarized empire.[3] In either case, the emphasis has been rupture. Both the practice of land tenure and the law governing it have been thought to fit these narratives of rupture: many studies have concluded that the land itself had become virtually private property, either through *malikane* or *waqf*.[4] Likewise, some scholars have argued that *kanun* became defunct in the eighteenth century because *kanun* – sometimes characterized as 'feudal' because of its association with the *timar* system – was a law unsuited to an increasingly monetized and commercialized economy.[5] Whether this rupture was evidence of decline or early modern transformation depended on whether the historian was of Eurocentric or of revisionist inclinations.

Eighteenth-century fatwas tell a very different story of the land law. First, rather than a story of provincial fragmentation or decentralization, it tells a story of increasing coherence as a more uniform approach to the law that emerged among the muftis and was more widely shared across greater swaths of the empire. In addition, the story of land law in the eighteenth century is not one of legal rupture where *kanun* fell into abeyance to be 'replaced' by the more commercially oriented law of the sharia. On the contrary, there was pronounced continuity with the harmony tradition as it had been shaping in the sixteenth and seventeenth centuries. In fact, it is arguable that much of the 'classical' land law only became relatively uniform in application and widespread in juridical practice in the eighteenth century, not before. In the many texts transmitting land law, there was broader consensus of the law's various provisions, how to apply them and the determining role of the sultan's orders. The model of harmonization pioneered by Baha'i Mehmed – deferential to the sultan's orders generally and only rarely embracing the *şeyhülislam*'s power to make amendments – remained intact on most issues. Opinions on transactions continued to fall on a spectrum whose contours had already emerged in the time of Şeyhülislam Hocasa'deddinzade Es'ad Efendi (served 1615–22 and 1623–5). The quintessential analogist, he had approved a wide array of transactions on *miri* land unless they caused quantifiable harm, while at the opposite end of the spectrum Ebu's-Su'ud and the autonomists maintained that *miri* land could only be transacted in a limited number of ways. More so than on other issues, there was still some tension between analogists and autonomists on the scope of allowable transactions in the eighteenth century, though among muftis analogism seems to have gained the upper hand. Nevertheless, the dramatic differences between muftis like Pir Mehmed, Vani Efendi and Es'ad Efendi that were characteristic of the seventeenth century were largely gone, and although not all differences of opinion were eradicated, the scope of the muftis' disagreements was narrower than it had been in the previous century. The differences between Arabs and Rumis also diminished, as the harmony tradition took hold in some Arabic-speaking provinces. This process of dissemination was uneven; while it is unclear how prevalent the harmony tradition became in provinces such as Greater Syria, it is clear that it was making inroads there and had spread beyond the lands of Rum.

Second, the fatwas qualify the extent to which it is proper to speak of a trend of privatization, and to what extent this 'privatizing' was a break with past precedent. No later than the early seventeenth century, the harmony tradition included a spectrum of both analogists and autonomists (see Chapter 3). In one area of the law, transactions, analogism had become the dominant approach by the eighteenth century. This development was not a break with preceding practice or a repudiation of the *kanun*, it was a realignment of majority and minority views within the harmony tradition. Given the wider scope of transactions analogists embraced, the ascendance of analogism could be read as a liberalization of transaction law that made the *mutasarrif* more like an owner. However, some caution is warranted in such a conclusion. The ability of the *mutasarrif* to transact more widely did not mean that he was now transacting freely; the muftis had also empowered the deputy to stop any transaction or usage of the land which might decrease the revenues. Hence, the muftis did not move to concentrate property rights exclusively in the hands of either the cultivator or the deputy, rather they continued to affirm that each had a separate and valid layer of rights and that a proper balance of these rights was necessary for the funding of the treasury.

The eighteenth century was an age of *mutasarrifs* holding lifelong, transactable and inheritable bundles of property rights, of whom the *ayan* were only one group. Of the various lifelong tenures on immovable property associated with the commercialism of the eighteenth century (*gedik*, *ijaratayn*, *malikane*), two of these mirrored the *kanun*'s formulation of *tasarruf* on *miri* and land (see Chapter 1);

the eighteenth-century iterations of *gedik*, though a different bundle, evolved in close dialogue with *ijaratayn*.[6] Hence the more standardized, lifelong property rights for *mutasarrifs* pioneered by the *kanun* were more likely a facilitator of rising commercialism than an obstacle to it. Continuing to wrestle with the question of how the disparate sources of the land law fit with one another, the eighteenth-century Ottoman ulema found further reason to facilitate transaction. *Kanun* and the law that was built upon it did not disappear in response to rising commercialism; rather, the harmony tradition already contained the tools for strengthening the transactional capability of the *mutasarrifs*.

To be sure, fatwas cannot answer all our questions about land law in the eighteenth century. They give no sense of what was 'typical' in any of the locations where they were issued. How much of the land was actually subject to the system of *tapu* and transactions through deputy permission, all of which had become so widely accepted among muftis in the eighteenth century? The amount of *miri* land held as *çiftliks*, or plantation-like farms, by the military class had expanded in the eighteenth century; presumably such individuals did not pay *tapu* or request permission to transact, although the fatwas give little clue about how *tasarruf* of *miri* land worked once it fell into the hands of privileged classes such as ulema and soldiers.[7] In other words, the diversity of tenures among the tax-extracting class in the eighteenth century makes it difficult to assess how much of the empire's lands were actually subject to the rules of possession that existed so coherently across the textual edifice of Ottoman law. Still, the fatwas attest that the *miri* regime and the textual tradition governing it was very much alive, functioning and evolving in the eighteenth century. Whether or not most land in the empire was governed as the fatwas specified, the consensus that emerged in this textual tradition of what the land law was and how to apply it would have a significant impact on the legal trends of the following century.

Background

The greater uniformity of land tenure law observed in fatwas from Syria, Anatolia and Rumelia clearly resulted from the circulation of the increasing number of legal texts that adhered to the harmony tradition. Many of these texts were produced in the seventeenth century, meaning that the muftis of the eighteenth century now encountered the land law in a number of different textual forms that would have been unavailable or in short supply in earlier times.[8] The manual compiled by Mehmed Sakızi, *Surrat al-Fatawa*, may well have been the most prominent of these. It was widely read and cited on land matters among the provincial muftis.[9] As a manual of *fiqh*, it was higher ranking in the Hanafi hierarchy of textual authority than fatwa collections, and its circulation played a seminal role in exposing scholars and muftis to Sakızi's vision of the harmony tradition. In Rumelia and Anatolia, muftis like Ahmed el-Mostari (d. 1776) of the town of Mostar in Bosnia-Herzegovina read and incorporated the fatwas of previous *şeyhülislams*, not only Ebu's-Su'ud, but also more recent holders of the office like Menteşzade 'Abdürrahim (*şeyhülislam* for seventeen months in 1715–16), who continued to 'build' their fatwas from the *kanun* and the fatwas of their predecessors.[10] As we will see in the next chapter, the fatwas on *miri* land attributed to ʿAbdürrahim would have a profound impact on the 1858 Land Code.[11] By 1737, fatwas on *miri* land and *waqf* issued by ʿAbdürrahim and a number of seventeenth-century *şeyhülislam*s would be gathered together in the compilation *Fetava-yı Cami*ʿ *ül-Icareteyn*, which would also be cited by provincial muftis.[12]

In addition, the *Kanun-ı Cedid* and other texts like it brought the muftis direct knowledge of the *kanun*s in addition to the fatwas that were built from them. A number of these *kanuns* were cited by the mufti of Erzurum, Seyid İbrahim Edhem Efendi (d. 1776), as part of his citations for his own fatwas.[13] Dated copies of the *Kanun-ı Cedid* suggest that it was only after the first quarter of the eighteenth century that it was widely in circulation, and its strongly autonomist inclinations would continue to find advocates in the *ilmiye* into the early nineteenth century.[14] The circulation of this text in this period supports the observations of several recent scholarly studies that have argued that *kanun*s and sultanic legal directives did not become irrelevant in the eighteenth century because the sultans ceased to issue the kinds of *kanunname*s that were so ubiquitous in the sixteenth century; in fact, these legal directives were incorporated into different textual genres where they had not previously appeared.[15] There is no better demonstration of the increasingly wide diffusion of the harmony tradition and its incorporation into Ottoman fatwas than to compare the land tenure fatwas of Vani Mehmed Efendi with his eighteenth-century successors as mufti of Erzurum, Seyid İbrahim Edhem (d. 1776) and ʿAbdurrahman Efendi el-Erzurumi (d. 1810).[16] While Vani had not acknowledged the land of Erzurum as *miri*, nor the taxation of the province as governed by the sultan's registers, both İbrahim Edhem and ʿAbdurrahman showed a thorough familiarity and acceptance of the *miri* regime, and a deference towards the sultan's orders.

There were some differences in the paths that the harmony tradition travelled on its way into Damascene fatwas. As noted in the previous chapter, Ibn ʿAbidin attested that Syrian muftis were largely unfamiliar with fatwa collections circulating in the Turkish language. In Damascus, the muftis knew of the sultan's textual orders from working with the court (where the administration enforced these orders) and a textual lineage that differed somewhat from that of Rum. The Damascene muftis' increasing familiarity with the harmony tradition was often directly traceable to the academic texts or fatwa compilations that rendered the sultan's orders into Arabic. As we will see, works like Haskafi's *al-Durr al-Muntaqa* as well as Sakızi's *Surrat al-Fatawa* were instrumental in bringing *firmans*, *kanuns* and eventually the fatwas built from them, to the Arabic-speaking provinces. In this way, the greater adherence to the harmony tradition across the breadth of the empire was a result of the changes to the 'texts of *fiqh*' described in the previous chapter. These academic Hanafi texts had accepted the rethinking of the *bayt al-mal* proposed by Ebu's-Suʿud and, by integrating the *kanun*s and *firman*s governing land, had brought them to the attention of Arabic-speaking audience.[17] Although there is evidence that some ulema, particularly in Egypt, continued to emphasize the supremacy of local custom over that of the empire, the general trend towards increasing cohesion gives the impression that the Ottoman *mashriq* was adopting a more uniform approach to the land law.

Convergence

The circulation of these numerous texts containing the sultan's directives led to an unsurprising result: to survey the fatwas of eighteenth- and early-nineteenth-century *şeyhülislams* and provincial muftis from Mostar, Erzurum and Damascus is to be impressed by how much they have in common. Across these provinces, there was a broad consensus of the features of the cultivators' property-rights bundle and the powers of the treasury's deputy. Egypt shared some of the same features but departed from them often enough to suggest that it was not as integrated into the harmony tradition as in the other three provinces. In all of these provinces it was commonly accepted that much of the lands, especially plowlands, belonged to the treasury and were thus designated *miri*, *amiriya* or *sultani*. The bundle of rights that the cultivator possessed was typically discussed under the generic term of *tasarruf* throughout Rumelia and Anatolia, while in Damascus an indigenous term for the bundle, *mashadd maska*, was used.[18] This term was not used in other parts of greater Syria,[19] but in Damascus, it was used for the cultivator's bundle of rights on both treasury land and *waqf* land, as these two bundles were essentially similar in character for the Syrians, just as *tapu* had provided a single tenure regime for both *miri* and *waqf* land in Rumelia and Anatolia. Although the more fully elaborated legal regimes governing *miri* land and *waqf* property held by *ijaratayn* had diverged on post-mortem transmission and on some issues of the cultivator's ability to make changes to the property without the consent of its administrator, the muftis continued to see some amount of similarity between *waqf* property and *miri* land, and to debate the degree of this similarity throughout the eighteenth century.

In these three regions, there was notable consensus about the rights of the cultivator's bundle and its special regime of transactions beginning from the middle of the eighteenth century. In Damascus, Martha Mundy and Richard Saumarez Smith have identified an important transformation that occurred at precisely this time: before the mid-eighteenth century, Damascene muftis did not discuss *mashadd maska* in terms of its similarities or differences with other Hanafi property rights and bundles like *kirdar* and *haqq al-qarar*, or for that matter with terms like *tapu* or *tasarruf* that were prevalent in the texts adhering to the harmony tradition.[20] Muftis such as 'Abd al-Rahman al-'Imadi (d. 1641)) and 'Abd al-Ghani al-Nabulusi (d. 1730) defined *mashadd maska* as '*'urf* of the peasants': a peculiarly local phenomenon having nothing to do with terms in the books of *fiqh* or the practices prevailing in other parts of the empire.[21] However, beginning with the tenure of Hamid al-'Imadi (d. 1758), a mufti who was also one of the most famous Damascene scholars of the century, the muftis began to situate their local practice more systematically within the wider parameters of Hanafi and Ottoman property concepts, including what I have called the harmony tradition.[22] Mundy and Smith attribute this transition to broader changes in administrative documentation and a corresponding desire of the muftis to limit property rights on *miri* land.[23]

There is another factor that should be highlighted in this transition, however: as the eighteenth-century Damascene muftis began to discuss how *mashadd maska* related to *miri tasarruf*, *tapu* and so on, they usually cited the juridical texts that guided their thinking in these matters. The works that they credited with shaping these rulings that shifted their terminology from the purely local to the more widely imperial idiom had only been composed in the mid- to late seventeenth century: they were Sakızi's *Surrat al-Fatawa* and Haskafi's *al-Durr al-Muntaqa*.[24] In other words, the Damascene muftis' engagement with the harmony tradition can usually be traced to the presence of the harmony tradition in the Hanafi texts of *fiqh* that was discussed in the previous chapters. As a result, the way that the Damascene jurists understood the cultivator's bundle generally drew closer to that of their Rumi colleagues in the eighteenth century. Hamid al-ʿImadi cited Sakızi's *Surrat al-Fatawa* on a number of issues: his understanding of the ten-year rule; of invalid transactions on *miri* land such as gift, sale and substitution; of the loss of the land if it was not worked for three years and of the need for the deputy's permission to transfer the bundle of rights.[25] He also affirmed that fellow villagers were to be offered the *tasarruf* or *mashadd maska* of a land before it was offered to an outsider.[26] His successor, ʿAli al-Muradi (d. 1771) – who explicitly integrated the sultan's order-giving texts into his work – affirmed both the necessity of transfer with permission and the invalidity of a creditor seizing cultivation rights.[27] With a broad consensus settling around these issues, it is clear that a more standardized approach to land tenure had emerged in the provincial traditions of *ifta'* not only in Rumelia and Anatolia but also in Damascus.

This is not to say that local understandings of *mashadd maska* were entirely subsumed by scholarly currents issuing from the *ilmiye*. In one key way, *mashadd maska* was conceptualized quite distinctly from *tasarruf* of *miri* land as articulated in the harmony tradition. In the lands of Rum, payment of the *tapu* fee in exchange for lifelong cultivation rights was at the heart of the process for securing the cultivator's bundle. In Damascus, the idea of a fee in exchange for the bundle would never become a defining feature of how *mashadd maska* was acquired. In some fatwas, the Damascene muftis conceptualized the acquisition of *mashadd maska* as delegation (*tafwid*) by the treasury deputy; in others, the bundle was acquired through labour invested in the land, analogous or even overlapping with the concept of *kirdar*.[28] While the first position was the dominant understanding in the harmony tradition, no Damascene jurists who took this view ruled that a *tapu*-like payment was required for a valid transfer, despite the muftis' acceptance that a transfer required permission of the deputy.[29] Ibn ʿAbidin's commentary on Hamid al-ʿImadi's fatwas is the first text that mentions a fee in connection with post-mortem transmission for daughters and other family members with the right to pre-empt.[30] Despite the lack of attention it received in the fatwas, we learn from a fleeting mention in one of Ibn ʿAbidin's other juridical works that a large upfront payment followed by the smaller yearly tax or rental payments was in fact a normative arrangement in Damascus as it was the lands of Rum.[31] In other words, actual practice in the Damascene hinterland of Ibn Abidin's era may have more closely approximated the normative practice of the empire's core lands than the fatwas revealed. While the fatwas attached no legal weight to the fee, Ibn Abidin's juridical works make clear that the specific property rights bundle first systematically articulated in the sixteenth century – consisting of lifelong *tasarruf* in return for a large fee plus regular subsequent payments – was present in Damascus on both *miri* land and *waqf*. Given that Damascus had no pre-Ottoman *tapu* tradition, this outcome is striking.

As a general matter, the scope of mufti disagreement, while still present, had narrowed considerably. In the seventeenth century, one of the matters that had divided the muftis was how the deputy could respond if the cultivator failed to obtain permission before erecting buildings or planting trees or vines. From the middle of the seventeenth century, the dominant position among the *şeyhülislams* had been that of the autonomists, which gave the deputy leeway to reverse these changes whether or not they reduced the revenue; this position was presented as the consensus in the nineteenth-century compendium *Cami' ül-İcareteyn*.[32] There are only a few eighteenth-century fatwas that deal with this problem directly, and they indicate that there was still lingering discomfort among provincial muftis on this issue. For that matter, Hamid al-'Imadi gave a fatwa disputing that there was even a need for a cultivator with *mashadd maska* to receive permission from a deputy or *mutawalli* before planting a tree.[33] Even Ahmed el-Mostari, well versed in the *şeyhülislams*' fatwas, expressed some equivocation on this issue. For instance, in one fatwa, Ahmed el-Mostari addressed this issue in square conformity with the autonomists:

Question:	Without permission, Zayd transfers land to 'Amr, who plants a vineyard. Can the *sipahi* uproot the vineyard and reverse the transfer?
Answer:	Yes, if it was planted without his permission.[34]

While he adhered to the *kanun*'s plain meaning when dealing with the vineyard, he ruled differently on a similar question:

Question:	Working as partners, a few people build post stations (*menzilhaneler*) on a bit of a field that is one of the cultivated fields belonging to Zayd the *sipahi*'s *timar*. They did not ask his permission, so is Zayd then able to destroy the post stations and remove them?
Answer:	He can only take a fair fee for that place from those people. (*Ancak ol yerin ecr-i mis̱lini ol kimesnelerden alır.*)

Here, he seems to say that the *sipahi* cannot destroy the buildings, but can only charge the partners a fee for its presence there. It is unclear why he allowed the deputy such latitude in the first fatwa, only to deny it in the second. Post stations provided an important public service to the empire and not only provided mail services but were the crucial infrastructure for provisioning troops during war.[35] It may have been for this reason that he refused to allow its destruction. In any case, it indicates that Mostari, who clearly accepted the dominant view of the autonomists in the first fatwa, did not find it applicable in all circumstances.

The issue of post-mortem transmission of *tasarruf* provides yet another example of the way consensus continued to grow between Syrians and Rumis about what the sultan had ordered and its status as law. It is an apt illustration of how earlier generations of Syrian ulema presumed that the land directives issued as *kanun* did not govern Syria, while later ones presumed that it did. In the seventeenth century, one way in which the Syrians differed markedly from the Rumis was in their continued exclusion of females in the awarding of *mashadd maska*. As late as the middle of the eighteenth century, the Damascene muftis were nearly unanimous in ruling that a woman could not take the *mashadd maska* of a deceased male relative, including her father.[36] We have seen that the renowned Hamid al-ʿImadi had familiarity with the harmony tradition and affirmed its relevance to Damascene practice in a number of other issues, yet when it came to post-mortem transmission, he gave no consideration to the sultan's orders.[37] When ʿAli al-Muradi began his tenure as mufti (*c.* 1758), however, the line of transmission designated in the *kanun* began to be observed in Damascus. Haskafi's commentary on *Multaqa'l-Abhur* proved to be a key text for transmitting *kanun*s on the land law into the juridical discourse of the Damascenes: in one fatwa, ʿAli al-Muradi indicated that he had become aware of the sultan's transmission law by reading this work.[38] Haskafi had recorded *kanun*s that included the transmission rules, but he seemed to believe that they pertained to the lands of Rum, not the Arab provinces (see Chapter 4). One can see ʿAli al-Muradi as prefiguring Ibn ʿAbidin's conclusion that the sultan's rules of transmission were operative on *miri* land generally by holding that the sultan's transmission law was as applicable in Damascus as it was in the lands of Rum.

While the Syrians showed signs that they increasingly believed that the sultan's orders should guide local practice on *miri* land, it is unclear to what extent other eighteenth-century muftis of the Arab provinces were moving in the same direction.[39] In particular, this eventual acceptance by the Damascenes of the sultan's transmission law appears to have had no counterpart in Egypt. In all likelihood, this nonconformity stemmed from the administrative exceptionalism that prevailed in Egypt as much as any scholarly proclivities for resisting instruction from Istanbul. From its conquest, Ottoman land tenure practices in Egypt were exceptional; Egypt had never been subject to the *timar* system but was administered instead through revenue blocks (*muqataʿa*s), which were eventually managed as tax farms (*iltizam*).[40] Most of the legal community, Hanafi and non-Hanafi, took the position that the land belonged to the treasury, although both Shafiʿis and Malikis had developed a counterposition that it was common and valid to treat plowland as *milk*.[41] It is unclear to what extent features like *tapu* or the need for permission when transferring cultivation rights were observed.[42] There was no tradition in Egypt of collecting fatwas for posterity, and no eighteenth-century Hanafi fatwa collections addressing land law have survived.[43] Scholarly accounts have therefore depended on court records and narrative sources for information about cultivator tenure. There is a consensus that peasant cultivators did have a secure lifelong right to cultivate, and this right could be rented, and pawned in a transaction called *gharuqa* rather than *rahn*, and transferred (*faragh* or *isqat*).[44] Depending on the locality, there were different patterns of transmitting the cultivator's bundle at death.[45] Sons or other capable males were favoured, but if they were absent, women often did inherit. In some places, the land was divided according to *fara'id* – the division of freehold property among heirs as allocated by the *fiqh* – after death.

Tellingly, the eighteenth-century Maliki mufti of al-Azhar, al-Dardir, defended the lack of uniform practice, arguing that local custom should dictate the issue of inheriting treasury land's usage.[46] The sultan, he maintained, could not overrule custom, even on treasury land. This view was not out of step with the Egyptian Hanafis. The sixteenth-century Egyptian ulema – including the great Hanafi jurist Ibn Nujaym – regarded many aspects of Ottoman legal practice and much of the *kanun* to be the custom of Rumelia and Anatolia, and therefore subordinate to local custom in the lands of Egypt, or simply not applicable there because Egypt had its own custom.[47] Similarly, 'Abd al-Rahim b. Abu'l-Lutf (d. 1692), the Hanafi mufti of Jerusalem in the late seventeenth century, also wrote that usage of the lands and houses on lands belonging to the treasury belonged exclusively to those residents in the village according to what they had agreed upon with one another.[48] Hence, it was the custom of the village that governed usage rights, and 'Abd al-Rahim seemed unaware that the sultan or his administrators might have issued legal texts that governed such usages. As we have seen, this was a position that some Damascene Hanafis also held until the mid-eighteenth century but which seems to have been less commonly held after that time.

Dardir's view that local custom overruled the sultan's orders is a striking reminder that the breadth of legal power that the sultan claimed over *miri* land did not flow automatically from the theory that the land belonged to the treasury. Here again, it brings to mind how different was the scope of power claimed for the sultans in a text like the *Kanun-ı Cedid* versus the more modest powers awarded to the sultan by the preceding Hanafi jurists. The Egyptian tenure regime makes plain that there was indeed room for a great deal of divergence in tenure law, even when the muftis generally agreed that the status of the land was ownership by the treasury. It is therefore remarkable how much convergence is evident between Damascus and the lands of Rum in the eighteenth century. In particular, the differences between Egypt and Damascus were more profound in the eighteenth century than were those between Damascus and Bosnia; this alone should complicate any ideas that there was an Arab-versus-Rumi approach to land law.

That being said, there are two issues – the plow-breaking fee and forcible return – which have left some with the impression that the Rumi ulema were more likely to indulge the sultan's authority in ways that the Arabs considered a violation of the sharia.[49] However, such an impression is less warranted than it would appear at first glance. The first issue was the tax levied on cultivators who did not plant their land and which was known as the 'plow-breaking' fee (in Arabic, *kasr al-faddan* and in

Turkish, *çift bozan resmi*). The Arab ulema condemned this fee as illicit, but the Rumis did not.[50] This disagreement was not the result of a general inclination of the Rumis to accept any order from the sultan as conforming to the sharia and an opposing inclination among Arabs to look askance at it. In fact, this disagreement was the most profound consequence that arose from the existence of the two competing frameworks of treasury land among the Ottoman Hanafis.[51] The Rumis followed Ibn ʿAlaʾ al-Ansari in seeing the fees due on land as having the dual character of both tax and rent; the Arabs viewed these payments exclusively as rent, following Ibn al-Humam – or rather, Ibn Nujaym's reading of Ibn al-Humam.[52] The Rumis then took the position that the payment was to be seen as *kharaj*, even though the land itself was not *kharaji*, and required of the land's possessor.[53] It was therefore licit to demand a payment on land that was capable of production whether or not the cultivator worked it. The Arabs maintained that the payment on *miri* land was not *kharaj* in any way: it was only rent.[54] Because there was no contract obliging a specified payment, rent could fall due on the cultivator only if the land was worked. The peasant was therefore not responsible for paying anything to the treasury or its agents if he did not cultivate and could not be fined for failing to plant. This difference was not erased with time, and because it sprang from essentially different understandings of the payment, it remained a divisive topic into the nineteenth century.[55] Although this was, properly speaking, an Arab rejection of one of the provisions in the *kanun*, it did not demonstrate a greater Arab fastidiousness about applying the sharia but revealed instead the consequence of the differing interpretive traditions prevalent in the Arab lands and the lands of Rum.

The plow-breaking fee remained a controversy reflecting a profound disagreement; but the more controversial issue was the deputy's ability to forcibly return cultivators to villages where they had previously lived. In fatwas and the texts of *fiqh* penned by the Arabs, there were numerous denunciations of this practice as oppressive.[56] Even though no such denouncements among the Rumi ulema have surfaced, the nearly impenetrable silence of the Rumis on the subject is striking. Fatwas issued by Rumi muftis on this topic are surprisingly scarce; some even seem to skirt the issue. Balizade, for example, transmitted a fatwa confirming that taking *ispence* from a runaway cultivator was licit, but he did not record any fatwas addressing the question of whether the runaway could be forcibly returned.[57] Forcible return did have a staunch defender in Pir Mehmed; it is his fatwas that populate the section on forcible return in the *Kanun-ı Cedid*.[58] Aside from Pir Mehmed, one does not find Rumi muftis giving fatwas that explicitly attest that it is permissible.[59] Instead, the few fatwas left by Rumi muftis that address the subject ruled exclusively about what was *not* permissible. For example, *Neticetü'l-Fetava* and the collected fatwas of the mufti ʿAbdurrahman Efendi el-Erzurumi (d. 1810) each contain a single fatwa stating that the cultivator does not have to return if ten years have elapsed.[60] In a fatwa diametrically opposed to one given by Pir Mehmed, *Şeyhülislam* Yenişehirli ʿAbdullah (in office 1718–30) maintained that a *sipahi* was not able to force the children of a man who had once lived in his *timar* village to move from their native place back to the *timar* village.[61] This fatwa was essentially identical to one written in Damascus by the seventeenth-century mufti Ismaʿil al-Haʾik (d. 1702), who, when faced with a similar situation, wrote that it was not necessary and that the sultan did not require it.[62] In other words, aside from the ever-accommodating Pir Mehmed, it is not at all clear that the Rumi muftis would give fatwas that explicitly sanctioned this power, even if they did not frontally challenge it. In this, they were much like their Syrian counterparts who held the official position of mufti.[63]

Expansive transactions: Permission and analogism

In the eighteenth century, there were no significant changes to land tenure law with regard to the permitted usage of the land or post-mortem transmission of the bundle of rights. In intervivos transactions, however, the muftis coalesced more at the analogist end of the spectrum: several eighteenth-century jurists authorized the expanded variety of transactions for *tasarruf* of *miri* land that Es'ad Efendi had embraced, but which had been opposed by the autonomists. In effect this meant that the eighteenth-century jurisprudence of transactions owed as much or more to Es'ad Efendi as it did to Ebu's-Su'ud Efendi. For the muftis, the allure of analogism may well have been due to the increasing commercialization of agriculture and monetarization of the fisc described in Chapter 1. However, the solutions that the muftis offered to these realities should caution us from the conclusion that commercial pressure must lead inexorably to private property or to ruptures with an 'outdated' legal infrastructure. With one exception, none of these transactions was new to the harmony tradition, and all continued to affirm the importance of the separate layers of property rights that belonged to the cultivator and the deputy. The seventeenth-century muftis had insisted that the deputy's permission powers must be consistent with his mandate of preserving revenues, and this definitional rigour around permissions appears to have been key to the ascendance of analogism; the deputy's permission was to be the key component for validity among the muftis who allowed a wider range of transactions. As we will see, there was some resistance within the *ilmiye* to some of these transactions, and it raises interesting questions about how members of the *ilmiye* determined what to do when *şeyhülislams* and authoritative sources provided conflicting precedent.

Ebu's-Su 'ud had approved only a small number of transactions, such as the transfer and the free transmission of land to sons or to the daughter with *tapu*. Keeping the order of *miri* land entirely separate from that of freehold, he prohibited the majority of transactions applicable to *milk*. An eighteenth-century judge helpfully summed up the result: 'It is invalid for a judge to give a judgment (*hüccet*) transacting *miri* land through sale (*bey'*), pawn (*rehn*) … gift (*hiba*), rent (*icar*), endowment (*vakıf*), or substitution (*istibdal*) or any transaction other than entrusting (*vedi'a*) and lending (*i'are*).'[64] Es'ad Efendi, on the other hand, had given fatwas allowing both substitution and pawn of *miri tasarruf*.[65] He also allowed variations on transfers such as conditional transfer (*faragh bi'l-shart*) and deathbed transfer (*faragh marad al-mawt*).[66] Conditional transfer was a transfer whose validity was contingent upon the fulfillment of some attached condition; if the condition was not met, the transfer was invalidated. Baha'i explicitly rejected conditional transfer for *miri* land, but the lack of autonomist fatwas dealing with deathbed transfer leaves it unclear that autonomists condemned it.[67] Hanafi law prohibited deathbed sale for *milk* property because it was often used as a strategy to avoid the inheritance laws; fatwas allowing this transaction on *miri* land therefore accentuated the difference between *miri* and *milk*, hence it may have been acceptable to autonomist sensibilities.

Muftis of the eighteenth century, both the *şeyhüislams* and the provincial muftis, more often appeared closer to Es'ad Efendi than to Ebu's-Su'ud on the scope of transactions. Many fatwas allowed substitution, pawn, conditional transfer and deathbed transfer while none of them categorically prohibited these transactions.[68] A number of muftis appeared to go further than Es'ad in challenging Ebu's-Su'ud's prohibitions by ruling that a cultivator could rent or lease (*ijara*) his land to someone else if he was not present in the village.[69] While the term 'rent' was new for this arrangement, the muftis understood this 'rental' to be no different from what *kanun*s and earlier muftis had called 'entrusting': it was a situation where the cultivator was absent and in need of someone else to farm the land and pay the tax.[70] These fatwas continued to apply the *kanun*'s stipulation that the absent *mutasarrif* must be in regular touch to affirm that he was alive and his land was not therefore due for *tapu*. As a general matter, the scope of transactions in the eighteenth century stayed within the bounds set by Es'ad Efendi in the early seventeenth, and his rationale prevailed within them: if the deputy and treasury were financially unharmed by a transaction, then they should not interfere.

The movement of the eighteenth-century muftis towards analogism meant, in some cases, turning away from well-established autonomist precedents. The transaction that best illustrated this kind of break was the exchange of the *mutasarrif*'s land rights in return for a loan that was called pawn (*rahn*) or transfer with redemption (*faragh bi'l-wafa'*).[71] Fatwas allowing these forms of pawn or mortgage on *miri* land were not widespread among the eighteenth-century muftis: most collections do not contain fatwas addressing the issue.[72] However, the *şeyhülislam* 'Abdürrahim gave several fatwas allowing it with the deputy's permission and following him, so did Ahmed el-Mostari.[73] If the cultivator paid back the sum, he could reassume his rights on the land; but as long as he could not, the lender or his heirs simply kept the *tasarruf*.[74]

Question:	With the permission of the *sipahi*, Zayd pawns (*rehn*) his field, taking a money loan from 'Amr. When Zayd dies childless, is the deputy able to give the field [to someone else] with *tapu*?
Answer:	No.[75]

Of all the transactions that had become more commonly accepted, *rahn* represented the sharpest break with the trends set by prominent autonomists: first, pawn extended a transaction of *milk* property to *miri*; second, it had been explicitly invalidated for *miri* land by Ebu's-Su'ud;[76] Baha'i Mehmed had likewise rejected *faragh bi'l-wafa'* on *miri* land.[77] Third, it could also be viewed as overruling precedent that prohibited creditors from seizing *tasarruf* to discharge debt, although the eighteenth-century muftis who upheld the validity of *rahn* were aware of this prohibition set by the *kanun* and continued to abide by it as a general matter.[78]

One might conclude that the muftis moved towards acceptance of pawn simply because a more commercialized environment demanded it. This conclusion might well be accurate, yet it obscures that there was a consistency in the muftis' approach to transactions, and that it was built on the consensus about the role of the deputy's permission power that had consolidated in the previous century. Let us consider one of Es'ad Efendi's fatwas regarding pawn:

> Question: In return for a sum (of money), Zayd gave the fields in his possession to 'Amr in the name of pawn (*rehn*). If five years later, Zayd dies childless, is the deputy able to take those fields from 'Amr and give it with *tapu*?
>
> Answer: If he [Zayd] did this without the deputy's permission, then he [the deputy] can do that.[79]

As in other transactions of *miri* land, the deputy's permission was key to validity and enforceability. The muftis who allowed the expanded scope of transactions approved by Es'ad Efendi all agreed that their validity was contingent on the deputy's permission, and as a result the deputy's role as the guardian of the treasury's interest in the land attained a new prominence. Whereas the autonomists had taken the view that only those transactions specific to *miri* land and enumerated in the *kanun* were valid, the eighteenth-century muftis seem to have adopted a less restricted view of what transactions were prohibited so long as the deputy had received the opportunity to assess if they were harmless, and then given his consent.

As Chapter 3 demonstrated, Es'ad Efendi had successfully injected the standard of 'harm' as the test for whether the deputy's permission could be withheld for a transaction: the muftis universally observed it. The correlate that had emerged from this move was a consensus that on *miri* land as on *waqf* property, the deputy or *mutawalli* was authorized to refuse permission to the cultivator for any action, including a transfer, that resulted in revenue loss. On *miri*, one can find fatwas affirming the deputy's right to prohibit cultivators from digging up and selling rocks or cutting down trees that were attached to the land (*khudai*).[80] More consequential were the rulings that not only allowed intervention but also threatened the greatest penalty the deputy could impose: that of confiscation. 'Abdürrahim and 'Abdurrahman Efendi el-Erzurumi agreed that villagers needed the deputy's consent to change the use of land from agriculture to pasturing animals, and if the villagers insisted on pasturage, added 'Abdürrahim, the deputy could give the land to someone else.[81] These rulings were similar to those that allowed the *mutawallī* to refuse the cultivator's choices on *waqf* in similar circumstances: 'Abd al-Ghanī al-Nābulusī of Damascus ruled that if the cultivators on *waqf* land refused to pay a rent that was a 'fair rent', the *mutawalli* could tell them to either pay the fair rent or uproot what they had planted and surrender the land back to him.[82] In all these instances, the muftis could agree that if the revenue was threatened by the cultivator's action, the deputy's refusal to permit it would be valid.

The deputy both guarded the treasury's interest in the land's productivity and possessed a personal stake in preserving the revenues; like Es'ad Efendi, the muftis of the eighteenth century found it reasonable to allow a wider range of transactions trusting that the deputy would put a stop to any transaction that posed a threat to the treasury's (and the deputy's) claims on it. A good example of this approach was their handling of the one transaction they approved that had not appeared in the fatwas of Es'ad Efendi: the division of *tasarruf* among co-possessors (*taqsim*). In the *fiqh*, *taqsim* – usually referred to as *qisma* in the *fiqh* manuals – often took place because the law of inheritance could leave a single estate jointly owned by a number of partners. An heir who requested division (*qisma* or *taqsim*) of *milk* asked that his share in the estate be delineated for his exclusive ownership. On *miri* land, Ahmed el-Mostari and 'Abdurrahman Efendi el-Erzurumi confronted the issue when multiple brothers jointly possessed land transmitted from their father and desired to divide the land among themselves rather than possess it as partners.[83] Even though Ebu's-Su'ud had written that the fragmentation of family farms must be prevented, the law of post-mortem transmission as it developed in the *kanun* was not ideally suited for this purpose. If a deceased cultivator had multiple sons, they all inherited equal shares of *tasarruf* of their father's land; if there were no sons but multiple daughters, then all daughters had the opportunity to pay *tapu* and take the land, and so forth. There was a real possibility that, if multiple partners supported separate households, the inability to divide the land might lead to difficulties with production. By making division contingent on the deputy's permission rather than ruling it out, the muftis empowered the treasury's agent closest to the situation to determine whether the transaction threatened production or enhanced it.

The treatment of *ijaratayn* in the eighteenth century illustrates how, with regard to transactions, the muftis were treating *miri* land as analogous to *waqf*. Debbağzade Nu'man Efendi (d. 1809), a judge during the reign of Selim III (r. 1789–1807), composed a reference manual of fatwas that he most likely made for his own use in court. Summarizing the accepted transactions of *ijaratayn* that required permission from the *mutawalli*, he included all the transactions that muftis now commonly permitted on *miri*: transfer, deathbed transfer, transfer with redemption (*faragh bi'l-wafa'*) and division (*taqsim*).[84] Nu'man Efendi noted that Ibn al-Bazzaz forbade both *rahn* and *qisma* on *waqf* property and he provided some unattributed fatwas about *qisma* that forbade it.[85] He then explained that while *qisma* had been prohibited on *waqf* land in earlier times, *Şeyhülislam* Yenişehirli 'Abdullah had allowed it with the *mutawalli*'s permission when the *mutawalli* deemed it to be beneficial to the *waqf* (*vakfa nafi' olmakla*).[86] Nu'man Efendi's explanation for the reason *qisma* was accepted on *waqf* in his own time makes explicit why analogist muftis had gravitated towards allowing *taqsim* on *miri* land: there was no reason, the muftis had concluded, to pre-empt *mutasarrifs* from transactions that did not harm or even benefited the treasury and the deputy.

Like the *mutawalli*, these muftis concluded, the deputy should be empowered to make decisions according to his mandate rather than required to enforce a prohibition that served no purpose. The result was that on *miri* land, transactions that autonomists had not permitted became accepted through the permission of the deputy. It was justified by the same criterion that guided permissible and non-permissible action on *waqf*, and which had been championed by Es'ad Efendi: was there harm (or benefit) to the revenues?

While an analogist approach to transactions seems to have been widespread among eighteenth-century muftis, not all members of the *ilmiye* had adopted it. Some could not accept that a deputy's permission was enough to validate transactions that had been prohibited in the *kanun* or rejected by eminent authorities like Ebu's-Su'ud. Composed at the end of the eighteenth century or the beginning of the nineteenth, Nu'man Efendi's manual accepted the wide variety of transactions stated earlier in the text for *ijaratayn*, with the *mutwalli*'s permission. He also approvingly cited the fatwas of Yenişehirli 'Abdallah in support of these views.[87] For *miri* land however, he adhered to a staunchly autonomist view of transactions, rejecting pawn, rent and substitution.[88] Transmitting much of Ebu's-Su'ud's definition of *miri* land, Nu'man Efendi maintained that it was sui generis, and that judges were required to uphold the sharply different order of transactions sanctioned in the *kanun*. He transmitted only fatwas of Ebu's-Su'ud, Çatalcalı 'Ali, and Yenişehirli 'Abdullah that were consistent with the autonomist view of *miri* land. Such views show that an analogist approach to transactions remained contested in some quarters and that moving into the era of reform, the harmony tradition remained a spectrum of juridical opinion. While more muftis adhered to the analogist approach to transactions, the terms of the debate between autonomists and analogists remained stable, and the muftis remained squarely moored in the harmony tradition that had evolved in the previous century.

Conclusion

The history of the land law adds nuance to some of the dominant narratives of Ottoman development in the eighteenth century. If we want to identify the period in which the land tenure *kanun*s were most widely known and uniformly applied across the empire, we must look to the eighteenth century. Whether *kanun* as an ideal of statecraft still produced the reverence it had enjoyed in the sixteenth century, it had gained a more institutionalized status in the later period. Furthermore, decentralization was not entirely the order of the day. The broader dissemination of a standardized form of land tenure law supports the conclusion that the Ottoman domains were a more integrated legal environment in the eighteenth century than was the case in the sixteenth. Across much of the Ottoman *mashriq*, the muftis were informed of the sultan's orders, regarded them as the definitive source of the land law and viewed his law as operative in their own lands. Despite the Arab resistance to some aspects of Ottoman legal practice in the years following the conquest in 1516, the Damascenes showed an increasing adherence to the provisions of the *kanun*, and they produced fatwas largely identical to those of their Rumi peers by the middle of the eighteenth century. Even on the most controversial issues, there was less distance between them than has been realized.

A more 'normative' practice of the land law had emerged that was recognizably tied to the *kanuns* of the sixteenth and seventeenth centuries, but in transactions, this consensus was achieved through an analogist approach to building fatwas. In the fatwas of the Rumi muftis – both the *şeyhülislams* and those of the provinces – the transactional breadth associated with Es'ad Efendi was more frequently extended to the cultivator over the land in his or her possession. In all probability, this increased variety of accepted transactions corresponded to the commercialized nature of the Ottoman agriculture and a monetarized fisc. Rather than indicating a declining adherence to *kanun*, however, this wider array of transactions was rooted in the doctrine of permission developed by the muftis of the seventeenth century, a doctrine that was itself 'built' on the *kanun*. With regard to the deputy, the muftis continued to agree that his explicit permission was necessary for transactional validity. Furthermore, they expected that he exercise the power of permission in a way that was consistent with his mandate as recipient of and protector of the revenues of the *bayt al-mal*: if a transaction caused harm by reducing revenue, the deputy could prohibit it. The principle that the land law existed to protect treasury revenues and should be practised in a way that furthered that goal was deeply enshrined during this period.[89] This consensus validated the state's most crucial power over the land, yet simultaneously allowed the *mutasarrif* of *miri* land to transact more widely so long as the land's revenues were not threatened.

Previous studies have concluded that the proliferation of various types of lifelong *tasarruf* in the eighteenth century meant the rise of a de facto private property. Similarly, a number of studies have viewed the definition of *tasarruf* in the 1858 Land Code as private property.[90] As will become clear in the next chapter, a full century before the code's assembling, all of the pieces from which it would be assembled had made an appearance in either the fatwas or *kanuns* issued by members of the imperial bureaucracy. Nevertheless, there is reason for caution in designating the *tasarruf* of this century as 'private property' or viewing it as a step towards an inevitable rise of private property. In transactions the *mutasarrif* had greater leeway, but the deputy still held formidable power to control any changes to the land, such as planting trees or erecting buildings. The deputy furthermore had charge of all assets – such as rocks and free-growing (*hudai*) trees – that were attached to the land. Indeed, the multilayered forms of control over immovable property seemed, on the whole, to have adapted to greater commercialism and shown resilience. When one examines the intertwined claims on either *miri* or *waqf* at this time – a tangle of *gedik* holders, *mutawallis* and deputies, *mutasarrifs* and their subletters, outside investors and the like – it is hard to view this complex tableau as a natural prelude towards the concentration of property rights into a single person who could be deemed an owner. Neither *waqf* nor *miri* appeared to be merging with or even particularly influenced by the legal category of *milk*; instead, the question of whether *miri* land and *waqf* property were basically similar legal entities retained its centrality and the contours of the *mutasarrif*s bundle remained of a distinct legal character.

Chapter 6

FROM HARMONY TO UNIFORMITY: DEFENSIVE SOVEREIGNTY AND THE OTTOMAN NINETEENTH-CENTURY REFORMS

In 1858, the administration of Sultan ʿAbdülmecid I issued a Land Code (*Arazi Kanunnamesi*) that claimed to be the single, definitive statement on the law governing *miri* land and large amounts of land held in *waqf*. The Land Code itself was created by a committee, known as the Meclis-i Vala-yi Ahkam-ı Adliye (Supreme Council of Judicial Ordinances, hereafter, the Council), formed for the express purpose of crafting such rules and headed by the venerable Ahmed Cevdet Paşa (d. 1895).[1] The introduction to the Code stated that the land had been governed previously by *kanuns* issued in the time of Sultan Süleyman and the fatwas given by the *şeyhülislams*, but the new times now called for improvements: 'New events have come to pass and circumstances have changed. For this reason, it is necessary to reform (*ıslah*) the *kanuns* and the land according to these circumstances and events and to add the necessary provisions and to make the necessary adjustments according to the demands of time and situation.'[2]

The change in times and circumstances to which the statement alluded was that the balance of power between the Ottomans and their imperial rivals to the west and north had, by the end of the eighteenth century, shifted markedly in favour of the latter. Two years prior to the Land Code's release, the Paris Treaty ending the Crimean War had guaranteed Ottoman territorial integrity in order to secure the geopolitical interests of the Great Powers of Europe.[3] As such, it was an acknowledgement that the Ottoman Empire was unable to effectively defend its territory. Since the eighteenth century, the Ottomans had progressively lost legal jurisdiction over European citizens operating within its borders and the Ottoman subjects – most often non-Muslims – who had adopted European protection.[4] As a result of the Anglo-Ottoman Commercial Agreement of 1838, the empire was locked into unfavourable terms of trade, first with Britain and then, by extension, virtually every other European country.[5] This yawning gap between the capabilities of the Ottoman Empire and its peers had evolved rapidly; it is unlikely that the Ottomans of 1758 could or would have predicted that their empire would face challenges of this magnitude just a century later.

Beginning in 1839, the Ottoman response to these threats was the Tanzimat, a programme that James Gelvin describes as part of a broader Middle Eastern strategy of modernization known as 'defensive developmentalism'.[6] This characterization of the Tanzimat as 'defensive', in an expansive sense, is a valuable lens for understanding its goals. The administrative, legal, military, educational and infrastructural transformation that the reformers attempted to implement sought to defend the empire's territorial integrity, its capability to raise revenues and to field an army, and its sovereignty over people and things within its borders.[7] Beyond these concrete goals of defending territory and wealth, there was a different kind of defensiveness at work. That the empire was clearly operating at a disadvantage in relation to its non-Muslim – as opposed to Muslim – rivals now imbued its conflicts with the sense that Muslims and even Islam itself were under threat. The empire's reformers were aware that some European rivals considered Islam to be responsible for the relative weakness of their position, and they were forced to wrestle with such views.[8] Although some of the leading architects of the Tanzimat were not particularly interested in preserving the Islamic character of Ottoman state and society, there were many reformers of both liberal and authoritarian political inclinations who were.[9] Although these reformers did not seek to diminish the role of Islam in Ottoman life, the Tanzimat's legal reforms would mean that Hanafi *fiqh* was not to play as dominant a role in the legal system.[10] Already in 1850 the Ottomans had adopted a commercial code based on the French Commercial Code of 1807.[11] Adopting other European codes to govern more areas of Ottoman life was a real possibility; there was now a debate among reformers about whether to introduce a civil code borrowed from France.[12] One can then understand the legislative activity of the reforming Ottoman state as defensive with regard to Islam in at least two senses: it defended and preserved a space in which to be Muslim, and it defended the new ways that Muslims had to live in this space as authentically Islamic.

Historians have differed markedly on whether the Code's project was conservative or revolutionary, and whether it introduced private property or represented a 'return' to state control of property.[13] While there are rampant disagreements among scholars about the Code and its consequences, such disagreements should not obscure the fact that there is a fair amount of consensus about it in some areas; for instance, historians generally believe that the Code was intended to ensure a steady flow of tax revenues.[14] Given that the reform projects would be expensive to implement and that Ottoman sovereign debt was rising precipitously, the need for greater revenue was particularly acute; having already entered into treaties that dismantled government monopolies and did not allow it to raise tariffs on imports, the empire could neither raise funds through means which had been successful in the past, nor could it pursue rapid industrialization.[15] Raising more revenue from taxpayers tending the land was, therefore, all the more urgent.

Studies of the Land Code have identified a number of features introduced by the Code and its siblings – the *Tapu* Law of 1858 and the Title Deed (*Tapu Senedi*) Regulations of 1860 – which were likely intended to facilitate assessing and collecting agricultural taxes: the process of mandatory registration of land possession and all transactions; the assigning of sole responsibility over the land and its taxation liability to specified individuals and the insistence on proper documentation as a condition of the state's recognition and enforcement of claims.[16] These novelties have justifiably received much scholarly attention, for they changed the *administration* of the land law rather dramatically. These changes were, in addition, consistent with the model of 'rational' administration so dominant among nineteenth-century states.[17] The Ottomans, it would seem, had embraced a model of the modern state and its administration that was indistinguishable from the norms prevailing elsewhere. These observations raise two questions: first, was the content of the law transformed as substantially as its administration? And second, if the Ottoman reformers' vision of a modern state and society was interchangeable with that of France, Germany or Japan, where did such a vision leave pre-existing institutions?

We should start by recognizing that the content of the Code – both in terms of the property relations and its significance for legal history – is best understood by the Code's defensive character. First, there was little change to the property rights of the *mutasarrif*: as part of a larger strategy of imperial defence, the Council did not abandon the empire's indigenous tradition of the cultivator's *tasarruf* in the 1858 Land Code but once again affirmed its centrality to the constitution of the empire. The Land Code was no more liberal in the rights it granted the *mutasarrif* than the muftis of the eighteenth century had been: the layer of rights that allowed the treasury or its agent to intervene in the name of maintaining productivity and revenue was preserved intact. In all probability, the dire needs of the treasury for more income made these powers all the more relevant, and a more attractive property regime than one enshrining private property. In fact, the configuration of property rights granted to the *mutasarrif* is the Code's most conservative feature. If this is a surprise, perhaps it should not be: Ahmed Cevdet Paşa, the Council head, famously remarked that if a nation exchanged its own basic laws – which were its very heart – for the laws of others, it would annihilate itself.[18] As a bundle of property rights connecting people to land and buildings for the past 300 years, there were few institutions more durable or more quintessentially Ottoman than the lifelong *tasarruf* held by tenants and cultivators across the empire. With minor modification, the Code preserved it as a paradigmatic relationship between state and subject: that of a taxpayer with secure tenure.

While the Code did little to change property rights, it cannot be described as lacking in innovation. The Code played a part in creating a new, 'generic' Ottoman legal subject devoid of class or religious distinction. As with most 'Old Regimes', the Ottoman Empire had not possessed a single legal or political category of Ottoman subjects prior to the nineteenth century. Political and legal status was determined by whether one belonged to *reaya* (tax-paying subject) or *askeri* (military tax-exempt) groups along with other factors like occupation, place of residence and religious affiliation. Reformers, by contrast, sought to impose the authority of the state and its laws equally upon all Ottoman subjects; in particular, they sought to impose on each individual 'the singular, general taxation claim of the state', as Huri Islamoğlu has argued.[19] This goal meant the elimination of specific privileges that differentiated classes from one another or entitled certain groups to special treatment. While Islamoğlu maintains that the Land Code introduced private property in furtherance of these goals, I contend that the Code's drafters accomplished this 'generalizing' mission without introducing a new concept of property. Rather, the Code would define the familiar *tasarruf* of *miri* land not as a bundle of rights proper to the *reaya* or any other specific class but as one available to any and all Ottoman subjects. Where there had been layers of property rights, now there would be only the bundle that had belonged traditionally to the peasant cultivators of the land. The result was that all subjects who wanted access to the land and its revenues could acquire it only through this one, standardized, legal means.

Finally, the Code itself was far more indicative of the trends that would impact the practice of law in the Muslim world than is usually acknowledged. Scholars have not always sufficiently appreciated that the Code is largely a codification of pre-existing land law. This book has argued repeatedly for the importance of understanding the evolution of the land law as a textual tradition. This importance becomes easier to understand when we realize that the Land Code in its entirety was assembled from this textual tradition that it was designed to supersede. While its civil code counterpart, the Mecelle, is generally thought to be the first codification of the *fiqh*, the Land Code has a strong claim on this distinction. Scholars of Islamic law have argued that codification of the *fiqh* changed the nature of Islamic legal practice in fundamental ways, although the scope and nature of such transformation remains deeply disputed.[20] In general, such scholars have seen codification as responding to the need for a more accessible articulation of the law or as the transfer of legal authority from the jurists to the state. The 1858 Land Code, on the other hand, offers a different perspective on codification and the way it transformed the law.

In the production of the Land Code, codification was the transfer of law-making power from the empire's Old Regime personnel and institutions to the Council created by the New Regime. Formerly, officials like *nişancıs* and muftis, in dialogue with independent scholars, had made land law in the sultan's name; now it was the Council alone among the sultan's administrators who were delegated this authority. This transfer marked a new, more direct administrative procedure for making and enacting law, one which implemented a stark distinction between state and subject. The Council's mandate was to see that codification produced a law that would uphold the reformers' objectives. In particular, it illuminates how the Council was able to sculpt the law to reflect particular priorities without actually introducing substantively new material. Such sculpting could be accomplished through the adoption of certain fatwas and precedents for inclusion in the Code while others were set aside, but more importantly, the format of the Code provided the Council with a tool for further accentuating the kinds of precedents that fit its agenda. The complex, layered textual edifice weaving together multiple authorities would be compressed into a single voice and a single text of law that obscured both the nature of the preceding legal order and the interventions of the Council. Moreover, the Code's assemblers were prescient judges of the criteria that would become increasingly central to establishing the Islamic credentials of law enacted by the state: the authority of the *fiqh*.

Miri Tasarruf: *Stability in a sea of change*

We may speculate about the intentions of the Council and what its members hoped the Code would accomplish, but one thing is clear: the Council chose not to substantially rethink the terms of lifelong *tasarruf*, nor the treasury's powers on the land. What the Council did change was how the treasury would exercise its powers. In the decades preceding the Code's compilation, reformers had taken steps to homogenize the empire's subjects in fact and in law. Many Ottoman statesmen were worried about the legal immunities enjoyed by foreign nationals and Ottoman subjects who had obtained foreign protection, but there was little that could be done to reverse this. They turned their attention to eroding the special status of the various *askeri* groups, seeking to literally 'subjugate' them, or, turn them into ordinary subjects. Concerned that its elite *ayan* had become overmighty subjects beyond the reach of state authority, the administrations of Mahmud II and 'Abdülmecid I confiscated large *çiftliks* and offered the land to peasant cultivators in the 1830s and 1840s.[21] The janissaries, who had long enjoyed privileges with regard to tax and penal law, were destroyed in 1826 and thereafter abolished. Likewise, the *timar* system was abolished along with the hereditary military class of *sipahis*. Tax farming was officially eliminated in 1839, although it would in fact continue to exist because the treasury lacked the personnel to dispense with it.[22] The message of such actions was clear: like God, the modernizing state had no partners and would brook no rivals.[23]

It is this context of military reform and the homogenizing civilianization of society that explains the Land Code's most obvious break with past precedent – which is, curiously, one of the least remarked upon aspects of the Code. Namely, the Code abolished the legal status of the deputy (*sahib al-ard*), which would no longer be part of the vocabulary of the 1858 Land Code. But the disappearance of the term itself did not entail the disappearance of the treasury agent – now called *me'mur* (the official) – who had a strong presence in the Code. No term conjures up more Weberian imagery: the *me'mur* was the embodiment of impersonalized, rationalized, nineteenth-century bureaucracy.[24] Although he retained most of the oversight powers that his predecessor, the deputy (*sahib al-ard*), had possessed, the *me'mur* was a salaried official with no personal interest in the land and little discretionary authority; he merely carried out the *kanun*. Among other things, the *me'mur* was charged with making sure that agricultural land did not lie idle. If a *mutasarrif* died without designated heirs for transmission and his land escheated to the treasury, the *me'mur* was charged with finding a new possessor.[25] In the past, the *kanun*s had declared that in this situation the deputy was '*mukhtar*' or '*mukhayyar*': free to choose whom he wanted if none of the successors specified in the *kanun* was present.[26] In the Code and the Tapu Regulations, on the other hand, the *me'mur* was charged with making sure that the land was put up for public auction, and he, as *me'mur*, was to have no voice in deciding the next *mutasarrif*. As this provision and many others like it made clear, the *me'mur* was not *mukhtar*; as his name implied, he carried out orders.

In contrast to the definition of the treasury agent, the Code's definition of *tasarruf* was not innovative. On the one hand, the Code did not concentrate property rights into a single 'owner-like' person – at least, it did not move further in this direction than the eighteenth-century muftis had envisioned. On the other hand, the Code did not – for the most part – enhance the treasury's rights or restore lapsed prerogatives. Generally, the Code preserved the cultivator's bundle that most muftis of the empire's eastern Mediterranean provinces had come to know and affirm by the eighteenth century, including its terminology; the Code defined this bundle of rights as *tasarruf* and the person possessing these rights as a *mutasarrif*.[27] Cultivated land was for the most part *miri* land, with its *raqaba*, or ultimate right of disposal, belonging to the treasury.[28] The basic elements of possession remained the same: one paid *tapu* to become the land's *mutasarrif* and in return had secure possession for life with all the attendant rights that had accumulated to the *mutasarrif* over the past three centuries.[29] That said, there were a handful of consequential changes. Some of these took a few discrete steps towards greater liberty, but it is hard to see a general trend in this direction. At least one break with precedent limited the *mutasarrif*'s control over the land rather than expanding it.

In terms of provisions that appeared to 'liberalize' *tasarruf*, the most famous measure – the long unpopular provision of forcible return – did not find a place in the Code. Additionally, the number of appointed heirs in post-mortem transmission who could take *tasarruf* freely, that is, without paying *tapu*, also increased, which took away a prerogative of the treasury and also decreased its revenue claims (Art. 59). Another liberalizing move in the Code merely completed a process of transformation around transfers, which had begun more than two centuries earlier. With military men defined in the Land Code and more generally as regular tax payers, there was no valid reason remaining for the *me'mur* to refuse permission (*izin*) for a transfer: the Code explicitly stated that the *mutasarrif* could transfer 'to anyone whom he wishes'.[30] The *me'mur* had no authority to reject the transfer, his granting of *izin* – now more a 'permit' than a 'permission' – was defined as completing the official process attached to a transfer: that of registering the act and issuing the necessary documentation.[31] The Code thus declared that intervivos transfers from one *mutasarrif* to another were free of any encumbrance beyond the payment of the *tapu* fee, with the caveat that village residents in need of land could pre-empt the sale as their ancestors had done since the seventeenth century.[32] Given that Es'ad Efendi, Mostari Ahmed and other muftis had regarded the deputy as a *me'mur* in this issue since the early seventeenth century, this was a codification of a long prevalent position. While not insignificant, the number of provisions increasing the *mutasarrif*s freedom of action remained small.

Not all the Code's innovations resulted in a *mutasarrif* who appeared more like an owner of private property: in Art. 21, the Code declared that if one had usurped land in another's *tasarruf*, then control of the land was to be restored to the rightful possessor. However, if the taxes were paid on the land, neither the *me'mur* nor the *mutasarrif* could seek compensation from the usurper, either for damage to the land or a fee equivalent to rent that could have been collected.

This article contradicted the fatwas of the eighteenth-century muftis who had addressed this subject – Mostari Ahmed and Erzurumlu 'Abdurrahman – both of whom had ruled that a *mutasarrif* could demand compensation from a usurper for damage.[33] It is revealing that the drafters of the Code chose to define the *mutasarrif* as someone who was not entitled to such compensation. Late Hanafi doctrine held that owners of *milk* land could demand compensation if a usurper had caused damage to or deterioration of the land.[34] While eighteenth-century muftis had extended this right to *mutasarrifs* of *miri* land, the Code withdrew it. According to the Code, the only entity with a monetary claim upon the usurper was the treasury, and this claim was limited to the amount assessed for the taxes. If the taxes had been paid, the usurper had met his one obligation and the treasury, via its agent the *me'mur*, could seek nothing further. The rightful possessor of the land, by contrast, had no claim upon the usurper. This article prohibited those who held the title of *mutasarrif* but who themselves neither cultivated the land nor paid its taxes from extracting a payment from someone who did perform the labour and pay the taxes. While the Code allowed the *mutasarrif* to rent the land to someone else to cultivate it, a person's use of the *mutasarrif's* land did not by itself generate an obligation to pay the *mutasarrif*; rather it generated an obligation to pay tax to the treasury. The Code's provision in Art. 21 meant that it was not possible for a *mutasarrif* to enjoy the protections that the law afforded an owner of a revenue-bearing property for rent (*mu'add li-l-istighlāl*), where simply by use of the property the usurper incurred an obligation to pay the owner. By withholding this protection, the Code continued to define *tasarruf* of *miri* land primarily as a bundle of rights for personal use by the *mutasarrif* which was secured through the payment of taxes. In this case, a break with eighteenth-century precedent served then to create greater consistency with the preceding conceptualization of the relationship between the *mutasarrif* and the treasury.

The least understood aspect of continuity in the Code is its regime of transactions. In this arena as in others, the Council was considering the muftis' opinions across the centuries rather than viewing sixteenth-century texts as the 'true' incarnation of law that must be reinstated. As we have seen previously, the eighteenth century witnessed conflicting views among the ulema on the scope of transactions, but the muftis were generally in alignment with Es'ad Efendi's tendency to allow more transactions than were enumerated by the *kanun*. With some modification, the Council chose to codify the more liberal terms of transaction that the eighteenth-century analogist muftis had endorsed, but the Code did not further liberalize these terms. Accepting and incorporating this wider variety of transfers – deathbed transfer, conditional transfer, transfer with redemption – the Code also confirmed the ability of the *mutasarrif* to rent (*ijara*) or loan (*'ariya*) the land or for multiple possessors to divide it (*taqsim*) with the *me'mur's* permission (Art. 8, 15, 114, 116, 120, Land Code). While it permitted the transfer with redemption, the Code banned *rahn* (Art. 116, Land Code). Given the juridical disputes over *rahn*, this was a pragmatic choice: it allowed the transaction under the rubric that had been approved by Yenişehirili 'Abdallah for *waqf*, but avoided terminology that had been thoroughly rejected in the autonomist tradition.[35] Adhering to the prevalent opinion in the fatwas of the previous century, the Code ruled that in a transfer with redemption, a *mutasarrif* could not take his land back from the creditor until the debt had been paid; if the *mutasarrif* died, his successor with claim to the land must discharge the debt before he could take the land (Art. 118, Land Code).[36] The Code furthermore took a position on debt familiar from the fatwas of Mostari Ahmed and construed *faragh bi'l-wafa'* as a special case entitling a creditor to the land's possession.[37] As a general matter, land could still not be seized by a creditor, either in life or after death (Art. 115, Land Code). Although later amendments would give creditors more opportunity to seize land in return for unpaid debt, the Code itself did not depart from precedent in such matters.

As a final observation, there was little change in the Code's configuration of the treasury's powers over the land and the *mutasarrif*'s use of it; of the changes that were introduced only one shifted the balance of rights towards the *mutasarrif*, while the others slightly shifted it in favour of the treasury. Retaining a strong layer of rights for the treasury was likely a conscious decision: since the Code was part of a broader administrative agenda to raise tax revenue, there was little incentive to scale back the treasury agents' longtime authority to intervene in the cultivators' decisions about the land's use. The primary limitation – formerly enforced by the deputy, but now enforced by the *me'mur* – was still the same: if the land was left unworked for three years, the *me'mur* could confiscate it (Art. 68, Land Code), although there was no article granting the *me'mur* authority to confiscate the land if the *mutasarrif* chose to pasture his animals on it. Beyond that, the prerogatives that the *me'mur* enforced were a litany of the familiar: endowing *miri* land as *waqf* was prohibited (Art. 121, Land Code); and permission from the *me'mur* was necessary to perform all the modifications (building, planting trees, extracting minerals and rocks, etc.) that had previously required the deputy's permission (Art. 25, 28, 106, 107, Land Code). These provisions had not lapsed and been reintroduced; instead, the fatwa tradition from the previous centuries shows that they had been continually observed.[38] Derived from a provision long applied to *waqf* land, a minor new restraint was imposed on the *mutasarrif*: a prohibition on digging up the soil and making tiles from it (Art. 12, Land Code). A more notable example where the Code widened the scope of the treasury's control was that the *me'mur* had the right to tear down unauthorized buildings without the ten-year limit on this power that had previously been part of the *kanun* (Art. 31, Land Code). This change is particularly remarkable given the seventeenth-century controversy over this provision, and the signs that even in the eighteenth century, a mufti like Mostari Ahmed appeared to have some misgivings about it. However, considered as a whole, the new measures introduced both minor expansions and a minor pruning of the treasury's powers, leaving the previous balance between the treasury agent and the *mutasarrif* fairly intact. The *me'mur*'s ability to restrict the *mutasarrif*'s scope of action to protect the treasury's rights was relatively unchanged from that of the deputy in previous centuries.

In summary, the Code's preservation of this mostly unreconstructed *tasarruf* suggests that the Council found it a proper balance of rights for the emerging order of state and individual subject. The *mutasarrif*'s freedom to use and transact the land was extensive, but there was no pretense of 'absoluteness' in its construction.[39] Retaining the treasury's previous powers to intervene in productivity and usage was a choice that was well aligned with the empire's attempts to rapidly develop its economy.[40] Alterations to *tasarruf* that liberalized the bundle would follow throughout the next sixty years: the *bayt al-mal*'s ability to limit the *mutasarrif*s usage would be whittled down by later amendments to the Code, thus identifying the end of the nineteenth century as the moment that the Ottomans finally 'kneeled down before the shrine of modern private property'.[41] However, as late as the early twentieth century, the land law's commentators – —both domestic and foreign – continued to see land possession as distinct from 'ownership' and more in the vein of a heritable leasehold.[42] Even as the notion of private property gained ascendance and *tasarruf* of *miri* was reconfigured in its image, the bundle of rights remained somewhat difficult to harmonize with this new legal category just as it had presented difficulties to the older prevailing categories like *kharaji*, loan or rental. To the empire's final years, legal practitioners found *miri tasarruf* to be idiosyncratic in character, and struggled to theoretically map it.

Creating a normal subject

If *tasarruf* of the land had changed little, the identity of who was eligible to become a *mutasarrif* had changed considerably. A key innovation of the Land Code was its erasure of the class of deputies and the presentation of all Ottoman subjects as potential *mutasarrifs* rather than the class of peasant cultivators. The *Kanunname of Budin* had presented the cultivators' bundle as appropriate for their role in securing a prosperous order. The eighteenth century had been an age of many kinds of *mutasarrifs* holding bundle of lifelong rights, and their variations had largely mirrored the stratified nature of old regime order: *gedik* existed for craftsmen, *malikane* for members of the *askeri*, *ijaratayn* for urban tenants and *tasarruf* of *miri* land for the *reaya* (peasant cultivators). The rights and responsibilities of the *mutasarrifs* had reflected the Ottoman political conviction that it was proper for different kinds of people to play different roles for the polity to function: in order for there to be social and political harmony, every person needed to play the appointed role correctly.[43] The Land Code, on the other hand, presented a body politic not in need of harmony, but of uniformity.

In the past – including the eighteenth century – *askeri* acquisition of the cultivator's *tasarruf* had been regarded as problematic in *kanun*s and fatwas.[44] The basis for this disapproval had been the concern that the primary source of tax revenue – *miri* land – would make its way into the hands of a class immune from taxation. It was not the Code itself that abolished the privileges attached to military service; other administrative actions had done so or were in the process of doing so.[45] Nevertheless, the Code did specify some of the many consequences of this 'deprivileging' of military personnel. The question in previous centuries about whether *miri* land was still subject to *tapu* and to permissions once it had fallen into *askeri* hands was now definitively settled in the Code: all *mutasarrifs* had the same rights and responsibilities, the latter including *tapu*, obtaining permissions and paying taxes. The two provisions in the Code dealing with *çiftlik*s confirmed that such holdings were large but were otherwise ordinary farms: the buildings, livestock and equipment were *milk*, but the land itself was *miri* and thus subject to normal devolution and the *tapu* fee (Art. 131, Land Code). Now that military personnel were ordinary subjects, their obtaining *tasarruf* posed no threat to revenues, at least theoretically. As a result, the Code contained no discriminatory measures that limited the opportunity of military men to become *mutasarrifs*. The opposite was, in fact, true: the Code contained special provisions allowing the former *sipahi* class to claim *tasarruf* of the private farms they had held on *timar* lands (Art. 129, Land Code). Additionally, the Code provided unprecedented assistance to veterans in acquiring *tasarruf* of *miri* land.[46] Article 58, moreover, forbade a soldier's land from being transferred to another because his service caused him to be absent from his land. Soldiers were thus no longer a fiscal threat; on the contrary, the Code cast them as loyal, tax-paying subjects who deserved reward for their service.

While the Code reflected the erasure of *askeri* class legal privileges, it simultaneously bore witness to the emergence of a different legally and fiscally privileged group whose access to *miri tasarruf* was prohibited much as the privileged *askeri* class had been in previous centuries. The Code facilitated access to land for those who had served in the military for the prescribed term or longer (a group composed exclusively of Muslims, the vast majority of whom were Turks).[47] By contrast, there were restrictions that made it more difficult for non-Muslims to obtain *miri tasarruf*.[48] In particular, Art. 111 forbade Ottoman subjects who had relinquished Ottoman nationality and become foreign protégés from retaining *tasarruf* of *miri* land in their possession. Such a provision was far more likely to affect Ottoman non-Muslims than Muslims, as it was usually Christians and Jews who acquired European protection that exempted them from the sultan's laws and taxes.

Since foreign nationals were beyond the reach of the Ottoman attempts at levelling its subjects, it is not surprising that they were excluded from acquiring *tasarruf*. Under pressure from a number of European ambassadors to reconsider, the Ottomans extended the right to obtain *tasarruf* to foreigners in 1867 but only after the latter agreed to give up some of their extraterritorial privileges: foreigners would be subject to the Land Code, which would be adjudicated in Ottoman secular courts.[49] Moreover, foreign *mutasarrifs* would pay the same taxes as Ottoman subjects.[50] This transformation of foreigners into persons qualified to be *mutasarrifs* demonstrates that the long-standing Ottoman goal of keeping *miri tasarruf* in the hands of taxpayers remained as important a priority as it had ever been. What was new was that Ottoman soldiers were noted in the Code as those who could be assimilated to the position of an ordinary taxpayer. Foreign nationals and their protégés, on the other hand, were prevented from acquiring *tasarruf* until the agreement reached with the affected foreign states allowed for their nationals to be assimilated as taxpayers.

In summary, the Code bestowed one bundle of rights to land upon all Ottoman subjects and prevented those who were not legally subject to the sultan and exempt from taxation from obtaining the bundle. By framing *miri tasarruf* as a perquisite of Ottoman nationality, and making no distinction to class and status differences that had existed in the recent past, the Code sharply diverged from prior practice of the law. The Code's formulation of *tasarruf* meant that elite office holders and peasant cultivators were henceforth legally indistinguishable and that it was equally valid for either to hold *tasarruf* of the land. Although it is beyond the scope of this work to discuss the results, the Code clearly triggered a clash between cultivators and the class of previously tax-farming or *timar*-holding elite over who would become the legally recognized *mutasarrif*. With their former 'layer' of rights eliminated, elites henceforth sought the only bundle that the law provided: that of the land's *tasarruf*.

Codifying Islamic law

Question: Zayd dies childless while a *mutasarrif* of a *miri* field. When the deputy offers [the field] to his brother 'Amr saying, 'pay the *tapu* and take it', 'Amr declines to do so. If the deputy then gives the field to Bakr, can 'Amr, who now regrets his decision, intervene and take it?

Answer: No.

Precedent: 'Amr did not request it, and his right to the *tapu* was forfeit. 'The transfer is forfeit and there is no second chance', as the *Hidaya* puts it. And it is thus in the *kanun-ı sultani*. 'We are ordered to obey the *ulu'l-amr*', is in the *Durar*. And Ebu's-Su'ud al-'Imadi gave a fatwa that he who balks at paying the fee to take the land at the time when the fee is due has forfeited his right. And what was forfeit will not be suffered to return to him. This is recorded in the fatwas of the collection of Feyzullah Efendi.[51]

Where did the land law reside prior to the Code's composition in 1858? In this fatwa, the nineteenth-century *'alim* Gedizli Mehmed Efendi (d. 1837) composed the paragraph of precedent that he saw as guiding the answer provided by an eighteenth-century *şeyhülislam*.[52] Gedizli Mehmed's citations show a trend that would continue into the twentieth century: its ulema were no autonomists. They tended to view the land law as deeply rooted in Hanafi *fiqh* and would find precedent for the land law in books of *fiqh* that preceded the rise of the harmony tradition – such as *Durar al-Ghurar* – and even the rise of the empire, such as the *Hidaya*.[53] Nevertheless, the sultan's directives were also cited: Gedizli Mehmed pointed to the *kanun* and the need to obey it because it was issued on the sultan's authority, showing the continuing concern for deference. For good measure, he included one of Ebu's-Su'ud Efendi's fatwas that was built off the sultan's orders, and whose validity was attested by its presence in the fatwa collection of another *şeyhülislam*, Feyzullah Efendi (served briefly in 1688, then again 1695–1703). Despite its brevity, the paragraph of citations reveals that the Ottomans of the nineteenth century found that the land law and the principles governing it were drawn from multiple legal textual forms that drew together the sultan's authority and that of the sharia. Numerous works expounding on the fit between this multitude of texts had been composed since the sixteenth century, and the citations bore witness to the complexity of the textual edifice governing *miri* land by the middle of the nineteenth century.

The textual complexity of the land law has often been sidelined in historical accounts of the 1858 Land Code and its origins. Most historians have judged the degree of continuity between the 1858 Code and past legal practice by focusing purely on the question of whether the Code was consistent with *kanuns* issued in the past.[54] This approach has obscured both the nature of the law of *miri* land in the previous two centuries and the reason that assembling the Code from it represented a profound intervention into its character. As previous chapters have demonstrated, the sultan's orders and *kanuns* had become deeply interwoven with Hanafi jurisprudence in increasingly intricate ways since the sixteenth century. The law governing the land was defined not only by orders issued from the sultan but also by the fatwas that were 'built upon' those orders – as both Ibn 'Abidin and the Code's introduction would put it.[55] In order to create a text that could satisfy its needs, the Code's compilers often turned to these fatwa collections or to the broader body of *fiqh* expounding *miri* land to construct the law adopted in the Code.[56] The content of numerous articles in the Code can be linked to preceding practices authorized in fatwas: the specificities of how the ten-year rule was to operate, the rights of partners who shared *tasarruf* and the consequences ensuing from transfers that were incomplete.[57] In fact, one of the most influential sources for the Code appears to have been the fatwas of Şeyhülislam 'Abdürrahim. Not only did the regime of transactions that the Code adopted (see earlier in the text) bear strong resemblance to those in 'Abdürrahim's fatwas, but his prohibitions on burying corpses on *miri* land and delineating the rights of the mentally incapacitated were also incorporated in the Code.[58] The Code did not spring from the *kanunnames* as they had been issued in the sixteenth and early seventeenth centuries but from the broader legal construct governing *miri* land that had evolved over the seventeenth and eighteenth centuries and was constituted by a multitude of interlocking texts.

Once we understand how the law of *miri* land was constructed from dialogue across these texts, it is clear that the Code's project was, among other things, an initial foray into codifying Hanafi *fiqh*. The Land Code, composed roughly a decade prior to the Mecelle, was compiled from a textual tradition saturated with Hanafi legal reasoning in its application and textually located in genres of Hanafism. From this tradition that included minority and majority opinions, and textual forms including *kanuns*, fatwas and scholastic commentary, the Council produced one text that was a single, homogenous, statement of law. There are three ways in which it makes sense to think of this document as a codification of Hanafi *fiqh* that was something of a test run for the transformation of the Hanafi corpus into a civil law-like code. First, the Land Code declared in the introduction that it abrogated all other texts, nullifying all its predecessors. All precedents existing in the fatwas that were not chosen for the Code were thus eliminated. This move, a classic feature of codification, ensured greater uniformity of legal practice. Second, unlike the multi-genre legal tradition from which it was composed, the Code presented all of its content as equally authoritative. The previous tradition had many voices with different levels of authority attached to them – as we have seen, there was even some debate about the priority that various textual forms carried – but the Code spoke with the single voice of the Council in articles that were each of equal weight.[59] Third, the Code drew not only on fatwas, but on the manuals of *fiqh* that were the most authoritative texts of the Hanafi school. The extent to which the manuals were incorporated into the Land Code has not been well appreciated and lends more weight to the view that the Land Code can be deemed a work of Islamic law.

The fatwas were more numerous and more diverse than the *kanun*s in the range of options that they offered the Council. By choosing to enact some in the Code and to ignore others, the Council intervened in the law to end the autonomist–analogist debates and increase predictability in ways that fit with reformist objectives. One such example already identified in the previous section was the validating of *faragh bi'l-wafa'* and invalidating of *rahn*. However, the most consequential example of such sculpting was the prominent positioning of the rights of exclusion in the Code. The *kanun*s of previous centuries seldom contained provisions governing the relations between cultivators.[60] By contrast, the Code is full of statutes detailing how the *mutasarrif* could exclude other cultivators from use of the land, and the majority of these 'rights of exclusion' had not been established by *kanun*s but in the fatwas built on the *kanun*s. These fatwas established the right to forbid others from grazing animals on the *mutasarrif's* fallow fields;[61] the right to keep others from grafting free-growing trees on the land;[62] the right to stop others from using the *mutasarrif*s pasture lands[63] and the right to destroy buildings that an outsider had built on the *mutasarrif*s land.[64] The *kanun* had little to say about woodlands (*koru*) or about the right of *mutasarrif*s to exclude others from their use, but the Code's articles concerning woodlands were indebted to fatwas such as those preserved in the *Kanunname of Ahmed Khan* and the fatwa compilations of *Şeyhülislams* Çatalcalı 'Ali and Menteşzade 'Abdürrahim.[65] In these issues, the muftis had posited such rights for the *mutasarrif*s from the process of making law that was built upon the *kanun*: a reminder that the muftis were makers of the law as well as its interpreters.

The Code's incorporation of these rights of exclusion shows how the process of codification allowed the Council to reshape the law without adding new rights or provisions per se. Huri Islamoğlu has argued that the Code's adoption of such rights of exclusion was a key part of the reformers' efforts to assign exclusive and clearly demarcated property rights to each *mutasarrif*, a move that also helped to define exclusive liability for taxation.[66] Although most of the exclusionary rights were not new, Islamoğlu was right to note that in the Code they had attained a particularly prominent role in defining *tasarruf*. Most of the rights of exclusion were established in the first section of the first chapter of the Code, the section that delineated the most essential rights constituting *tasarruf*. The *kanunname*s of centuries past often gave pithy definitions of the peasant's bundle of rights on *miri* land, but the rights of exclusion had never been included in these definitions.[67] A careful enumeration of such rights in the first section of the Code suggests that the Council had thoroughly catalogued all such rights that were posited in the fatwas and ensured that they were included. By contrast, the Council declined to include any reference to the few circumstances where seventeenth- and eighteenth-century muftis had ruled that one *mutasarrif* had an ability to limit another *mutasarrif*s control over his own land or attached *milk* property.[68] This attentiveness to the inclusion of fatwa-based precedent that fit the reformers objectives, while ignoring such precedent that did not, was one method that the Council had at its disposal for crafting the law in ways consistent with its goals.

But selectively embracing some precedents and ignoring others was not the only tool that the Council possessed to sculpt the law. Prior to the assembling of the Code, the land law had consisted of *kanun*s, orders, *firman*s, fatwas and scholastic analysis mixed together in texts that attempted to establish how they fit with one another to produce the law. A text like the *Kanun-ı Cedid* assigned the dominant role to the *kanun*s and *firman*s, which it highlighted by the visual arrangement of the text: a single *kanun* or *firman* on a topic was presented, followed by fatwas illuminating application in specific cases, or by drawing conclusions based on the rule articulated in the *kanun*. Explaining the status of fields that were not plowed, the *Kanun-ı Cedid* declares: 'Nothing will be taken from such fields that are retained in fallow for a year or two when the herb grows that they call *kelembe*. But in the third year, a tithe will be taken. This does not need to be written in the defter .... A *kanun* from the time of Katip Latifi Cafer Çelebi.'

'Question: Fields in the *tasarruf* of a few people are cultivated one year. Then, if herbs or grass grow there and Zayd the *sipahi* wants to graze his cattle on it, can these people [the *mutasarrifs*] prevent him from doing so?

Answer: They can. Baha'i Mehmed.'[69]

In this example, the *kanun* merely states that *kelembe* will be taxed in the third year, while the fatwa elaborates further and states that the possessors can exclude others from using it. In illuminating the *mutasarrif*s rights and responsibilities in this situation, the text contained both *kanun* and fatwa, but the distinct character of those two textual forms and a presentation that placed them in relationship to one another was preserved in such texts.

By contrast, the Land Code did not preserve such differences in its format. Just as the many ranks of Ottomans were becoming a legally homogenized mass of subjects, so too was the multi-genre tradition of land law becoming a homogenized, single category of law. Article 11 states, 'The herb known as *kelembe* grows on a field which is left fallow according to its capacity. If someone possesses that field with *tapu*, then only its possessor may make use of the herb and may forbid others from entering the field or grazing their animals on it.' In the Code, the source of the article's content (did it derive from *kanun*? from the *fiqh*?) was obscured, and the selected provisions were all rendered equally enjoined by state authority. The Code left no trace of its multiple sources or the debate about how they fit together. Incorporated into the Code, the rights of exclusion became equally 'legal' and indistinguishable from the Code's provisions that had their origins in *kanun*. With its entirely homogenous presentation, the Code had no need for harmonization.

Finally, the Council did not confine itself to *kanuns* and the fatwas built from the sultan's orders to craft the Code's content; at times, its members drew on the manuals of *fiqh*. The Code's provisions dealing with *taqsim* are particularly illustrative of the occasions when the Council employed this broader approach. There were no *kanuns* that dealt with it, but *Şeyhülislam* 'Abdürrahim, Erzurumlu 'Abdurrahman, and Mostari Ahmed had all given fatwas affirming that *taqsim* was valid only if the deputy gave permission.[70] None of them explained how permission was to work in this specific case; if there were any criteria the deputy was supposed to apply beyond the general test of whether a transaction caused revenue depletion, the muftis did not expound these. By contrast, the Code adopted very specific language determining what procedure the *me'mur* must follow in Article 15 of the Land Code. First, he must determine if the land was partitionable (*kabil-i taksim*), meaning that if it were divided into individual shares among the partners, each share would still be of viable use for its individual holder (*müşteriklerden her birinin hisse-yi müfrezesiyle intifa' mümkün olup*). If it met this criterion, it was to be divided proportionally as specified by the sharia or, as the Code put it, 'in some equitable way'. If it did not meet these criteria, the partition could not be carried out. The determination that the *me'mur* was to make before partition – a careful assessment of the productive viability of the new holdings that would be created – was entirely in keeping with his position as treasury agent and guardian of the land's productive capacity. It was consistent with the understanding of the deputy's role and also with Ottoman concern about the consequences of land fragmentation that had been articulated since the sixteenth century.[71] But the care that the text took to make explicit how exactly the *me'mur* was to meet these objectives was new and consistent with the tendency to turn the *me'mur*'s job into a rote process of carrying out procedure.

In order to construct a procedure with the necessary detail, the Council turned to the manuals of *fiqh*. The formulation in Art. 15 was notable for its resemblance to language in the *fiqh* manuals regulating the process of *qisma*. For instance, a fatwa by Hamid al-'Imadi recorded in *al-'Uqud al-Durriyya* treated a circumstance where one of multiple heirs to an estate of land and crops asked for the division of his share. The questioner specified that the land was partitionable (*qabila li'l-qisma*) and that each heir would be able to viably use his share after the partition (*wa yantafi' kull bi-nasibihi ba'd al-qisma*), and that a proper proportionality of each share was possible (*al-mu'adala mumkina*) and that the partition would not change the productivity (*wa'l-manfa'a la tatabaddal*). The mufti had responded that in this case, the partition was warranted.[72] In short, the criteria specified in the Code were gleaned from 'Imadi's ruling – or perhaps some other like it – in the Code's article on *taqsim*. Once again, the change from the previous legal regime was minimal, arguably an elaboration in detail more than a change per se. Yet it had a purpose beyond simply creating greater clarity in how to apply the law; it also directed the *me'mur* to enforce the law in a way that guarded viability and productivity in landholding, a concern of reformers and their predecessors alike.

By the time Cevdet Paşa and the Council began work on the Mecelle, they had already acquired some experience in the process of rendering the *fiqh* into a Code. Cevdet had seen the potential of codification not only to clarify but also to enjoin some courses of action while blocking alternatives. The Council was able to make such interventions in the Land Code proclaiming that it had done little if any innovating, a claim that was simultaneously both accurate yet misleading.[73] In the sense that it was a code assembled from pre-existing textual traditions, the 1858 Land Code did not differ greatly from its predecessor (the *Kanun-ı Cedid*), which had also melded previous materials to create an authoritative and comprehensive version of the law, one that conformed to one set of priorities and silenced others.[74] This similarity might caution us from overexaggerating the difference between modern regimes of legality and their predecessors, but some things were indisputably different between the *Kanun-ı Cedid* and the Land Code: the *Kanun-ı Cedid* did not abrogate all preceding legal texts and invalidate all precedents outside those of its own four corners. Additionally, the *Kanun-ı Cedid* showcased the multiplicity of lawmakers who participated in the land law's construction on the sultan's behalf and the many textual forms that enacted law. In the Code, though, this intricate configuration was erased, just as it would be in the Mecelle. The stripping of the features that identified the content as *kanun* or fatwa marked the most visible break between the working of the law in the Old Regime versus that of the New Regime.

Defending Islam: From 'built on the kanun*' to 'built on the* fiqh*'*

For centuries, Ottoman sultans had presented themselves as responsible for protecting and enacting the sharia, leading some administrators and subjects to ponder whether the dynasty's adherence to its *kanun* was consistent with its commitment to sharia. But in the nineteenth century, a somewhat different drama was playing out as reformers and administrators debated what role sharia should play in the legal institutions of the empire. What the 1858 Land Code portends for the future of Islamic law is rarely discussed because the land law is presumed to have had at most a tenuous relationship with the *fiqh* or other things Islamic. Such views have meant that the significance of the Land Code's resituating of land law vis-à-vis the *fiqh* has been overlooked.

As an early attempt to recreate sharia texts in the format of a modern *kanunname* with numbered articles, the 1858 Land Code was one of the first pieces of reform legislation to deal with familiar provisions cast in an unfamiliar format. The result was an important change in the formulation of the law governing *miri* land. Previously, texts like the *Kanun-ı Cedid* had taken pains to express the Islamic character of the law and to establish its conformity with sharia. In addition to invoking the duty of a sultan to provide order for the world, the opening section that framed the text authorized the sultan – or as the later parts of the text clarified, his appointed bureaucrats – to create legislation for the land by virtue of its belonging to the treasury. In the Code, by contrast, the Council would demonstrate the land law's connection to sharia by creating a stronger facial resemblance between the *fiqh* and the provisions in the Code. The 1858 Land Code contained no framing that explained the relationship between the Code and the sharia or the body of the *fiqh* as a whole. Perhaps the Council believed that such explanations were no longer necessary; by the mid-nineteenth century, the ulema had recognized the sultan and his officials as the legislators for *miri* land for centuries.[75] Having disappeared from the frame, the sharia's authority was increasingly projected in the statutes themselves. The Code introduced a number of modifications and further elaboration of usage rights or transactions, and the net result of these modifications was to bring the land law into closer conformity with the order of *fiqh*. In an age where the *fiqh* was losing its centrality in Ottoman legal practice and there was greater anxiety about the relationship between Islam and the new legislation, the Code was more visibly tethered to the *fiqh* than its antecedents had been.

In some cases, it was the articulation of new priorities that brought the land law into greater alignment with a sharia sensibility. One of these was the law of post-mortem transmission, one of the few areas of land law that saw extensive revision in the nineteenth century.[76] While the 'line of transmission' designated in the *kanun* in the late sixteenth and seventeenth centuries bore some resemblance to succession laws in the *fiqh*, the Code's transmission law had a far more pronounced resemblance to the *fiqh*. This change has garnered much attention in previous works, so it needs no lengthy examination here.[77] A less remarked-on change of this kind was the Code's articulation of limits on the legal personhood of minors and people who were deemed to lack compos mentis. Since the fifteenth century the *kanun* had contained provisions about orphaned minors and the safeguarding of their rights to their father's land; no later than the sixteenth century, fatwas had created specific avenues for the asserting of these rights.[78]

It was Art. 52 that grappled with the *kanun*s and fatwas issued previously about orphaned minors. The article bestowed upon both minors and the mentally incapacitated the principal right that orphans had previously possessed, namely, that their lands should not be given to others and that if they were, then the ward had ten years upon maturity (or recovery of mental faculties) to reclaim them.[79] However, there was an important qualification added that brought this law into greater conformity with the *fiqh*'s general empowerment of guardians to sell the property of their ward if they could credibly claim that it was necessary to pay for the orphan's maintenance or inherited debt.[80] Namely, the guardians were empowered to transfer *miri* land that constituted an integral part of a *çiftlik* if they were selling the *çiftlik* in its entirety to maintain the ward. In this case, as Art. 52 decreed, the ward would *not* have the ability to reclaim the land upon maturity or recovery of mental faculties. Such a rule was consistent with the way that guardianship generally worked in Hanafi *fiqh*: when a guardian sold his ward's *milk* property, such as a home or commercial rental property, this sale was not reversible unless the former ward could prove that the sale had not been necessary.[81] This restriction on the ward's ability to regain his father's *miri* land reshaped the law in the image of the *fiqh* and in this case made the *miri* land of a *çiftlik* more comparable to *milk*.

The Code therefore asserted the land law's Islamic character in a very different way from that of the *Kanun-ı Cedid*. This shift was a powerful testament to the way that 'modernization' of the field of law was to play out in Middle Eastern states: if law was to possess a claim to an unassailably Islamic pedigree, its origins had to be located in the *fiqh*. It is clear that the Code's early commentators of the late nineteenth and early twentieth centuries no longer saw the land law's *kanuns* and *firmans* as distinct from but in harmony with sharia. The land law was, in their writings, derived directly from *fiqh* and sharia. Halis Eşref, one of the most authoritative commentators on the Code (and later, the Mecelle), wrote, 'because the Land Code is built on the rules of *fiqh*, foundational knowledge of the Code cannot be acquired without at least a cursory knowledge of the shar'i issues that the Code is built upon'.[82] He noted that it was necessary to explain the 'sharia and historical bases' of the *kanuns* issued by the sultans with regard to land. Another well-known commentator, Hoca Eminefendizade, wrote:

> Orders like those of the land law are derived from sharia principles. In order to write a commentary on such a *kanun*, it is necessary to have a full knowledge of the lofty science of *fiqh*, and to know the fatwas given by the sublime state's *şeyhülislams* on the subject of *miri* land is the most important thing … the *kanun* cannot be more just than the commandments of the sharia. There are no commandments of greater perfection than those of the principles of the *fiqh*. For this reason most of the commandments of these *kanuns* are taken from the books of *fiqh*. The others are commandments that were selected on the basis of general interest (*maslaha*).[83]

This shift in understanding, to one where the sharia and *fiqh* were the primary sources of the land law, should not be dismissed as the tendentious reasoning of commentators who themselves wished to defend the immaculately Islamic nature of the sultan's law. Rather, the Land Code's assembling from 'sharia texts' like fatwa collections and the introduction of synoptic material from the *fiqh* manuals (which themselves expounded the order of *miri* land that the Land Code was codifying) made such a claim plausible for its commentators.

Roughly a century earlier, Ibn 'Abidin had noted that land law fatwas were built off the sultan's orders. For Eşref and Hoca Eminefendizade, the sultan's orders were built off the *fiqh*. Formulating the relationship between the sultan's directives and the body of Hanafi *fiqh* had been an enduring project even as it became largely uncontroversial from the late seventeenth century. But in the nineteenth century, things had changed, as the Land Code itself stated at the outset. The sultan's ability to 'do things in a special way' was no longer specific to land tenure or penal law; rather, the sultan's ability to reorder the world was far more pervasive. The sultan could, and had, adopted codes of law for enforcement that were foreign in every sense of the word. In a context where the sultan could enact law that had no Islamic historicity, locating the land law's origins in *fiqh* secured its Islamic mooring. This creation of a more squarely *fiqh*-based genealogy for the land law was a portent of how laws (and other things) would be judged to be Islamic or not Islamic in the modern age. By declaring that land law was based on the *fiqh*, the nineteenth-century commentators finally mooted the question that had dogged the Ottomans for centuries about whether the *kanun* and sharia were in harmony. After 1858, they were declared to be one and the same.

Conclusion

The 1858 Land Code was a project of defensive development that created a law to meet new demands for tax revenue and the ordering of relations between the state and its subjects. While the Code changed little about the bundle of rights that constituted *tasarruf*, it did change the definition of eligibility for *tasarruf*. Whereas it had been a perquisite of the *reaya*; it was now a privilege of Ottoman nationality, which entailed responsibility for obeying laws and paying taxes. Property rights had trickled up the social ladder of the Old Regime, and when the diverse Ottoman social classes were homogenized into a single subject, the prototypical lifelong *tasarruf* – that of the peasant's right to the land – was standardized and offered to all, thus marking a final chapter in the diffusion of property rights across the Ottoman population.

The Code also aimed to defend the Ottoman state's reforms as preserving Islam and the sharia. Not surprisingly, the transformation of the land law into the Code illustrated a number of trends that would characterize the reconfiguring of 'Islamic law' in the modern period. Transferred from its Old Regime custodians to those of the New, it was subtly shaped through codification to reflect priorities important to reformers, like individuation or maintaining productivity. In a move that would elide the complex nature of pre-reform legal edifice, the many voices that had contributed to the law were compressed into the singular voice of the Code: the intricacy of a law that had been in a shared venture between sultans, scholars and multiple textual forms would now disappear. Legal sovereignty trended towards the same homogenization that marked the Ottoman legal subject. The enlarged and relatively uncontroversial role for the sultan in lawmaking that emerged in the nineteenth century suggests that he no longer needed a frame like that provided in the *Kanun-ı Cedid* to justify his legal autonomy. But the sultan's authority having burst the frame, the law he enacted was more ambiguously Islamic in character; therefore, the Council enhanced the Code's Islamic credentials through a more direct resemblance to the *fiqh*. Conformity with the *fiqh*, always an important principle for the ulema, was taking a newly definitive role in the conception of a specifically Islamic legality.

CONCLUSION

The Ottoman Empire was a polity that remained agrarian until its dissolution in the twentieth century, and Ottoman land tenure practices have therefore played a dominant role in the historical narratives that explain its experience. The older narratives of Ottoman decline (or failed modernization) emphasized the breakdown of the *timar* system, the turn away from *kanun* and the emergence of illicit private estates and *waqf*s. Today, the rehabilitated narrative of Ottoman history that seeks to better understand Ottoman durability and adaptation is no less predicated on a particular understanding of land tenure evolution. The revised narrative emphasizes that Ottoman longevity is due in no small part to a pragmatic seventeenth-century fiscal-military reorganization and a relative privatization of agricultural revenues in the eighteenth century. There is still a tendency, even among revisionists, to see the Ottoman Empire of the sixteenth century as the apex of a classical order, one characterized by universalist ambitions and patrimonial inclinations, even if realities on the ground required accommodation. This order comprised institutions that, while effective for the governing of the empire prior to the mid-sixteenth century, were unfit for the challenges of the following centuries. The 'classical' institutions were thus slowly abandoned to be replaced by newer ones better suited for a larger, more monetized empire facing increasingly vigorous opponents.

This book has asked the reader to reimagine the narrative of the empire's passage from the sixteenth to the nineteenth centuries. It has posited the sixteenth century not as the height of an order that would pass away but as the beginning of a particular bundle of property rights conveying lifelong *tasarruf* that would play a dominant role for the rest of Ottoman history in governing residence and occupation of land and buildings. Over the course of the seventeenth and eighteenth centuries, this peculiar formation of property rights took root and grew within the empire's legal texts, trickling up from the peasant cultivators to a wide array of Ottoman subjects before its codification and extension to all who were subject to the sultan's legal jurisdiction in the nineteenth century. The institutionalization of this bundle was due in large part to the labours of the ulema across the empire. First, they accepted that the orders issued by the sultan must guide the fatwa as well as the *hüccet*. Second, they actively participated in the process of incorporating and transmitting the sultan's directives in new ways to wider audiences. From the sixteenth century, the sultan's legislative power was increasingly deeply rooted in both administrative and scholastic legal texts, reshaping the Hanafi doctrine of treasury land and how the mufti was to discern the law when issuing a fatwa. In the nineteenth century, the legal texts and practices that had exercised tremendous influence on Ottoman life for the last three centuries were adapted to meet contemporary challenges.

In response to the depictions of the Ottoman sultanate as despotic, Ottoman historians have long argued that even if the sixteenth-century sultan spoke like an absolutist, he did not have sufficient tools at his disposal to govern like one. Many scholars have called attention to the way that the elites of his provinces were integrated into the structures of governance or were able to maintain some measure of independent control over their own stations and possessions. Less attention has been paid to the integration of the peasantry in these structures or to the transformative potential of that integration. It was the sultanate of Süleyman, with its wide-ranging aspirations to control the empire's resources, that instituted the form of lifelong secure tenure that would become so widespread throughout the Ottoman domains in its various iterations. It is ironic that the lifelong *tasarruf* granted by *tapu* – the legal structure upon which the conventions of private property would later be moored – found its origins in those figures often deemed most hostile to any private right that might limit the sultan's control: Sultan Süleyman and Ebu's-Su'ud Efendi.

If *kanun*, itself a complex institution, came to be identified as the order established by the sovereign authority of the dynasty, one question this book has considered is how the jurists regarded this order and what impact its provisions had on the jurists' own lawmaking activities. Ottoman historians are merely the latest set of scholars to ponder such questions; the Ottomans themselves were deeply immersed in conceptualizing how the sultan's orders and the texts enacting them were related to the sharia and the textual forms scripting sharia. In the case of land tenure, designating the lands of the *bayt al-mal* as a space wherein the sultan could claim a new terrain free of juridical precedent for inscribing his own law proved to be one effective way for conceptualizing how the two fit together: or as later Ottomans put it, how they harmonized. The sultan was no longer a trustee making ad hoc decisions about the land, as the great Hanafi scholars of the past had conceived of the relationship between the sultan and the treasury. Rather, he and his complex bureaucracy could create and enforce permanent laws that broke with precedent.

The question of how the *kanun* fit with jurisprudence in the governance of *miri* land was not resolved in the sixteenth century; it was in constant negotiation over the following centuries. The body of *kanun*s governing land tenure expanded considerably in the late sixteenth and early seventeenth centuries, further extending direct dynastic control over peasant cultivators and reducing the discretion of *sipahi*s and other treasury deputies. But most importantly, the seventeenth century was defined by a series of controversies over the way harmony was to be understood or to what extent it actually existed. Analogists and autonomists advanced different interpretive traditions for the fit between the sultan's orders and the practice of Hanafi jurisprudence, with a consensus emerging at mid-century that leaned towards the deference of autonomism on most issues but inclined towards analogism in some issues attached to transactions. This moment coincided with the integration of the sultan's directives on land tenure into the academic texts of the Hanafis, marking a growing consensus among the empire's Hanafi ulema that the sultan's orders superseded local practice and were to be imposed on treasury-owned land throughout the empire. Within these academic texts, the doctrine of *miri* land began to force a reconsideration of the Hanafi position on how the treasury acquired such lands. To understand how far scholarly opinion had consolidated around the juridical validity of *miri* land, we must look to an unlikely source of its affirmation: the *Kanunname of Candia*. The author of this specific text rejected the *tapu* fee and the rest of the taxation associated with the *miri* regime, but he did not denounce claiming land for the treasury at the moment of conquest as an unlawful innovation (*bid'a*). Although the author praised the decision of Mehmed IV not to do so and instead to emulate the example of the pious caliph 'Umar, the author shied away from condemning a practice that had been proclaimed as valid by the hero of the Ottoman *selefi* movement, Mehmed Birgevi. This reaction revealed how profoundly the views of the Ottoman scholastic community had come to accept the reconfiguring of the law in the image of Ottoman administrative practice.

This study has also departed from prevailing characterizations of the eighteenth century as a time when proliferation of *çiftlik*s and *malikane*s meant that the legal regime of *miri* land had attenuated and become irrelevant. In fact, the eighteenth century may be fairly described as 'the age of *mutasarrifs*', when the various bundles of lifelong *tasarruf* were possessed by a wide and socially diverse group of Ottoman subjects. The first such bundle had been birthed through the reconciliation of *tapu* as a practice of the cadastral register and with *tapu* as a practice in the fatwa and *hüccet*. Thereafter, it had trickled up the social ladder to endow commercial and residential renters on *waqf* property, and tax-farming *ayan*, with the same secure lifelong rights that peasants enjoyed on the land. By the mid-eighteenth century, these lifelong *mutasarrif*s could be seen in the cities and the countryside throughout the Ottoman domains. The layered rights of these *mutasarrif*s meant that the *ayan*'s control over the land left room for the peasant cultivator's layer of rights to remain robust. The fatwas attest not only that the peasant cultivator continued to enjoy the protections of the past, but that muftis also tended to grant him the wider latitude to transact what analogists of the early seventeenth century had pioneered, including conditional transfers, division of holdings and the collateralization of *tasarruf* in return for a loan. This degree of latitude in transactions aroused some controversy within the *ilmiye*, but it would find acceptance in the codification of the 1858 Land Code. In continuity with previous centuries, muftis continued to give rulings maintaining a balance between the possession rights of the cultivator and the right of the treasury and its deputy to the land's produce.

This book has also presented a challenge to the widespread notion that *kanun* as a textual tradition no longer carried the authority it had possessed in the past. If the eighteenth century did not see a proliferation of new *kanunname*s, both fatwa collections and academic texts of jurisprudence were more likely than those of previous centuries to incorporate *kanuns*, orders and observations of jurists that practice should comply with them. Additionally, the land regime as defined by the *kanun* and the interpretive tradition of the fatwas was more uniformly understood and more widely attested across the Ottoman domains in the eighteenth century than it had been in the sixteenth. It was not until the middle of the eighteenth century that there was a shift in Syria from regarding the *miri* regime as the local custom of Anatolia to the law of the empire; the scope and reach of the texts that testified to the validity of the *miri* land regime were truly imperial.

The paradigm of harmony had always suggested a world of difference and multiplicity where things needed to work with one another in a complementary fashion, as statecraft literature had expounded by reference to the body politic and the circle of justice. As political theories emphasizing the ordering of differences fell from favour in the nineteenth century, the age of conceptualizing land tenure law as harmony drew to a close. The shift introduced in the 1858 Land Code was not in its definition of *tasarruf* (often misleadingly translated in English language studies as 'ownership') but rather in its definition of who could be a *mutasarrif*. The Code marked a passage from an age of multiple *mutasarrifs* into an age of uniformity and homogenization. While the peasant cultivator's form of *tasarruf* was inscribed in the 1858 Land Code with little alteration from its eighteenth-century form, it was no longer a bundle of rights for one class of people which promoted their living in social harmony with other, different groups. Instead, the Code's *tasarruf* presented a singular mould for the generic Ottoman subject. The image of the body politic with its different humours requiring balance was no longer a potent paradigm for the order of the Ottoman realm. The Ottoman bureaucratic imagination was now inclined towards the image captured in the frontispiece of Hobbes's *Leviathan* (1651): a mass of undifferentiated individuals composing the body politic (see Chapter 1). The Code's *tasarruf* remained consistent with its precedents, but over time it was amended in ways that incrementally reduced the treasury's power to intervene in the cultivator's usage and facilitated the ability of creditors to seize land for unpaid debt. Although the Code increasingly conformed to the ideals of private property, early-twentieth-century commentaries continued to regard it as not entirely assimilated to private property, though in that regard it is likely to have been representative of norms prevailing everywhere, including in Europe.

It is also clear that the Code did not reintroduce a long-lost legislative sovereignty to the sultan. Various members of the sultan's personnel in the chancery and *ilmiye* had been making the land law since the sixteenth century; in the mid-nineteenth century, it was simply a different, more concentrated group of personnel who took over the task under the aegis of the Supreme Council of Judicial Ordinances. Like the sultan's subjects, the law itself underwent a homogenizing compression: the polyvocal and multilayered nature of the law that had defined texts like the *Kanun-i Cedid* became a singular, homogenized voice of law in the Code. The land law, which had previously combined texts across multiple genres in the way that it executed legal power, was now embodied in a Code, which reduced all of these genres to 'sources' that offered choices for selection or omission. While previous generations had theorized whether and how *kanun* and sharia harmonized to create the law, any difference between the two was now, like so many other differences in the modern era, not to be admitted. The homogenization of both the subject of the law and the law itself was a self-defensive gesture; but in defending its 'own' institutions and affinities, reformers transformed both the institutions and the understanding of the ways they had functioned in the past.

In offering this narrative of land law over three centuries, this study has attempted to replace an entrenched narrative that links a powerful sovereignty with a lack of property rights. It provides instead a narrative of a powerful sovereignty that instituted an extremely consequential regime of property rights. This book has also argued that the evolution of the land law and the sovereign's place within it is not a matter separate from the history of Islamic law; it is instead very much a part of it. Above all, it has attempted to trace the various visions of harmony that informed the law governing the vast fields and plowlands that gave the empire its wealth, its might and its sense of destiny.

NOTES

Introduction

1 D. A. Howard, 'Historical Scholarship and the Classical Ottoman Ḳānūnnāmes', *Archivum Ottomanicum* 14, 1995–6, 87.

2 Most copies end with a *firman* (sultanic edict) dating to 1084 H/1673 CE, and because this *firman* often appears in the company of other *firmans* issued at roughly the same time, this date is most likely correct. However, the copy published in MTM ends with the date the manuscript was transcribed: 'the end of sacred Muharram, in the year 1129'. This is the earliest copy date I have seen. When subsequent copies were made from it, the transcribers mistakenly attributed the *firman* to 1129 H rather than to 1084 H, and so a number of copies made from this copy preserve their lineage through the mistaken dating of the *firman*. These copies include an untitled *Kanun-ı Cedid*, SYK Fatih 3505, copied 1216; 'Kitab-ı Kanun-ı Cedid', SYK Reşid Efendi 278/1, 1–110; and '*Kanunname*' SYK Yazma Bağışlar 1181, copied 1183.

3 For some of these many copies see Halil Inalcik, 'Kanunname', EI[2], 565, and Ahmet Akgündüz, *Osmanlı Kanunnâmeleri ve Hukukî Tahlilleri* (Istanbul: FEY Vakfı Yayınları, 1990), 1, 17–40.

4 To mention only a few Ömer Lûtfi Barkan, *Türk Toprak Hukuku Tarihinde Tanzimat Ve 1274 (1858) Tarihli Arazi Kanunnamesi* (Istanbul: Maarıf Matbaası, 1940); Halil İnalcik, 'Land Problems in Turkish History', *Muslim World* 45, no. 3 (1955): 221–8; Halil İnalcik, *İslam Arazi Ve Vergi Sisteminin Tesekkülü Ve Osmanlı Devrindeki Şekillerle Mukayesesi* (Istanbul: Osman Yalçın Matbaası, 1959); Ömer Lûtfi Barkan, *Türkiye'de Toprak Meselesi Toplu Eserler I* (Istanbul: Gözlem Yayınları, 1960); and Halil İnalcik, *An Economic and Social History of the Ottoman Empire*, vol. 1, 1300–600 (Cambridge: Cambridge University Press, 1997).

5 These heuristic models include Jean Bodin's seigneurial monarchy; the Oriental despotism of Renaissance humanists and their successors and Max Weber's patrimonialism and its peculiarly Islamic variant of sultanism. For the models themselves, see Jean Bodin, *The Six Bookes of a Commonweale a Facsimile Reprint of the English Translation of 1606 Corrected and Supplemented in the Light of a New Comparison with the French and Latin Texts*, ed. Kenneth Douglas McRae (Cambridge, MA: Harvard University Press, 1962), 201; Lucette Valensi, *The Birth of the Despot: Venice and the Sublime Porte*, trans. Arthur Denner (Ithaca, NY: Cornell University Press, 2009); Bryan S. Turner, *Weber and Islam a Critical Study* (Boston, MA: Routledge & Kegan Paul, 1974), 77. On the applicability of such models to the sixteenth-century Ottoman Empire see Halil Inalcik, 'Comments on "Sultanism": Max Weber's Typification of the Ottoman Polity', *Princeton Papers in Near Eastern Studies* 1 (1992): 49–72 and Baki Tezcan, *The Second Ottoman Empire: Political and Social Transformation in the Early Modern World* (New York: Cambridge University Press, 2010), 10.

6 See Halil İnalcik, 'Islamization of Ottoman Laws on Land and Land Tax', in *Festgabe an Josef Matuz Osmanistik-Turkologie-Diplomatik*, ed. Christa Fragner and Klaus

Schwartz (Berlin: Klaus Schwarz Verlag 1992), 101–18; Colin Imber, *Ebu's-Su'ud: The Islamic Legal Tradition* (Edinburgh: Edinburgh University Press, 1997), 115–38; Colin Imber, 'The Law of the Land', in *The Ottoman World*, ed. Christine Woodhead (New York: Routledge, 2012), 41–56; and Snjezana Buzov, 'The Lawgiver and His Lawmakers: The Role of Legal Discourse in the Change of Ottoman Imperial Culture' (PhD Diss., University of Chicago, 2005), 77–134; Heather L. Ferguson, *The Proper Order of Things: Language, Power, and Law in Ottoman Administrative Discourses* (Redwood City, CA: Stanford University Press, 2018), 72–105.

7 For a notable (and rare) dissent on this issue, see Haim Gerber, *The Social Origins of the Modern Middle East*, Acls Humanities E-Book (Boulder, CO: L. Rienner Mansell Publishing, 1987), 69–71.

8 Barkan, *Türk Toprak Hukuku;* Gabriel Baer, 'The Evolution of Private Landownership in Egypt and the Fertile Crescent', in *The Economic History of the Middle East, 1800–1914*, ed. C. Issawi (Chicago: University of Chicago Press, 1966), 80–90; Kemal H. Karpat, 'The Land Regime, Social Structure, and Modernization in the Ottoman Empire', in *Beginnings of Modernization in the Middle East: The Nineteenth Century*, ed. William R. Polk and Richard L. Chambers, Publications of the Center for Middle Eastern Studies (Chicago: University of Chicago Press, 1968), 69–90; Halil Cin, *Osmanlı Toprak Düzeni Ve Bu Düzenin Bozulması*, 4th edn (Ankara: Berikan Ofset Matbaa, 2016).

9 Inalcik, 'Land Problems in Turkish History'; Kenneth Cuno, 'The Origins of Private Ownership of Land in Egypt: A Reappraisal', *International Journal of Middle Eastern Studies* 12, no. 3 (1980): 245–75; Peter Sluglett and Mariam Farouk-Sluglett, 'The Application of the 1858 Land Code in Greater Syria: Some Preliminary Observations', in *Land Tenure and Social Transformation in the Middle East*, ed. Tarif Khalidi (Beirut: American University of Beirut Press, 1984), 409–21; E. A. Aytekin, 'Agrarian Relations, Property and Law: An Analysis of the Land Code of 1858 in the Ottoman Empire', *Middle Eastern Studies* 45, no. 6 (2009): 935–51. For a different approach that emphasizes the code's individuation of property right as a strategy of state-building, see Huri Islamoğlu, 'Property as a Contested Domain: A Reevaluation of the Ottoman Land Code of 1858', in *New Perspectives on Property and Land in the Middle East*, ed. Roger Owen (Cambridge, MA: Harvard University Press, 2000), 3–61.

10 H. A. R. Gibb and Harold Bowen, *Islamic Society and the West: A Study of the Impact of Western Civilization on Moslem Culture in the Near East* (London: Oxford University Press, 1950), 173–99 and Bernard Lewis, 'Some Reflections on the Decline of the Ottoman Empire', *Studia Islamica* 1 (1958): 111–27.

11 Some recent works aiming to reframe the 'big picture' include Karen Barkey, *Empire of Difference: The Ottomans in Comparative Perspective* (New York: Cambridge University Press, 2008); Tezcan, *The Second Ottoman Empire* and James L. Gelvin, *The Modern Middle East: A History*, 5th edn (New York: Oxford University Press, 2020).

12 Kenneth Cuno's work is among the most influential in this regard, but his views have undergone some modification. Although he earlier took the position that elites who purchased tax farms possessed something like ownership rights of the land, he later understood their rights to be restricted to revenue claims rather than the land itself. See Kenneth Cuno, 'The Origins of Private Ownership of Land in Egypt: A Reappraisal', *International Journal of Middle Eastern Studies* 12, no. 3 (1980): 245–75; Kenneth Cuno, *The Pasha's Peasants: Land, Society, and Economy in Lower Egypt, 1740–1858* (Cambridge: Cambridge University Press, 1992), 34–8; and Kenneth Cuno, 'Ideology and Juridical Discourse in Ottoman Egypt: The Uses of the Concept of Irṣād',

Islamic Law and Society 6, no. 2 (1999): 136–63. Others have focused on stronger property rights and rising use of juridical terminology in documents. See Molly Greene, 'An Islamic Experiment? Ottoman Land Policy on Crete', *Mediterranean Historical Review* 11, no. 1 (1996): 60–78; Dina Rizk Khoury, 'Administrative Practice between Religious Law (Shari'a) and State Law (Kanun) on the Eastern Frontiers of the Ottoman Empire', *Journal of Early Modern History* 5, no. 4 (2001): 305–30; Sabrina Joseph, *Islamic Law on Peasant Usufruct in Ottoman Syria: 17th to Early 19th Century* (Boston, MA: Brill, 2012).

13 Martha Mundy and Richard Saumarez Smith, *Governing Property, Making the State: Law, Administration, and Production in Ottoman Syria* (London: I.B. Tauris, 2007).

14 Earlier scholars saw this shift as resulting at least in part from decay in 'secular' Ottoman authority and the rise of 'religious fanaticism', see Uriel Heyd, *Studies in Old Ottoman Criminal Law*, ed. V. L. Ménage (Oxford: Clarendon Press, 1973), 154–7; Richard Repp, 'Qānūn and Sharī'a in the Ottoman Context', in *Islamic Law: Social and Historical Contexts*, ed. Aziz Al-Azmeh (London: Routledge, 1988), 131–2. Later adherents have shown skepticism towards 'fanaticism' and emphasized instead that a combination of military, political or economic factors led to the irrelevance of *kanun* and a corresponding rise in the position of the sharia. See Tezcan, *The Second Ottoman Empire*, 19–36.

15 Particularly important has been the notion of archive as a way of thinking about sovereignty's constitution and law-making authority. See Brinkley Morris Messick, *Sharīʿa Scripts: An Historical Anthropology* (New York: Columbia University Press, 2018); Reem A. Meshal, *Sharia and the Making of the Modern Egyptian: Islamic Law and Custom in the Courts of Ottoman Cairo* (New York: American University in Cairo Press, 2014), 103–39; Timothy J. Fitzgerald, 'Reaching the Flocks: Literacy and the Mass Reception of Ottoman Law in the Sixteenth-Century Arab World', JOTSA 2, no. 1 (2015): 5–20; Guy Burak, 'Evidentiary Truth Claims, Imperial Registers, and the Ottoman Archive: Contending Legal Views of Archival and Record-Keeping Practices in Ottoman Greater Syria (Seventeenth–Nineteenth Centuries)', BSOAS 79, no. 2 (2016): 233–54 and '"In Compliance with the Old Register": On Ottoman Documentary Depositories and Archival Consciousness', JESHO 62, nos. 5–6 (12 November 2019): 799–823; Ferguson, *The Proper Order of Things*.

16 Richard C. Repp, *The Müfti of Istanbul: A Study in the Development of the Ottoman Learned Hierarchy* (Atlantic Highlands, NJ: Ithaca Press, 1986), 62–8; Guy Burak, 'According to His Exalted Ḳânûn: Contending Visions of the Muftiship in the Ottoman Province of Damascus (Sixteenth to Eighteenth Centuries)', in *Societies, Law and Culture in the Middle East: 'Modernities' in the Making* (Warsaw: De Gruyter Open, 2015), 74–86.

17 Messick, *Sharīʿa Scripts*, 21–3.

18 Ibid., 25, 167–75.

19 Inalcik, 'Kanunname', EI[2.], 565.

20 Reinhard Schulze, 'The Birth of Tradition and Modernity in 18th and 19th Century Islamic Culture: The Case of Printing', *Culture and History* 16 (1997): 34–6. Some examples of the texts that are collections of *kanun-ı cedid* but are different from the *Kanun-ı Cedid* are *Kanunname-i Cedid Budur*, SYK Esad Efendi 586/2, 16–29, and *Kanunname-i Cedid der (…) fima yeteʿallik bi'l-arazi*, SYK Mirişah Sultan 440/6, 48–61.

21 Some examples include Joseph Schacht, *An Introduction to Islamic Law* (Oxford: Clarendon Press, 1982), 209–11; Wael B. Hallaq, *The Impossible State: Islam, Politics, and Modernity's Moral Predicament* (New York: Columbia University Press, 2013), 50; and Haim Gerber, *Islamic Law and Culture, 1600–1840* (Boston, MA: Brill, 1999), 46–60.
22 Rudolph Peters, 'What Does It Mean to Be an Official Madhhab? Hanafism and the Ottoman Empire', in *The Islamic School of Law: Evolution, Devolution, and Progress*, ed. P. J. Bearman, Rudolph Peters and Frank E. Vogel, Harvard Series in Islamic Law 2 (Cambridge, MA: Islamic Legal Studies Program, Harvard Law School, 2005), 147–58; Reem Meshal, 'Antagonistic Sharī'as and the Construction of Orthodoxy in Sixteenth-Century Ottoman Cairo', *Journal of Islamic Studies* 21, no. 2 (2010): 183–212; Guy Burak, *The Second Formation of Islamic Law: The Hanafi School in the Early Modern Ottoman Empire* (New York: Cambridge University Press, 2015), 18, 62–4, 207; Samy Ayoub, *Law, Empire and the Sultan: Ottoman Imperial Authority and Late Ḥanafī Jurisprudence* (Oxford: Oxford University Press, 2020); James Baldwin, *Islamic Law and Empire in Ottoman Cairo* (Edinburgh: Edinburgh University Press, 2017).
23 Inalcik, 'Islamization', 101–18.
24 Inalcik, 'Ḳānūn', EI^2, 559–60; Ö. L. Barkan, *XV ve XVI Incı Asırlarda Osmanlı Imparatorluğund Zirai Ekonominin Hukuki Ve Malî Esasları*. Vol. 1, *Kanunlar* (Istanbul: Bürhaneddin Matbaası, 1943), *xx*; Heyd, *Studies in Old Ottoman Criminal Law*, 180–3; Richard Repp, 'Qānūn and Sharī'a', 128; Imber, *Ebu's-Su'ud*, 51.
25 Abdullah Demir, *Devlet-i Aliyye'nin Büyük Hukukçusu Şeyhülislam Ebussuud Efendi* (Istanbul: Ötüken, 2006), 83; Boğaç A. Ergene, 'Qanun and Sharia', in *Ashgate Research Companion to Islamic Law*, ed. Rudolph Peters and Peri Bearman (Burlington, VT: Ashgate, 2014), 114–17.
26 Burak, *The Second Formation of Islamic Law*, 18, 62–4, 207.
27 Susan Reynolds has argued that the convention of referring to 'tenure' in the medieval period and 'property' in the modern era leads to an exotification and misunderstanding of medieval land law and its property rights. See Reynolds, 'Tenure and Property in Medieval England', *Historical Research* 88, no. 242 (2015): 563–76.
28 Although it is often stated that the strict separation of persons and things is inherent to the notion of property, this has been historically accurate in the continental tradition more so than the Anglo-American, where this distinction is not absolute. See O. Kahn-Freund, 'Introduction', in Karl Renner, *The Institutions of Private Law and Their Social Functions* (New Brunswick, NJ: Transaction Publishers, 2010), 19–21.
29 On property as a bundle, see C. Reinold Noyes, *The Institution of Property* (New York: Longmans, Green and Co., 1936), 310–11.
30 Lawrence C. Becker, *Property Rights: Philosophic Foundations* (Boston, MA: Routledge and K. Paul, 1977), 18–19.
31 The decoupling of labour from possession had occurred by the end of sixteenth century. Women were not considered to be cultivators, yet the *kanun* allowed brotherless daughters to pre-empt all other claims to their father's land by 1568, as we will see in Chapter 2; *sipahis* were warned not to confiscate their lands if they were kept under cultivation. By 1595, a person could leave the village and not lose his possession right if he kept in touch with the village authority and the land was worked by someone else. See MTM 91–2.
32 Martha Mundy writes that 'although office may arise from property or property from office, the two terms build from different core notions', in Islamic juridical writing. She goes on to define this difference: 'Unlike ownership … office can never

be imagined or naturalized as a simple dyad of person and thing. Rather office entails a triad of persons and things in which a person delegates to another a power over other persons or things. And again, unlike ownership, office is generally, if not always, conceived as revocable by the superior person in the chain of delegation.' See Martha Mundy, 'Ownership or Office? A Debate in Islamic Hanafite Jurisprudence over the Nature of the Military "Fief", from the Mamluks to the Ottomans', in *Law, Anthropology and the Constitution of the Social: Making Persons and Things*, ed. A. Pottage (Cambridge: Cambridge University Press, 2009), 146 n. 11.

33 For examples of studies that usefully employ concepts like 'layers' or 'webs', see Dror Ze'evi, *An Ottoman Century: The District of Jerusalem in the 1600s* (Albany: SUNY Press, 1996), 115–39; Engin Akarlı, 'Gedik: A Bundle of Rights and Obligations for Istanbul Artisans and Traders, 1750–1840', in *Law, Anthropology, and the Constitution of the Social: Making Persons and Things*, ed. Alain Pottage and Martha Mundy (Cambridge: Cambridge University Press, 2004), 168–70; Siraj Sait and Hilary Lim, *Land, Law and Islam: Property and Human Rights in the Muslim World* (New York: Palgrave Macmillan, 2006), 54–79.

34 Although the Napoleonic Code of 1804 attempted to bring a legally absolute ownership to land, there were enormous difficulties with determining which of the multiple interested persons could claim ownership. See Donald R. Kelley and Bonnie G. Smith, 'What Was Property? Legal Dimensions of the Social Question in France (1789–1848)', *Proceedings of the American Philosophical Society* 128, no. 3 (1984): 200–30. In England, land law still retains a number of peculiarities that distinguishes land from other kinds of property, although these were reduced in successive legislative acts that began in 1833 and concluded with the Settled Land Act of 1925. See A. W. Brian Simpson, *A History of the Land Law*, 2nd edn (New York: Clarendon Press, 1986), 270–90.

35 Robert W. Gordon, 'Paradoxical Property', in *Early Modern Conceptions of Property*, ed. John Brewer and Susan Staves (New York: Routledge, 1995), 97–8; Paschal Larkin, *Property in the Eighteenth Century: With Special Reference to England and Locke* (New York: H. Fertig, 1969); Gregory S. Alexander, 'Time and Property in the American Republican Legal Culture', *New York University Law Review* 66, no. 2 (1991): 273–352.

Chapter 1

1 Noel Malcolm, 'The Title Page of *Leviathan* Seen in a Curious Perspective', in *Aspects of Hobbes* (Oxford: Oxford University Press), 200–33.

2 There is an immense literature on this issue for early modern Europe, to which Alan Ryan, *Property and Political Theory* (New York: B. Blackwell, 1984) may serve as a useful introduction. For a critique of the way that the theorists of the sovereignty–property distinction created a temporal 'other' in the Middle Ages and a spatial 'other' in the non-Western world, see Kathleen Davis, *Periodization and Sovereignty: How Ideas of Feudalism and Secularization Govern the Politics of Time* (Philadelphia: University of Pennsylvania Press, 2008).

3 Jean Bodin, *The Six Bookes of a Commonweale: A Facsimile Reprint of the English Translation of 1606 Corrected and Supplemented in the Light of a New Comparison with the French and Latin Texts* (Cambridge, MA: Harvard University Press, 1962), 201–2.

4 Halil Inalcik, *An Economic and Social History of the Ottoman Empire*, ed. Halil Inalcik with Donald Quataert (Cambridge: Cambridge University Press, 1994), 1: 115; F. G. Milkova, 'Sur la teneur et le caractère ce la propriété d'état des terres miriye dans l'empire ottoman du XVe au XIXe Siècles', *Études balkaniques* 5 (1966): 155–75; Gyula Káldy-Nagy, 'The First Centuries of the Ottoman Military Organization', *Acta Orientalia Academiae Scientiarum Hungaricae* 31, no. 2 (1977): 147–62; Ömer Lütfi Barkan, 'Timar' in *Türkiye'de Toprak Meselesi Toplu Eserler 1* (Istanbul: Gözlem Yayınları, 1960), 817–28.

5 For a recent study of the Ottoman and Hapsburg Empires as contrasting ideal types of patrimonialism and aristocracy, see Jane Burbank and Frederick Cooper, *Empires in World History: Power and the Politics of Difference* (Princeton, NJ: Princeton University Press, 2010), 117–48.

6 Ali Yaycioglu, *Partners of the Empire: The Crisis of the Ottoman Order in the Age of Revolutions* (Redwood City, CA: Stanford University Press, 2016).

7 Halil Inalcik, 'State, Sovereignty and Law during the Reign of Süleymân', in *Süleymân the Second and His Time*, ed. Halil Inalcik and Cemal Kafadar (Istanbul: Isis Press, 1993), 88–9; and Linda T. Darling, *A History of Social Justice and Political Power in the Middle East: The Circle of Justice from Mesopotamia to Globalization* (New York: Routledge, 2013), 129, 140.

8 Usually, *gazi* is translated as 'holy-warrior', a term that is confusing given that it can include non-Muslim warriors. For an explanation of the term's evolution in the Ottoman context, see Linda T. Darling, 'Christian-Muslim Interaction on the Ottoman Frontier: Gaza and Accommodation in Early Ottoman History', in *Ottoman Mosaic: Exploring Models for Peace by Re-exploring the Past*, ed. Kemal H. Karpat (Seattle: Cune Press, 2010), 103–20.

9 Halil Inalcik, '"Stefan Duşan'dan Osmanlı Imparatorluğuna: Asırda Rumeli'de Hristiyan Sipahiler Ve Menşeleri', in *Fuad Köprülü Armağanı: 60. Doğum Yılı Münasebetiyle Fuad Köprülü Armağanı* (Istanbul: Dil ve Tarih Coğrafya Fakültesi Yayını, 1953), 207–48; Heath Lowry, *The Nature of the Early Ottoman State* (Albany: State University of New York Press, 2003); Mariya Kiprovska, 'The Mihaloğlu Family: Gazi Warriors and Patrons of Dervish Hospices', *Osmanlı Araştırmaları* 32 (2008): 193–222.

10 Father-to-son transmission seems to have been practised from the genesis of the system, but Süleyman created regulations designed to ensure that successive generations were performing the necessary military service. See Irène Beldiceanu-Steinherr, 'Loi Sur La Transmission Du Timar', *Turcica* 11 (1978).

11 Halil Inalcik, 'Ottoman Methods of Conquest', *Studia Islamica* 2 (1954): 114–16.

12 Halil Inalcik, *The Ottoman Empire: The Classical Age, 1300–1600*, 2nd edn (London: Phoenix, 1995), 115.

13 Colin Imber, *The Ottoman Empire, 1300–1650: The Structure of Power* (Basingstoke: Palgrave, 2002), 200–1.

14 Milkova, 'Sur la teneur': 155. Although a number of scholars consider this date accurate, there is no consensus; for a fuller discussion about the introduction of the *miri* category in the Ottoman Empire, see Snjezana Buzov, 'The Lawgiver and His Lawmakers: The Role of Legal Discourse in the Change of Ottoman Imperial Culture' (PhD Diss., University of Chicago, 2005), 89.

15 For the origins of the doctrine of treasury ownership, see Frede Løkkegaard, *Islamic Taxation in the Classic Period with Special Reference to Circumstances in Iraq* (Copenhagen: Branner & Korch, 1950). For Saljuk practice, see Osman Turan,

'Türkiye Selçuklularında Toprak Hukuku. Miri Topraklar Ve Husûsî Mülkiyet Şekilleri', *Belleten* 12 (1948). Some historians believe that the Byzantine land tenure practices such as *pronoia* grants were the basis for the Ottoman land regime in the provinces that had previously belonged to the Byzantine Empire; see Imber, in *Ottoman Empire, 1300–1650*, 194–5, and John R. Barnes, *Introduction to Religious Foundations in the Ottoman Empire* (Leiden: Brill, 1986), 24–8. For a systematic assessment of Byzantine influence, see Mark C. Bartusis, *Land and Privilege in Byzantium: The Institution of Pronoia* (New York: Cambridge University Press, 2012), 589–95.

16 Douglas E. Streusand, *Islamic Gunpowder Empires in World History* (Boulder, CO: Westview Press, 2010), 85.

17 Abdul-Rahim Abu-Husayn, 'The Iltizam of Mansur Furaykh: A Case Study of Iltizam in Sixteenth-Century Syria', in *Land Tenure and Social Transformation in the Middle East*, ed. Tarif Khalidi (Beirut: American University of Beirut, 1984).

18 Oktay Özel has pointed out that the freehold property (*milk*) in this grant was not the land itself, but rather the revenues, and that the peasants living in *temlik* villages for the most part had ordinary *tapu* tenure, which will be discussed later in the text. See Oktay Özel, 'Limits of the Almighty: Mehmed II's "Land Reform" Revisited', JESHO 42, no. 2 (1999): 232–3. While this distinction between land as *milk* versus revenues as *milk* may have been clear to some administrators, muftis occasionally gave fatwas that give the impression that they believed the land itself to be *milk* in such a grant. For instance: 'The sultan makes *milk* of land, mountains, villages, farms and all of the revenues of these, meaning the fees either in whole or in part, for a man who is a warrior. It has remained thus, true *milk*, moving to his children and his children's children …' see Bālīzādah Muṣṭafā b. Süleymān (d. 1662), '*Mizān al-Fatāwā*', SYK Yenicami 675, 27a. The growth of the *miri* system and the relatively smaller number of such grants after the sixteenth century may have meant the end of such questions.

19 Káldy-Nagy, 'The First Centuries of the Ottoman Military Organization', 148; Ömer Lütfi Barkan, 'Osmanlı Imparatorluğunda bir iskân ve kolonizasyon metodu olarak vakıflar ve temlikler. I. Istila devrinin kolonizator turk dervisleri ve zaviyeler', *Vakıflar Dergisi* II (1942): 359–62; Rifa'at Ali Abou-El-Haj, 'Power and Social Order: The Uses of the Kanun', in *The Ottoman City and Its Parts: Urban Structure and Social Order*, ed. Irene A. Bierman, Rifa'at Ali Abou-el-Haj and Donald Preziosi (New Rochelle, NY: A. D. Caratzas, 1991), 81.

20 Colin Imber, 'The Status of Orchards and Fruit Trees in Ottoman Law', in *Studies in Ottoman History and Law* (Istanbul: Isis Press, 1996), 207–16.

21 Barnes, *Introduction to Religious Foundations*, 45–8. For an exploration of the juridical evolution in attitude towards this kind of *waqf*, see Cuno, 'Ideology and Juridical Discourse', 136–63.

22 Sultan Mehmed II dismantled a number of *waqf*s that he claimed had illegally been endowed from treasury land, although his action was later reversed. See Özel, 'Limits of the Almighty', 226–46. For a broader perspective on the circumstances that led multiple fifteenth-century Muslim rulers to revoke or consider revoking the *waqf*s in their realms, see Christopher Markiewicz, *The Crisis of Kingship in late Medieval Islam: Persian Emigres and the Making of Ottoman Sovereignty* (New York: Cambridge University Press, 2019), 55–7.

23 The initiation of these trends is frequently located in the reign of Mehmed II (r. 1444–6 and 1451–81). See Cemal Kafadar, *Between Two Worlds: The Construction of*

the Ottoman State (Berkeley: University of California Press, 1995), 96–7; Inalcik, *The Ottoman Empire: The Classical Age*, 18, 27–9.

24 Özel, 'Limits of the Almighty'; Aleksandar Fotić, 'The Official Explanation for the Confiscation and Sale of Monasteries (Churches) and Their Estates at the Time of Selim II', *Turcica* 26 (1994): 33–54.

25 For *baştina timar*, see Inalcik, 'Stefan Duşan'dan Osmanlı Imparatorluğuna', 235–41, and Tom Papademetriou, *Render unto the Sultan: Power, Authority, and the Greek Orthodox Church in the Early Ottoman Centuries* (Oxford: Oxford University Press, 2015), 56. For *malikane divani*, see Ömer Lütfi Barkan, 'Türk-İslâm Toprak Hukuku Tatbikatını Osmanlı İmparatorluğu'nda Aldığı Şekiller: Mâlikâne-Divani Sistemi', in *Türkiye'de Toprak Meselesi* (Istanbul: Gözlem Yayınları, 1960), 151–208, and Oktay Özel, *The Collapse of Rural Order in Ottoman Anatolia: Amasya 1576–1643* (Leiden: Brill, 2016), 22.

26 Halil Inalcik, 'Ottoman Methods of Conquest', *Studia Islamica* 2 (1954): 119.

27 Douglas Howard, 'The Ottoman Timar System and Its Transformation 1563–1656' (PhD Diss., University of Michigan, 1987), 85–90.

28 Ibid.

29 Inalcik, 'State, Sovereignty and Law', 99–102.

30 Colin Imber has stated that Ebu's-Su'ud ruled that *miri* land could be confiscated from the peasant at any time, see Imber, *Ebu's-Su'ud*, 127–8. The fatwa that serves as the basis of this conclusion – which can be found in MTM, 55–6 – does say that with compensation in the form of tax reduction, peasant fields can be taken if the treasury has need. Dror Ze'evi has stated that in principle, the sultan could transfer cultivators to different plots or take them and assign them to others, see Ze'evi, *Ottoman Century*, 136. Some historians have pointed out that in the fourteenth to sixteenth centuries, sultans ordered population resettlements known as *sürgün*, whereby a percentage of households or even entire villages were transferred within the empire for security or repopulation considerations. See Ömer Lütfi Barkan, 'Osmanlı İmparatorluğunda Bir İskân ve Kolonizasyon Metodu Olarak Sürgünler', *İstanbul Üniversitesi İktisat Fakültesi Mecmuası*, part 1, vol. 11 (1949–50): 524–69; part 2, vol. 13 (1952): 56–79; and part 3, vol. 14 (1953–4): 209–36.

31 Halil Inalcik, 'Suleiman the Lawgiver and Ottoman Law', *Archivum Ottomanicum* 1 (1969): 105–38; Josef Matuz, *Das Kanzleiwesen Sultan Süleymans Des Prächtigen* (Wiesbaden: F. Steiner, 1974); Richard C. Repp, *The Müfti of Istanbul: A Study in the Development of the Ottoman Learned Hierarchy* (London: Ithaca Press, 1986); Peters, "What Does It Mean to Be an Official Madhhab', 147–58; Buzov, *The Lawgiver and His Lawmakers*; Abdurrahman Atçıl, *Scholars and Sultans in the Early Modern Ottoman Empire* (Cambridge: Cambridge University Press, 2017); Ferguson, *The Proper Order of Things*, esp. chap. 2.

32 For the contracts, see Inalcik, *Economic and Social History of the Ottoman Empire*, 109.

33 According to Snjezana Buzov, the grand vizier Ibrahim Pasha attempted to abolish or alter land tenure practices that he viewed as contrary to the sharia, while the *şeyhülislam*, Kemalpaşazade Efendi, who held office from 1526 to 1534, favoured the opposite approach and maintained that existing taxes and transactions largely aligned with the requirements expounded in the *fiqh*. See Buzov, 'The Lawgiver and His Lawmakers', 46–106; see also Katharina Anna Ivanyi, *Virtue, Piety and the Law: A Study of Birgivi Mehmed Efendi's* al-Ṭarīqa al-muḥammadiyya (Leiden, The Netherlands: Brill, 2020), 231.

34 Repp, *The Müfti of Istanbul*, 278–9; Katib Çelebi, *The Balance of Truth*, trans. G. L. Lewis (London: George Allen and Unwin, 1957), 128.

35 Nev'izâde Atâî, 'Hadaiku'l-Hakaik fî Tekmilet'ş-Şakâik', in *Şakaik-ı Nu'maniye ve Zeyilleri*, ed. Abdülkadir Özcan (Istanbul: Çağrı Yayınları, 1989), 2:185.

36 While *kanun* is sometimes understood narrowly as a 'law', other readings emphasize that 'dynastic custom' or 'dynastic practice' in a very wide sense may be a better general definition. Some foundational studies and those attempting to better understand and historicize the nuances of *kanun* include Halil Inalcik, 'Kutadgu Bilig'de Türk ve Iran siyaseti nazariye ve gelenekleri', in *Reşid Rahmeti Arat İçin* (Ankara: Türk Kültürünü Araştırma Enstitüsü, 1966), 259–75; Inalcik, 'Süleyman the Lawgiver': 107–9; Baki Tezcan, 'The "Kânûnnâme of Mehmed II": A Different Perspective', in *The Great Ottoman-Turkish Civilisation*, ed. Kemal Çiçek (Ankara: Yeni Türkiye, 2000), 657–65; Abou-El-Haj, 'Power and Social Order', 77–102; Buzov, 'The Lawgiver and His Lawmakers', 122–32; Ferguson, *The Proper Order of Things*, 104–5.

37 Cornell H. Fleischer, *Bureaucrat and Intellectual in the Ottoman Empire: The Historian Mustafa Âli (1541–1600)* (Princeton, NJ: Princeton University Press, 1986), 8; Hüseyin Yılmaz, 'The Sultan and the Sultanate: Envisioning Rulership in the Age of Süleymān the Lawgiver (1520–1566)' (PhD Diss., Harvard University, 2005), 271–2, 377–85). It has long been recognized that this position was not unanimous, even among the administrative elite and members of the dynasty; see Cemal Kafadar, 'The Myth of the Golden Age', in *Süleymân the Second and His Time*, ed. Halil Inalcik and Cemal Kafadar (Istanbul: Isis Press, 1993), 37–48; and Buzov, *Lawgiver and His Lawmakers*, 46–76.

38 Inalcik, 'State, Sovereignty and Law', 88; Buzov, *Lawgiver and His Lawmakers*, 123, 130–2; Kaya Şahin, *Empire and Power in the Reign of Süleyman: Narrating the Sixteenth-Century Ottoman World* (Cambridge: Cambridge University Press, 2013), 215–30.

39 For a sophisticated explanation on the link between bureaucracy and the political ideal of justice, see Ferguson, *The Proper Order of Things*, 250–76. See also note 7, earlier.

40 The eighteenth-century mufti of Tripoli refers to an owner of a freehold house and piece of land in this way: '*mutasarrif fihuma bi'l-milk*'. See ʿAbdallāh al-Khalīlī, *Fatāwā*, PUSC Garrett no. 507Y, 85b.

41 For instance, Ebu's-Suʿud describes a transfer as taking a sum of money for his 'right of *tasarruf*', see MTM 53 and Inalcik, *An Economic and Social History*, 1: 112. The language of *tasarruf* is so ubiquitous in the sources that historians often take it as synonymous with peasant tenure. For example, Amy Singer, *Palestinian Peasants and Ottoman Officials: Rural Administration around Sixteenth-Century Jerusalem* (Cambridge: Cambridge University Press, 1994), 12.

42 As Colin Imber has observed, Ebu's-Suʿud did reserve the right of confiscation for the treasury if need arose; see note 30 earlier. However, it would be strange to find a state that refused to claim an eminent domain-like power for itself; see Susan Reynolds, *Before Eminent Domain: Toward a History of Expropriation of Land for the Common Good* (Chapel Hill: University of North Carolina Press, 2010). The question is under what circumstances and how frequently such a power was invoked. To the extent that fatwas from the sixteenth through eighteenth centuries present a documentary record of such practices, they overwhelmingly treat legally valid expropriation as a result of leaving the land unworked for three years rather than as a result of treasury need.

Sipahis were clearly not authorized to confiscate a cultivator's land and simply claim that the treasury's need required it.

43 There is some dispute about the origin of the word itself, see Mehmet Zeki Pakalin, 'Tapu', in *Osmanli tarih deyimleri ver terimleri sözlügü* (Istanbul: Milli Eğitim Evi, 1972), 22: 399. In his various works, Halil Inalcik translates *tapu* as 'lease', though some scholars prefer 'title', which is also the definition for the term in modern Turkey. Cf. Inalcik, *An Economic and Social History* 1:108–10 and Colin Imber, 'The Law of the Land', in *The Ottoman World*, ed. Christine Woodhead (New York: Routledge, 2013), 43.

44 MTM, 305–6.

45 The Ottomans would attempt to limit the amount that could be charged for *tapu* to a year's worth of the land's produce; see MTM, 69. There is evidence that *sipahis* nevertheless demanded excessive amounts, see Ali Açıkel, 'XV-XVI. Yüzyıllarda Artukabad Kazasının Sosyal Yapısı', *Atatürk Üniversitesi Türkiyat Araştırmaları Enstitüsü Dergisi*, no. 25 (2004): 188.

46 Muhammad Wohidul Islam, 'Al-Mal: The Concept of Property in Islamic Legal Thought', *Arab Law Quarterly* 14, no. 4 (1999): 363; Wael B. Hallaq, *Sharia: Theory, Practice and Modern Transformation* (Cambridge: Cambridge University Press, 2009), 247–8.

47 MTM, 50.

48 Inalcik believes that stopping records of 'sale' and *waqf* in *miri* land and establishing proper documentation for *miri* transactions was the leading concern of Ebu's-Su'ud. See Inalcik 'Islamization', 107–9.

49 References to the powers of the landlord as derived from his status as the sultan's agent can be found no later than the seventeenth century. See Ṣādıḳ ibn Muḥammed Sāḳızī, 'Ṣurrat al-Fatāwā', PDL, 180b; see also Chapters 3 and 6, this book.

50 The conventional valuation of a *timar* in the fifteenth century was about 1,000 *akçes*, while a *zeamet* was valued between 20,000 and 100,000 *akçes* and a *has* was valued over 100,000 *akçes*. See Inalcik, *An Economic and Social History*, 141.

51 Uriel Heyd, *Studies in Old Ottoman Criminal Law*, ed. V. L. Ménage (Oxford: Clarendon Press, 1973), 176–7.

52 See note 40.

53 For example, MTM, 53.

54 Muḥammad Amīn Ibn 'Ābidīn, *al-'Uqūd al-Durriyh fī Tanqīḥ al-Fatāwā al-Ḥāmidiyya*, ed. Muḥammad 'Uthmān (Beirut: Dār al-Kutub al-'Ilmiyya, 2008), 2:358.

55 Mundy and Smith, *Governing Property*, 16–19. Examining Birgevi's criticims of the land tenure regime in detail, Katharina Ivanyi argues that in addition to the *tapu* fee, Birgevi was deeply opposed to the order of succession and the inability of debtors to lay claim to the cultivator's land. However, the latter two critiques were only valid if the land was the cultivator's freehold property, whereas his criticism of the *tapu* fee was particularly biting because the *tapu* fee, in his view, was inconsistent with either treasury ownership or individual ownership. See Ivanyi, *Virtue, Piety and the Law*, 226–30.

56 John Barnes has argued that such a view is in fact accurate; prior to the sixteenth century there was nothing that can be regarded as a general Ottoman legal practice with regard to land. See Barnes, *Introduction to Religious Foundations*, 32–3.

57 On a view of this period as one of multiple crises leading to a new imperial configuration see Tezcan, *The Second Ottoman Empire*. On various aspects of the

crisis see Sam White, *The Climate of Rebellion in the Early Modern Ottoman Empire* (New York: Cambridge University Press, 2011); Halil Inalcik, 'The Socio-Political Effects of the Diffusion of Fire-Arms in the Middle East', in *War, Technology and Society in the Middle East*, ed. Vernon J. Parry and Malcolm Yapp (New York: Oxford University Press, 1975), 195–217; Mustafa Akdağ, *Celâlî Isyanları (1550–1603)* (Ankara: Ankara Universitesi Basimevi, 1963); Oktay Özel, 'Population Changes in Ottoman Anatolia during the 16th and 17th Centuries: The Demographic Crisis Reconsidered', IJMES 36, no. 2 (2004): 183–205.

58 Halil Inalcik, 'Military and Fiscal Transformation in the Ottoman Empire, 1600–1700', *Archivum Ottomanicum* 6 (1980): 288–9; see also Gábor Ágoston, *The Last Muslim Conquest: The Ottoman Empire and Its Wars in Europe* (Princeton, NJ: Princeton University Press, 2021), 315–24.

59 Baki Çakır, *Osmanlı Mukataa Sistemi (XVI-XVIII. Yüzyıl)* (Istanbul: Kitabevi, 2003), 117; Inalcik, 'Military and Fiscal Transformation', 328.

60 BOA MAD 4181, Tax Farm Register, 8.

61 Howard, Douglas A., 'Ottoman Historiography and the Literature of "Decline" of the Sixteenth and Seventeenth Centuries', *Journal of Asian History* 22, no. 1 (1988): 62.

62 For the reliance of Ottoman histories on Ottoman notions of decline, see Howard, 'Ottoman Historiography', 73–7. A more critical approach to the texts of the seventeenth-century decline writers and their conclusions began with works like Roger Owen, 'The Middle East in the Eighteenth Century – an "Islamic" Society in Decline? A Critique of Gibb and Bowen's *Islamic Society and the West*', *Review of Middle East Studies* 1 (1975): 101–12; Abou- Rifaat Ali El-Haj, 'The Ottoman Nasihatname as a Discourse over Morality', in *Mélanges, Professeur Robert Mantran*, ed. Abdeljelil Temimi (Zaghouan, Tunisie: Centre d'Ètudes et de recherches ottomanes, morisques, de documentation et d'information, 1988), 17–30.

63 Inalcik, 'Military and Fiscal Transformation', 311–13 and 330–1; Linda T. Darling, *Revenue-Raising and Legitimacy: Tax Collection and Finance Administration in the Ottoman Empire, 1560–1660* (New York: Brill, 1996), 2–21, 301–2; Mehmed Genç, 'Osmanlı Maliyesinde Malikâne Sistemi', in *Osmanlı Imparatorluğund Devlet Ve Ekonomi* (İstanbul: Ötüken, 2000), 99–117; Ariel Salzmann, *Tocqueville in the Ottoman Empire: Rival Paths to the Modern State* (Boston, MA: Brill, 2004), 122–75; Barkey, *Empire of Difference*, 226–63.

64 Linda Darling has shown that the narrative of a dramatic shift from *timar*s to tax farms rests on surprisingly few empirical studies; she has furthermore concluded that the data of at least fifteen provinces defy the account that the *timar* system was shrinking and becoming obsolete. See Linda Darling, 'Historicizing the Ottoman Timar System: Identities of Timar-Holders, Fourteenth to Seventeenth Centuries', *Turkish Historical Review* 8 (2017): 145–73.

65 The agricultural revenues in the province of Damascus were largely dominated by tax farming in the seventeenth century, but Damascus provides a poor example of a transition from *timar*s to tax farms. Relatively few villages had been designated *timar*s in the sixteenth century, but of those that were, almost all of them continued to be *timar*s into the eighteenth century. See the cadastral survey of 1569–70 (BOA TT 479), 207–384, and compare with *timar* registers from 1662–3 (BOA MAD 15393) and 1711–17 (BOA MAD 21512). Proliferation of *çiftlik*s has been documented primarily in the Balkans; see Traian Stoianovich, 'Land Tenure and Related Sectors of the Balkan Economy, 1600–1800', *Journal of Economic History* 13, no. 4 (1953); Khristo Gandev, 'L'apparition des rapports capitalistes dans l'économie

rurale de la Bulgarie du nord-ouest au cours Du Xviiie Siècle', *Études Historiques* 1 (1960); and Bruce W. McGowan, *Economic Life in Ottoman Europe Taxation, Trade and the Struggle for Land, 1600–1800* (New York: Cambridge University Press and Maison des Sciences de l'Homme, 1981).

66 For historians of the Balkan provinces in particular, there was a question of how the Ottomans fit into a wider historiography of Eastern Europe, with its emphasis on early peripheralization in an emerging capitalist world economy due to the grain trade (see n. 64).

67 See the various essays, particularly that of Gilles Veinstein, in *Landholding and Commercial Agriculture in the Middle East*, ed. Çağlar Keyder and Faruk Tabak (Albany: SUNY Press, 1991).

68 The 1858 Land Code states that tax farmers did grant lands with *tapu*, see 'Arazi Kanunnâmesi' in *Mukayeseli Islam ve Osmanlı Hukuku Külliyatı*, ed. Ahmet Akgündüz (Diyarbakir: Dicle Üniversitesi Hukuk Fakültesi Yayınları, 1986), 684, article 3. There was some discussion among the muftis of Damascus about which tax collectors had such powers (see Mundy and Smith, *Governing Property*, 25). Likewise, Çatalcalı 'Ali Efendi ruled that a *mukataacı*'s permission was necessary to erect a building on *miri* land, see Çatalcalı 'Alī Efendi, "Fetāvā," SYK Esad Efendi 1072, 299b.

69 See Menteşzāde 'Abdürraḥīm, *Fetāvā-yi 'Abdürraḥīm* (Ḳonsṭanṭīnīye [Istanbul]: Dār üṭ-ṭıbā'at ül-Ma'mūret üs-Sulṭāniye, 1243 [1827]), 2: 511. For a *mukataacı* with such authorization, see the fatwa of *Şeyhülislam* Hacı Veliyüddin Efendi (d. 1768) in Dürrīzāde Meḥmed 'Ārif b. Muṣṭafā and Gedizli Meḥmed Efendi, *Netīcetü'l-Fetāvā* with an Arabic nüḳūl added by Gedizli Meḥmed Efendi (İstanbul: Darü'ṭ-Ṭıba'āti'l-'Āmīre, 1237 [1822]), 674. Despite its attribution to Dürrīzāde, *Netīcetü'l-Fetāvā* is a collection of eighteenth-century fatwas given by a number of *şeyhülislams*.

70 Çatalcalı 'Alī Efendi, '*Fetāvā*', SYK Esad Efendi 1072, 299b.

71 According to Baki Çakır, 'Being a *mültezim* did not provide the person with military privilege. If he sought such a privilege, its specification in the *iltizam* (tax farm) agreement and the state's acceptance of it were both necessary.' See Çakır, *Osmanlı Mukataa Sistemi*, 117. On the other hand, Linda Darling notes that in the seventeenth century it was common for bidders on tax farms to demand an office with military status as a condition of the revenue contract. See Darling, *Revenue-Raising and Legitimacy*, 149–50.

72 For example Sarı Mehmet Paşa and Walter Livingston Wright, *Ottoman Statecraft: The Book of Counsel for Vezirs and Governors (Naṣā'iḥ ül-Vüzera ve'l-Ümera) of Sari Meḥmed Pasha, the Defterdār* (Princeton, NJ: Princeton University Press, 1935), 118–20; Kâtip Çelebi, *Destur ül-'Amel li-Islah ül-Khalel* (Delhi: Facsimile Publisher, 1864), 9–11.

73 Reşat Kasaba, *A Moveable Empire: Ottoman Nomads, Migrants, and Refugees* (Seattle: University of Washington Press, 2009), 52–83; Cengiz Orhonlu, *Osmanlı İmparatorluğu'nda Aşiretlerin İskânı* (Istanbul: Edebiyat Fakültesi Basımevi, 1963); Rifa'at A. Abou-El-Haj, 'The Formal Closure of the Ottoman Frontier in Europe: 1699–1703', *Journal of the American Oriental Society* 89, no. 3 (1969): 467–75.

74 On wealth acquisition specific to tax farming see Mehmet Genç, 'A Study of the Feasibility of Using Eighteenth-Century Ottoman Financial Records as an Indicator of Economic Activity', in *The Ottoman Empire and the World Economy*, ed. Huri Islamoğlu-Inan (Cambridge: Cambridge University Press, 1987), 358; and Salzmann, *Tocqueville in the Ottoman Empire*, 60–71; for trade see Nikolai Todorov, *The Balkan City, 1400–1900* (Seattle: University of Washington Press, 1983), 149–50. Despite

these developments, historians are divided as to whether, overall, the economy was expanding before 1770. See Yaycioglu, *Partners of the Empire*, 36–7, and note 66, 307.

75 There were a number of property rights bundles that bestowed either long-term tenure or lifelong tenure upon the recipient that were typically based on the tenant using his own funds to improve or establish a right to engage in productive activity on *waqf* property. The meanings of these terms changed considerably from the sixteenth to the eighteenth centuries, and varied in the way they were practised in the Ottoman domains. Their histories are therefore complex, and exploring them is beyond the scope of this work. They include *sukna*, *gedik*, *hikr*/*muqata'a* and *khiluw*.

76 This is equally true of the bundles like *gedik* and *khiluw* that will not be dealt with in this chapter. On the role of the approval of and implementation of *gedik* in Istanbul by officials of the sultan's *divan*, see Akarli, '*Gedik*'. For a mufti's approval of *gedik* and *khiluw* because they fulfill a genuine social need of people and therefore a sound practice see Muḥammad Amīn ibn 'Ābidīn, *Ḥāshiyyat Ibn 'Ābidīn Radd Al-Muḥtār 'alā al-Durr al-Mukhtār* (Bayrouth [Beirut]: Dār iḥyā' al-turath al-'arabī, 2010[1431]), 9: 30–31.

77 For a recent, comprehensive study of *ijaratayn* see Süleyman Kaya, *Osmanli Hukukunda İcâreteyn* (Istanbul: Klasik, 2014). Kaya notes that the term *ijaratayn* is seldom seen before the eighteenth century, although the muftis referred to the more ambiguous terms of 'rent by *mu'accele* and *mü'eccele*' that could mean either rent for a finite term or lifelong rental; see Kaya, *İcâreteyn*, 82–4. Earlier authoritative studies include Ahmet Akgündüz, *Islâm Hukukunda Ve Osmanlı Tatbikatında Vakıf Müessesesi* (Ankara: Türk Tarih Kurumu Basımevi, 1988), 354–90; Barnes, *Introduction to Religious Foundations*, 54–9; Klaus Kreiser, 'Icareteyn: Zur "Doppelten Miete" im Osmanischen Stiftungswesen', *Journal of Turkish Studies* 10 (1986): 219–26.

78 Kaya, *İcâreteyn*, 192.

79 This remained the majority opinion of the Hanafis in the academic texts of *fiqh* into the nineteenth century; see Luqman Haji Abdullah, 'The Classical Islamic Law of Waqf: A Comparative Approach' (PhD Diss., University of Edinburgh, 2005), 144–5.

80 Kaya, *İcâreteyn*, 69.

81 See M. Hamdi Elmalı and Nazif Öztürk, *Elmalı M. Hamdi Yazır Gözüyle Vakıflar (Ahkâmu'l-Evkaf)* (Ankara: Türkiye Diyanet Vakfı Matbaacılık ve Ticaret İşletmesi, 1995), 268–9; and Barnes, *Introduction to Religious Foundations*, 52. Hüseyin Hatemi notes the *miri* terminology for delegation 'tefviz', succession 'intikal' and transfer 'ferağ'; see Hüseyin Hatemi, *Önceki ve Bugünkü Türk Hukuku'nda Vakıf Kurma Muamelesi* (Istanbul: Fakülteler Matbası, 1969), 80. Süleyman Kaya, after an exhaustive study of the many 'intermediate' property rights in the Hanafi tradition such as *kirdar*, *gedik* and *sukna*, concludes that *ijaratayn* is like the extension of *tapu* from land to buildings. See Kaya, *İcâreteyn*, 72.

82 This is clear from fatwas from the sixteenth and early seventeenth centuries, where peasants working *waqf* land routinely are referred to as holding it by *tapu*. Examples of *şeyhülislams* treating the presence of *tapulu* tenure on *waqf* land as unremarkable are *Şeyhülislam* Hocāsa'deddīnzāde Es'ad Efendi (d. 1625), see Es'ad Efendi, '*Fetāvā-yi Müntahabe*', SYK Kasidecizade 277, 182b; *Şeyhülislam* Zekeriyezade Yahya Efendi (d. 1644), see Meşrebzāde Meḥmed 'Ārif Efendi (d. 1858), *Fetāvā-yi Cāmi' ül-İcāreteyn* (İstanbul: Darü'ṭ-Ṭıba'āti'l-'Āmīre, 1252 [1837]), 117, 137; *Şeyhülislam* Baha'i Mehmed Efendi (d. 1654), see Ahmet Akgündüz, *Osmanlı Kanunnâmeleri ve Hukukî Tahlilleri* (Istanbul: FEY Vakfı, 1990), 9:437 no. 297 and 9:443 no. 344; and *Şeyhülislam* Feyzullah Efendi (d. 1703), see Kaya, *İcâreteyn*, 68 n. 239.

83 Ebu's-Su'ud himself gave fatwas acknowledging that when *waqf* land was held by *tapu*, the *mutawalli* held similar powers to those of the *sahib al-ard*. See Kaya, *İcâreteyn*, 68.
84 Meşrebzāde Meḥmed 'Ārif, *Fetāvā-yi Cāmi' ül-Icāreteyn* (İstanbul: Darü'ṭ-Ṭıba'āti'l-'Āmīre, 1252 [1837]), 137.
85 Ottoman historians often associate the *tapulu* tenure exclusively with *miri* land because of its systematic legal exposition as an element of the *timar* system in the sixteenth century. However, the *tapu* tenure clearly pre-dated its sixteenth-century formulation and was found widely within the Anatolian and Balkan provinces on lands that did not support *timars* or did so only in part, including both *waqf* and *tamlik* lands; see Barnes, *Introduction to Religious Foundations*, 47.
86 Ḥaṣkafī, 'Alā' al-Dīn (al-), and 'Abd al-Raḥmān ibn Muḥammad Shaykhzada, *Majma' al-Anhur fī Sharḥ Multaqā al-Abḥur: wa ma'ah al-Durr al-Muntaqā fī Sharḥ al-Multaqā*. 4 vols (Bayrūt [Beirut]: Manshūrāt Muḥammad 'Alī Bayḍūn: Dār al-Kutub al-'Ilmīyah, 1419 [1998]), 1:665.
87 For evidence suggesting that *ijaratayn* existed as early as the sixteenth century, see Ahmet Akgündüz, *Islâm Hukukunda Ve Osmanlı Tatbikatında Vakıf Müessesesi* (Ankara: Türk Tarih Kurumu Basımevi, 1988), 357–9. For the opposing viewpoint see Kaya, *Icâreteyn*, 83–4.
88 Barnes, *Introduction to Religious Foundations*, 54; Hatemi, *Önceki ve Bugünkü Türk Hukuku'nda Vakıf*, 79; Akarlı, 'Gedik: A Bundle of Rights and Obligations', 181–2.
89 Hatemi, *Önceki ve Bugünkü Türk Hukuku'nda Vakıf*, 79–80, n. 41.
90 Barnes, *Introduction to Religious Foundations*, 55. James Baldwin notes several instances of *ijaratayn* in the court records of seventeenth-century Cairo; Baldwin, *Islamic Law*, 89.
91 The standard of what benefited the *waqf*, as opposed to what was a necessity for its survival, was employed by *Şeyhülislam* 'Abdürrahim Efendi, who served as *şeyhülislam* from 1715 to 1716, in validating the rental of *waqf* property by way of *mu'accele* and *mü'eccele*, see Meşrebzāde, *Fetāvā-yı Cāmi' ül-İcāreteyn*, 57.
92 Erol Özvar, *Osmanlı Maliyesinde Malikane Uygulaması* (İstanbul: Kitabevi, 2003), 17–18.
93 BOA MAD 9486, Tax Farm Register, 161.
94 Genç, 'Osmanlı Maliyesinde Malikâne Sistemi', 107. The move to confine the *malikane* to the military class may have been a reaction to the criticism of officials like Defterdar Mehmed Pasha, who saw the *malikane* as diverting tax revenues that should be used for war in order to line the pockets of great men of state who were not combatants. See Defterdar Sarı Mehmet Paşa, *Zübde-i Vekayiât: Tahlil Ve Metin (1066–1116/1656–1704)*, ed. Abdülkadir Özcan (Ankara: Türk Tarih Kurumu Basımevi, 1995), 513.
95 Genç, 'Osmanlı Maliyesinde Malikâne Sistemi', 107.
96 Ariel Salzmann notes that other male relatives of the deceased also were frequently able to exercise this pre-emptory right, see Salzmann, 'An Ancien Régime Revisited: "Privatization" and Political Economy in the Eighteenth-Century Ottoman Empire', *Politics and Society* 21, no. 4 (1993): 402.
97 Baki Çakır, *Osmanlı Mukataa Sistemi (XVI–XVIII. Yüzyıl)* (Istanbul: Kitabevi, 2003), 163. From 1735, there was a fee of 10 per cent of the *mu'accele* due on this transaction; Genç, 'Osmanlı Maliyesinde Malikâne Sistemi', 108.
98 Suraiya Faroqhi, 'Crisis and Change, 1590–1699', in *An Economic and Social History of the Ottoman Empire*, ed. Halil Inalcik with Donald Quataert (Cambridge: Cambridge University Press, 1994), 2: 537–8.

99 Özvar, *Osmanlı Maliyesinde Malikane*, 172–3.
100 Genç, 'Osmanlı Maliyesinde Malikâne Sistemi', 99–117; Salzmann, 'An Ancien Régime Revisited', 405–8; Virginia Aksan, 'Ottoman Military Power in the Eighteenth Century', in *Writing the Ottomans into World History* (Istanbul: Isis Press, 2016), 308–9; Linda Darling, 'Public Finances: The Role of the Ottoman Centre', in *The Cambridge History of Turkey: The Later Ottoman Empire, 1603–1839*, ed. Suraiya Faroqhi, vol. 3 (Cambridge: Cambridge University Press, 2006), 127–9.
101 Genç, 'Osmanlı Maliyesinde Malikâne Sistemi', 116–17.
102 Madeline C. Zilfi, *The Politics of Piety: The Ottoman Ulema in the Postclassical Age (1600–1800)* (Minneapolis: Bibliotheca Islamica, 1988), 233–5; Salzmann, 'Ancien Régime Revisited': 402–5; Salzmann, *Tocqueville in the Ottoman Empire*, 108–10; Dina Rizk Khoury, *State and Provincial Society in the Ottoman Empire: Mosul, 1540–1834* (Cambridge: Cambridge University Press, 1997), 114–17; Barkey, *Empire of Difference*, 233–4; Yaycioglu, *Partners of the Empire*, 67–86.
103 Ariel Salzmann, 'The Old Regime and the Ottoman Middle East', in *The Ottoman World*, ed. Christine Woodhead (New York: Routledge, 2013), 416–19.
104 Yaycioglu, *Partners of the Empire*, 117–56; Deena R. Sadat, 'Rumeli Ayanlari: The Eighteenth Century', *The Journal of Modern History* 44 (1972): 351; Barbara Jelavich, *History of the Balkans* (New York: Cambridge University Press, 1983), 1: 73–5.
105 Khoury, *State and Provincial Society*, 58–72. Khoury notes that when interests diverged later in the eighteenth century, the alliance of local elite families and central administration fractured.
106 Rejecting comparisons with the Magna Carta, Barkey nevertheless emphasizes that the state's dealing with the *ayan* collectively was a significant political innovation. See Barkey, *Empire of Difference*, 223–4.
107 Yaycioglu, *Partners of the Empire*, 212. Yaycioglu speculates that Mahmud himself 'signed on' to the document but all that is known for certain is that he visited the committee drawing up the document and thereby suggested his support for their work. See *Partners of the Empire*, 204.
108 Virginia Aksan, 'The Ottoman Absence from the Battlefields of the Seven Years' War', in *Writing the Ottomans into World History* (Istanbul: Isis Press, 2016), 271–93.
109 Barnes, *Introduction to Religious Foundations*, 56–9; Akarlı, '*Gedik*', 190–6.

Chapter 2

1 'The Ulu'l-amr (people of authority) have a great deal of right to make decisions on this kind of lands.' Akgündüz, *Osmanlı Kanunnâmeleri*, 7:664. Many scholars refer to limited or bounded spaces in the *fiqh* wherein temporal authority is given wide latitude to make decisions. See Hallaq, *Sharia Theory*, 361; Hallaq, *The Impossible State*, 63–9. Ahmet Akgündüz and Halil Cin specifically link the sultan's power to fill in the 'gaps' in the shari'a with the legitimacy of the land law; see Halil Cin, *Osmanlı Toprak Düzeni Ve Bu Düzenin Bozulması* (Ankara: Berikan Yayınevi, 2016), 4:32; Ahmet Akgündüz, *Osmanlı Kanunnâmeleri*, 1:45–55.
2 Taqī al-Dīn Ibn Taymiyya, *al-Siyāsā al-Shar'īyya fī Iṣlāḥ al-Rā'ī wa al-Ra'īyya.* ([Cairo], Egypt: Dār al-Kutub al-'Arabī bi-Miṣr, 1374 [1955]), 38–62.
3 Frank E. Vogel, *Islamic Law and Legal System: Studies of Saudi Arabia* (Leiden: Brill, 2000), 335. On Ibn Taymiyya and the scope of decision-making authority for rulers,

see Baber Johansen, 'A Perfect Law in an Imperfect Society: Ibn Taymiyya's Concept of "Governance in the Name of the Sacred Law"', in *The Law Applied: Contextualizing the Islamic Sharīʿa: A Volume in Honor of Frank E. Vogel*, ed. P. J. Bearman, Wolfhart Heinrichs and Bernard G. Weiss (London: I.B. Tauris, 2008), 259–94.

4 Guy Burak, 'Between the Ḳānūn of Qāytbāy and Ottoman Yasaq: A Note on the Ottomans' Dynastic Law', *Journal of Islamic Studies* 26, no. 1 (2015): 1–23. The question of how this law-making power intersected with the authority of the jurists was not a settled matter.

5 See Marion H. Katz, 'Pragmatic Rule and Personal Sanctification in Islamic Legal Theory', in *Law and the Sacred*, ed. Austin Sarat, Lawrence Douglas and Martha Merrill Umphrey (Stanford, CA: Stanford University Press, 2007), 93. Ibn Taymiyya's antipathy to the Mongol *yāsā*, from which he justified the claim that they were infidels and that it was licit to kill them, has often been seen as a reflection of his dislike for the Mongols. See Thomas Raff, *Remarks on an Anti-Mongol Fatwa by Ibn Taimiya* (Leiden: Brill, 1973). The position is consistent with his broader belief that only God can make lasting and unchallengeable laws that humans must obey.

6 Even the issue of what persons were eligible to receive funds from the treasury had some guidelines attached to it in the *fiqh*. There was general agreement that combatants were eligible, as were the ulema. For a detailed discussion of how Hanafi views on qualified recipients had evolved, see Muḥammad Amīn ibn ʿĀbidīn, *Ḥāshiyyat Ibn ʿĀbidīn Radd al-Muḥtār ʿalā al-Durr al-Mukhtār* (Beirut: Dār iḥyāʾ al-turath al-ʿarabī, 2010 [1431]), 6:265.

7 Ömer Lütfi Barkan, *Kanunlar*, *xli*; Barkan, 'Caractère Religieux et Caractère Séculier des Institutions Ottomanes', in *Contributions à l'histoire économique et sociale de l'empire ottoman*, ed. Jean-Louis Bacqué-Grammont and Paul Dumont (1983), 18–22; İnalcik, 'Islamization of Ottoman Laws', 106–7; Akgündüz, *Osmanlı Kanunnâmeleri*, 1:138–42; Imber, *Ebu's-Suʿud*, 36–7. However, Snjezana Buzov adamantly disagrees. Although she judges Ebu's-Suʿud to be sincere, she also gives another compelling reason to assign significance to his endeavours: the movement of *kanun* into texts generated by the ulema. See Buzov, 'The Lawgiver and His Lawmakers: The Role of Legal Discourse in the Change of Ottoman Imperial Culture' (PhD Diss., University of Chicago, 2005), 80, 96–100.

8 Lauren A. Benton, *A Search for Sovereignty: Law and Geography in European Empires, 1400–1900* (Cambridge: Cambridge University Press, 2010); Tamar Herzog, *Frontiers of Possession: Spain and Portugal in Europe and the Americas* (Cambridge, MA: Harvard University Press, 2015).

9 To name merely a few examples of this vast literature: Luke Clossey, 'Faith in Empire: Religious Sources of Legitimacy for Expansionist Early Modern States', in *Politics and Reformations: Communities, Polities, Nations, and Empires: Essays in Honor of Thomas A. Brady, Jr.*, ed. Christopher Ocker, Michael Printy, Peter Starenko and Peter Wallace (Boston, MA: Brill, 2007), 571–88; Paolo Prodi, *The Papal Prince, One Body and Two Souls: The Papal Monarchy in Early Modern Europe* (Cambridge: Cambridge University Press, 1987); David Parker, 'Sovereignty, Absolutism and the Function of the Law in Seventeenth-Century France', *Past & Present* no. 122 (1989): 36–74; A. London Fell, *Origins of Legislative Sovereignty and the Legislative State* (Cambridge, MA: Gunn & Hain, 1983), 4:239; Luc Foisneau, *Politique, Droit et théologie chez Bodin, Grotius et Hobbes* (Paris: Kimé, 1997); Daniel Engster, *Divine Sovereignty: The Origins of Modern State Power* (DeKalb: Northern Illinois University Press, 2001).

10 Gülru Necipoğlu, 'Süleyman the Magnificent and the Representation of Power in the Context of Ottoman-Hapsburg-Papal Rivalry', *The Art Bulletin* 71, no. 3 (1989): 401–27; Cornell Fleischer, 'The Lawgiver as Messiah: The Making of the Imperial Image in the Reign of Süleymân', in *Soliman Le Magnifique Et Son Temps: Actes Du Colloque De Paris Galeries Nationales Du Grand Palais 7–10 Mars 1990/Süleymân the Magnificent and His Time: Acts of the Parisian Conference Galeries Nationales Du Grand Palais 7–10 March 1990*, ed. Gilles Veinstein (Paris: Documentation Française, 1992), 159–77; Kathryn Babayan, *Mystics, Monarchs, and Messiahs: Cultural Landscapes of Early Modern Iran* (Cambridge, MA: Harvard University Press, 2002); Sanjay Subrahmanyam, 'Turning the Stones Over: Sixteenth-Century Millenarianism from the Tagus to the Ganges', *Indian Economic & Social History Review* 40, no. 2 (2003): 129–61; Eva Orthmann, 'Court Culture and Cosmology in the Mughal Empire: Humāyūn and the Foundations of the Dīn-I Ilāhī', in *Court Cultures in the Muslim World: Seventh to Nineteenth Centuries*, ed. Jan-Peter Hartung and Albrecht Fuess (Abingdon: Routledge, 2011), 202–20; A. Azfar Moin, *The Millennial Sovereign: Sacred Kingship and Sainthood in Islam* (Columbia University Press, 2012); Kaya Şahin, *Empire and Power in the Reign of Süleyman: Narrating the Sixteenth-Century Ottoman World* (Cambridge: Cambridge University Press, 2013), 186–213; Hüseyin Yılmaz, *Caliphate Redefined: The Mystical Turn in Ottoman Political Thought* (Princeton, NJ: Princeton University Press, 2018); Christopher Markiewicz, *The Crisis of Kingship in Late Medieval Islam: Persian Emigres and the Making of Ottoman Sovereignty* (New York: Cambridge University Press, 2019).

11 Anderson considers the revival of Roman law, with its concept of property as a civil matter and its public legal authority concentrated in the emperor, as crucial for Europe's legal development. See Perry Anderson, *Lineages of the Absolutist State* (New York: Verso, 2013), 28. For other appraisals, see Gerald Strauss, *Law, Resistance, and the State: The Opposition to Roman Law in Reformation Germany* (Princeton, NJ: Princeton University Press, 1986); Benjamin Straumann, 'Early Modern Sovereignty and Its Limits', *Theoretical Inquiries in Law* 16, no. 2 (2015): 423–46. More recently scholars have taken an interest in the revival's relation to colonial rule, see A. Fitzmaurice, *Sovereignty, Property and Empire, 1500–2000* (Cambridge: Cambridge University Press, 2014).

12 Many of these, such as Cardinal Wolsey of England and Cardinals Richelieu and Mazarin of France, are so well known in the countries where they served that their names are familiar to the general public, just as Ebu's-Su'ud's name is widely known today in Turkey. See Joseph Bergin, *The Politics of Religion in Early Modern France* (New Haven, CT: Yale University Press, 2014), 15; C. V. Wedgwood, *Richelieu and the French Monarchy* (London: Hodder & Stoughton Ltd., 1949); Patrick J. Hornbeck II, *Remembering Wolsey: A History of Commemorations and Representations* (New York: Fordham University Press, 2019). For the papacy as a new model of 'absolutist' rule see Prodi, *The Papal Prince* and Harold J. Berman, *Law and Revolution: The Formation of the Western Legal Tradition* (Cambridge, MA: Harvard University Press, 1983).

13 Fleischer, *Bureaucrat and Intellectual*, 34–6; Christine Woodhead, 'Scribal Chaos? Observations on the Post of Re'isülküttab in the Late Sixteenth Century', in *The Ottoman Empire: Myths, Realities, and Black Holes Contributions in Honor of Colin Imber*, ed. E. Kermeli and O. Özel (Istanbul: Isis Press, 2006), 156, n. 3.

14 Hüseyin Yılmaz, 'Containing Sultanic Authority: Constitutionalism in the Ottoman Empire before Modernity', *Osmanli Arastirmalari/Journal of Ottoman Studies* 45 (2015): 231–64; and Şahin, *Empire and Power*, 28–30 and 216–17.
15 Ferguson, *Proper Order of Things*, 276.
16 This is the term used by Abdurrahman Atçıl in his study of the formation of the *ilmiye*. See Atçıl, *Scholars and Sultans*. Earlier works charting the functions and formation of the *ilmiye* have also focused on its highly hierarchical, bureaucratic character. For example, see Ismail Hakkı Uzunçarşılı *Osmanlı Devletinin Ilmiye Teşkilâtı* 3. Baskı ed. (Ankara: Türk Tarih Kurumu Basımevi, 1988) and Repp, *Müfti of Istanbul*.
17 Repp, *Müfti of Istanbul*, 297–304.
18 However, reflecting the views of the mid-twentieth century, Barkan and Repp both doubted that a 'religious' official like the *şeyhülislam* would have been requested to make detailed explanations of land tenure law that were incorporated in *kanunnames*. They believed that Ebu's-Su 'ud must have held a chancellery position when he wrote the statements that appear in kanunnames for Budin and Thessaloniki and Skopje. See Barkan, *Kanunlar, xxiv-xlii, l-liii*; Richard Repp, 'Qānūn and Sharī'a in the Ottoman Context', in *Islamic Law: Social and Historical Contexts*, ed. Aziz Al-Azmeh (London: Routledge, 1988), 132–6.
19 Descriptions of the specifically Hanafi approach to land classification and tax before the Ottoman period can be found in Hossein Modarressi Tabataba'i, *Kharāj in Islamic Law* (London: Anchor Press, 1983), 109–12 and Baber Johansen, *Islamic Law on Land Tax and Rent: The Peasants' Loss of Property Rights as Interpreted in the Hanafite Legal Literature of the Mamluk and Ottoman Periods* (London: Croom Helm, 1988), 8, 7–12. Many works that present an overview of the subject fail to recognize the differences between the pre- and non-Ottoman Hanafis and the other Sunni schools on these issues, for example Ziaul Haque, *Landlord and Peasant in Early Islam: A Study of the Legal Doctrine of Muzara'a or Share Cropping* (Islamabad: Islamic Research Institute, 1977), 188–98.
20 Imber, *Ebu's-Su'ud*, 116–17; Modarressi Tabataba'i, *Kharāj in Islamic Law* (London: Anchor Press, 1983), 187–8; Løkkegaard, *Islamic Taxation in the Classic Period*, 72.
21 Johansen, *Islamic Law on Land Tax and Rent*, 8, noted that this does not seem to be well understood. What he fails to mention is that the confusion is attributable in part to the shift of the Ottoman Hanafis on this question, for Ebu's-Su'ud was to create an option that did not require the land to become milk, and this position would be adopted as the doctrine of the school.
22 Halil Inalcik's understanding of the *waqf*-like character of *kharaji* land is explicitly influenced by al-Shāfi'ī, see Inalcik, *Islam Arazi ve Vergi Sisteminin Tesekkülü Ve Osmanlı Devrindeki Şekillerle Mukayesesi* (Istanbul: Osman Yalçın Matbaası, 1959), 5.
23 Johansen, *Islamic Law on Land Tax and Rent*, 11.
24 A. Ben Shemesh, ed., *Taxation in Islam. Volume III: Abū Yūsuf's Kitāb al-Kharāj* (Leiden: E. J. Brill, 1969).
25 Barnes wrote that Abu Yusuf does sound as though he considers the land more like a *waqf* than freehold, even if the Hanafi school insisted it was the latter. See Barnes, *Introduction to Religious Foundations*, 26–8. Other scholars have tried to understand 'Umar's actions and to what extent they instituted a new practice of landholding; see Løkkegaard, *Islamic Taxation*, 18–19, 31–7; Ziaul Haque, *Landlord and Peasant*, 129–31; 189–92; Ali Abd al-Kader, 'Land, Property and Land Tenure in Islamic Law',

The Islamic Quarterly 5, no. 1 (1959): 9; Modarressi Tabataba'i, *Kharāj in Islamic Law*, 78–93.

26 Johansen, *Islamic Law on Land Tax and Rent*, 82–5.

27 See, for example Fakhr al-Dīn Qāḍīkhān al-Uzjandī al-Farghānī, *Fatāwā Qāḍīkhān fī Madhhab al-Imām al-A'zam Abī Ḥanīfah Al-Nu'mān*, ed. Sālim Mustafa al-Badrī (Beirut: Dār al-Kutub al-'Ilmiyya, 2009), 3:536.

28 Ibn al-'Alā' al-Anṣārī, *al-Fatāwā al-Tātārkhāniyya*, 5:424.

29 The work in question is Ibn al-Humām, *Sharḥ Fatḥ al-Qadīr* (Cairo: 1356 H) 4: 362.

30 Johansen, *Islamic Law on Land Tax and Rent*, 84–5.

31 Johansen, *Islamic Law on Land Tax and Rent*, 81. Mundy, 'Ownership or Office?', 142–65; Johansen, 'Can the Law Decide?', i 143–64.

32 Johansen, *Islamic Law on Land Tax and Rent*, 85–93 and Kenneth Cuno, 'Was the Land of Ottoman Syria Miri or Milk? An Examination of Juridical Differences within the Hanafi School', *Studia Islamica* 81 (1995): 121–52.

33 Even though some seventeenth-century Rumi ulema were clearly familiar with Ibn al-Humām's work, none of them invokes him when discussing land in the treasury. One might tentatively say that this continued into the eighteenth and nineteenth centuries among the Rumis; the late-eighteenth-century mufti of Erzurum, 'Abdurrahman Efendi, mentioned *Fatawa Qadikhan* and *al-Fatawa al-Tatarkhaniyya* frequently in his fatwas, but not the Egyptians Ibn Nujaym and Ibn al-Humām. See 'Abdurraḥmān Efendi el-Erzurumī, *Sefînetü'l-Fetāvā*, SYK H. Hüsnü Paşa 332, 398–414.

34 Imber, *Ebu's-Su'ud*, 120.

35 MTM 57–8.

36 Although it is unclear exactly when the practice of claiming new land for the *bayt al-mal* was initiated as an administrative practice, it was documented as part of legal and administrative procedure no later than its adoption in the *Kanunname of Budin* (see Chapter 1).

37 In fact, the dominant concern of the jurists in their discussions of treasury land was what actions the sultan could take to pursue his valid entitlement to the land's *kharaj*. See Qāḍīkhān, *Fatāwā Qāḍīkhān*, 3:536; Ibn al-Bazzaz, *al-Fatāwā al-Bazzāziyya*, 1:83; Farīd al-Dīn 'Ālim ibn 'Alā' al-Anṣārī, *al-Fatāwā al-Tātārkhāniyya*, ed. Sajjad Ḥusayn (Karātshī, Bākistān: Idārat al-Qur'ān wa-al-'Ulūm al-Islāmīyah, 2003), 5:424–5.

38 For the Hanafis, *kharaj* was a burden due from the land whether or not the land was kept cultivated. Failure to pay was one of the primary means through which lands entered the custody of the treasury: if a proprietor was unable or unwilling to pay the tax, the imam could confiscate the land and allow another to work it to pay the *kharaj*. See Modarressi Tabataba'i, *Kharaj in Islamic Law*, 94–5; see also the citations in the note earlier, which affirm this understanding.

39 See note 8.

40 For example Inalcik, 'Islamization of Ottoman Laws', 106–7 and Greene, 'An Islamic Experiment?': 64.

41 See, for example, Muḥammad Amīn ibn 'Ābidīn, *Ḥāshiyyat Ibn 'Ābidīn Radd al-Muḥtār 'alā al-Durr al-Mukhtār* (Beirut: Dār iḥyā' al-turath al-'arabī, 2010/1431), 6:224; Zayn al-'Ābidīn Ibrahīm Ibn Nujaym, 'al-Tuḥfa al-Marḍiyya fī al-Arāḍī al-Miṣriyya', in *Rasā'il Ibn Nujaym*, ed. Khalīl al-Mays (Beirut: Dār al-Kutub al-'Ilmiyya, 1980), 51.

42 One of the more detailed treatments of the subject is that of 'Alim ibn 'Ala' al-Ansari, who nevertheless is quite brief. See al-Anṣārī, *al-Fatāwā al-Tātārkhāniyya*, 5:424–5.

43 For a discussion of the positions of important Hanafis on the issue, see Ibn 'Abidīn, *Radd Al-Muḥtār*, 6:224.
44 Johansen, *The Islamic Law on Land Tax*, 11.
45 MTM 51.
46 MTM 53.
47 MTM 57.
48 Ibn al-Bazzāz, *al-Fatāwā al-Bazzāziyya*, 1:83.
49 Al-Anṣārī, *al-Fatāwā al-Tātārkhāniyya*, 5:424.
50 Johansen, *Islamic Law on Land Tax*, 66. The most influential text crediting Qadikhan with establishing the rule that a ten-year period of residence proves occupancy is Ṣādiq Muḥammad Sāqizī, 'Ṣurrat al-Fatāwā', PDL, 180b.
51 Ibn 'Abidin traces this doctrine to *Qunyat al-Munya li-Tatmim al-Ghunya* by Najm al-Din al-Zahidi al-Ghazmini (d. 1260). See Ibn 'Ābidīn, 'Taḥrīr al-'Ibāra fīman huwwa awlā bi'l-Ijāra', in *Majmu'at Rasā'il Ibn 'Ābidīn*, ed. Muḥammad 'Azāzī (Beirut: Dār al-Kutub al-'Ilmiyya, 1971), 2: 207.
52 This formulation of *kirdar* had crystallized no later than the fifteenth century, in the *Jami' al-Fusulayn* of Badr al-Din Mahmud b. Qadi Simawna. See Kaya, *Osmanli Hukukunda Icâreteyn*, 52; and also Muḥammad Amīn Ibn 'Ābidīn, *al-'Uqūd al-Durriyya fī Tanqīḥ al-Fatāwā al-Ḥāmidiyya* (Dār al-Kutub al-'Ilmiyya, 2008), 2:345–6; Muḥammad Amīn ibn 'Umar, 'Taḥrīr al-'Ibāra Fīman Huwwa Awlā Bi'l-Ijāra', in *Majmū'at Rasā'il Ibn 'Ābidīn*, ed. Muḥammad 'Azāzī, 2: 214–15 (Beirut: Dar al-Kotob al-Ilmiyah, 2014).
53 '*Ẓahīrü'l-Ḳuḍāt*', Akgündüz, *Osmanlı Kanunnameler*, 9: 425, 426.
54 Baber Johansen was struck by the way that the Central Asian custom of renting without a lease eventually supplanted the dominant understanding in the Hanafi school that a lease was a necessary condition of a valid rental. See Johansen, 'Coutumes locales et coutumes universelles aux sources des règles juridiques en droit Musulman Hanéfite', in *Contingency in a Sacred Law: Legal and Ethical Norms in the Muslim Fiqh* (Boston, MA: Brill, 1999), 163–71.
55 Of these, it was what Inalcik terms the 'general *kanunnames*' that dealt most explicitly with property rights of the cultivators. Such *kanunnames* were issued in the reigns of Bayezid II (r. 1481–1512) and Selim I (r. 1512–1520); see Inalcik, 'Ḳānūnnāme', EI^2, 565. Another such *kanunname* is attributed to Mehmed II, but is thought to be a later compilation dating either to the sixteenth or even the seventeenth century; see Baki Tezcan, 'The "Kânûnnâme of Mehmed II": A Different Perspective', in *The Great Ottoman-Turkish Civilisation Vol. 3 Philosophy, Science and Institutions*, ed. Kemal Çiçek (Ankara: Yeni Türkiye, 2000), 657–65. Süleyman was to issue more than one general *kanunname*, and the first may have been issued as early as 1523 according to Akgündüz, *Osmanlı Kanunnâmeleri*, 4:294. Although there were a number of *kanunnames* made for specific provinces by this time – with many examples published in Barkan, *Kanunlar* and Akgündüz, *Osmanlı Kanunnâmeleri* – relatively few of them dealt with tenure and transactions; the majority were focused solely on taxation.
56 Anton Minkov, 'Ottoman Tapu Title Deeds in the Eighteenth and Nineteenth Centuries: Origin, Typology and Diplomatics', *Islamic Law and Society* 7, no. 1 (2000): 65–101; Suraiya Faroqhi, 'Land Transfer, Land Disputes and Askeri Holdings in Ankara (1592–1600)', in *Mémorial Omer Lutfi Barkan* (Paris: Librairie d'Amérique et d'Orient, 1980), 87–100.
57 MTM 56–7.
58 See MTM 51, 52, 53.

59 See Chapter 4, pp. 84–5 and Chapter 5, pp. 95–6.
60 In '*al-Tuḥfa al-Marḍiyya fī'l-Arāḍī al-Miṣriyya*', Ibn Nujaym explains that the lands have escheated to the treasury. Thereafter, the sultan as their custodian is able to sell them, and hence all the *waqf*s of Egypt and all the land held by individuals as *milk* was legally sold to them by the sultan from treasury land. More so than Ebu's-Su'ud, he argued that after the land entered the treasury, it lost its *kharaji* status. Thus, after the sultan sold it, it could not become *kharaji* a second time, meaning that no tax whatsoever is owed on it. His ultimate conclusion was that no one in fact owed taxes on the land: the peasants who farm it pay rent. Ibn Nujaym, Zayn al-'Ābidīn Ibrāhīm, '*Al-Tuḥfa al-Marḍiyya fī'l-Arāḍī al-Miṣriyya*', in *Rasā'il Ibn Nujaym*, ed. Khalīl al-Mays (Beirut: Dār al-Kutub al-'Ilmiyya, 1980), 50–64 (esp. 54).
61 For Ebu's-Su'ud's grappling with these questions, see Mundy, 'Ownership or Office?', 163–4.
62 Rates on grain-producing land were typically either an eighth or a fifth of the harvest; see Inalcik, 'Islamization', 110.
63 Ferguson, *The Proper Order of Things*, 132.
64 Heyd and Ménage, *Studies in Old Ottoman Criminal Law*, 183–7; Peters, 'What Does It Mean?', 151–3.
65 Imber, *Ebu's-Su'ud*, 45; Ferguson, *The Proper Order of Things*, 87–90.
66 Akgündüz, *Osmanlı Kanunnâmeleri*, 2:48.
67 Bālīzādah Muṣṭafā b. Sulaymān, '*Mīzān al-Fatāwā*', SYK Yenicami 675, 30a.
68 A term that in Turkish typically means temporal authority; it is derived from a term in Arabic that is typically rendered as custom, but has a broader sense of something that is widely acknowledged as correct practice. See discussion of this term in the context of jurisprudence, p. 72, Chapter 4. For its significance in Ottoman legal usage see Halil Inalcik, 'Osmanlı Hukukuna Giriş: Örfi-Sultani Hukuk Ve Fatih'in Kanunları', *Ankara Üniversitesi SBF Dergisi* 13, no. 2 (1958): 102–26.
69 '*Bayezid Kanunnamesi*', Akgündüz, *Osmanlı Kanunnâmeleri*, 2:66.
70 This exception occurs in the *Kanunname of Candia*, discussed in chap. 4.
71 Yunus Koç argues that sultans had a great deal of authority to change specific taxation rates or practices, although he notes that sultans did this typically in response to complaints lodged by peasants; when they did so they justified the change on the grounds that the old practice had not been in conformity with the shari'a or with the *kanun*, or both. See Yunus Koç, 'Early Ottoman Customary Law: The Genesis and Development of Ottoman Codification', in *Shattering Tradition: Custom, Law and the Individual in the Muslim Mediterranean*, ed. Walter. Dostal and Wolfgang Kraus (London: I.B. Tauris, 2005), 105–7.
72 MTM 50.
73 In Karaman, brothers in *musha'* holdings could take the share of a deceased brother. See Ö. L. Barkan, *XV ve XVI Incı Asırlarda Osmanlı Imparatorluğund Ziraı Ekonominin Hukuki Ve Malî Esasları*. Vol. 1, *Kanunlar* (Istanbul: Bürhaneddin Matbaası, 1943), 46. In this case, the brother may have been living in a joint-family household with his deceased brother, a pattern that Kenneth Cuno has identified among more prosperous landholding families in Ottoman Egypt where the same order of succession was favoured. See Cuno, *The Pasha's Peasants*, 74; and Kenneth Cuno, 'Joint Family Households and Rural Notables in 19th-Century Egypt', *International Journal of Middle East Studies* 27, no. 4 (1995): 491–3. In Izvornik, the deceased's full or paternal half-brother was recognized as heir if there were

no surviving son, and he was able to pay the *tapu* due. See Akgündüz, *Osmanlı Kanunnâmeleri*, 5:302.

74 "*Zahīrü'l-Kudat*," Akgündüz, *Osmanlı Kanunnameler*, 4:309. The same prohibition appears in Bayezid II's *kanunname*, ibid., 2:67.

75 Ibn al-Bazazz states specifically that the imam entrusts a man (*rajul*) with the care of treasury land. See Ibn al-Bazzāz, *al-Fatāwā al-Bazzāziyya*, 1:83. The mufti of Skopje, Pir Mehmed (d. 1611), was not categorical that men should prevail over women, but wrote that when the deputy has a choice between men and women, that 'the rules favor men'. See Akgündüz, *Osmanlı Kanunnâmeleri*, 9:400. The Syrian muftis were, with few exceptions, unanimously against female inclusion in *tasarruf* until the eighteenth century. See Malissa Taylor, 'Keeping Usufruct in the Family. Popular and Juridical Interpretations of Ottoman Land Tenure Law in Damascus', *Bulletin d'Études Orientales* 61, 'Damas médiévale et ottomane' (2012): 429–43. Kenneth Cuno has demonstrated that in eighteenth-century Egypt, a woman would inherit *tasarruf* only if there was no 'capable' male left in the household. See Cuno, *The Pasha's Peasants*, 74–5. In Egypt, the trend towards favouring men and excluding women gained ground in the nineteenth century under the muftiship of Muhammad al-Mahdi al-Abbasi. See Muḥammad al- 'Abbāsī al-Mahdī al-Miṣrī, *al-Fatāwā al-Mahdīyya fī al-Waqā'i' al-Miṣriyya* ([al-Qahira]: Dār al-kutub wa al-wathā'iq al-qawmīyya bi'l-Qāhira, 2015), 4:10, 129.

76 Compare MTM 50, with al-Anṣārī, *Fatāwā Tātārkhāniyya*, 5:424–26, and Ibn Nujaym, '*Al-Tuḥfa al-Marḍiyya*', 53.

77 MTM 66. See also Barkan, *Türk Toprak Hukuku*, 25.

78 The *Ma'ruzat* are legal questions that were reportedly put before Süleyman by Ebu's-Su'ud for him to resolve. Scholars are not entirely sure if Suleyman's involvement is in fact apocryphal. In any case, the text proclaims that it was drawn up for one of Süleyman's successors, so it may contain legal decisions that postdate the reign of Süleyman. On this text see Heyd, *Criminal Law*, 183–5; Repp, 'Qānūn and Sharī'a', 136–8; and Haim Gerber, *State, Society, and Law in Islam: Ottoman Law in Comparative Perspective* (Albany: State University of New York Press, 1994), 88–92.

79 Such is the case in *irth*, or inheritance rules of the *fiqh*. Moreover, both Süleyman's *kanunname* and fatwas from the sixteenth and seventeenth century show that women did come forward to demand what they saw as their rightful inheritance after the father's death. It is not clear that this was the case of the Christians of the Balkans and Greece. In the Cyclades, Kasdagli writes that male offspring inherited paternal property, while females inherited maternal property. See Aglaia E. Kasdagli, 'Family and Inheritance in the Cyclades, 1500–1800: Present Knowledge and Unanswered Questions', *History of the Family* 9, no. 3 (2004): 270.

80 This petition is preserved in the *Kanun-ı Cedid*, MTM 68, and was adopted in the *Kanunname of Izvornik and Srebrinica*, believed to date roughly to the same time. See Akgündüz, *Osmanlı Kanunnâmeleri*, 5:302. It would also be incorporated into an important work of jurisprudence in the seventeenth century. See 'Alā' al-Dīn al-Ḥaṣkāfī, *al-Durr al-Muntaqā*, printed on the margin of 'Abd al-Raḥmān ibn Muḥammad Shaykhzādah, *Majma' al-anhur fī sharḥ multaqā'l-abḥur* (Beirut: Dār al-Ma'rifa, 1960), 1:665.

81 Alan Duben, 'Turkish Families and Households in Historical Perspective', *Journal of Family History* Spring (1985): 83–4; Kenneth Cuno speculates that joint-family household patterns in Egypt emerged among families with large holdings precisely to raise the chances that a male heir would be produced in each generation and thus prohibit the break-up of the holding. See Cuno, 'Joint Family Households and Rural

Notables in 19th-Century Egypt', *International Journal of Middle East Studies* 27, no. 4 (1995): 492–3.

82 Making law that need not rely on time-honoured practice for legitimacy is often considered a key characteristic of legislative sovereignty, see Dieter Grimm, *Sovereignty: The Origin and Future of a Political and Legal Concept*, trans. Belinda Cooper (New York: Columbia University Press, 2015), 17.

83 For instance, the addition of the deceased's sister to the line of transmission, the conditions of residence attached to her succession and then the later modifications made with regard to residence were recorded in the *Kanun-ı Cedid* as responses to petitions submitted in 1594 and 1632 or 1633. See MTM 71.

84 Roughly a quarter of the *Kanun-ı Cedid* deals with post-mortem transmission questions, see MTM, 61–80. Female *mutasarrifs* could only be succeeded by a son, MTM 63–4.

85 MTM, 62–3.

86 Beshara Doumani has written of family *waqfs* as family charters. Of the endowment charters in Ottoman Tripoli he has written that 'Taken together, these choices express, among other things, the endower's vision of what constituted family, how it should be reproduced, and its proper place in the material and spiritual worlds.' See Doumani, *Family Life in the Ottoman Empire: A Social History* (Cambridge: Cambridge University Press, 2017), 104. The dynasty, through its regulation of access to *miri* land, appeared to be doing much the same thing.

87 I intentionally use the terminology of Wael Hallaq and Brinkley Messick to describe this passage from the specific to the general, or what Messick terms from the 'archive' to the 'library'. Throughout, my point is that the Hanafi jurists did not conceive of a sultan having the latter kind of power. On 'stripping' see Wael B. Hallaq, 'From Fatwās to Furū': Growth and Change in Islamic Substantive Law', Islamic Law and Society 1, no. 1 (1994): 44–5; Brinkley Morris Messick, *Sharīa Scripts: An Historical Anthropology* (New York: Columbia University Press, 2018), 171–3.

88 MTM, 53.

89 Barbara Arneil, *John Locke and America. The Defense of English Colonialism* (Oxford: Oxford University Press 1996); Herzog, *Frontiers of Possession*, and Herzog, 'Did European Law Turn American? Territory, Property and Rights in an Atlantic World', in *New Horizons in Spanish Colonial Law: Contributions to Transnational Early Modern Legal History*, ed. Thomas Duve and Heikki Pihlajamäki, *Global Perspectives on Legal History*, vol. 3 (Frankfurt am Main: Max Planck Institute for European Legal History, 2015), 76; Kathleen Davis, *Periodization and Sovereignty: How Ideas of Feudalism and Secularization Govern the Politics of Time* (Philadelphia: University of Pennsylvania Press, 2008), 57–8.

90 Herzog, 'Did European Law Turn American?', 88.

91 An example of the latter are the fees and prohibitions related to marriage. See Meshal, 'Antagonistic Sharī'as': 197–201. See also Samy Ayoub, 'The Sultan Says: State Authority in the Late Hanafi Tradition', *Islamic Law and Society* 23, no. 3 (2016): 239–78; and Baldwin, *Islamic Law*, 72–98.

Chapter 3

1 Halil Inalcik, 'Ḳānūnnāme', EI[2], 565–6; Inalcik, 'Islamization', 115–16; Imber, *Ebu's-Su'ud*, 51.

2 There were some dissenters, as we have already seen in the case of Mehmed Birgevi. Another example of a dissenter is Vani Mehmed Efendi (d. 1685), the mufti of Erzurum, whose fatwas will be examined in this chapter.
3 Muḥammad Amīn ibn 'Ābidīn, *Al-'Uqūd al-Durriyya fī Tanqīḥ al-Fatāwā al-Ḥāmidiyya*, ed. Muḥammad 'Uthmān (Beirut: Dār al-Kutub al-'Ilmiyya, 2008), 2:358: '*mabniyyatun 'ala awamira sultaniyyatin*'.
4 Barkan, *Kanunlar*, xxxix; Uriel Heyd and V. L. Ménage, *Studies in Old Ottoman Criminal Law* (Oxford: Clarendon Press, 1973), 187–90; M. Macit Kenanoğlu, 'Osmanlı Devleti'nde Kanun-Fetva Ilişkisi Ve Örfi Fetva Kavramı', in *Osmanlı Hukukunda Fetva*, ed. Süleyman Kaya, Yunus Uğur, and Mustafa Demiray (Istanbul: Klasik, 2018), 111–48.
5 Scholarly analysis of this phenomenon has changed considerably over the years as a result of the re-examination of the 'decline' thesis. For important contributions see Ferguson, *The Proper Order of Things*, 258–76; Baki Tezcan, 'Law in China or Conquest in the Americas: Competing Constructions of Political Space in the Early Modern Ottoman Empire', *Journal of World History* 24, no. 1 (2013): 107–34; Ali Abou-El-Haj, 'Power and Social Order', 77–102; Fleischer, *Bureaucrat and Intellectual*, 191–200; Howard, 'Ottoman Historiography': 52–77; Pál Fodor, 'State and Society, Crisis and Reform, in 15th–17th Century Ottoman Mirror for Princes', *Acta Orientalia Academiae Scientiarum Hungaricae* 40, no. 2/3 (1986): 217–40; Bernard Lewis, 'Ottoman Observers of Ottoman Decline', *Islamic Studies* 1, no. 1 (1962): 71–87.
6 Akgündüz, 'Kanûnnâme Padishahi', *Osmanlı Kanûnnâmeleri*, 9: 491–535; Ayn-i Ali, *Kavânîn-i Âl-i Osman der hülâsa-i mezâmin-i defter-i dîvân*, ed. M. Tayyib Gökbilgin (Istanbul: Enderun Kitabevi, 1979); Robert Anhegger, 'Hezarfen Hüseyin Efendi'nin Osmanlı Devlet Teşkilâtına Dâir Mülâhazaları', *Tükiyat Mecmuası* x, no. 1951–3 (1953): 365–93 and Hezarfen Hüseyin Efendi, *Telhîsü'l-beyân fî kavânîn-i Âl-i Osmân*, ed. Sevim Ilgürel (Ankara: Türk Tarih Kurumu Basımevi1998); Eyyubî Efendi, *Eyyubî Efendi Kānûnâmesi: Tahlil ve Metin*, ed. Abdülkadir Özcan (İstanbul: İstanbul Üniversitesi Kütüphane, 1994); and Akgündüz, 'Aziz Efendi Kanûnnâmesi', *Osmanlı Kanûnnâmeleri*, 10:181–219.
7 Uriel Heyd, *Studies in Old Ottoman Criminal Law*, ed. V. L. Ménage (Oxford: Clarendon Press, 1973), 216; Başak Tuğ, *Politics of Honor: Sexual Violence and Socio-Legal Surveillance in the Eighteenth Century* (Leiden: Brill, 2017), 63–4.
8 Barkan, *Kanunlar*, xxxix–xl; Repp, 'Qānūn and Sharī'a', 126–7; Akgündüz, *Osmanlı Kanûnnâmeleri*, 11:39.
9 Fleischer, *Bureaucrat and Intellectual*, 227. For the role of *nişancı* and its evolution in the bureaucracy, see Christine Woodhead, 'After Celalzade: The Ottoman Nişancı c. 1560–1700', in *Studies in Islamic Law: A Festschrift for Colin Imber*, ed. Andreas Christmann and Robert Gleave (Oxford: Oxford University Press, 2007), 295–312.
10 For instance, the *Kanun-ı Cedid* inscribes the *kanunname* made by the *nişancı* Okçuzade Şah Mehmed Efendi (d. 1630) in its entirety. Okçuzade served as *nişancı* five times from 1599 to 1623 or 1624. For his life and career, see Christine Woodhead, 'Ottoman Inşa and the Art of Letter-Writing: Influences upon the Career of the Nişancı and Prose Stylist Okçuzade (d. 1630)', *Osmanlı Araştırmaları* VII–VIII (1988): 143–59.
11 Rhoads Murphey interprets the issuing of this *kanunname* as a gesture of establishing sovereignty during the reign of Ahmed I, who was more inclined to pursue peace than wage war. See Murphey, 'Continuity and Discontinuity in Ottoman Administrative Theory and Practice during the Late Seventeenth Century', *Poetics Today* 14, no.

2 (1993): 425. The preamble of the *Kanunname of Ahmed Khan* suggests that the first version of this text was completed on 16 February 1609. Extant copies include material from much later in the seventeenth century, including the work of Baha'i Efendi and Yahya Efendi. See '*Ḳānūnnāme-yi Aḥmed Han*', SYK Esad Ef. 851/3, f. 54–69.

12 For instance, the *Mu'allimzade Kanunnamesi* is named for Mu'allimzade Mahmud Çelebi (d. 1579), who served as *nişancı* for a year between 1576 and 1577; see Ismail Hami Danışmend, *Izahlı Osmanlı Tarihi Kronolojisi* (Istanbul: Türkiye Yayınevi, 1971), 599. Nevertheless, the text contains numerous *firmans* dated to the 1580s. The copy SYK Lala Ismail 109 is dated 1017 AH (1608 or 1609).

13 Barkan, *Kanunlar, xxvii.*

14 Mundy and Smith, *Governing Property*, 246, n. 20.

15 Burak, *Second Formation*, 41, 135–9; Yavuz Aykan, 'From the Hanafi Doxa to the Mecelle: The Mufti of Amid and Genealogies of the Ottoman Jurisprudential Tradition', in *Forms and Institutions of Justice: Legal Actions in Ottoman Contexts* (Istanbul: Institut français d'études anatoliennes, 2018).

16 Woodhead, 'After Celalzade', 297–9. Inalcik viewed the transfer of authority over land issues as moving from the *nişancı* to the şeyhülislam in the reign of Ahmed I (1603–17). See Inalcik, 'Ḳānūnnāme', EI[2], 566.

17 Woodhead, ibid.; Inalcik, ibid.; Barkan, *Kanunlar*, xvii, xix.

18 Burak, *The Second Formation*, chapters 1 and 2; Burak, 'According to His Exalted Ḳânûn: Contending Visions of the Muftiship in the Ottoman Province of Damascus (Sixteenth-Eighteenth Centuries)', in *Society, Law, and Culture in the Middle East: 'Modernities' in the Making*, ed. Dror Ze'evi and Ehud Toledano (Warsaw: De Gruyter Open Ltd, 2015), 74–86; Atçıl, *Scholars and Sultans*, 5–8; Richard Repp, 'The Altered Nature and Role of the Ulema', in *Studies in Eighteenth Century Islamic History*, ed. Thomas Naff and Roger Owen (Carbondale: Southern Illinois University Press, 1977), 277–87.

19 Heyd wrote that the *şeyhülislam* 'possessed, and often used, the right to issue a fetvā declaring a certain firman or kanun invalid because it was contrary to the shari'a', see Heyd, *Studies in Old Ottoman Criminal Law*, 186–7. In matters of land tenure, however, I have never seen a fatwa issued by a *şeyhülislam* that does this. When the *şeyhülislam* departed from the plain meaning of a *kanun* or an earlier *şeyhülislam*'s ruling, he did not draw attention to the departure.

20 Yılmaz, 'Containing Sultanic Authority': 247.

21 The format of the *Kanun-ı Cedid* has moved several historians to state that even though fatwas may be contained in a *kanunname*, these fatwas did not attain the legal weight of *kanun* as issued by the sultan. See Barkan, *Kanunlar, xxiv-xlii, l-liii* and Repp, 'Qānūn and Sharī'a', 133–5.

22 There is some discrepancy among the biographers about his floruit; see Şükrü Özen, 'Pîr Mehmed Üskübî', TDVIA.

23 The most influential of these is *Mu'inü'l-müfti fi'l-cevab ale'l-müstefti*; for copies see Şükrü Özen, 'Osmanlı Dönemi Fetva Literatürü', *Türkiye Araştırmaları Literatür Dergisi* 3, no. 5 (2005): 307.

24 Published in Akgündüz, *Osmanlı Kanunnâmeleri*, 9:394–483; at least three manuscript copies exist: SYK Esad Efendi 852; SYK Esad Efendi 587, 129b–173a and SYK Lala Ismail 106, 113b–173a.

25 Uriel Heyd, 'Some Aspects of the Ottoman Fetvā', BSOAS 32, no. 1 (1969): 46. The sultan's order to the mufti of Balıkesir, dated 1594, claims that it is ordering the

resumption of long-standing precedent, that is that provincial muftis were to show their reasoning and cite authorities for their decisions in their fatwas.

26 '*Arāżī-yi Harāciye ve öşriye ḥaḳḳında ḳānūn ve fetvālar*', SYK Bağdatlı Vehbi 569, 1–64.

27 Since fatwas deal with the hypothetical rather than the particular, the question uses particular names as part of its legal formulation. 'Zayd' is male person 1, while "Amr' is male person 2, and 'Hind' is female person 1.

28 Ibid., 15b.

29 Quran, 4:59.

30 '*Ẓahīrü'l-Ḳuḍāt*', Akgündüz, *Osmanlı Kanunnameler*, 9:396.

31 Ibid., 9:397. The mufti's incorporation of administrative documents into his decision-making process supports recent work arguing that an 'archival consciousness' was visible in Ottoman administrative process from the seventeenth century. See Guy Burak, '"In Compliance with the Old Register": On Ottoman Documentary Depositories and Archival Consciousness', *Journal of the Economic and Social History of the Orient2* 62, nos. 5–6 (2019): 799–823.

32 "*Ẓahīrü'l-Ḳuḍāt*," Akgündüz, *Osmanlı Kanunnameler*, 9: 403.

33 Ibid., 9:396 and 9:397.

34 On the life and influence of Vani Mehmed Efendi see the essays in Mehmet Yalar and Celil Kiraz eds, *Ulusal Vânî Mehmed Efendi Sempozyumu: 7–8 Kasim 2009, Kestel-Bursa: Bildiriler* (Bursa: Emin Yayınları, 2011); for his influence at the court of Mehmed IV see Marc Baer, *Honored by the Glory of Islam* (New York: Oxford University Press: 2008), 105–19. For a study of his fatwas see Ömer Faruk Köse, 'The Fatwa Collection of an Ottoman Provincial Mufti, Vani Mehmed Efendi (D. 1685)' (Master's Thesis, Boğaziçi University, 2015).

35 Vanī Meḥmed Efendi, '*Fetava-yi Bistamī*', IU 989, 123b. Asked if a *sipahi* could stop a cultivator from selling a house, Vani wrote that the land, not just the house, was the cultivator's freehold: '*Wa yajūz al-ishtirā' bay' arāḍīhā li-āna mamlūka lahum*.' He cites Firişte 'Izz al-Din b. Amin al-Din, a scholar known as Ibn Malak, who lived and taught in Tire in the late fourteenth and early fifteenth centuries; see Ömer Faruk Akün, 'Firishte-Oghlu', EI^2, 923.

36 Barkan, *Kanunlar*, 63–5.

37 Vanī Meḥmed Efendi, '*Fetava-yi Bistamī*', 26b.

38 The practices of 'Umar had been a focal point in Hanafi teaching on land tenure since the earliest works of land tenure were composed; see Chapter 2, p. 35. To one seemingly straightforward question about the rate of *kharaj* applying to a vegetable garden, Vani Mehmed responded with a three-page excursis surveying the opinion of a number of Hanafi authorities and noting that it had been the practice of 'Umar to impose *kharaj*. He cites Muhammad al-Shaybani (d. 805); the *Hidaya* of 'Ali bin Abi Bakr al-Marghinani (d. 1196 or 1197); the *Fatawa Tatarkhaniyya* of al-Ansari; the *Kafi fi furu' al-Hanafiyya* of al-Hakim al-Shahid Muhammad b. Muhammad (d. 945); and the *Sharh Mukhtasar al-Tahawi* of 'Ala' al-Din b. Muhammad b. Isma'il al-Isbijabi (d. 1140). See Vanī Meḥmed Efendi, '*Fetāvā-yi Bistamī*', 20a–22b.

39 In addition to the sources cited in the notes earlier, he routinely cites the *Durar al-Hukkam fi Sharh Ghurar al-Ahkam* of Molla Hüsrev (d. 1480).

40 An example refers to the *sipahis* as the persons to whom the cultivator, Zayd, pays his *kharaj*: '*harācını ṭaraf salṭanet'den tevkīl sipāhīlere her sene eda eylese …*', see Vanī Meḥmed Efendi, '*Fetāvā-yi Bistamī*', 16b. Moreover, another fatwa affirms that it is valid for the sultan to assign *kharaj* to a particular person (fol. 24b).

41 'Arāžī-yi Harāciye ve öşriye ḥaḳḳında ḳānūn ve fetvālar', 20b–21a.
42 See John Makdisi, 'The Kindred Concepts of Seisin and Ḥawz in English and Islamic Law', in *The Law Applied: Contextualizing the Islamic Shari'a: A Volume in Honor of Frank E. Vogel*, ed. P. J. Bearman, Wolfhart Heinrichs and Bernard G. Weiss (London: I.B. Tauris, 2008) for a discussion of the similarity of replevin and *istihqaq*.
43 The vocabulary of 'istihqaq' would be seen in the fatwas of some eighteenth-century muftis, but it generally designated those who had a pre-emptive claim to *tapu*. These muftis would discuss who has the 'right of *tapu*' (*haqq-ı tapu*) after death, such as Erzurumlu 'Abdurrahman the late eighteenth-century mufti of Erzurum. See 'Abdurraḥmān, *Sefīnetü'l-Fetāvā*, 407 and 410. The Bosnian mufti Mostari Ahmed refers to 'the possessors of *istihqaq*' (*erbāb-ı istihqāq*), see Aḥmed el-Mostarī, '*Fetāvā-yi Aḥḥmediyye*', 209a, while Şeyhülislam Yenişehirli Abdallah (d. 1743) uses a slightly different term, *haqq-ı tapu sahıbları*, with the same meaning. See Yeñişehirli 'Abdullāh, *Beḥcetü'l-Fetāvā ma'an-nüḳūl* (İstanbul: Maṭba'a-i 'Āmīre, 1289 [1872]), 641.
44 There are examples of other Ottoman provincial muftis, such as the 'Abd al-Rahim b. Abu'l-Lutf al-Husayni al-Qudsi (d. 1692) of Jerusalem, that affirm that office or its perquisites cannot be inherited, although the issue comes up more frequently when the heirs of a *sipahi* lay claim to revenues that had not been collected when he died. See See al-Ḥusaynī, '*al-Fatāwā al-Raḥīmīyya fī wāqi'āt al-sādah al-ḥanafiyya*', PUSC Islamic Manuscripts, Garrett no. 3198Y, 53a and 53b.
45 Pir Mehmed noted its special stature in one of his fatwas: 'His [the son's] father's *tapu* lands are considered to be like inherited *milk* [*Atasının tapulu yeri mülk-i mevrûs gibi i'tibâr olunur*]'. A *kanun* with this wording can be found in the 1528 *Kanunname of Bolu*, see Halil Cin, *Osmanlı Toprak Düzeni Ve Bu Düzenin Bozulması* (Ankara: Berikan Yayınevi, 2016), 240. This rule also appears in the *Bayezid Kanunname*. See Akgündüz, *Osmanlı Kanunnâmeleri*, 2:65. For Pir Mehmed's citation, see '*Arāžī-yi Harāciye ve öşriye ḥaḳḳında ḳānūn ve fetvālar*', 13b.
46 '*Ẓahīrü'l-Kuḍāt*', Akgündüz, *Osmanlı Kanunnameler*, 9:414.
47 There appears to be less discrepancy on the date of the text than the floruit of Sakızi; some authorities claim he died as early as 1649 and others as late as 1688. See Tahsin Özcan, 'Sâdık Mehmed Efendi, Sakızı', TDVİA.
48 See chap. 5, p. x on the eighteenth-century muftis who cite this work. To this list we could also add Muhammad al-'Abbasi al-Mahdi of Egypt, who served as grand mufti to the Khedives from 1847 to 1897. See 'Abbāsī al-Mahdī, *al-Fatāwā al-Mahdiyya fī al-Waqā'i' al-Miṣriyya* ([al-Qahira]: Dār al-kutub wa al-wathā'iq al-qawmiyya bi'l-Qāhira, 2015), 4:122–23.
49 Ṣādiq Muḥammad Sāqizī, "*Ṣurrat al-Fatāwā*," PDL, 180b.
50 See 'Abdurraḥmān el-Erzurumī, '*Sefīnetü'l-Fetāvā*', SYK H. Hüsnü Paşa, 332, 399 and Ḥāmid al-'Imādī, '*al-Fatāwā al-Ḥāmidiyya*', ZAL 5656, 455. The former was the mufti of Erzurum at the end of the eighteenth century, the latter was the mufti of Damascus, about whom, see Chapter 5.
51 MTM 305.
52 MTM 317.
53 See Menteşzāde 'Abdürraḥīm, *Fetāvā-yi 'Abdürraḥīm* (Ḳonstanṭīnīye [Istanbul]: Dār üṭ-ṭıbā'at ül-Ma'mūret üs-Sulṭāniye, 1243 [1827]), 508. In one fatwa, he maintains that the *sipahi* should give the cultivator a chance to pay *tapu* before giving the land to someone else, but in the second he writes that the cultivator cannot stop the deputy from giving the land to an outsider. Sun'ullah's fatwa does not state how much time has passed but affirms that without '*temessük*', meaning here the appropriate process

of permission and *tapu* to secure it, the *sipahi* can take it away and give it to someone else with *tapu*. See MTM 81.

54 The bureaucratic complexity of the Ottoman Empire would seem to defy Weber's typologies of patrimonialism and sultanism, which he defined as arbitrary personal rule. Nevertheless, some important scholarly works continue to find it a useful way to characterize the Ottoman regime. See Burbank and Cooper, *Empires in World History*, 117–48; Karen Barkey, 'The Ottoman Empire (1299–1923): The Bureaucratization of Patrimonial Authority', in *Empires and Bureaucracy in World History: From Late Antiquity to the Twentieth Century*, ed. Peter Crooks and Timothy Parsons (Cambridge: Cambridge University Press, 2016), 102–26.

55 Lütfi Bayraktutan, *Şeyhülislâm Yahya: Hayatı, Edebî Kişiliği, Sanatı, Eserleri ve Divanından Seçmeler* (Istanbul: Kültür Bakanlığı, 1990), 8–9.

56 He held three terms: 21 May 1622–4 October 1623; 22 May 1625–10 February 1632 and 7 January 1634–27 February 1644. See Bayram Ali Kaya, 'Yahya Efendi, Zekeriyyazade', TDVİA.

57 MTM 59. Okçuzade is believed to have been a beneficiary of Yahya Efendi's patronage, see Woodhead, 'Ottoman Inşa and the Art of Letter-Writing: Influences Upon the Career of the Nişancı and Prose Stylist Okçuzade (d. 1630).' *Osmanlı Araştırmaları/ Journal of Ottoman Studies* 7 (1988): 147, 152–3.

58 It was Yahya who gave the younger man the pen name of Baha'i. Muḥammad al-Amīn al-Muḥibbī, *Khulāṣat al-Athar fī A'yān al-Qarn al-Ḥādi 'Ashar* (Beirut: Dār al-Kutub al-'Ilmiyya, 2006), 4:4.

59 His first term lasted nearly two years: 18 July 1649–2 May 1651, and the second from 16 August 1652–2 January 1654. See Mehmet İpşirli and Mustafa İsmet Uzun, 'Bahâî Mehmed Efendi', TDVİA.

60 His comments can be found on the margins of a manuscript copy of the *Tarih-i Hind-i Garbi*, the illustrated book about the discovery of America and other wonders of the world. See Thomas D. Goodrich, 'Marginalia – a Small Peek into Ottoman Minds', *Journal of Turkish Studies* 29, no. 1 (2005): 181–99. For an analysis of both Yahya and Baha'i as poets, see Elias John Wilkinson Gibb, *A History of Ottoman Poetry: Volume III 1520–1600*, ed. Edward Granville Browne (London: Luzac, 1958-[1967]), 273–93 and 294–300.

61 For the Kadizadelis, see Chapter 4, pp. 76–7.

62 Semiramis Cavusoglu, 'The Kadizadeli Movement: An Attempt of Seri'at -Minded Reform in the Ottoman Empire' (PhD Diss., Princeton University, 1990), 129–41.

63 Bünyamin Punar, 'Kanun and Sharia: Ottoman Land Law in Şeyhülislam Fatwas from Kanunname of Budin to Kanunname-i Cedid' (MA thesis, Istanbul Şehir University, 2015), 85–6.

64 Punar, 'Kanun and Sharia', 85, 102.

65 The most vivid illustration of the difference between declaring a transaction invalid versus declaring it reversible comes in a fatwa from Es'ad Efendi. In a number of fatwas he rules that a transfer without permission is not valid (mu'teber) but then was asked if it was valid to transfer a *waqf* field without the *mutawalli*'s permission. He replied, '*vakıf ḥaqqında olmaz, 'adm-ı racū' ḥaqqında olur*': that is, 'with regard to *waqf*, it is not, but with regard to the lack of reversibility, it is'. See Hocāsa'deddīnzāde Es'ad Efendi, '*Fetāvā-yi Müntahabe*', SYK Kasidecizade 277, 179a–179b. Its invalidity does have consequences, such as failing secure transmission rights for the unauthorized cultivators' children or other heirs (fol. 179b), but a *sipahi*'s reversal of the transaction is not a valid action.

66 MTM 52.
67 '*Arāzīye Müte'allik Ḳānūnnāme*', SYK Esad Efendi 846, 172.
68 MTM 83, 87–8. This same *kanun* is present in the *Kanunname of Ahmed Khan*, but it refers only to the buildings and omits the part about the trees. '*Ḳānūnnāme-yi Aḥmed Han*', SYK Esad Ef. 851/3, f. 57a.
69 Akgündüz 9:440–1.
70 For example, MTM 90: 'Question: Because Zayd has not farmed the field in his possession for more than three years, the *sipahi* is giving it to someone else by *tapu*. If Zayd can offer the same amount of *tapu*, is he able to take the land [again]? Answer: Since there is a sultanic order, he is. Written by Yahya Efendi.'
71 Es'ad Efendi, '*Fetāvā-yi Müntahabe*', 183.
72 Punar provides evidence that the two were linked in Es'ad Efendi's mind by showing the similarities between his rulings on waqf land with those on *miri* land. See Punar, 'Kanun and Sharia', 85–6, n. 251 and 252.
73 Luqman Haji Abdullah believes this to be the majority position of the Hanafi school, see Abdullah, *The Classical Islamic Law of Waqf: A Comparative Approach* (Edinburgh: University of Edinburgh Press, 2005), 152; Süleyman Kaya notes that both prominent *ilmiye* personnel, such as Şeyhülislam 'Abdürrahim (d. 1716) and influential 'independent' muftis like the Palestinian Khayr al-Din al-Ramli (d. 1671) took this position. See Kaya, *Icâreteyn* (Istanbul: Klasik, 2014), 48.
74 The *kanunname* that is the basis for the *Kanunname of Ahmed Khan*, issued in 1609, appears to be among the earliest of *kanunnames* that were made for members of the *ilmiye*. Especially on issues like this one, where the *kanun* governing the destruction of buildings and trees appears to date to a post-Süleyman and Ebu's-Su'ud era, there is a question of how *ilmiye* personnel would have been apprised of new rules emanating from the *nişancı*'s office.
75 A number of Es'ad Efendi's fatwas do not say yes or no, but rather 'it's the purview of the sultan's order', (*emr-i sultani mufavvazdır*) suggesting that he recognized the sultan's authority in the matter, but that he did not know what, if any, orders had been issued (e.g. '*Fetāvā-yi Müntahabe*', 183b). Also, he gave some fatwas that suggest a loose grasp on the later provisions of the *kanun*, ruling that a cultivator who acquired his brother's share in a holding that they previously farmed together must pay *tapu* for it (fol. 182a). Usually in such a situation, brothers shared a holding that had been transmitted from their deceased father. According to Pir Mehmed, the sultan had ordered that in this case, the brother would not have to pay *tapu*. See MTM 77.
76 Tezcan, *The Second Ottoman Empire*, 63–78; and Baki Tezcan, 'The Ottoman Mevali as "Lords of the Law"', *Journal of Islamic Studies* 20, no. 3 (2009): 383–407.
77 Es'ad Efendi famously refused to give a fatwa declaring it permissible for Osman II kill his brothers. See Burak, *The Second Formation of Islamic*, 47.
78 Chapter 5 will revisit this issue in the fatwas of eighteenth-century muftis and texts, pp. 93–4.
79 MTM 119.
80 MTM 80.
81 Among the muftis examined in this chapter, only Yahya Efendi allows that a *mutawalli* of a *waqf* (so perhaps the deputy on *miri* land as well?) may refuse a permission and insist that the present tenant remain. See this chapter n. 92.
82 The questioner asks which transfer is valid if Zayd transfers first to 'Amr without permission and then to Bakr with permission. Ruling in favour of 'Amr, the mufti wrote, 'If the transfer to 'Amr causes no harm, the deputy is ordered to permit it to

'Amr (*'Amr'a tefvīż żarar yoğsa, ṣāḥıb-ı arż 'Amr'a izinle me'mūrdur*).' See Es'ad Efendi, '*Fetāvā-yi Müntahabe*', 179a.

83 '*Ẓahīrü'l-Ḳuḍāt*', Akgündüz, *Osmanlı Kanunnameler*, 9:451; see also discussion of this fatwa in Mundy and Smith, *Governing Property*, 250, n. 80.

84 Akgündüz, *Osmanlı Kanunnâmeleri*, 9:452–3.

85 '*Ẓahīrü'l-Ḳuḍāt*', Akgündüz, *Osmanlı Kanunnameler*, 9:439.

86 Cf. 'Abdürraḥīm, *Fetāvā-yi 'Abdürraḥīm* (Ḳonsṭanṭīnīye [Istanbul]: Dār üṭ-ṭıbā'at ül-Ma'mūret üs-Sulṭāniye, 1243 [1827], 2: 515 and Minḳarīzāde Yaḥyā Efendi, '*Fetāvā*', SYK Hamidiye 610, 501a. The published volume of 'Abdürrahim's fatwas was compiled by Gedizli Mehmed Efendi (d. 1837 and also known as Mehmed el-Gedusi) in 1827' see Özen, 'Osmanlı Dönemi': 301–2. The fatwas on *miri* land that Gedizli attributed to 'Abdürrahim in this publication are replicated in their entirety in SYK Hamidiye 610. Problematically, the latter work proclaims to be the collected fatwas of *Şeyhülislam* Minkarizade Yahya (served 1662–74) in the title and on the first page of the text. However, the table of contents attributes the fatwas to 'Abdürrahim. I have consulted three copies of the compilation of Minkarizade's fatwas assembled by his student and fatwa assistant (*fetva emini*) Şerifzade 'Ata'ullah Mehmed Efendi (d. 1715), and none of the *miri* land fatwas that appear in Hamidye 610 is present in these manuscripts (SYK Pertevniyal 342, SYK M Hilmi F Fehmi 59 and IU T3244). On 'Ata'ullah Mehmed's compilation, generally considered to be reliable in its attribution and known as *Fetāvā-yi 'Ata'iye*, see Özen, 'Osmanlı Dönemi Fetva Literatürü', 297–8. Given the ambiguity of Hamidiye 610 and the lack of corroborating evidence for attributing them to Minkarizade, I have therefore chosen to treat these fatwas as belonging to 'Abdürrahim, although with the caveat that this is not entirely certain.

87 The key concern that 'Abdürrahim expressed is that agricultural taxes could not be collected from these tax-exempt individuals. There was a general agreement among Ottoman officials that *çiftlik* possessors did have to pay property taxes such as *avarız*, although it is not as clear that they were equally liable for agricultural taxes. See Malissa Taylor, 'Forcing the Wealthy to Pay Their Fair Share? The Politics of Rural Taxes in 17th-Century Ottoman Damascus', *Journal of the Economic and Social History of the Orient* 62, no. 1 (2019): 35–66.

88 Aḥmed el-Mostarī, '*Fetāvā-yi Aḥmediyye*', SYK Kasidecizade 290, 211b. The precedent Mostari cites is credited as the chapter on sharecropping (*kitab al-muzar'a*) in a work he refers to as *al-Fara'id*, perhaps the commentary on *Multaqā'l-Abḥur* written by Ebu'l-Berekat Sivasi (d. 1638).

89 Meşrebzāde, *Fetāvā-yı Cāmi' ül-İcāreteyn*, 306. This compendium treated both *ijaratayn* and *miri* land. The published version of the text was extensively edited, checked and arranged by Meşrebzade at the behest of Şeyhülislam Sıdkızade Ahmed Reşid (d. 1834). An earlier version (or versions) had been in circulation since 1737. See Özen, 'Osmanlı Dönemi': 274.

90 Meşrebzāde, *Cāmi' ül-İcāreteyn*, 302, 303–4.

91 Meşrebzāde, *Cāmi' ül-İcāreteyn*, 302.

92 Barkan believed that not only the *Kanun-ı Cedid* but also the vast majority of *kanunnames* were not law codes issued by the dynasty: these were collections of individual statues compiled by private individuals. See Barkan, *Kanunlar*, xxii–xxvii.

93 Anton Minkov finds that the development of *tapu* documentation follows a similar chronology. The classical *tapu* document began to take its form in the mid-sixteenth

century but did not reach its standard form until the second half of the seventeenth century. See Minkov, 'Islamic Law and Society': 67.

Chapter 4

1 Most *kanunnames* do not specify whether the land is *miri* or some other category; they simply record the tax regime associated with *miri* land. However, some also confirmed the post-mortem transmission rights; see Barkan, *Kanunlar*, 'Koca İli Livası Kanunu', 33–4; 'Yeni İl Kanunu', 78–80; 'Gürcistan Kanunnamesi', 197–8.

2 Non-Muslims who accept living within the community of Islam have accepted *dhimma*, a status that distinguishes them from non-Muslims but extends specific legal protections to them. Works of Hanafi *fiqh* generally required 'people of *dhimma*' to pay *jizya*, a poll tax, as well as the *kharaj* land tax.

3 '*The Kanunname of Candia*', BOA TT 825, 2–3. See the translated published copies in Barkan, *Kanunlar*, 350–3; and Akgündüz, *Osmanlı Kanunnâmeleri*, 10:940–3.

4 Molly Greene, *A Shared World: Christians and Muslims in the Early Modern Mediterranean* (Princeton, NJ: Princeton University Press, 2000), 28; and Eugenia Kermeli, 'Caught in between Faith and Cash: The Ottoman Land System of Crete, 1645–1670', in *The Eastern Mediterranean under the Ottoman Rule: Crete, 1645–1840. Halcyon Days in Crete 6: A Symposium Held in Rethymno, 13–15 January 2006*, ed. Antonis Anastasopoulos (Rethymnon: Crete University Press, 2008), 38–41.

5 Yahya Efendi wrote that if a land was conquered by the sword, *jizya* was imposed on the people, and the land stayed in their possession, then the land is *kharaji*. As their *milk*, it devolved to their heirs and the *sipahi* could not give it to someone else with *tapu*. See Şeyhülislâm Şerīfzāde 'Aṭa'ullah Meḥmed Efendi, '*Revāyiḥu'z-zekiye fī Fihrisi'l-fetāvā't-Türkiye*', IU T3244, 116b–117a.

6 The register created for Mytilene in 1670, published in Akgündüz, *Osmanlı Kanunnâmeleri* 10:957–66, is the closest match to that of '*The Kanunname of Candia*'. A later *kanunname* for Mytilene dating to 1709 is similar, and published in Barkan, *Kanunlar*, 332–8. There are two other *kanunnames* dating to the 1670s: one governing a number of Aegean islands (Akgündüz, *Osmanlı Kanunnâmeleri*, 10:945–54), and a second for the island of Taşöz (Akgündüz, *Osmanlı Kanunnâmeleri*, 10:945–54 and 10:955–6), both of which are more of a combination between the *miri* regime and the *kharaji* one.

7 See Repp, 'Qānūn and Sharī'a', 132–3; Greene, 'An Islamic Experiment?': 60–78; Khoury, 'Administrative Practice': 305–30; Tezcan, *Second Ottoman Empire*, 24–5.

8 On the campaign to recapture the Morea, see J. von Hammer-Purgstall, *Histoire de L'Empire Ottoman depuis son origine jusqu'à nos jours*, trans. J. Hellert (Istanbul: Isis, 2000), 13:140–7. On the *kanunname*, see Fariba Zarinebaf, John Bennet, and Jack L. Davis, eds., 'A Historical and Economic Geography of Ottoman Greece', *Hesperia Supplements* 34 (2005): 1–328.

9 Barkan, *Kanunlar*, 326.

10 The *kanunname*'s compilation in the Morea was still ongoing in September 1716, a year after the conquest; Mustafa Naima, who had been involved in assigning *timars* and *zeamets* for the *kanunname*, had died, and an order from that month confirmed that he would be replaced because the work was not yet complete; see Lewis V.

Thomas, *A Study of Naima* (New York: New York University Press, 1972), 52. Dated copies of the *Kanun-ı Cedid* began to appear in early 1717.

11 It was unclear whether the Ottomans were still committed to preserving the *kharaji* regime in the Aegean islands by 1715. The islands of Aigina, Tenos and Cerigo were recaptured from Venice in that year, and the tax imposed was that of the Ottoman tithe rather than *kharaj*. See Machiel Kiel, 'The Smaller Aegean Islands in the 16th–18th Centuries according to Ottoman Administrative Documents', in *Between Venice and Istanbul: Colonial Landscapes in Early Modern Greece*, ed. Siriol Davies and Jack L. Davis (Princeton, NJ: American School of Classical Studies at Athens, 2007), 38–40.

12 See Chapter 5, pp. 89, 92, and 94.

13 Samy Ayoub, *Law, Empire and the Sultan: Ottoman Imperial Authority and Late Ḥanafī Jurisprudence* (Oxford: Oxford University Press, 2020), 22, 66.

14 Ibid., 65–93; Ayoub, 'The Sultan Says': 239–78.

15 Yavuz Aykan, *Rendre la justice à Amid: procédures, acteurs et doctrines dans le contexte ottoman du XVIIIème siècle* (Leiden: Brill, 2016), 183–4.

16 Burak, 'Evidentiary Truth Claims': 233–54; Burak, '"In Compliance with the Old Register"': 799–823.

17 Martha Mundy, 'On Reading Two Epistles of Muhammad Amin Ibn 'Abidin of Damascus', in *Forms and Institutions of Justice: Legal Actions in Ottoman Contexts*, ed. Yavuz Aykan and Işık Tamdoğan (Istanbul: OpenEdition Books, 2018), paragraph 20.

18 Ayman Shabana, *Custom in Islamic Law and Legal Theory: The Development of the Concepts of 'urf and 'ādah in the Islamic Legal Tradition* (New York: Palgrave Macmillan, 2010), 111–24; Ahmed Fekry Ibrahim, 'Customary Practices as Exigencies in Islamic Law: Between a Source of Law and a Legal Maxim', *Oriens* 46, nos. 1–2 (2018): 222–61; Ayoub, *Law, Empire, and the Sultan*, 4–5.

19 Wael B. Hallaq, 'A Prelude to Ottoman Reform: Ibn 'Ābidīn on Custom and Legal Change', in *Histories of the Modern Middle East: New Directions*, ed. I. Gershoni, Y. Hakan Erdem, and Ursula Woköck (Boulder, CO: Lynne Rienner Publishers, 2002), 37–61; Gerber, *Islamic Law and Culture*, 105–15; Baber Johansen, 'Secular and Religious Elements in Hanafite Law: Function and Limits of the Absolute Character of Government Authority', in *Contingency in a Sacred Law: Legal and Ethical Norms in the Muslim Fiqh* (Leiden: Brill, 1999), 163–71; Shabana, *Custom in Islamic Law*, 111–24; Ayoub, *Law, Empire and the Sultan*, 103–6.

20 Usually, the sultan's writ to which the scholars defer adopts one pre-existing path of action while proscribing others; rarely does it introduce a novel path of action. See the examples with regard to delegating office and a woman's ability to marry a man of lesser social standing in Ayoub, *Law, Empire, and the Sultan*, 84.

21 Ibid., 71.

22 Mundy, 'On Reading Two Epistles', paragraph 14.

23 To name just a few, '*Kanun-ı Cedid der Beyan-ı Tapu*', SYK Hacı Mahmud 5657 is dated 1122 AH (1710); '*Kanunname-yi Cedid fima yete'allık bi'l-'arazi*', SYK Mihrişah 440/6, f. 48–61 is dated 1101 AH (1690); and '*Münşeat*' SYK Esad Efendi 3835/1, f. 1–101 is dated 1121 AH (1709 or 1710). Although several of these have '*kanun-ı cedid*' in the title, they are different compilations from the text I refer to as the *Kanun-ı Cedid*. Also, both *Zahirü'l-Kudat* and three extant copies of the *Kanunname of Ahmed Khan* (SYK Ayasofya 2894, SYK Esad Efendi 846 and SYK Esad Efendi 851) contain or append fatwas of *Şeyhülislam* Baha'i Mehmed, hence they were assembled no earlier than the second half of the seventeenth century.

24 For a detailed timeline of the composition of this *kanunname*, see Ersin Gülsoy, 'Osmanlı Tahrir Geleneğinde Bir Değişim Örneği: Girit Eyâleti'nin 1650 Ve 1670 Tarihli Sayımları', in *Pax Ottomana: Studies in Memoriam Prof. Dr. Nejat Göyünç*, ed. Kemal Çiçek (Haarlem: SOTA; Ankara: Yeni Türkiye, 2001), 184–6.

25 Ibid., 194.

26 Repp, 'Qānūn and Sharī'a', 132; Gilles Veinstein, 'Le Législateur ottoman face à l'insularité: l'enseignement des kânûnnâme', in *Insularités ottomans*, ed. Nicolas Vatin and Gilles Veinstein (Paris [Istanbul]: Maisonneuve & Larose; Institut français d'études anatoliennes, 2004), 91–110.

27 Those who believe the island's regime primarily reflected commercialization or fiscal change include Greene, 'An Islamic Experiment': 60–78; Kermeli, 'Caught in between Faith and Cash'; and Elias Kolovos, 'Beyond "Classical" Ottoman Defterology: A Preliminary Assessment of the Tahrir Registers of 1670/71 Concerning Crete and the Aegean Islands', in *The Ottoman Empire, the Balkans and the Greek Lands: Toward a Social and Economic History*, ed. Elias Kolovos, Phokion Kotzageorgis and Sophia Laiou (Istanbul: Isis Press; Gorgias Press, 2010), 201–36.

28 The texts of substantive or positive law are called branches (*furu'*) to distinguish them from the texts of roots (*usul*) that refer to Islamic legal theory. That the branches are derived from the roots is implied, though much of the scholarship on Islamic law views the relationship between theory and positive law as more complex than this. See Wael B. Hallaq, *A History of Islamic Legal Theories: An Introduction to Sunnī Uṣūl Al-Fiqh* (Cambridge: Cambridge University Press, 1997), 130–43; Robert Gleave, 'Deriving Rules of Law', in *The Ashgate Research Companion to Islamic Law*, ed. Rudolph Peters and Peri Bearman (Farnham: Ashgate, 2014), 65.

29 Hallaq, *History of Islamic Legal Theories*, 153–5; Ayoub, *Law, Empire and the Sultan*, 8; Ibn 'Abidin wrote a poem explaining the weight of the different sources within the Hanafi juridical tradition that highlights the importance of the manuals; see Norman Calder, 'The "ʿuqūd rasm al-muftī" of Ibn ʿĀbidīn', *Bulletin of the School of Oriental and African Studies, University of London* 63, no. 2 (2000): 215–28.

30 The short works were known as *mukhtasar*, and the longer as *mabsut*. See Hallaq, *Sharia: Theory, Practice*,180–83. For an argument that the development of the *mukhtasar* genre was a way of maintaining a cohesive doctrine among jurists, see Mohammad Fadel, 'The Social Logic of Taqlīd and the Rise of the Mukhataṣar [*sic*]', *Islamic Law and Society* 3, no. 2 (1996): 193–233.

31 Wael B. Hallaq, 'From Fatwās to Furūʿ: Growth and Change in Islamic Substantive Law', *Islamic Law and Society* 1, no. 1 (1994): 29–65; Schacht, *Introduction to Islamic Law*, 74–5.

32 Burak, *Second Formation of Islamic Law*, 122–56.

33 For the impact of these texts on Ebu's-Su'ud's formulation of the land law, see Chapter 2. On the formation of a specifically Ottoman Hanafi canon of which these scholars were a part, see Burak, *Second Formation of Islamic Law*, esp. 71–100.

34 Molla Hüsrev's *Durar al-Hukkam fi Sharh al-Ahkam*; al-Timurtashi's *Tanwir al-Absar wa-Jami' al-Bihar* and Ibn Nujaym's *al-Bahr al-Ra'iq sharh Kanz al-Daqa'iq*.

35 See Chapter 2, p 35–6.

36 '*The Kanunname of Candia*', BOA TT 825, 2.

37 '*The Kanunname of Candia*', 3.

38 Caroline Finkel, *Osman's Dream: The History of the Ottoman Empire* (New York: Basic Books, 2007), 196–252; Gabriel Piterberg, *An Ottoman Tragedy: History and Historiography at Play* (Berkeley: University of California Press, 2003); Karen Barkey,

Bandits and Bureaucrats: The Ottoman Route to State Centralization (Ithaca: Cornell University Press, 1994); Oktay Özel, 'The Reign of Violence: The *Celalis* C. 1550–1700', in *The Ottoman World*, ed. Christine Woodhead (New York: Routledge, 2012), 184–202.

39 The Koprülüs have often received praise from historians, who typically view them as ruthless but effective. See Ahmed Refik Altınay, *Köprülüler* (Istanbul: Türkiye Ekonomik ve Toplumsal Tarih Vakfı, 2001); Norman Itzkowitz, *Ottoman Empire and Islamic Tradition* (Chicago: University of Chicago Press, 1972), 77–85; Suraiya Faroqhi, 'Crisis and Change, 1590–1699', in *An Economic and Social History of the Ottoman Empire, vol. 2 1600–1914*, ed. Suraiya Faroqhi (Cambridge: Cambridge University Press, 1994), 419–20. For a different view, see Marc Baer, *Honored by the Glory of Islam: Conversion and Conquest in Ottoman Europe* (New York: Oxford University Press, 2008), 78–80. The reaction of the Köprülüs' contemporaries was decidedly mixed: see Derin Terzioğlu, 'Sufi and Dissident in the Ottoman Empire: Niyazi Misri (1618–1694)' (PhD Diss., Harvard University, 1999), 336–41.

40 Ekin Tuşalp Atiyas, 'The "Sunna-Minded" Trend', in *A History of Ottoman Political Thought up to the Early Nineteenth Century: A Concise History*, ed. Marinos Sariyannis (Rethymno, Greece: Foundation for Research and Technology-Hellas, Institute for Mediterranean Studies, 2015), 98–122.

41 On the *Kadızadeli* movement see Ahmet Yaşar Ocak, 'II. yüzyılda Osmanlı İmparatorluğu'nda dinde tasfiye (puritanizm) teşebbüslerine bir bakış: Kadızâdeliler hareketi', *Türk Kültürü Araştırmaları*, 17–21/1–2 (1979–1983), 208–25; Madeline C. Zilfi, 'The Kadızadelis: Discordant Revivalism in Seventeenth-Century Istanbul', *Journal of Near Eastern Studies* 45 (1986): 251–69; Necati Öztürk, 'Islamic Orthodoxy among the Ottomans in the Seventeenth Century: With Special Reference to the Qadi-Zade Movement' (PhD Diss., University of Edinburgh, 1981); Semiramis Çavuşoğlu, 'The Kâdîzâdeli Movement: An Attempt of Şeriat-Minded Reform in the Ottoman Empire' (PhD Diss., Princeton University, 1990); Marinos Sariyannis, 'The Kadızadeli Movement as a Social and Political Phenomenon: The Rise of a "Mercantile Ethic"?' in *Political Initiatives from the Bottom-Up in the Ottoman Empire. Halcyon Days in Crete VII, A Symposium Held in Rethymno, 9–11 January 2009*, ed. Antonis Anastasopoulos (Rethymno: Crete University Press, 2012), 263–89.

42 A number of scholars have addressed the question of why the compatibility of sharia and *kanun* became so acrimoniously debated in the mid- to late seventeenth century. Many studies see it as rooted in social and economic change, while others are more inclined to take seriously the ideological component. See Abou-El-Haj, 'Power and Social Order', 77–102; Kafadar, 'The Myth of the Golden Age', 37–48; and Tezcan, *The Second Ottoman Empire*, 48–59. For a comprehensive review of the literature espousing the second position, see Atiyas, 'The "Sunna-Minded" Trend', 112–20.

43 On Birgevi's protest see Ivanyi, *Virtue, Piety and the Law*, 222–32; on the 1696 *firman* see Abou-El-Haj, 'Power and Social Order', 99.

44 Atiyas, 'The "Sunna-Minded" Trend', 113–18.

45 Rifa'at Abou-El-Hajj has argued that the questioning of the *kanun*'s rectitude was an epiphenomenal manifestation of the rise of a new elite challenging the old order and its codified privileges. See Abou-El-Haj, 'Power and Social Order' and also Abou-El-Haj, 'The Ottoman Nasihatname', 17–30. Similarly, Molly Greene has speculated that the Köprülü family approved of declaring the land of Crete to be *milk* in part because it allowed them to establish large, truly private estates there. See Greene, *A Shared World*, 27–8.

46 For Minkarizade, see 'Minḳarīzāde Ḳānūnnāmesi', SYK Hacı Mahmud Efendi 1238/3, 69–88; for Çatalcalı, Şeyhülislam Çatalcalı 'Alī b. Meḥmed Efendi, 'Fetāvā', Yazma Bağışlar 2303, 404–10.
47 Feyżullāh b. Meḥmed Efendi, Fetāvā-yi Feyżiye ma'an-Nuḳūl (İstanbul: Darü't-Ṭıba'āti'l-'Āmīre, 1266 [1850]):16–21, 570–2.
48 Imber, Ebu's-Su'ud, 270.
49 Tahsin Özcan, 'Şeyhîzâde', TDVİA.
50 Muḥammad al-Amīn al-Muḥibbī, Khulāṣat al-Athar fī a'yān al-qarn al-ḥādi 'ashar (Beirut: Dār al-Kutub al-'Ilmiyya, 2006), 4:63–65.
51 'Abd al-Razzāq ibn Ḥasan Bayṭār, Ḥilyat al-Bashar fī Tarīkh al-Qarn al-Thālith 'Ashar (Damascus: [publisher not identified], 1962–64), 3:1230–9; Gerber, Islamic Law and Culture, esp. chapters 6 and 7; Hallaq, 'A Prelude to Ottoman Reform'.
52 J. Schacht, 'al-Ḥalabī', EI², 90.
53 'Alā' al-Dīn al-Ḥaṣkafī and 'Abd al-Raḥmān ibn Muḥammad Shaykhzādah, Majma' al-Anhur fī Sharḥ Multaqā al-Abḥur: wa ma'ah al-Durr al-Muntaqā fī Sharḥ al-Multaqā. 4 vols (Bayrūt [Beirut]: Manshūrāt Muḥammad 'Alī Baydūn: Dār al-Kutub al-'Ilmiyya, 1419 [1998]), 1:664.
54 Ebu's-Su'ud had laboured to clarify the difference between the tithe of the fiqh and that of the register in a number of fatwas. See Imber, Ebu's-Su'ud, 125–6, and Ferguson, The Proper Order of Things, 130–1.
55 Ḥaṣkafī and Shaykhzādah, Majma', 1:664–5.
56 Burak, The Second Formation of Islamic Law, 155–6; Ayoub, Law, Empire and the Sultan, 86–90.
57 Ḥaṣkafī and Shaykhzādah, Majma', 1:665.
58 Ayoub notes his attentiveness to the Ma'ruzat in particular; see Ayoub, Law, Empire and the Sultan, 89–90.
59 There are a number of places in this section where he distinguishes between the order prevailing in 'the land in Rum' and that prevailing 'in our lands' (fī biladina). Ḥaṣkafī and Shaykhzādah, Majma', 1:663–6.
60 For a broad perspective on Ibn 'Ābidīn's scholarly interests and career, see Gerber, Islamic Law and Culture. For his position as a transitional figure, see Hallaq, 'A Prelude to Ottoman Reform'.
61 Cuno, 'Was the Land of Ottoman Syria Miri or Milk?', 137–42.
62 He wrote that some villages or farmlands were known to be property of the bayt al-mal, but that it should not be presumed that as a general rule cultivators were not owners, see Ibn 'Ābidīn, Ḥāshiyyat, 6:221. In the province of Damascus, the peasants generally regarded grain-growing lands as miri, and those given to arboriculture, viniculture or irrigated gardens of other kinds to be milk. This was not entirely consistent with an Ottoman understanding of miri land, and the 1548 kanunname for Syria reflected this tension; see Barkan, Kanunlar, 221, item 8, where the kanunname specifies that if a land is sultani and the villagers have planted vines or orchards on it only to later put such lands back to the plow, they cannot claim that these lands are milk. Additionally, it was on the latter type of land (gardens and orchards) that disputed claims of ownership arose, see Imber, 'The Status of Orchards and Fruit-Trees': 763–74; Samir Seikaly, 'Land Tenure in 17th Century Palestine: The Evidence from the Al-Fatāwā Al-Khairiyya', in Land Tenure and Social Transformation in the Middle East, ed. Tarif Khalidi (Beirut: American University of Beirut, 1984), 401–2; Cuno, 'Was the Land of Ottoman Syria Miri or Milk?', 145–50.

63 Like Şeyhizade, Ibn 'Abidin either did not know or chose not to record the transmission law in all its intricate detail. Ibn 'Abidin's phrasing of the way that the daughter and brother can take the land is indicative of how he understands the *tapu* fee: it is an advance on the rent.
64 Ibn 'Ābidīn, *Ḥāshiyyat*, 6:221.
65 Nabulusi, who wrote a commentary on Birgevi's *al-Tariqa al-Muhammadiyya*, responded to Birgevi's description of Ottoman land practices by contrasting the practices prevailing in the Damascene hinterland; see al-Nābulusī and Meḥmed al-Birkawī, *al-Ḥadīqa al-Nadiya Sharḥ al-Ṭarīqa al-Muḥammadiya wa'l-Sīra al-Aḥmadiya* (Beirut: Dār al-Kutub al-'Ilmiyya, 1971), 5:504. Ibn 'Abidin, by contrast, makes multiple statements identifying the sultan's order as a source of law for *miri* land. See Ibn 'Ābidīn, *Al-'Uqūd al-Durriyya*, 2:358.
66 Johansen, *Islamic Law on Land Tax and Rent*, 80–97; see also Cuno, 'Was the Land of Ottoman Syria *Miri* or *Milk*?'
67 Nābulusī and Birkawī, *al-Ḥadīqa al-Nadiya*, 5:499–500.
68 Atiyas, 'The "Sunna-Minded" Trend', 100–4, 114–15.
69 Katharina Ivanyi emphasizes that Birgevi's acceptance of the 'rental' paradigm was not enthusiastic. See Ivanyi, *Virtue, Piety and the Law*, 229.
70 Ibid., 5:500.
71 Dürrīzāde Meḥmed 'Ārif b. Muṣṭafā, *Netīcetü'l-Fetāvā*, 681.
72 Ḥaṣkafī and Shaykhzādah, *Majma'*, 1:664.
73 Ḥaṣkafī and Shaykhzādah, *Majma'*, 1:663.
74 Ibid.
75 Ibn 'Ābidīn, *Ḥāshiyyat*, 6:220.
76 Ḥaṣkafī and Shaykhzādah, *Majma'*, 1:664.
77 For the Morea, see n. 6; for Podolia, see Dariusz Kołodziejczyk, *The Ottoman Survey Register of Podolia (Ca. 1681) = Defter-i Mufassal-i Eyalet-i Kamaniçe*, vol. 2 (Cambridge, MA: Harvard Ukrainian Research Institute, 2004). For Tabriz, see Fariba Zarinebaf-Shahr, 'Tabriz under Ottoman Rule (1725–30)' (PhD Diss., University of Chicago, 1991).

Chapter 5

1 Donald Quataert, *The Ottoman Empire, 1700–1922* (Cambridge: Cambridge University Press, 2000), 110–37, esp. 128–32; Şevket Pamuk, 'The Ottoman Empire in the Eighteenth Century', *Itinerario* 24, nos. 3–4 (2000): 104–16; Pamuk, *A Monetary History of the Ottoman Empire* (Cambridge: Cambridge University Press, 2000), 159–71.
2 Bruce McGowan, 'The Age of the Ayans, 1699–1812', in *An Economic and Social History of the Ottoman Empire Volume Two 1600–1914*, ed. Suraiya Faroqhi (Cambridge: Cambridge University Press, 1997), 637–758; Karl Barbir, *Ottoman Rule in Damascus, 1708–1758* (Princeton, NJ: Princeton University Press, 1980), 43–6; Salzmann, 'An Ancien Régime Revisited', 393–423; Yaycioglu, *Partners of the Empire*, 65–115.
3 For the 'classical' view see Gibb and Bowen, *Islamic Society and the West*, 252–8; Inalcik, *The Ottoman Empire: The Classical Age*, 49–51. For the revisionists, see Genç, 'Osmanlı Maliyesinde Malikâne Sistemi'; Salzmann, 'An Ancien Régime Revisited'; and Barkey, *Empire of Difference*, 226–63.

4 For the land's appropriation as private property, see Barnes, *Introduction to Religious Foundations*, 54 and E. A. Aytekin, 'Agrarian Relations, Property and Law: An Analysis of the Land Code of 1858 in the Ottoman Empire', *Middle Eastern Studies* 45, no. 6 (2009): 945–7. For further examples see Introduction, p. 130, n.8.

5 On the tendency to associate rising commercialism with the dissolution of *kanun*, see Chapter 4, n. 5. Despite this tendency, a number of prominent historians who have written of a general decline in the status and practice of *kanun* did not believe that such a decline extended to land tenure *kanun* specifically. Halil İnalcik saw the *Kanun-ı Cedid* as the empire's operative land law until approximately 1700, Colin Imber believed it to be in effect until the 1858 Land Code. See Inalcik, 'Islamization of Ottoman Laws ', 115 and Imber, *Ebu's-Su'ud*, 270.

6 Seven Ağır and Onur Yıldırım, 'Gedik: What's in a Name?', in *Bread from the Lion's Mouth: Artisans Struggling for a Livelihood in Ottoman Cities*, ed. Suraiya Faroqhi (New York: Berghahn, 2015), 217–36; Ağır, 'The Rise and Demise of *Gedik* Markets in Istanbul, 1750–1860', *Economic History Review* 71, no. 1 (2018): 137–8; Akarlı, 'Gedik: A Bundle of Rights ', 166–200.

7 *Şeyhülislam* Menteşzade 'Abdürrahim (d. 1716) was close to unique in addressing a few issues related to the large farms known as *çiftliks* that were held by the *ayan*; see 'Abdürraḥīm, *Fetāvā-yi 'Abdürraḥīm* (Ḳonsṭanṭīnīye [Istanbul]: Dār üṭ-ṭıbā'at ül-Ma'mūret üs-Sulṭāniye, 1243 [1827]), 2: 520–2. A description of village taxation in late-eighteenth-century Serbia suggests that some *ayan* had no interest in depriving the peasants of their *tasarruf*; rather, the *ayan*'s goal was to take all the profits of agriculture rather than to establish a legal claim that they possessed the land rather than the cultivators. See Michael Ursinus, 'The Transformation of the Ottoman Fiscal Regime', in *The Ottoman World*, ed. Christine Woodhead (London: Routledge, 2013), 429–31.

8 Ibn 'Abidin's work highlights that his familiarity with the *kanun* came via his study of previous scholars who had incorporated it into their jurisprudence, and he had not felt compelled to familiarize himself with the *kanun* or the fatwas based on it for any external reason. See Gerber, *Islamic Law and Culture, 1600–1840*, 60.

9 For provincial citations of Sakızi, see two eighteenth-century muftis of Erzurum, Seyid İbrāhīm Edhem, *Nehriyetü'l-fetvā*, IU T1590, 297b, 303a; 'Abdurraḥmān Efendi el-Erzurumī, '*Sefinetü'l-Fetāvā*', 399, 402. The eighteenth-century muftis of Amid also cited Sakızi on land and other issues; see Yavuz Aykan, 'Comment al-hajj Mehmet s'est-il approprié un terrain récupéré à la suite de la décrue du Tigre? Le statut d'une terre vacante (arz-ı mübâha) devant un tribunal ottoman (Amid au XVIIIe siècle)', in *Appartenance Locale et Propriété au nord et au sud de la Méditerranée*, ed. Sami Bargaoui et al. (Aix-en-Provence, France: IREMAM, 2015), 47. The Damascene mufti Hamid al-'Imadi's citations of Sakızi will be discussed later. A manual assembled by an eighteenth-century scholar named Ibrahīm Raqim ibn Darwīsh Muḥammad (d. 1735), presumably for his own use, contains a section on *miri* land that transcribes the relevant section of *Surrat al-Fatawa*. See Ibn Darwīsh Muḥammad, '*Fatāwā*', PUSC Garret 4609Y, 35b–36a.

10 For instance, the section 'Explanation of land containing trees' in Aḥmed el-Mostarī '*Fetāvā-yi Aḥmediye*', SYK Kasidecizade 290, f. 222b–223b is copied in its entirety from 'Abdürrahim's fatwas, although Mostari does not cite him. See Menteşzāde 'Abdürraḥīm, *Fetāvā-yi 'Abdürraḥīm*, 2: 540–2.

11 There is some question as to whether ʿAbdürrahim authored these fatwas; see Chapter 3, n. 87. Whoever wrote them, their publication is likely one reason that they exercised such a formative impact on the 1858 Land Code.
12 On this text, see Özen, ʻOsmanlı Dönemiʼ: 274. For an example of a citation see İbrāhīm Edhem, *Nehriyetü'l-fetvā*, 92a.
13 For example, İbrāhīm Edhem, *Nehriyetü'l-fetvā*, 298a. A number of his fatwas referencing the *kanun* have been reproduced in M. Macit Kenanoğlu, ʻOsmanlı Devleti'nde Kanun-Fetva İlişkisi ve Örfî Fetva Kavramıʼ, in *Osmanlı Hukukunda Fetva*, ed. Süleyman Kaya (Istanbul: Klasik, 2018), 120–41.
14 This observation is based on a survey of roughly forty-five copies of the text held at the Süleymaniye Library in Istanbul, Istanbul University Library, and the Türk Tarih Kurumu Library. Of the dated copies, most appear to have been made between 1730 and 1840.
15 On *kanun*'s integration into manuals of *fiqh*, see Aykan, *Rendre la justice à Amid*, 183–4 and Ayoub, ʻThe Sultan Saysʼ: 239–78; on its integration into the *Ahkam* registers, see Tuğ, *The Politics of Honor*, 80–6; on its integration into the court registers in Cairo, see Baldwin, *Islamic Law and Empire*.
16 For these muftis see Şükrü Özen, "Osmanlı Dönemi Fetva Literatürü." *Türkiye Araştırmaları Literatür Dergisi* 3, no. 5 (2005): 267, 315.
17 Samy Ayoub states that the incorporation of sultanic orders into the manuals of *fiqh* is one of the chief characteristics of what he calls ʻlate Hanafismʼ. See Ayoub, *Law, Empire and the Sultan*, 66, and ʻ"The Sultān Says"ʼ, 239–78.
18 It is unclear when this term came into usage and whether it predated the Ottoman conquest. On the particularities of *mashadd maska*, see Joseph, *Islamic Law on Peasant Usufruct*, 106–19; Mundy and Saumarez Smith, *Governing Property*, 28–31; and Abdul-Karim Rafeq, ʻ"City and Countryside in a Traditional Setting: The Case of Damascus in the First Quarter of the Eighteenth Centuryʼ, in *The Syrian Land in the 18th and 19th Century: The Common and the Specific in the Historical Experience*, ed. Thomas Philipp, 295–332 (Stuttgart: Steiner, 1992).
19 There is no reference to this term in the fatwas of the great Palestinian mufti Khayr al-Din al-Ramli (1585–1671), known as *al-Fatawa al-Khayriyya*. Similarly, court records on land transactions in Jerusalem make no mention of it. See Ze'evi, *Ottoman Century*, 117–39. It is also absent from the fatwas of the mufti of Tripoli, ʿAbdullah al-Khalili (d. *c.* 1762). See Khalīlī, *Fatāwā*, PUSC MS Garrett no. 507Y, 55b–121a.
20 Mundy and Smith, *Governing Property*, 28–31, traces this transition. Some muftis like Ismaʿil al-Haʾik, while not citing either imperial orders or the *şeyhülislams*' fatwas, deployed concepts – and in his specific case, a vocabulary – that suggested some familiarity with such sources: he referred *miri* land as delegated (*fawwada*) to the cultivator on behalf of the imam with the deputy's permission, and described it as neither owned nor inherited. See Ismāʿīl al-Ḥāʾik, ʻ*Bāb Mashad Maska min Fatāwī* [*sic*] *al-Shaykh Ismāʿīl al-Ḥāyik* [*sic*]ʼ, ZAL 5677, 9b.
21 ʿAbd al-Rahman al-ʿImadi referred to it as such when defining the term for the head scribe at one of the law courts of Damascus. Ibn ʿAbidin would later inscribe this definition into his commentary on the fatwas of Hamid al-ʿImadi. See Ibn ʿĀbidīn, *al-ʿUqūd al-Durriyya fī Tanqīḥ al-Fatāwā al-Ḥāmidiyya*, ed. Muḥammad ʿUthmān (Beirut: Dār al-Kutub al-ʿIlmiyya, 2008), 2:344. Nabulusi argued that in the lands surrounding Damascus, *mashadd maska* existed on both lands that had an owner and that was held in *waqf*, and he classified lands belonging to the treasury as an entirely separate category. See al-Nābulusī, *al-Ḥadīqa al-Nadiyya*, 5:504.

22 Mundy and Smith, *Governing Property*, 28.

23 Ibid., 30–1.

24 They were also clearly in dialogue with the influential *al-Fatawa al-Khayriyya* of Khayr al-Din al-Ramli, another text of recent vintage. Al-Ramli had not used the terminology of the harmony tradition in his work, but had applied the Central Asian property right of *kirdar* to local practice in Palestine, and the muftis of Damascus would increasingly seek to understand this concept in relation to their local tradition as well. For al-Ramli's use of *kirdar* see Sabrina Joseph, 'An Analysis of Khayr Al-Din Al-Ramli's Fatawa on Peasant Land Tenure in Seventeenth-Century Palestine', *The Arab Studies Journal* 6/7, no. 2/1 (1998): 117–18; for Hamid al-'Imadi's view of *kirdar* and its difference from *mashadd maska* see Muḥammad Amīn Ibn 'Ābidīn, *al-'Uqūd al-Durriyya fī Tanqīḥ al-Fatāwā al-Ḥāmidiyya*, ed. Muḥammad 'Uthmān (Dār al-Kutub al-'Ilmiyya, 2008), 2:349.

25 For the first two, see al-'Imādī, '*al-Fatāwā al-Ḥāmidiyya*', ZAL 5656, 455b, and the others see 460a. Notable is his answer's adoption of '*sahib al-ard*' for the deputy and '*tasarruf/mutasarrif*' with regard to the cultivator and his usage, while the question does not use either of these terms and adheres to the more vernacular vocabulary associated with these terms in Damascus: '*takallum*' and its variants for the deputy, and *mashadd maska* for the cultivator's right.

26 This provision, which was part of the post-Süleyman *kanun*, appeared also in the fatwas of the Syrian jurist Hamid al-'Imadi. See al-'Imādī, '*al-Fatāwā al-Ḥāmidiyya*', ZAL 5656, 459.

27 'Alī Efendi al-Murādī, '*Majmū' Fatawa al-Muradiyya*', ZAL 2642, 326 and 327.

28 Muftis who describe it as a delegation include al-Ha'ik and al-'Imadi; see al-Ḥā'ik, '*Bāb Mashad Maska*', f. 9b; al-'Imādī, '*al-Fatāwā al-Ḥāmidiyya*', 455a, 457a, 460a. Nābulusī is more complex, arguing that *tasarruf* of the plowland held in a *timar* is delegated, but elsewhere he writes that *mashadd maska* is earned by working the land. See al-Nābulusī, '*Fatāwā al-Nābulusī*' ZAL 2684, f. 75a and al-Nābulusī, *Al-Ḥadīqa al-Nadiyya*, 5:504.

29 One of the few times that a fee is mentioned is in a fatwa by Muhammad al-'Imadi, who rules that the "*ushri*' (perhaps the tax farmer?) trying to obtain a fee on *waqf* land has no legal right, because the *mutawalli* is the person who gives permission. See al-'Imādī, '*Al-Nūr al-Mubīn fī Fatāwā al-'Imādiyīn*', ZAL 7508, f. 73a.

30 Ibn 'Ābidīn, *al-'Uqūd al-Durriyya*, 2:357.

31 Muḥammad Amīn Ibn 'Ābidīn, *Ḥāshiyyat Ibn 'Ābidīn Radd al-Muḥtār 'alā al-Durr al-Mukhtār* (Beirut: Dār iḥyā' al-turath al-'arabī, 2010/1431), 9:30.

32 Meşrebzāde Meḥmed 'Ārif Efendi, *Fetāvā-yı Cāmi' ül-İcāreteyn* (İstanbul: Darü'ṭ-Ṭıba'āti'l-'Āmire, 1837), 116–17.

33 Al-'Imādī, '*al-Fatāwā al-Ḥāmidiyya*', ZAL 5656, f. 462a.

34 Mostarī, '*Fetāvā-yi Aḥmediye*', 224b.

35 Rhoads Murphey, *Ottoman Warfare 1500–1700* (New Brunswick, NJ: Rutgers University Press, 1999), 98–9; Colin Heywood, 'The Ottoman Menzilhane and Ulak System in Rumeli in the Eighteenth Century', in *Türkiye'nin Sosyal ve Ekonomik Tarihi, 1071–1920*, ed. Osman Okyar and Halil Inalcik (Ankara: Meteksan, 1980), 179–86.

36 Several Damascenes cited Isma'il al-Ha'ik, who wrote that *miri* land was the provenance of men capable of using it productively, and that women had no part in it; see al-Ḥā'ik, '*Bāb Mashadd Maska*', f. 9b.

37 There was an anomalous case where Hāmid al-'Imadi permitted the *mutawalli* of a *waqf* to divide the land between the widow and the son of a deceased cultivator (see

'*al-Fatāwā al-Ḥāmidiyya*', 457), but with *miri* land he held that the deputy should exclude females wishing to claim a deceased relative's land; see Malissa Taylor, 'Keeping Usufruct in the Family', 429–43.

38 See '*Majmū' Fatāwā Murādiya*', 325, for his citation of al-Haskafi. See also p. 327 where he shows familiarity with the line of successors established in the *kanun*.

39 This can be difficult to gauge because not all surviving eighteenth-century fatwa collections deal with *miri* land. The fatwa collection of the mufti of Tripoli, 'Abdullah al-Khalili, contained almost no questions about it. This makes sense given that Tripoli's economy was based on irrigated agriculture and arboriculture in particular. See Khalīlī, *Fatawa*, f. 87b to 103b.

40 'Abd al-Raḥīm 'Abd al-Raḥman 'Abd al-Raḥīm, *al-Rīf al-Miṣrī fi'l-Qarn al-Thāmin 'Ashar*, second edn (Qalyūb, Egypt: Maṭābi' al-Ahrām al-Tijāriyya, 2004), 95–100; Stanford J. Shaw, "The Land Law of Ottoman Egypt (960/1553): A Contribution to the Study of Landholding in the Early Years of Ottoman Rule in Egypt," *Der Islam* 38, no. 1 (1963): 111–12.

41 For Shafi'is, see Cuno, 'Was the Land of Ottoman Syria *Miri* or *Milk*?', 139–40, and Cuno, *Pasha's Peasants*, 77–9. For the Maliki jurists, see Baber Johansen. 'Can the Law Decide That Egypt Is Conquered by Force? A Thirteenth-Century Debate on History as an Object of Study', in *Studies in Islamic Law: A Festschrift for Colin Imber*, ed. Andreas Christmann and Robert Gleave (Oxford: Oxford University Press, 2007), 143–64. Scholars studying Ottoman-era Egyptian court records note that the documentation of transactions is, in some cases, consistent with *miri* regulation in its phrasing – *isqat* and *faragh*, the terms for transfer – in other cases it uses terms of freehold (*milk*) and sale (*bay'*); see Ayman Aḥmad Maḥmūd, *al-Arḍ wa al-Mujtama' fi Miṣr fi'l-'aṣr al-'Uthmānī*, 923 H/1517–1069 H/1658 (al-Haram, Egypt: 'Ayn lil-Dirāsāt wa al-Buḥūth al-Insāniya wa al-Ijtimā'īya, 2008), 41–3.

42 Sāqizī attributes a fatwa to Ibn Nujaym where *tapu* and permission from the deputy were necessary, suggesting that Ibn Nujaym approved of these measures in Egypt. See Ṣādiq Muḥammad Sāqizī, '*Ṣurrat al-Fatāwā*', PDL, f. 181a. Several scholars have documented that even when the land's tax collection was in the care of tax farmers rather than combatants, the cultivators still required permission for intervivos transaction in the seventeenth and eighteenth centuries. See 'Abd al-Razzāq al-Hilālī, *Qiṣṣat al-Ard wa'l-Fallāḥ wa'l-Iṣlāḥ al-Zirā'ī fi 'l-Waṭan al-'Arabī* (al-Qāhira [Cairo]: Dār al-Kashāf, 1967), 28; Cuno, *Pasha's Peasants*, 34. In the fatwas of Muhammad al-'Abbasi al-Mahdi in the nineteenth century, there is no reference to either *tapu* or to some other kind of entry fee, although the permission of the '*hakim*' (a term meaning 'judge' in Syria but perhaps another term for 'deputy' in Egypt) is sometimes invoked. See Muḥammad al-'Abbāsī al-Mahdī al-Miṣrī, *al-Fatāwā al-Mahdiyya fi'l-Waqā'i' al-Miṣriyya* (al-Qahira [Cairo]: Dār al-kutub wa al-watha'iq al-qawmiyya bi'l-Qāhira, 2015), 4:11–16.

43 In his study of the archiving of eighteenth-century provincial fatwas, Guy Burak has no examples from Egypt to include. See Burak, 'Şeyhulislâm Feyzullah Efendi, the Ḥanafī Mufti of Jerusalem and the Rise of the Provincial Fatāwā Collections in the Eighteenth Century', *Journal of the Economic and Social History of the Orient* 64, no. 4 (4 June 2021): 377–403.

44 Ayman Maḥmūd, *al-Arḍ wa'l-Mujtama' fi Miṣr fi'l-'Aṣr al-'Uthmānī, 923 H/1517–1069 H/1658: Dirāsa Wathā'iqiyya* (al-Haram [Giza]: 'Ayn li'l-Dirāsāt wa'l-Buḥūth al-Insāniyya wa'l-Ijtimā'iyya, 2008), 148, 160–1; Stanford J. Shaw, *The Financial and Administrative Organization and Development of Ottoman Egypt, 1515–1798*

(Princeton, NJ: Princeton University Press, 1962), 20; Abd al-Rahim A. Abd al-Rahim, 'Land Tenure in Egypt and Its Social Effects on Egyptian Society: 1798–1813', in *Land Tenure and Social Transformation in the Middle East*, ed. Tarif Khalidi (Beirut: American University of Beirut, 1984), 237; 'Abd al-Raḥīm 'Abd al-Raḥman 'Abd al-Raḥīm, *Al-Rīf al-Miṣrī fi'l-Qarn al-Thāmin 'Ashar*, second edn (Qalyub, Egypt: Maṭābi' al-Ahrām al-Tijāriyya, 2004), 111–13.

45 Shaw, *Financial and Administrative*, 20; Cuno, *Pasha's Peasants*, 74–81.

46 Cuno, *Pasha's Peasants*, 77.

47 Meshal, 'Antagonist Sharī'as', 203–4, and Meshal, *Sharia and the Making of the Modern Egyptian*, 9–10. Although the Egyptian Hanafis may have rejected the ability of the sultan to make a general rule out of local custom, Baber Johansen states that the Central Asian Hanafis had done precisely that when they created a new doctrine of rent and usurpation from local custom. See Johansen, 'Coutumes locales', 163–71.

48 'Abd al-Raḥīm b. Abū'l-Luṭf, *al-Fatāwā al-Raḥīmīyya fī Wāqi'āt al-Sāda al-Ḥanafiyya*, PUSC Islamic Manuscripts Garrett no. 3198Y, 53b.

49 Some scholars believe the Arabs took a more rigorous approach to applying the sharia and, as a result, regarded at least some of the Ottoman *kanuns* regulating land tenure with greater skepticism than did their Rumi colleagues. Examples of scholars who attribute a general Arab skepticism towards the *kanun* include Michael Winter, 'The Islamic Profile and the Religious Policy of the Ruling Class in Ottoman Egypt', *Israel Oriental Studies* 10 (1983): 132–45; and Abd al-Karim Rafeq, 'The Syrian *'Ulama*, Ottoman Law and Islamic *Shari'a*', *Turcica* 26 (1994): 9–32. Reem Meshal argues that the characterization of the Arab ulema as champions of orthodoxy misses the point that the real tension between Egyptian ulema and the Ottoman administration was the latter's insistence on its role as the arbiter of orthodoxy; see Meshal, 'Antagonistic Sharī'as': 203. Guy Burak states that condemnation of provisions in the *kanun* by use of the Arabic pejorative term *yāsā* exposed the Arab antipathy towards the notion of a dynastic law; for the Ottomans, it was the source of the *kanun*'s legitimacy; see Burak, 'Between the Ḳānūn': 18–20.

50 Condemnation of the fee can be found in Ibn Nujaym's *al-Bahr al-Ra'iq*, and thereafter in every major work of Hanafi *fiqh* in Egypt and Syria. Ibn Nujaym, *al-Baḥr al-Rā'iq sharḥ Kanz al-Daqā'iq* (Cairo: 1894), 5:118.

51 See Chapter 2, pp. 41–2 and Chapter 4, pp. 84–5. Although a Rumi, Mehmed Birgevi agreed with the Arabs on this point; see Chapter 4, pp. 82–3.

52 See Chapter 4. Haskafi's *al-Durr al-Muntaqā* showed that he was aware of the Rumi interpretation but did not find it persuasive. See also Johansen, *Islamic Law*, 100.

53 Ebu's-Su'ud Efendi was adamant about this; see Chapter 2. Martha Mundy previously noted that the *kanun* collections and their Rumi interpreters considered this part of the *kanun* to be consistent with principles of *fiqh*; see Martha Mundy, 'Islamic Law and the Order of the State: The Legal Status of the Cultivator', in *Syria and Bilad Al-Sham under Ottoman Rule: Essays in Honour of Abdul-Karim Rafeq*, ed. Stefan Weber and Peter Sluglett (Boston: Brill, 2010), 403.

54 See Johansen, *Islamic Law on Land Tax and Rent*, 100–3.

55 It is arguable that Ibn 'Abidin actually equivocates on this issue. In *al-Radd al-Muhtar*, his commentary on Haskafi's *al-Durr al-Muntaqa*, he took the standard position of the Arab Hanafis that the payment was only rent, not *kharaj*. See Ibn 'Ābidīn, *Ḥāshiyyat Ibn 'Ābidīn*, 6:220. In his famous treatise on custom, *Nashr al-'arf fi bina ba'd al-ahkam 'ala al-'urf*, he noted that the cultivators of his own day were renters but that it had become acceptable to take the tithe or *kharaj* from them. See Ibn 'Ābidīn,

'*Nashr al-'arf fī binā ba'ḍ al-aḥkām 'alā al-'urf*, in *Majmū'at Rasā'il Ibn 'Ābidīn*, ed. Muḥammad al-'Azāzi (Beirut: Dār al-Kutub al-'Ilmiyya, 2014), 2:196.

56 Khayr al-Din al-Ramli's critique was well known by later Hanafis; see Ibn 'Ābidīn, *Ḥāshiyyat Ibn 'Ābidīn Radd al-Muḥtār*, 6:708. Nabulusi's fatwas against forcible return have been published; see Bakri Aladdin, 'Deux fatwas du Šayh 'Abd al-Ġanī al-Nābulusī', *Bulletin d'Études Orientales* 39–40 (1987–8): 7–37. An otherwise obscure mufti from the Biqā' Valley composed a lengthy treatise condemning the practice; see Yasīn al-Faraḍī bin Muṣṭafā, '*Kitab Nuṣrat al-Mutagharribīn 'an al-awṭan 'alā al-ẓuluma wa ahl al-'udwān*' Berlin: Staatsbibliothek MS Sprenger 907.

57 Bālīzādah Muṣṭafā b. Sulaymān, '*Mīzān al-Fatāwā*', SYK Yenicami 675, 30b.

58 The other main contributors, Bahai Mehmed Efendi and Yahya Efendi, do not appear to have given any fatwas dealing squarely with forcible return and validating its permissibility; the same appears to be true for their successors in the office of şeyhülislam.

59 Martha Mundy has concluded likewise, see Mundy, 'Ethics and Politics in the Law: On the Forcible return of the cultivator', in *İSAM Konuşmaları · Düşüncesi · Ahlak · Hukuk · Felsefe · Kelâm [İSAM Papers: Ottoman Thought · Ethics · Law · Philosophy-Theology]*, ed. Seyfi Kenan (Istanbul: TDV Yayın Matbaacılık, 2014).

60 These fatwas are a collection of eighteenth-century muftis, even though it is often unclear who authored each fatwa. See Dürrīzāde Meḥmed 'Ārif b. Muṣṭafā, *Netīcetü'l-Fetāvā*, with an Arabic *nüḵūl* added by Gedizli Meḥmed Efendi (İstanbul: Darü'ṭ-Ṭıba'āti'l-'Āmīre, 1237 [1822]), 681; 'Abdurraḥmān Efendi el-Erzurumī, '*Sefīnetü'l-Fetāvā*', SYK H. Hüsnü Paşa 332, 401b–402a.

61 Yenişehirli 'Abdullāh, *Beḥcetü'l-Fetāvā ma'an-nüḵūl* (İstanbul: Maṭba'a-i 'Āmīre, 1289 [1872]), 642. Pir Mehmed's fatwa had stated that the son – who had never resided in his father's village – could be forced to 'return' to the village because 'to whomever belongs the sheep belongs the lamb', MTM 306.

62 '*Fatāwā Banī 'Imād wa Ghayrihim*', ZAL 5864, f. 131b.

63 These muftis avoided frontally contradicting the *kanun*, although their rejection became more absolute from the middle of the eighteenth century. See Mundy and Smith, *Governing Property*, 32–7, and Mundy, 'Islamic Law and the Order of the State', 406–8.

64 Nu'mān Efendi, *Fetāvā'n-Nu'māniye*, 379.

65 On substitution see Es'ad Efendi, '*Fetāvā-yi Müntahabe*', 179b. See also Punar, 'Kanun and Sharia', 88–9. For pawn (*rahn*), see 179a, 179b and discussion later in the text.

66 On conditional transfer, see Es'ad Efendi, '*Fetāvā-yi Müntahabe*', 180. For deathbed transfer see '*Fetāvā-yi Müntahabe*', 180, 182.

67 MTM 89.

68 For pawn, see discussion later in the text. On substitution, see Menteşzāde 'Abdürraḥīm, *Fetāvā-yi 'Abdürraḥīm*, 533–3. On conditional transfer, see Kaya, ed., *Netîcetü'l-Fetâvâ*, 450–1, no. 2121. See also the multiple examples in 'Abdürraḥīm, *Fetāvā-yi 'Abdürraḥīm*, 532–3. On deathbed sale, see 'Abdürraḥīm, *Fetāvā-yi 'Abdürraḥīm*, 530, and'Abdurraḥmān Efendi el-Erzurumī, *Sefīnetü'l-Fetāvā*, 404.

69 Dürrīzāde/Gedizli, *Netīcetü'l-Fetāvā*, 676; Aḥmed el-Mostarī, '*Fetāvā-yi Aḥmediye*', 189b; and 'Abdürraḥīm, *Fetāvā-yi 'Abdürraḥīm*, 2:509.

70 The *kanun* endorsed this practice using the terms 'entrusting' (*amana*) or 'loan' (*'ariya*), and the seventeenth-century muftis had typically employed those terms as well; see MTM 88–9. Not all muftis embraced the term 'rent' to describe this situation in the eighteenth century: the mufti of Erzurum Seyid İbrāhīm Edhem Efendi

(d. 1776) rather idiosyncratically refers to this arrangement as Zayd commissioning (*sipariş*) ʿAmr to farm his land while he was absent. See Seyid İbrāhīm Edhem, *Nehriyetü'l-fetvā*, 298b. ʿAbdürrahim also used this term: ʿAbdürraḥīm, *Fetāvā-yi ʿAbdürraḥīm*, 2: 532.

71 These are not exactly alike as *rahn* may or may not involve the right of the creditor to use the object that has been pledged or pawned. In the transfer with redemption, the usage right is an intrinsic part of the transaction.

72 In Damascene fatwas from the seventeenth and eighteenth centuries, it only appeared in questions about land held in *waqf*, where it was permitted. For fatwas permitting *rahn*, see Ismāʿīl al-Ḥāʾik, (d. 1702), '*Bāb Mashad Maska*', f. 9b, and the fatwa authored by ʿAbd al-Raḥmān Muḥammad ʿImād al-Dīn (d. 1641) in '*Fatāwā Banī al-ʿImādī wa Ghayrihim*', ZAL 5864, f. 125a. The fatwa given by ʿAlī al-Murādī in '*Majmūʿ Fatāwā Murādiya*', ZAL 2642 f. 328, is somewhat ambiguous but suggests that *rahn* is valid if the *mutawalli* has permitted it.

73 ʿAbdürraḥīm, *Fetāvā-yi ʿAbdürraḥīm*, 2: 535 and Mostarī, '*Fetāvā-yi Aḥmediye*', 214b–216a.

74 Ahmed el-Mostari recorded a fatwa in which the lender died, and only after his daughters had been in possession of the land for sixteen years was the indebted *mutasarrif* able to repay the loan and reclaim the land. Mostarī, '*Fetāvā-yi Aḥmediye*', 214b.

75 ʿAbdürraḥīm, *Fetāvā-yi ʿAbdürraḥīm*, 535.

76 M. Ertuğrul Düzdağ, *Şeyhülislam Ebussuud Efendi Fetvaları: Kanunî Devrinde Osmanlı Devrinde Osmanlı Hayatı* (Istanbul: Kapı Yayınları, 2012), 219.

77 MTM 88; see also '*Ḳānūn-ı Cedīd*', SYK Bağdatlı Vehbi 569, 31.

78 The *kanun* specifically forbade a creditor to make a claim on the estate of a cultivator who died in debt. Creditors were prohibited from wresting the land from the possession of the cultivator's son (see MTM 65). In a normal transaction of *rahn*, the creditor can force a sale to reclaim his debt. See Hallaq, *Sharia*, 268. It does not appear that the Ottoman muftis would allow this in the case of pawned *tasarruf*. In any case, unless a specific agreement with the deputy's blessing had authorized an exchange of *tasarruf* for money, the muftis still affirmed that *tasarruf* could still not be used to discharge debt. Ahmed el-Mostari, who permitted *rahn* with the deputy's permission, nevertheless forbade a group of brothers from *taqsim* if the purpose was to create a portion that could be sold to repay debt. See Mostarī, '*Fetāvā-yi Aḥmediye*', 217a. Likewise, *Şeyhülislam* ʿAbdürrahim, who also gave copious fatwas allowing *rahn*, also gave a fatwa forbidding a creditor from seizing *miri tasarruf* to pay off debt. See ʿAbdürraḥīm, *Fetāvā-yi ʿAbdürraḥīm*, 2: 536. Other eighteenth-century muftis ruled similarly: see Dürrīzāde and Gedizli, *Netīcetü'l-Fetāvā*, 674. ʿAbdurraḥmān Efendi el-Erzurumī, '*Sefīnetü'l-Fetāvā*', 413–14; and in Damascus ʿAlī al-Murādī, '*Majmūʿ Fatāwā Murādiya*', 326.

79 Esʿad Efendi, '*Fetāvā-yi Müntahabe*', f. 179a.

80 Abdürrahim, *Fetāvā-yi Abdürrahim*, 550.

81 Abdurrahman Efendi el-Erzurumi, '*Sefinetü'l-Fetāvā*', 403.

82 ʿAbd al-Ghanī al-Nābulusī, '*Fatāwā al-Nābulusī*', ZAL 2684, f. 108b.

83 Aḥmed el-Mostarī, '*Fetāvā-yi Aḥmediye*', 216a–218b is a section entirely dedicated to *taqsim*; see also ʿAbdurraḥmān Efendi el-Erzurumī, '*Sefīnetü'l-Fetāvā*', 412. This transaction did not appear in any of the fatwas from Damascus. ʿAbbasi al-Mahdi of Egypt forbade it both on *waqf* and *miri*; see ʿAbbāsī, *al-Fatāwā al-Mahdiyya*, 4:314.

84 For the sections on the *mutasarrif*s right of *faragh*, see Debbāğzāde Nuʿmān Efendi, *Fetāvā'n-Nuʿmāniye*, SYK Esad Ef. 1080, 346b–349b.
85 Nuʿmān Efendi, *Fetāvā'n-Nuʿmāniye*, 352a.
86 Nuʿmān Efendi, *Fetāvā'n-Nuʿmāniyee*, 353b.
87 Nuʿmān Efendi, *Fetāvā'n-Nuʿmāniye*, 347b–348b.
88 Nuʿmān Efendi, *Fetāvā'n-Nuʿmāniye*, 379.
89 Kenneth Cuno, noting the ulema's defence of 'unsound' endowments and the rights of the rentier class generally in eighteenth-century Egypt, also found extensive reference to the mandate of the *bayt al-mal* and its legitimation of contemporary practices. See Cuno, 'Ideology and Juridical Discourse in Ottoman Egypt', 136–63.
90 See Introduction, n. 9, for a list of such works.

Chapter 6

1 On the Council, see, Stanford J. Shaw, 'The Central Legislative Councils in the Nineteenth-Century Ottoman Reform Movement before 1876', *International Journal of Middle East Studies* 1, no. 1 (1970): 51–4. On Cevdet Paşa, see Harold Bowen, 'Aḥmad Djewdet Pas̲h̲a', EI^2, 284-286.
2 Akgündüz, *Mukayeseli Islam ve Osmanlı Hukuku Külliyatı*, 679. Hereafter, all references to the Land Code in the notes refer to this copy.
3 M. Şükrü Hanioğlu, *A Brief History of the Late Ottoman Empire* (Princeton, NJ: Princeton University Press, 2008, 78–83.
4 Bruce Alan Masters, *Christians and Jews in the Ottoman Arab World: The Roots of Sectarianism* (New York: Cambridge University Press, 2001), 74–9; Eldem, 'Capitulations and Western Trade', in *The Cambridge History of Turkey Vol. 3 The Later Ottoman Empire 1603–1839*, ed. Suraiya Faroqhi (Cambridge: Cambridge University Press, 2006), 319–21; Turan Kayaoğlu, *Legal Imperialism: Sovereignty and Extraterritoriality in Japan, the Ottoman Empire, and China* (New York: Cambridge University Press, 2010), 104–28. However, in the later nineteenth century, the Ottomans did see some success in limiting how foreign Muslims could access the privileges of the capitulatory regime. See Lale Can, 'The Protection Question: Central Asians and Extraterritoriality in the Late Ottoman Empire' (IJMES) 48, no. 4 (2016), 679–99.
5 Charles P. Issawi, ed., *The Economic History of the Middle East: 1800–1914: A Book of Readings* (Chicago: University of Chicago Press, 1966), 38–55; Donald Quataert, 'Part IV The Age of Reforms 1812–1914', in *An Economic and Social History of the Ottoman Empire Vol. 2 1600–1914*, ed. Halil Inalcik with Donald Quataert (Cambridge: Cambridge University Press, 1994), 825–7; Roger Owen, *The Middle East in the World Economy, 1800–1914* (New York: Methuen, 1981).
6 Gelvin, *The Modern Middle East*, 70–88.
7 For a holistic yet dated treatment of the Tanzimat and the officials who crafted its policies see Roderic H. Davison, *Reform in the Ottoman Empire, 1856–1876* Princeton Legacy Library (Princeton, NJ: Princeton University Press, 1976). For important studies on various aspects of it see Ilber Ortaylı, *Tanzimat devrinde Osmanlı mahallî idareleri, 1840–1880* (Ankara: Türk Tarih Kurumu, 2000); Virgina H. Aksan, *Ottoman Wars 1700–1870: An Empire Besieged* (London: Routledge, 2013), 313–42, 376–83, 402–16; Daniel Panzac, 'Tanzimat et santé publique: Les débuts du conseil sanitaire de

l'Empire ottoman', in *Population et santé dans l'Empire ottoman (XVIIIe-XXe siècles)*, ed. Daniel Panzac (Istanbul: Isis, 1996), 77–85.

8 The influential British diplomat Stratford Canning was among these. However, there were other European statesmen who encouraged Ottoman reformers to 'stay Turks' and continue to regard Islamic law as an essential part of the empire's institutional infrastructure. See Niyazi Berkes, *The Development of Secularism in Turkey* (New York: Routledge, 1998), 148–9.

9 On the attitudes of 'Westernizing' reformers to religion, see Şerif Mardin, *Religion and Social Change in Modern Turkey: The Case of Bediüzzaman Said Nursi* (Albany: State University of New York Press, 1989), 113. On liberal reform and Islam, see also Mardin, *The Genesis of Young Ottoman Thought* (Princeton, NJ: Princeton University Press, 1962). On Islam and the politics of autocracy, see Selim Deringil, *The Well-Protected Domains: Ideology and the Legitimation of Power, 1876–1909* (New York: I.B. Tauris, 1999), 44–67.

10 Some ulema opposed the Tanzimat on these grounds, but there were also reformers and their supporters in the ranks of the ulema, see, Uriel Heyd, 'The Ottoman Ulema and Westernization in the Time of Selim III and Mahmud II', in *The Modern Middle East: A Reader*, ed. Albert Hourani, Philip S. Khoury and Mary C. Wilson (Berkeley: University of California Press, 1993), 29–60.

11 Niyazi Berkes, *Development of Secularism*, 161–2.

12 Ahmed Cevdet Paşa, *Tezakir, 1–12*, ed. Cavid Baysun (Ankara: Türk Tarih Kurumu Basımevi, 1953), 63; Hallaq, *Sharia: Theory, Practice, Transformations*, 406–7. there is debate among historians about the extent to which French law influenced either Ottoman penal law and the new court systems introduced by the Tanzimat, as Hallaq claims. Ehud Toledano sees the 1850 Penal Code and Omri Paz the criminal courts that were established in tandem with it as essentially indigenous projects despite their departures from past practice. See Toledano, 'The Legislative Process in the Ottoman Empire in the Early *Tanzimat* Period: A Footnote', *International Journal of Turkish Studies* 11, no. 2 (1980): 99–108; Paz, 'Documenting Justice: New Recording Practices and the Establishment of an Activist Criminal Court System in the Ottoman Provinces (1840-Late 1860s)', *Islamic Law and Society* 21, no. 1–2 (2014): 81–113. Nevertheless, scholars such as Avi Rubin continue to argue that French legal practice had a profound effect on Ottoman legal reform. See Rubin, 'Legal Borrowing and Its Impact on Ottoman Legal Culture in the Late Nineteenth Century', *Rechtliche Anleihen und ihr Einfluss auf die osmanische Rechtskultur im späten 19. Jahrhundert* 22, no. 2 (2007): 279–303.

13 See Introduction, p. 2, notes 8 and 9.

14 Not coincidentally, the Council responsible for crafting the Code had also taken control of provincial taxation as one of its first official acts. See Paz, 'Documenting Justice', 93–4. Noting the scholarly consensus on the revenue-raising objective of the Code, Donald Quataert added the qualification that stability appears to have been just as important an objective as raising revenues. It is true that the Land Code reduced *tapu* revenues for many people seeking to acquire land; this made sense not from a fiscal standpoint but from a social one. See Quataert, *Economic and Social History*, 857.

15 Owen, *Middle East in the World Economy*, 61–4, 104–8; Issawi, ed., *Economic History of the Middle East*, 38–59.

16 Barkan, *Türk Toprak Hukuku Tarihinde Tanzimat Ve 1274 (1858)*, 61; Doreen Warriner, 'Land Tenure Problems in the Fertile Crescent', in Issawi, *Economic History of the Middle East*, 71–8; Sluglett and Farouk-Sluglett, 'The Application of the 1858 Land Code', 409–21; Cin, *Osmanlı Toprak Düzeni Ve Bu Düzenin Bozulması*, 121; Islamoğlu, 'Property as a Contested Domain', 3–61; Mundy and Smith, *Governing Property*, 43.

17 The classic statement on this ideal of administration can be found in Max Weber, *Economy and Society: A New Translation*, ed. and tr. Keith Tribe (Cambridge, MA: Harvard University Press, 2019), 347–54. For a study of the Ottoman pursuit of this administrative ideal see Carter Vaughn Findley, *Bureaucratic Reform in the Ottoman Empire: The Sublime Porte 1789–1922* (Princeton: Princeton University Press, 1980).

18 Cevdet Paşa, *Tezakir*, 63.

19 Islamoğlu, 'Property as a Contested Domain', 24. The desire to create a single Ottoman legal subject is typically remarked on in the Ottoman attempts at creating at a subject devoid of religious specificity; see, for example, Hanioğlu, *Brief History*, 74. Both the 1856 imperial rescript and an 1863 decree designed to limit the number of Ottomans seeking foreign protection were to emphasize that all Ottoman subjects had the same rights, see Will Hanley, 'What Ottoman Nationality Was and Was Not', in *The Subjects of Ottoman International Law*, ed. L. Can et al. (Bloomington: Indiana University Press, 2020), 61–2. However, from 1839 there were efforts to end the legal and social distinction between *askeri* and *reaya*. These included eliminating both the perquisites of military class like the lifelong tax farm and liabilities faced by the *askeri* class in their status as slaves such as confiscation of their estates and summary judgement rather than trial. See K. Kıvanç Karaman and Şevket Pamuk, 'Ottoman State Finances in European Perspective, 1500–1914', *Journal of Economic History*, LXX (2010), 593–629 and Carter Vaughn Findley, *Ottoman Civil Officialdom: A Social History* (Princeton: Princeton University Press, 1989), 25–6.

20 Typically, this transition has been understood as one from an indigenous jurists' law to a Western-inspired, modern statutory law. See N. J. Coulson, *A History of Islamic Law* (New Brunswick, NJ: Aldine Transaction, 2011), 149–53; Aharon Layish, 'The Transformation of the Sharīʿa from Jurists' Law to Statutory Law in the Contemporary Muslim World', *Die Welt des Islams* 44, no. 1 (2004): 85–113; Hallaq, *Sharia*, 411, 443–99. The paradigm, however, is shifting; see Avi Rubin, 'Modernity as a Code', 828–56; Ayoub, 'The Mecelle, Sharia, and the Ottoman State', 121–46; Anver M. Emon 'Codification and Islamic Law: The Ideology Behind a Tragic Narrative', *Middle East Law and Governance* 8, nos. 2–3 (2016): 275–310; Burak, 'Ottoman Islamic Law and "Early Modernity"', JOTSA 7, no. 1 (2020): 17–19.

21 Çağlar Keyder, 'Small Peasant Ownership in Turkey: Historical Formation and Present Structure', *Review (Fernand Braudel Center)* 7, no. 1 (1983): 61.

22 Stanford J. Shaw, 'The Nineteenth-Century Ottoman Tax Reforms and Revenue System', *International Journal of Middle East Studies* 6, no. 4 (1975): 421–59. Nadir Özbek has argued that the reformers were not intent on rooting out all forms of tax farming, but rather were focused on fiscal centralization, and found ways to adapt tax farming to these goals. See Özbek, 'Tax Farming in the Nineteenth-Century Ottoman Empire: Institutional Backwardness or the Emergence of Modern Public Finance?', *Journal of Interdisciplinary History*, XLIX, no. 2 (Autumn, 2018): 219–45.

23 However, many historians who have studied the implementation of the Tanzimat argue that despite the reformers' goals, in practice there remained a need to come to

terms with local leaders and their interests. For a recent example of such studies, see Yönca Köksal, *The Ottoman Empire in the Tanzimat Era: Provincial Perspectives from Ankara to Edirne* (London: Routledge, 2019).

24 Carter Vaughn Findley traces use of the term '*me'mur*' to roughly the time of the Rescript of Gülhane in 1839, which is often considered to have initiated the first phase of the Tanzimat. For Findley, this marks the beginning of the bureaucracy's passage from a patrimonial bureaucracy staffed by the sultan's slaves to a rational bureaucracy staffed by civil officials. See Findley, *Ottoman Civil Officialdom*, 25–7.

25 Art. 64, Land Code. Unless otherwise noted, all further references to the Land Code can be found in the copy published in Akgündüz, *Mukayeseli İslam Ve Osmanlı Hukuku Külliyatı*, 681–715.

26 See, for example, MTM 59.

27 Akgündüz, *Mukayeseli İslam Ve Osmanlı Hukuku Külliyatı*, 685–6.

28 Because of the priority given to individuation in the Code, the Code made a new distinction between cultivated land and pasture land. In the past, both had been treated as *miri*, but pasture lands held by villages rather than by specific individuals were classified in the Code as '*metruke*' (Art. 5, Land Code).

29 That is, all the familiar rules about transfers with permission, loan or rental, the ability to be absent and retain possession, the ability to plant trees or build buildings with permission; the ability for fellow villagers to preempt the acquisition of an outsider.

30 Art. 36, Land Code: '*dilediği kimseye farig olabilir*'.

31 The Tapu Law states in Art. 21 that if everything is in order, the transfer and the documentation thereof is to be issued without delay; see Stanley Fisher, *Ottoman Land Laws: Containing the Ottoman Land Code and Later Legislation Affecting Land; with Notes and an Appendix of Cyprus Laws and Rules Relating to Land* (New York: H. Milford, Oxford University Press, 1919), 47.

32 As before, co-villagers had a year to make their claim; see Art. 45, Land Code.

33 'Abdurraḥmān el-Erzurumī, *Sefīnet*, 401b. Ahmed el-Mostari has multiple fatwas stating that a *mutasarrif* or his heirs can demand compensation for deterioration or damage from a usurper. See Mostarī, '*Fetāvā-yi Aḥmediye*', 212a–212b.

34 Earlier Hanafi authorities had rejected that a usurper owed use-value of the thing usurped to the owner, but late Hanafis reversed this, ruling that usurpers were liable for consuming profits or inflicting damages on the property; see Ayoub, *Law, Empire, and the Sultan*, 144–6. On the evolution of the usurper's obligation to pay an equivalent of rent see also Johansen, *Islamic Law on Land Tax and Rent*, 107–11, 123.

35 See Chapter 5, p. 101; Yenişehirli 'Abdullāh, *Beḥcetü'l-Fetāvā*, p. 640.

36 Compare with fatwas discussed in chapter 5, p. 98.

37 The Code did introduce a new provision allowing the cultivator to empower the creditor to sell the holding and repay himself from the proceeds if the cultivator could not pay back the debt. See Art. 117, Land Code. There was no legal way for the creditor to the force the cultivator to take this course, but one can easily imagine that the creditor might find ways to pressure the cultivator to do so.

38 A number of studies have read the Code as a 'reassertion' of state powers, which had existed in the sixteenth century only to disappear in the seventeenth and eighteenth centuries; see Gabriel Baer, 'Land Tenure in Egypt and the Fertile Crescent, 1800–1950', in *Economic History of the Middle East and North Africa*, ed. Charles Issawi (New York: Columbia University Press, 1982), 79–90; Karpat, 'The Land Regime', 86.

39 In this, the Code differed from some of the other global attempts at land law reform that took place in the nineteenth century. The Napoleonic Code proclaimed

private property to be absolute, but in practice, property rights on land remained overlapping and contested in nineteenth-century France. See Donald R. Kelley and Bonnie G. Smith, 'What Was Property? Legal Dimensions of the Social Question in France (1789–1848)', *Proceedings of the American Philosophical Society* 128, no. 3 (1984): 200–30.

40 Although Barkan saw the Land Code as a return to an earlier tradition of law rather than a continuity with the recent past, his characterization of the *miri* regime as a 'nationalization' of the empire's land does not strike me as entirely wrongheaded when applied to the 1858 Land Code. The latter defended Ottoman claims to legal and fiscal sovereignty in much the same way and for the same reasons that 'developing' states undertook the nationalization of natural resources in the twentieth century. See Ömer Lütfi Barkan, 'Türkiye'de Toprak Meselesinin Tarihi Esasları', *Türkiye'de Toprak Meselesi Toplu Eserler 1* (Istanbul: Gözlem Yayınları, 1960), 127.

41 Mundy and Smith, *Governing Property*, 41.

42 *Tapu* is still the advance on what is essentially a rental contract between the *mutasarrif* and the treasury. See Halis Eşref, *Şerḥ-i Ḳānūn-ı Arāżī* ([Istanbul]: Der Sa'ādet (Maḥmūd Bey) Maṭba'ası, 1889), 39. That *miri tasarruf* was a heritable lease was also the opinion of the British authorities applying the Land Code on Cyprus; see also Fisher, *Ottoman Land Laws*, 3.

43 As it has appeared in the literature of the 'circle of justice' or the images of the 'body politic' in political tracts and works of advice for sultans. Linda Darling, *A History of Social Justice and Political Power in the Middle East: The Circle of Justice from Mesopotamia to Globalization* (New York: Routledge, 2013), 1–11, 146–8; Kâtip Çelebi, *Düstur el-'Amel li-Islah el-Halel* (Istanbul: 1280/1863), 7–9; Mustafa Naima, *Tarih-i Naima* (Kostantiniye [Istanbul]: Darü't-tibaatı'l-Amire, 1834), 27–30.

44 This was the one circumstance in which an eighteenth-century mufti ruled that a deputy was correct to refuse a transfer. Furthermore, *kanun*s restricting the deputy's ability to give *tasarruf* to members of his family continued to be cited by the muftis, see Menteşzāde 'Abdürraḥīm, *Fetāvā-yi 'Abdürraḥīm*, 2: 514–15.

45 Quataert, *Ottoman Empire, 1700–1922*, 64–8; Stanford J. Shaw and Ezel Kural Shaw, *History of the Ottoman Empire and Modern Turkey* (New York: Cambridge University Press, 1977), 2:14–16, 19–27, 49.

46 Since the Edict of Gülhane in 1839, the term of service for a normal conscript or volunteer was set at five years. See Erik Jan Zürcher, 'The Ottoman Conscription System, 1844–1914', *International Review of Social History* 43, no. 3 (1998): 437–49, 439. Article 67 of the Code stated that if a man who had served at least five years in the military had the *haqq-ı tapu* on a piece of land, five *dönüm*s of the land would be granted to him free of *tapu*.

47 Hakan Erdem, 'Recruitment for the "Victorious Soldiers of Muhammad" in the Arab Provinces, 1826–1828', in *Histories of the Modern Middle East*, ed. I. Gershoni, H. Erdem and U. Woköck (Boulder, CO: Lynne Rienner 2002), 189–94. The religio-ethnic composition of the military remained heavily Turkish and Muslim despite recruitment in the Arab provinces and the opening of conscription to Christians in 1853.

48 Art. 109 adopted an old provision of the *kanun*, declaring that in post-mortem transmission, only Muslims were eligible to take the *tasarruf* of a deceased Muslim; Art. 110 prohibited foreign subjects from succession to *tasarruf*.

49 Kayaoğlu, *Legal Imperialism*, 127–8.

50 Fisher, *Ottoman Land Laws*, 57–9.

51 This fatwa is unattributed, but it is part of the collection of eighteenth-century fatwas known as *Neticetü'l-Fetava*. See Dürrīzade Muḥammad 'Ārif b. Muṣṭafā and Gedizli Meḥmed Efendi, *Netīcetü'l-Fetāvā*, 677–8.

52 Also known as Mehmed Gedüsi, he compiled a number of fatwa collections for publication and appended precedent (*nüḳul*) to a number of these. See Abdullah Ceyhan, 'Osmanlı Devri Müderris, Kadı ve Fetva Eminlerinden Gedizli Hafız Mehmed Efendi', *Diyanet İlmi Dergi* 11, no. 3 (1993): 11–24.

53 The *Hidaya* was composed by Burhan al-Din al-Marghinani (d. 1197), one of the great Central Asian Hanafi ulema. The *Durar al-Ghurar* was composed by Molla Hüsrev (d. 1480), one of the first Ottoman ulema to write works that were widely read and cited by Hanafis outside the empire.

54 This is not true of Mundy and Smith, *Governing Property*, but is true of Barkan, *Türk Toprak Hukuku*; Cin, *Osmanlı Toprak Düzeni Ve Bu Düzenin Bozulması*, fourth edn (Ankara: Berikan Ofset Matbaa, 2016), and Haim Gerber, *The Social Origins of the Modern Middle East*, ACLS Humanities E-Book (Boulder, CO: L. Rienner Mansell Publishing, 1987), 69–72.

55 See Chapter 3, p. 50. For the Code's introduction where the fatwas are described as built upon the *kanun*s issued in Süleyman's era, see Land Code, Introduction.

56 Cevdet Paşa acknowledged as much. See Islamoğlu, 'Property as a Contested Domain', 11.

57 The fatwas on these subjects are too numerous to list in full; a few representative examples are given here. See Chapter 3 for the ten-year rule and compare with Art. 78, Land Code. For one of the many issues concerning the rights of partners, compare Erzurumlu 'Abdurraḥmān, *Sefīnetü'l-Fetāvā*, 404, and Art. 41, Land Code. See Dürrīzāde and Gedizli Meḥmed, *Netīcetü'l-Fetāvā* for the procedure finalizing transfers and also anonymous eighteenth-century fatwas on pp. 677, 678, 680 and 681. Cf. Art. 37–9 in the Land Code.

58 For his fatwas on transactions see Chapter 5, pp. 98–100. For the prohibition against burying corpses on *miri* land see *Şeyhülislām* Menteşzāde 'Abdürraḥīm, *Fetāvā-yi 'Abdürraḥīm*, 2: 550. Cf. Art. 33 in the Land Code. For the rights of the mentally incapacitated see *Fetāvā-yi 'Abdürraḥīm*, 2: 530–31. Cf. Art. 50–3 in the Land Code.

59 Brinkley Messick refers to the format of a modern Code as 'closed', in contrast to the textual tradition of *fiqh* characterized by its openness to interpretation. See Messick, *The Calligraphic State: Textual Domination and History in a Muslim Society* (Berkeley: University of California Press, 1993), 56. This description strikes me as accurate, yet it does not capture that the process of closing the text was not a neutral one.

60 There were some such provisions, but they were few in number. By the seventeenth century, though, one of the most 'muscular' of such powers was that a *kanun* empowered cultivators to pull up trees or vines planted on their land by usurpers (MTM 87). The Code allowed the *me'mur* to uproot in this case, upon request from the *mutasarrif* (see Art. 35, Land Code).

61 Cf. Art. 11, Land Code, with anonymous fatwa '*Ḳānūnnāme-yi Aḥmed Han*' SYK Esad Ef. 851, 62b, and a similar fatwa of Baha'i Mehmed Efendi, MTM 89.

62 Cf. Art. 27, Land Code with fatwa, 'Abdürraḥīm, *Fetāvā-yi 'Abdürraḥīm*, 2: 541.

63 Cf. Art. 24, Land Code with fatwas in Çatalcalı 'Alī Efendi, '*Fetāvā-yi 'Alī Efendi*'," SYK Esad Efendi 1072, 297a and Aḥmed el-Mostarī, '*Fetāvā-yi Aḥmediye*', 221a–221b.

64 Cf. Art. 35, Land Code with fatwa, 'Abdürraḥīm, *Fetāvā-yi 'Abdürraḥīm*, 2: 552.

65 Cf. Arts. 19 and 30, Land Code, with an anonymous fatwa '*Ḳānūnnāme-yi Aḥmed Han*', 72; and fatwas of 'Abdürraḥīm, *Fetāvā-yi Abdürraḥīm*, 2: 541, and Çatalcalı, '*Fetāvā-yi 'Alī Efendi*', 298a.

66 See Huri Islamoğlu, 'Property as a Contested Domain', 30–1.

67 Examples of various attempts to define the contours of the cultivator's rights can be found in the *kanunnames* for Budin and for the Morea. For both of these texts, see Barkan, *Kanunlar*, 296 and 326 respectively.

68 A few fatwas had posited some modest ability of fellow villagers and neighbours to intervene: an anonymous fatwa in '*Ḳānūnnāme-yi Aḥmed Han*', 74, allows a *mutasarrif* to cut the branch of a tree belonging to his neighbour on adjacent land because its shadow keeps his grass from growing. Similarly, Ibrahim Edhem of Erzurum ruled that if someone decided to remove his *milk* cutwater from a stream, he could be stopped if it harmed the *sipahi* and villagers. See İbrāhīm Edhem, *Nehriyetü'l-Fetvā*, 302a–302b.

69 MTM 89.

70 On *taqsim*, see Chapter 5, p. 100.

71 While Mundy and Smith see the Code's adoption of *taqsim* as an important rupture with the past that 'rendered obsolete the notion of a viable agricultural lot' (see Mundy and Smith, *Governing Property*, 46), I find this article striking for the opposite reason. The Code's specification that *taqsim* cannot be carried out if an unworkable fragmentation will occur is a testament not only to the continuity of this concern, but of the newly urgent need to maximize taxation revenues that likely kept this concern relevant in the nineteenth century.

72 Ibn 'Ābidīn, *al-'Uqūd al-Durriyya*, 2:297.

73 Both Cevdet Paşa and his influential biographer Şerif Mardin made this claim on the basis that the land law was assembled from the pre-existing textual tradition; see Ebul'ula Mardin, *Medenî Hukuk Cephesinden Ahmet Cevdet Paşa* (İstanbul: Turkiye Diyanet Vakfi Yayinlari, 2012), 36. Such a claim adumbrated both the profound transformation of the law's administration and the more subtle sculpting of the law that occurred through codification.

74 Avi Rubin (and others) objects to calling any premodern text a code; see Avi Rubin, 'Modernity as a Code: The Ottoman Empire and the Global Movement of Codification', *Journal of the Economic and Social History of the Orient* 59, no. 5 (2016): 839–40. Yet the *Kanun-ı Cedid* fits the criteria that Rubin considers to be the hallmark of modern codes: it is succinct, rationally organized and comprehensive (829). His characterization of *kanunnames* as addressing only particular localities instead of the empire as a whole is inaccurate; the *Kanun-ı Cedid* does indeed address the empire as a whole even though it is composed of texts originally issued to govern specific localities.

75 Additionally, in the newly perilous circumstances of the time, Ottoman administrators and ordinary subjects alike looked to the state to take necessary action to defend itself and its subjects; for the state to assume the authority to enact new laws had never been less controversial; Gerber, *Islamic Law and Culture*, 50–2; Akgündüz, *Osmanlı Kanunnâmeleri Ve Hukukî Tahlilleri*, 1:55.

76 These laws were not all new in 1858, changes had been happening since the 1840s, see Cin, *Osmanlı Toprak*, 242–4, and Mundy and Smith, *Governing Property*, 44–5.

77 Works in the previous note and Barkan, *Türk Toprak Hukuku Tarihinde Tanzimat*, 45–7, 73–86.

78 MTM 65–6.

79 Prior to the nineteenth century, only male orphans had ten years from the time of maturity to claim their father's land; females had ten years from the death of the father. The *kanun* did not state that the deputy or guardian was forbidden to transfer, only that the orphan had the right to undo such transfers. However, the muftis ruled that if a deputy tried to grant the land to someone else and the guardian of the minor protested, the transfer could be stopped. See the fatwas of Baha'i Mehmed and Mostari Ahmed forbidding the deputy to give the land to another while the orphan was a child in '*Ḳānūn-ı Cedīd*', SYK Bağdatlı Vehbi 569, 15b, and Aḥmed el-Mostarī, '*Fetāvā-yi Aḥmediye*', 213a, respectively. Later fatwas would extend the orphan's right to reclaim *miri* land to all minors and the mentally disabled, the position which the Code too would adopt. See 'Abdürraḥīm, *Fetāvā-yi 'Abdürraḥīm*, 2: 525–8, 530–1.

80 The dominant view of the 'late' Hanafis was that immoveable property of the orphan could be sold only if there was need, such as lack of other funds for his maintenance, see Ibn 'Ābidīn, *al-'Uqūd al-Durriyya*, 2: 508, 509–10. In Ottoman courts, "need" was documented in cases where a guardian sold his ward's immoveable property, see Mahmoud Yazbak, 'Muslim Orphans and the Sharī'a in Ottoman Palestine according to Sijill Records', *Journal of the Economic and Social History of the Orient* 44/2 (2001): 130–1.

81 If the orphan could prove that there had been no need for the sale, he could reverse it. See Ibn 'Ābidīn, *al-'Uqūd al-Durriyya*, 2: 510. For sale of moveable property, orphans typically needed to sue their guardians and show the latter's mismanagement in order to recover funds from the sale of their assets. For examples of such cases in Kayseri and Konya, see Necmettin Aygün, 'Nikâh Akdi ve Vasîlik Bağlamında Aksaray ve Çevre Yerleşimlerde Kadınlar ile Çocukarın Hak Arama Hukuku (1742–1743)', in *Mutefekkir, Faculty of Islamic Sciences* 5/10 (2018): 247–66, 258. For such cases in Aleppo, see Margaret L. Meriwether, 'The Rights of Children and the Responsibilities of Women: Women as Wasis in Ottoman Aleppo 1770–1840', in *Women, the Family, and Divorce Laws in Islamic History*, ed. A. E. A. Sonbol (Syracuse: Syracuse University Press, 1996), 228–30, 226–7.

82 Eşref, *Şerhi Kanun-ı Arazi*, 8.

83 'Alī Ḥaydar Hocā Emīnefendizāde, *Şerḥ-i Cedīd li-Ḳānūn il-Erāzī* (İstanbul: A. Asadourian) Şirket-i Mürettibiye-yi Maṭba'ası, 1321 [1903 or 1904]. [The passage before the ellipsis comes from pp. 2–3 of the introduction. The portion after ellipsis comes from p. 6.]

SELECTED BIBLIOGRAPHY

Unpublished sources

Archival sources

Prime minister's archives, Istanbul Turkey (Başbakanlık Arşivi)

Tapu Tahrir Defterleri (BOA TT) 479, 825, 1371.
Maliye'den Müdevver (BOA MAD) Tax Farm Registers 4181, 9486, 15393, 21512.

Manuscript sources

The following abbreviations are used in the text and bibliography: Süleymaniye Yazma Eser Kütüphanesi, Istanbul (SYK); İstanbul Üniversitesi Nadir Kitabler Kütüphanesi, Istanbul (IU); Asad National Library of Syria, *Ẓāhiriyya* collection, Damascus (ZAL); Princeton Digital Library (PDL); Princeton University Special Collections (PUSC).

Kanunnames and other anonymous texts

Arāzīye Müte'allik Ḳānūnnāme. SYK Esad Efendi 846, 172–80.
Fetāvā. SYK Esad Efendi 587/5, f. 151–64. Anonymous compilation of fatwas attributed to Ebu's-Su'ud Efendi, Pir Mehmed and Baha'i Mehmed Efendi.
Ḳānūn-ı Cedīd. SYK Bağdatlı Vehbi 551/1, 1–71.
Ḳānūn-ı Cedīd. SYK Bağdatlı Vehbi 569/1, 1–64.
Ḳānūn-ı Cedīd. SYK Fatih 3505, 1–73.
Ḳānūn-ı Cedīd. SYK Hacı Mahmud 1245.
Ḳānūn-ı Cedīd der Beyān-i Tapu. SYK Hacı Mahmud 5657.
Ḳānūnnāme ve Ḥılye-yi Ḥaḳḳānī ve ghayrihi min et-Tevārīh. SYK Fatih 5424/1, 1–49.
Ḳānūnnāme-yi Aḥmed Han. SYK Esad Ef. 851/3, 54–69.
Ḳānūnnāme-yi Cedīd bu dur. SYK Esad Ef. 586/2, 16–29.
Ḳānūnnāme-yi Cedīd Ebu's-Su'ud Efendi Hażretleri. SYK Reşid Efendi 277/1, 1–36.
Ḳānūnnāme-yi Cedīd fīmā yete'allıḳ bi'l-'arāżī. SYK Mihrişah 440/6, f. 48–61.
Minḳarīzāde Ḳānūnnāmesi. SYK Hacı Mahmud Efendi 1238/3, f. 69–88.
Münşe'at. SYK Esad Efendi 3835.
Sulṭān Süleymān Han zamānında ve Şeyhülislām Ebū's-Su'ūd Efendi aṣrında olan ḳānūnnāmelerdir. IU 9623.

Texts with authors

Bālīzādah, Muṣṭafā b. Sulaymān. *Mīzān al-Fatāwā*. SYK Yenicami 675.
Çatalcalı, *Şeyhülisām* 'Alī b. Meḥmed Efendi. *Fetāvā-yi 'Alī Efendi*. SYK Esad Efendi 1072.

Çatalcalı, *Şeyhülislām* 'Alī b. Meḥmed Efendi. *Fetāvā*. SYK Yazma Bağışlar 2303.
Debbāğzāde, Nu'mān Efendi. *Fetāvā'n-Nu'māniye*. SYK Esad Efendi 1080.
Ebū Ca'fer. *Tapu Müte'allik Fetvālar*. SYK Yazma Bağışlar 1438/1, f. 1–38.
el-Erzurumī, 'Abdurraḥmān Efendi. *Sefīnetü'l-Fetāvā*. SYK H. Hüsnü Paşa 331–2.
al-Faraḍī, Yasīn bin Mustafā. *Kitab Nuṣrat al-Mutagharribīn 'an al-awṭan 'alā al-ẓuluma wa ahl al-'udwān*. Berlin Staatsbibliothek MS Sprenger 907.
al-Ḥā'ik, Ismā'īl. *Bāb Mashad Maska min Fatāwī al-Shaykh Ismā'īl al-Ḥāyik*. ZAL 5677.
Hocāsa'deddīnzāde, *Şeyhülislām* Es'ad Efendi. *Fetāvā-yi Müntahabe*. SYK Kasidecizade 277.
al-Ḥusaynī al-Ḥanafī, 'Abd al-Raḥīm b. Abū'l-Luṭf b. Isḥāq b. Muḥammad. *Al-Fatāwā al-Raḥīmiyya fī wāqi'āt al-sāda al-ḥanafiyya*. PUSC Islamic Manuscripts, Garrett no. 3198Y.
İbrāhīm Edhem, Seyid. *Nehriyetü'l-Fetvā*. IU T1590.
Ibn Darwīsh Muḥammad, Ibrāhīm Rāqim. *Fatāwā*. PUSC Islamic Manuscripts Garret 4609Y.
al-'Imādī, 'Abd al-Raḥmān Muḥammad, 'Alī İbrāhīm 'Abd al- Raḥmān al-'Imādī and Muḥammad İbrāhīm 'Abd al- Raḥmān al-'Imādī. *Al-Nūr al-Mubīn fī Fatāwā al-'Imādiyīn*. ZAL 7508.
al-'Imādī, Ḥāmid 'Alī Ibrahīm. Al-Fatāwā al-Ḥāmidiyya. ZAL 5656.
al-'Imādī, Muḥibb al-Dīn, 'Abd al-Raḥmān Muḥammad al-'Imādī, 'Alī İbrāhīm 'Abd al- Raḥmān al-'Imādī, Muḥammad İbrāhīm 'Abd al- Raḥmān al-'Imādī, 'Alā' al-Dīn Muḥammad, 'Imād al-Dīn al-'Imādī and Ḥusām al-Dīn al-Rūmī. *Fatāwā Banī al-'Imādī wa Ghayrihim*. ZAL 5864.
al-Khalīlī, 'Abdallāh. *Fatāwā*. PUSC Islamic Manuscripts, Garrett no. 507Y, 55b–121a.
Minḳarīzāde, *Şeyhülislām* Yaḥyā Efendi. *Fetāvā*. SYK Hamidiye 610.
el-Mostarī, Aḥmed Efendi. *Fetāvā-yi Ahmediye*. SYK Kasidecizade 290.
al-Murādī, 'Alī and Ḥusayn al-Murādī. *Majmū' Fatāwā Murādiyya*. ZAL 2642.
al-Nābulusī, 'Abd al-Ghanī. *Fatāwā al-Nābulusī*. ZAL 2684.
Sāqizī, Ṣādiq Muḥammad. *Ṣurrat al-Fatāwā*. PDL.
Sāqizī, Ṣādiq Muḥammad. *Ṣurrat al-Fatāwā*. SYK Esad Efendi 797.
al-Shurunbulālī, Ḥasan b. 'Ammār. *Ḥāshiyyat Shaykhnā al-Shaykh Ḥasan al-Shurunbulālī 'alā al-Durar wa'l-Ghurar*. SYK Murad Molla 794.
Şerīfzāde, *Şeyhülislām* 'Aṭā'ullāh Meḥmed Efendi. *Fetāvā-yi 'Aṭā'iye*. SYK M Hilmi F Fehmi 59.
Şerīfzāde, *Şeyhülislām* 'Aṭā'ullāh Meḥmed Efendi. *Fetāvā-yi 'Aṭā'iye*. SYK Pertevniyal 342.
Şerīfzāde, *Şeyhülislām* 'Aṭā'ullāh Meḥmed Efendi. *Revāyiḥu'z-zekiye fī Fihrisi'l-fetāvā't-Türkiye*. IU T3244.
Üsküpī, Pīr Meḥmed. Ẓahīrü'l-Ḳuḍāt. SYK Esad Efendi 852.

Published primary sources

'Abbāsī al-Mahdī al-Miṣrī, Muḥammad al-. *Al-Fatāwā al-Mahdiyya Fī'l-Waqa'i' al-Miṣriyya*. Vol. 4. Cairo: Dār al-kutub wa al-wathā'iq al-qawmiyya bi'l-Qāhira, 2015.
'Abdullāh, *Şeyhülislām* Yeñişehirli. *Behcetü'l-Fetāvā ma'an-nüḳūl*. İstanbul: Maṭba'a-i 'Āmire, 1289 [1872].
'Abdürraḥīm, *Şeyhülislām* Menteşzāde. *Fetāvā-yi 'Abdürraḥīm*. Ḳonsṭanṭīnīye [Istanbul]: Dār üṭ-ṭıbā'at ül-Ma'mūret üs-Sulṭāniye, 1243 [1827].

Akgündüz, Ahmet. 'Arazi Kanunnâmesi'. In *Mukayeseli Islam ve Osmanlı Hukuku Külliyatı*, 678–715. Diyarbakir, Turkey: Dicle Üniversitesi, Hukuk Fakültesi, 1986.
Akgündüz, Ahmet. *Osmanlı Kanunnâmeleri ve Hukukî Tahlilleri*. 11 vols. Istanbul: FEY Vakfı, 1990.
Anṣārī, Farīd al-Dīn 'Ālim ibn 'Alā' al-Dīn al-. *Al-Fatāwā al-Tātārkhāniyya*. 5 vols. Karachi: Idārat al-Qur'ān wa'l-'Ulūm al-Islāmīyya, 2003.
Cevdet Paşa, Ahmed. In *Tezàkir*, edited by M. Cavid Baysun. 4 vols. Ankara: Türk Tarih Kurumu Basımevi, 1953–1967.
Defterdar Sarı Mehmed Paşa. *Zübde-i Vekayiât: Tahlil Ve Metin (1066–1116/1656–1704)*. Prepared by Abdülkadir Özcan. Ankara: Türk Tarih Kurumu Basımevi, 1995.
Dürrīzāde, Meḥmed 'Ārif b. Muṣṭafā. *Neticetü'l-Fetāva*, with an Arabic *nüḳūl* added by Gedizli Meḥmed Efendi. İstanbul: Darü'ṭ-Ṭıba'āti'l-'Āmīre, 1237 [1822].
Eşref, Halis. *Şerh-i Ḳānūn-ı Arāżī*. Istanbul: Mahmud Bey Matbaası, 1889.
Feyżullāh b. Meḥmed Efendi, *Fetāvā-yi Feyżiye ma'an-Nüḳūl* (İstanbul: Darü'ṭ-Ṭıba'āti'l-'Āmīre, 1266 [1850].
Ḥaṣkafī, 'Alā' al-Dīn al-, and Abd al-Raḥmān ibn Muḥammad Shaykhzada. *Majma' al-Anhur fi Sharḥ Multaqā al-Abḥur: Wa ma'ah al-Durr al-Muntaqā fi Sharḥ al-Multaqā*. 4 vols. Beirut: Manshūrāt Muḥammad 'Alī Bayḍūn, Dar al-Kotob al-Ilmiyah, H 1419 [1998].
Hocā Emīnefendizāde, 'Alī Ḥaydar. *Şerḥ-i Cedīd li-Ḳānūn il-Erāżī*. İstanbul: (A. Asadourian) Şirket-i Mürettibiye-yi Maṭba'ası, 1321 [1903 or 1904].
Ibn 'Ābidīn, Muḥammad Amīn ibn 'Umar. *Al-'Uqūd al-Durriyya Fī Tanqīḥ al-Fatāwā al-Ḥāmidiyya*. 2 vols. Beirut: Dar al-Kotob al-Ilmiyah, 2008.
Ibn 'Ābidīn, Muḥammad Amīn ibn 'Umar. *Ḥāshiyyat Ibn 'Ābidīn Radd al-Muḥtār 'Alā al-Durr al-Mukhtār*. Beirut: Dār iḥyā' al-turath al-'arabī, 1431 [2010].
Ibn 'Ābidīn, Muḥammad Amīn ibn 'Umar. 'Nashr al-'arf fī binā ba'ḍ al-aḥkām 'ala al-'urf'. In *Majmū'at Rasā'il Ibn 'Ābidīn*, edited by Muḥammad 'Azāzī, 2:153–203. Beirut: Dar al-Kotob al-lmiyah, 2014.
Ibn 'Ābidīn, Muḥammad Amīn ibn 'Umar. 'Taḥrīr al-'Ibāra Fīman Huwwa Awlā Bi'l-Ijāra'. In *Majmū'at Rasā'il Ibn 'Ābidīn*, edited by Muḥammad 'Azāzī, 2: 205–27. Beirut: Dar al-Kotob al-Ilmiyah, 2014.
Ibn Nujaym, Zayn al-'Ābidīn Ibrāhīm. *Al-Baḥr al-Rā'iq sharḥ Kanz al-Daqā'iq*. Vol. 5. Cairo: Al-Maṭba'ah al-Ilmīyah, H 1311 [1894 CE].
Ibn Nujaym, Zayn al-'Ābidīn Ibrāhīm. 'Al-Tuḥfa al-Marḍiyya Fī al-Arāḍī al-Miṣriyya'. In *Rasā'il Ibn Nujaym*, edited by Khalīl al-Mays, 50–64. Beirut: Dar al-Kotob al-Ilmiyah, 1980.
Kâtip Çelebi. *The Balance of Truth*. Translated by Geoffrey Lewis. London: Allen and Unwin, 1957.
Kâtip Çelebi. *Destūr ül-'Amel Li-Iṣlāḥ ül-Khalel*. Delhi: Facsimile Publisher, 1864.
Kołodziejczyk, Dariusz. *The Ottoman Survey Register of Podolia (ca. 1681) = Defter-i Mufassal-i Eyalet-i Kamaniçe*. 2 vols. Cambridge, MA: Harvard Ukrainian Research Institute, 2004.
Mantran, Robert, and Jean Sauvaget, eds. *Règlements fiscaux ottomans: Les provinces syriennes*. Paris: Adrien-Maisonneuve, 1951.
Meşrebzāde Meḥmed 'Ārif. *Fetāvā-yi Cāmi' ül-Icāreteyn*. İstanbul: Darü'ṭ-Ṭıba'āti'l-'Āmīre, 1252 [1837].
al-Nābulusī, 'Abd al-Ghanī and Meḥmed al-Birkawī. *Al-Ḥadīqa al-Nadiyya: Sharḥ al-Ṭarīqa al-Muḥammadiyya wa'l-Sīra al-Aḥmadiyya*. Beirut: Dar al-Kotob al-Ilmiyah, 1971.

Nev'îzâde Atâî. '*Hadâiku'l-Hakâik Fî Tekmilet'ş-Şakaik*'. In *Şakaik-i Nu'maniye ve Zeyilleri*, prepared by Abdülkadir Özcan, volume 2. Istanbul: Çağrı Yayınları, 1989.
Silāḥdār Fındıḳlı Meḥmed Ağa. *Silāḥdār Tarihi*. Vol. 2 [AH] *1095–1106*. Istanbul: Orhaniye Maṭbaʿası, 1928.

Published secondary works and unpublished dissertations and theses

Abd al-Kader, Ali. 'Land, Property and Land Tenure in Islamic Law'. *Islamic Quarterly* 5, no. 1 (1959): 4–11.
Abd al-Raḥīm, ʿAbd al-Raḥīm ʿAbd al-Raḥman. *Al-Rīf al-Miṣrī fī'l-Qarn al-Thāmin ʿAshar*. Second edn. Qalyub, Egypt: Maṭābiʿ al-Ahrām al-Tijāriyya, 2004.
Abou-el-Haj, Rifaʿat Ali. 'The Formal Closure of the Ottoman Frontier in Europe: 1699–1703'. *Journal of the American Oriental Society* 89, no. 3 (1969): 467–75.
Abou-el-Haj, Rifaʿat Ali. 'The Ottoman *Nasihatname* as a Discourse over "Morality"'. In *Mélanges Professeur Robert Mantran*, edited by Abdeljelil Temimi, 17–30. Zaghouan, Tunisia: Centre d'études et de recherches ottomanes, morisques, de documentation et d'information, 1988.
Abou-el-Haj, Rifaʿat Ali. 'Power and Social Order: The Uses of the Kanun'. In *The Ottoman City and Its Parts: Urban Structure and Social Order*, edited by Irene A. Bierman, Rifaʿat Ali Abou-el-Haj and Donald Preziosi, 77–102. New Rochelle, NY: Caratzas, 1991.
Abu-Husayn, Abdul-Rahim. 'The *Iltizam* of Mansur Furaykh: A Case Study of *Iltizam* in Sixteenth-Century Syria'. In *Land Tenure and Social Transformation in the Middle East*, edited by Tarif Khalidi, 249–56. Beirut: American University of Beirut, 1984.
Ağir, Seven. 'The Rise and Demise of *Gedik* Markets in Istanbul, 1750–1860'. *Economic History Review* 71, no. 1 (2018): 133–56.
Ágoston, Gábor. *Guns for the Sultan: Military Power and the Weapons Industry in the Ottoman Empire*. New York: Cambridge University Press, 2005.
Ágoston, Gábor. 'Knowledge, Technology and Warfare in Europe and the Ottoman Empire in the Early Modern Period'. In *Osmanlılar ve Avrupa: Seyahat, Karşılaşma ve Etkileşim: Erken Klasik Dönemden XVIII. Yüzyıl Sonuna Kadar*, edited by Seyfi Kenan. Istanbul: İslam Araştırmaları Merkezi, 2010.
Ahmed, Shahab. *What Is Islam? The Importance of Being Islamic*. Princeton, NJ: Princeton University Press, 2016.
Aigle, Denise. 'Le grand *jasaq* de Gengis-Khan, l'empire, la culture mongole et la *Sharīʿa*'. *Journal of the Economic and Social History of the Orient* 47, no. 1 (2004): 31–79.
Akarlı, Engin. '*Gedik*: A Bundle of Rights and Obligations for Istanbul Artisans and Traders, 1750–1840'. In *Law, Anthropology, and the Constitution of the Social: Making Persons and Things*, edited by Alain Pottage and Martha Mundy, 166–200. Cambridge: Cambridge University Press, 2004.
Akdağ, Mustafa. *Celâlî Isyanları (1550–1603)*. Ankara: Ankara Universitesi Basimevi, 1963.
Aksan, Virginia H. 'Ottoman Political Writing, 1768–1808'. *International Journal of Middle East Studies* 25, no. 1 (1993): 53–69.
Aladdin, Bakri. 'Deux fatwā-s du Šayh ʿAbd al-Ġanī al-Nābulusī (1143/1731): Présentation et édition critique'. *Bulletin d'études orientales* 39–40 (1987–8): 7–37.
Alexander, Gregory S. 'Time and Property in the American Republican Legal Culture'. *New York University Law Review* 66, no. 2 (1991): 273–352.

Anjum, Ovamir. *Politics, Law and Community in Islamic Thought: The Taymiyyan Moment*. Cambridge: Cambridge University Press, 2012.
Arjomand, Said Amir. 'Perso-Islamicate Political Ethic in Relation to the Sources of Islamic Law'. In *Mirror for the Muslim Prince: Islam and the Theory of Statecraft*, edited by Mehrzad Boroujerdi, 82–106. Syracuse, NY: Syracuse University Press, 2013.
Arneil, Barbara. *John Locke and America. The Defence of English Colonialism*. Oxford: Clarendon Press, 1996.
Atçıl, Abdurrahman. *Scholars and Sultans in the Early Modern Ottoman Empire*. Cambridge: Cambridge University Press, 2017.
Atiyas, Ekin Tuşalp. 'The "Sunna-Minded" Trend'. In *A History of Ottoman Political Thought up to the Early Nineteenth Century*, edited by Marinos Sariyannis, 233–78. Leiden: Brill, 2019.
Ayalon, David. 'The Great *Yāsa* of Chingiz Khān: A Reexamination (Part A)'. *Studia Islamica*, no. 33 (1971): 97–140.
Ayalon, David. 'The Great *Yāsa* of Chingiz Khān: A Reexamination (Part B)'. *Studia Islamica*, no. 34 (1971): 151–80.
Ayalon, David. 'The Great *Yāsa* of Chingiz Khān: A Reexamination (Part C1)'. *Studia Islamica*, no. 36 (1972): 113–58.
Ayalon, David. 'The Great *Yāsa* of Chingiz Khān: A Reexamination (Part C2). Al-Maqrīzī's Passage on the *Yāsa* under the Mamluks'. *Studia Islamica*, no. 38 (1973): 107–56.
Aykan, Yavuz. *Rendre La Justice à Amid: Procédures, acteurs et doctrines dans le contexte ottoman du XVIIIème siècle*. Leiden: Brill, 2016.
Ayoub, Samy. 'The *Mecelle*, Sharia, and the Ottoman State: Fashioning and Refashioning of Islamic Law in the Nineteenth and Twentieth Centuries'. *Journal of the Ottoman and Turkish Studies Association* 2, no. 1 (2015): 121–46.
Ayoub, Samy. '"The Sulṭān Says": State Authority in the Late Hanafi Tradition'. *Islamic Law and Society* 23, no. 3 (2016): 239–78.
Ayoub, Samy. *Law Empire and the Sultan: Ottoman Imperial Authority and Late Ḥanafī Jurisprudence*. New York: Oxford University Press, 2020.
Azmeh, Aziz al-. *Muslim Kingship: Power and the Sacred in Muslim, Christian, and Pagan Polities*. London: Tauris, 2001.
Baer, Gabriel. 'Land Tenure in Egypt and the Fertile Crescent, 1800–1950'. In *The Economic History of the Middle East, 1800–1914: A Book of Readings*, edited by Charles P. Issawi, 79–90. Chicago: University of Chicago Press, 1966.
Baer, Marc David. *Honored by the Glory of Islam: Conversion and Conquest in Ottoman Europe*. New York: Oxford University Press, 2008.
Baldwin, James E. *Islamic Law and Empire in Ottoman Cairo*. Edinburgh: Edinburgh University Press, 2017.
Barkan, Ömer Lûtfi. 'Caractère religieux et caractère séculier des institutions ottomanes'. In *Contributions à l'histoire économique et sociale de l'Empire ottoman*, edited by Jean-Louis Bacqué-Grammont and Paul Dumont, 11–58. Leuven, Belgium: Peeters, 1983.
Barkan, Ömer Lûtfi. 'Türk-İslâm Toprak Hukuku Tatbikatını Osmanlı İmparatorluğu'nda Aldığı Şekiller: Mâlikâne-Divani Sistemi'. In *Türkiye'de Toprak Meselesi*, 151–208. Istanbul: Gözlem Yayınları, 1960.
Barkan, Ömer Lûtfi. *Türk Toprak Hukuku Tarihinde Tanzimat ve 1274 (1858) Tarihli Arazi Kanunnamesi*. Istanbul: Maarıf Matbaası, 1940.
Barkan, Ömer Lûtfi. *XV ve XVI Incı Asırlarda Osmanlı Imparatorluğund Ziraı Ekonominin Hukuki Ve Malî Esasları*. Vol. 1, *Kanunlar*. Istanbul: Bürhaneddin Matbaası, 1943.

Barkey, Karen. *Bandits and Bureaucrats; The Ottoman Route to State Centralization*. Ithaca, NY: Cornell University Press, 1994.

Barkey, Karen. *Empire of Difference: The Ottomans in Comparative Perspective*. Cambridge: Cambridge University Press, 2008.

Barkey, Karen. 'The Ottoman Empire (1299–1923): The Bureaucratization of Patrimonial Authority'. In *Empires and Bureaucracy in World History: From Late Antiquity to the Twentieth Century*, edited by Peter Crooks and Timothy Parsons, 102–26. Cambridge: Cambridge University Press, 2016.

Barnes, John Robert. *An Introduction to Religious Foundations in the Ottoman Empire*. Leiden: Brill, 1986.

Bartusis, Mark C. *Land and Privilege in Byzantium: The Institution of Pronoia*. Cambridge: Cambridge University Press, 2012.

Bayraktutan, Lütfi. *Şeyhülislâm Yahya: Hayatı, Edebî Kişiliği, Sanatı, Eserleri ve Divanından Seçmeler*. Istanbul: Kültür Bakanlığı, 1990.

Beiner, Ronald. *Civil Religion: A Dialogue in the History of Political Philosophy*. New York: Cambridge University Press, 2011.

Beldiceanu-Steinherr, Irène. 'Loi sur la transmission du Timar'. *Turcica* 11 (1978): 78–102.

Benton, Lauren A. *A Search for Sovereignty: Law and Geography in European Empires, 1400–1900*. Cambridge: Cambridge University Press, 2010.

Bergin, Joseph. *The Politics of Religion in Early Modern France*. New Haven, CT: Yale University Press, 2014.

Berkes, Niyazi. *The Development of Secularism in Turkey*. New York: Routledge, 1999.

Burak, Guy. 'Between the *Ḳānūn* of Qāytbāy and Ottoman *Yasaq*: A Note on the Ottomans' Dynastic Law'. *Journal of Islamic Studies* 26, no. 1 (2015): 1–23.

Burak, Guy. *The Second Formation of Islamic Law: The Hanafi School in the Early Modern Ottoman Empire*. New York: Cambridge University Press, 2015.

Burak, Guy. 'The Second Formation of Islamic Law: The Post-Mongol Context of the Ottoman Adoption of a School of Law'. *Comparative Studies in Society and History* 55, no. 3 (2013): 579–602.

Burbank, Jane, and Frederick Cooper. *Empires in World History: Power and the Politics of Difference*. Princeton, NJ: Princeton University Press, 2010.

Buzov, Snjezana. *The Lawgiver and His Lawmakers: The Role of Legal Discourse in the Change of Ottoman Imperial Culture*. Edited by Cornell Fleischer. Chicago: University of Chicago Press, 2005.

Çakır, Baki. *Osmanlı Mukataa Sistemi (XVI–XVIIIi. Yüzyıl)*. Istanbul: Kitabevi, 2003.

Can, Lale, Michael Low, Kent F. Schull and Robert Zens, eds. *The Subjects of Ottoman International Law*. Bloomington: Indiana University Press, 2020.

Ceyhan, Abdullah. 'Osmanlı Devri Müderris, Kadı ve Fetva Eminlerinden Gedizli Hafız Mehmed Efendi'. *Diyanet İlmi Dergi* 11, no. 3 (1993): 11–24.

Cin, Halil. *Osmanlı Toprak Düzeni ve Bu Düzenin Bozulması*. 2nd edn. Istanbul: Boxaziçi, 1985.

Cin, Halil. *Osmanlı Toprak Düzeni ve Bu Düzenin Bozulması*. 3rd edn. Konya: Selçuk Üniversitesi Hukuk Fakültesi, 1992.

Cin, Halil. *Osmanlı Toprak Düzeni ve Bu Düzenin Bozulması*. 4th edn. Ankara: Berikan Yayınevi, 2016.

Coulson, N. J. *A History of Islamic Law*. New Brunswick, NJ: Transaction, 2011.

Crone, Patricia. *Slaves on Horses: The Evolution of the Islamic Polity*. Cambridge: Cambridge University Press, 2003.

Cuno, Kenneth M. 'Ideology and Juridical Discourse in Ottoman Egypt: The Uses of the Concept of *Irṣād*'. *Islamic Law and Society* 6, no. 2 (1999): 136–63.
Cuno, Kenneth M. *The Pasha's Peasants: Land, Society, and Economy in Lower Egypt, 1740–1858*. Cambridge: Cambridge University Press, 1992.
Cuno, Kenneth M. 'Was the Land of Ottoman Syria *Miri* or *Milk*? An Examination of Juridical Differences within the Hanafi School'. *Studia Islamica* 81 (1995): 121–52.
Danışmend, Ismail Hami. *Izahlı Osmanlı Tarihi Kronolojisi*. 5 vols. Istanbul: Türkiye Yayınevi, 1971–2.
Darling, Linda T. 'Christian-Muslim Interaction on the Ottoman Frontier: *Gaza* and Accommodation in Early Ottoman History'. In *The Ottoman Mosaic: Exploring Models for Peace by Re-exploring the Past*, edited by Kemal Karpat and Yetkin Yildirim, 103–18. Seattle, WA: Cune Press, 2010.
Darling, Linda T. 'Historicizing the Ottoman *Timar* System: Identities of *Timar*-Holders, Fourteenth to Seventeenth Centuries'. *Turkish Historical Review* 8, no. 2 (2017): 145–73.
Darling, Linda T. *A History of Social Justice and Political Power in the Middle East: The Circle of Justice from Mesopotamia to Globalization*. New York: Routledge, 2013.
Darling, Linda T. '*Nasihatnameler, Icmal Defterleri*, and the *Timar*-Holding Ottoman Elite in the Late Sixteenth Century'. *Osmanli Arastirmalari/Journal of Ottoman Studies* 43 (2014): 193–226.
Darling, Linda T. '*Nasihatnameler, Icma Defterleri*, and the *Timar*-Holding Ottoman Elite in the Late Sixteenth Century – Part 2, Including the Seventeenth Century'. *Osmanli Arastirmalari/Journal of Ottoman Studies* 45 (2015): 1–23.
Darling, Linda T. *Revenue-Raising and Legitimacy: Tax Collection and Finance Administration in the Ottoman Empire, 1560–1660*. Leiden: Brill, 1996.
Demir, Abdullah. *Devlet-i Aliyye'nin Büyük Hukukçusu Şeyhülislam Ebussuud Efendi*. Istanbul: Ötüken, 2006.
Deringil, Selim. *The Well-Protected Domains: Ideology and the Legitimation of Power in the Ottoman Empire, 1876–1909*. London: Tauris, 1999.
Eldem, Edhem. 'Capitulations and Western Trade'. In *The Cambridge History of Turkey*. Vol. 3, *The Later Ottoman Empire, 1603–1839*, edited by Suraiya Faroqhi, 283–335. Cambridge: Cambridge University Press, 2006.
Emon, Anver M. 'Codification and Islamic Law: The Ideology behind a Tragic Narrative'. *Middle East Law and Governance* 8, nos. 2–3 (2016): 275–309.
Emon, Anver M. 'Natural Law and Natural Rights in Islamic Law'. *Journal of Law and Religion* 20, no. 2 (2004–5): 351–95.
Engster, Daniel. *Divine Sovereignty: The Origins of Modern State Power*. DeKalb: Northern Illinois University Press, 2001.
Erdem, Hakan. 'Recruitment for the "Victorious Soldiers of Muhammad" in the Arab Provinces, 1826–1828'. In *Histories of the Modern Middle East: New Directions*, edited by Israel Gershoni, Hakan Erdem and Ursula Woköck, 189–94. Boulder, CO: Rienner, 2002.
Ezzati, Abul-Fazl. *Islam and Natural Law*. London: ICAS Press, 2002.
Faroqhi, Suraiya. 'The Fieldglass and the Magnifying Lens: Studies of Ottoman Crafts and Craftsmen'. *Journal of European Economic History* 20, no. 1 (1991): 29–59.
Faruki, Kemal. 'Legal Implications for Today of *al-Aḥkām al-Khamsa* (The Five Values)'. In *Ethics in Islam*, edited by Richard G. Hovannisian, 65–71. Malibu, CA: Undena, 1985.
Fell, A. London. *Origins of Legislative Sovereignty and the Legislative State*. Cambridge, MA: Gunn & Hain, 1983.

Ferguson, Heather L. *The Proper Order of Things: Language, Power, and Law in Ottoman Administrative Discourses*. Stanford, CA: Stanford University Press, 2018.

Fisher, Stanley. *Ottoman Land Laws: Containing the Ottoman Land Code and Later Legislation Affecting Land; with Notes and an Appendix of Cyprus Laws and Rules Relating to Land*. London: Oxford University Press, 1919.

Fitzgerald, Timothy J. 'Ottoman Methods of Conquest: Legal Imperialism and the City of Aleppo, 1480–1570'." PhD Diss., Harvard University Press, 2009.

Fleischer, Cornell H. *Bureaucrat and Intellectual in the Ottoman Empire: The Historian Mustafa Âli (1541–1600)*. Princeton, NJ: Princeton University Press, 1986.

Fleischer, Cornell H. 'From Şehzade Korkud to Mustafa Ali: Cultural Origins of the *Nasihatname*'. In *Proceedings of the Third Congress on the Social and Economic History of Turkey*, edited by Heath Lowry and Ralph Hattox, 67–77. Istanbul: Isis Press, 1990.

Fleischer, Cornell H. 'Royal Authority, Dynastic Cyclism, and "Ibn Khaldûnism" in Sixteenth-Century Ottoman Letters'. *Journal of Asian and African Studies* 18, nos. 3–4 (1983): 198–220.

Foisneau, Luc. *Politique, droit et théologie chez Bodin, Grotius et Hobbes*. Paris: Kimé, 1997.

Gandev, Christo. 'L'apparition des rapports capitalistes dans l'économie rurale de la Bulgarie du Nord-Ouest au cours du XVIII siècle'. *Études Historiques* 1 (1960): 207–20.

Gelvin, James L. *The Modern Middle East: A History*. 5th edn. New York: Oxford University Press, 2020.

Genç, Mehmet. 'Osmanlı Maliyesinde Malikâne Sistemi'. In *Osmanlı Imparatorluğunda Devlet ve Ekonomi*, 99–117. İstanbul: Ötüken, 2000.

Genç, Mehmet. 'A Study of the Feasibility of Using Eighteenth-Century Ottoman Financial Records as an Indicator of Economic Activity'. In *The Ottoman Empire and the world economy*, edited by Huri Islamoğlu-Inan, 345–73. Cambridge: Cambridge University Press, 1987.

Gerber, Haim. *Islamic Law and Culture, 1600–1840*. Leiden: Brill, 1999.

Gerber, Haim. *State, Society, and Law in Islam: Ottoman Law in Comparative Perspective*. Albany: State University of New York Press, 1994.

Gibb, H. A. R., and Harold Bowen. *Islamic Society and the West: A Study of the Impact of Western Civilization on Moslem Culture in the Near East*. London: Oxford University Press, 1950.

Greene, Molly. 'An Islamic Experiment? Ottoman Land Policy on Crete'. *Mediterranean Historical Review* 11, no. 1 (1996): 60–78.

Greene, Molly. 'The Ottomans in the Mediterranean'. In *The Early Modern Ottomans: Remapping the Empire*, edited by Virginia H. Aksan and Daniel Goffman, 104–16. Cambridge: Cambridge University Press, 2007.

Greene, Molly. *A Shared World: Christians and Muslims in the Early Modern Mediterranean*. Princeton, NJ: Princeton University Press, 2000.

Grimm, Dieter. *Sovereignty: The Origin and Future of a Political and Legal Concept*. Translated by Belinda Cooper. New York: Columbia University Press, 2015.

Griswold, William J. *The Great Anatolian Rebellion, 1000–1020/1591–1611*. Berlin: Schwarz Verlag, 1983.

Gülsoy, Ersin. 'Osmanlı Tahrir Geleneğinde Bir Değişim Örneği: Girit Eyâleti'nin 1650 ve 1670 Tarihli Sayımları'. In *Pax Ottomana: Studies in Memoriam Prof. Dr. Nejat Göyünç*, edited by Kemal Çiçek, 183–203. Haarlem: SOTA; Ankara: Yeni Türkiye, 2001.

Hagen, Gottfried. 'Legitimacy and World Order'. In *Legitimizing the Order The Ottoman Rhetoric of State Power*, edited by Hakan T. Karateke and Maurus Reinkowski, 55–83. Leiden: Brill, 2005.

Haji Abdullah, Luqman. 'The Classical Islamic Law of Waqf: A Comparative Approach'. PhD Diss., University of Edinburgh, 2005.
Hallaq, Wael B. *The Impossible State: Islam, Politics, and Modernity's Moral Predicament*. New York: Columbia University Press, 2013.
Hallaq, Wael B. 'A Prelude to Ottoman Reform: Ibn 'Abidin on Custom and Legal Change'. In *Histories of the Modern Middle East: New Directions*, edited by Israel Gershoni, Hakan Erdem and Ursula Woköck, 37–61. Boulder, CO: Rienner, 2002.
Hallaq, Wael B. *Sharia: Theory, Practice, Transformations*. Cambridge: Cambridge University Press, 2009.
Hammer-Purgstall, Joseph von. *Histoire de l'empire Ottoman, depuis son origine jusqu'à nos jours*. Translated by J. Hellert. Istanbul: Isis Press, 2000.
Hanioğlu, M. Şükrü. *A Brief History of the Late Ottoman Empire*. Princeton, NJ: Princeton University Press, 2008.
Haque, Ziaul. *Landlord and Peasant in Early Islam: A Study of the Legal Doctrine of Muzara'a or Share Cropping*. Islamabad: Islamic Research Institute, 1977.
Herzog, Tamar. 'Did European Law Turn American? Territory, Property and Rights in an Atlantic World'. In *New Horizons in Spanish Colonial Law: Contributions to Transnational Early Modern Legal History*, edited by Thomas Duve and Heikki Pihlajamäki, 75–95. Frankfurt am Main: Max Planck Institute for European Legal History, 2015.
Herzog, Tamar. *Frontiers of Possession: Spain and Portugal in Europe and the Americas*. Cambridge, MA: Harvard University Press, 2015.
Heyd, Uriel. 'The Ottoman Ulema and Westernization in the Time of Selim III and Mahmud II'. In *The Modern Middle East: A Reader*, edited by Albert Hourani, Philip S. Khoury and Mary C. Wilson, 29–61. Berkeley: University of California Press, 1993.
Heyd, Uriel. *Studies in Old Ottoman Criminal Law*. Edited by V. L. Ménage. Oxford: Clarendon Press, 1973.
al-Hilālī, Abd al-Razzāq. *Qiṣṣat al-Ard wa'l-Fallāḥ wa'l-Iṣlāḥ al-Zirā'ī fī 'l-Waṭan al-'Arabī*. al-Qāhira [Cairo]: Dar al-Kashāf, 1967.
Hornbeck, Patrick J., II. *Remembering Wolsey: A History of Commemorations and Representations*. New York: Fordham University Press, 2019.
Howard, Douglas A. 'The Ottoman Timar System and Its Transformation, 1563–1656'. PhD Diss., Indiana University, 1987.
Howard, Douglas A. 'Ottoman Historiography and the Literature of "Decline" of the Sixteenth and Seventeenth Centuries'. *Journal of Asian History* 22, no. 1 (1988): 52–77.
Howard, Douglas A. 'Historical Scholarship and the Classical Ottoman Ḳānūnnāmes'. *Archivum Ottomanicum* 14, 1995–6: 79–109.
Imber, Colin. *Ebu's-su'ud: The Islamic Legal Tradition*. Stanford, CA: Stanford University Press, 1997.
Imber, Colin. 'The Law of the Land'. In *The Ottoman World*, edited by Christine Woodhead, 41–56. New York: Routledge, 2012.
Imber, Colin. *The Ottoman Empire, 1300–1650: The Structure of Power*. Basingstoke: Palgrave Macmillan, 2002.
Imber, Colin. 'The Status of Orchards and Fruit-Trees in Ottoman Law'. In *Studies in Ottoman History and Law*, 207–16. Istanbul: Isis Press, 1996.
İnalcik, Halil. *An Economic and Social History of the Ottoman Empire*. Vol. 1, *1300–1600*. Cambridge: Cambridge University Press, 1997.

İnalcik, Halil. 'Islamization of Ottoman Laws on Land and Land Tax'. In *Festgabe an Josef Matuz: Osmanistik-Turkologie-Diplomatik*, edited by Christa Fragner and Klaus Schwartz, 101–18. Berlin: Schwarz Verlag, 1992.

İnalcik, Halil. 'Kutadgu Bilig'de Turk Ve Iran Siyaset Nazariye Ve Gelenekleri'. In *Reşid Rahmeti Arat Için*, edited by Resit Rahmeti Arat, 259–71. Ankara: Türk Kültürünü Araştırma Enstitüsü, 1966.

İnalcik, Halil. 'Military and Fiscal Transformation in the Ottoman Empire, 1600–1700'. *Archivum Ottomanicum* 6 (1980): 283–337.

İnalcik, Halil. *The Ottoman Empire: The Classical Age, 1300–1600*. Translated by Norman Itzkowitz and Colin Imber. London: Phoenix, 1995.

İnalcik, Halil. 'The Socio-Political Effects of the Diffusion of Fire-Arms in the Middle East'. In *War, Technology and Society in the Middle East*, edited by Vernon J. Parry and Malcolm Yapp, 195–217. London: Oxford University Press, 1975.

İnalcik, Halil. 'State, Sovereignty, and Law During the Reign of Süleymân'. In *Süuleymân the Second and His Time*, edited by Halil İnalcik and Cemal Kafadar, 59–92. Istanbul: Isis Press, 1993.

İnalcik, Halil. 'Stefan Duşan'dan Osmanlı Imparatorluğuna: Asırda Rumeli'de Hristiyan Sipahiler ve Menşeleri'. In *Fuad Köprülü Armağanı: 60. Doğum Yılı Münasebetiyle: Mèlanges Fuad Köprülü*, 207–48. Istanbul: Osman Yalçın Matbaası, 1953.

İnalcik, Halil. 'Suleiman the Lawgiver and Ottoman Law'. *Archivum Ottomanicum* 1 (1969): 105–38.

Islam, Muhammad Wohidul. 'Al-Mal: The Concept of Property in Islamic Legal Thought'. *Arab Law Quarterly* 14, no. 4 (1999): 361–8.

Islamoglu, Huri. 'Property as a Contested Domain: A Reevaluation of the Ottoman Land Code of 1858'. In *New Perspectives on Property and Land in the Middle East*, edited by Roger Owen, 3–61. Cambridge, MA: Harvard University Press, 2000.

Issawi, Charles P., ed. *The Economic History of the Middle East, 1800–1914: A Book of Readings*. Chicago: University of Chicago Press, 1966.

Ivanyi, Katharina Anna. *Virtue, Piety and the Law: A Study of Birgivī Meḥmed Efendi's* al-Ṭarīqa al-muḥammadiyya. Leiden: Brill, 2020.

Johansen, Baber. 'Can the Law Decide That Egypt Is Conquered by Force? A Thirteenth-Century Debate on History as an Object of Study'. In *Studies in Islamic Law: A Festschrift for Colin Imber*, edited by Andreas Christmann and Robert Gleave, 143–63. Oxford: Oxford University Press, 2007.

Johansen, Baber. 'Coutumes locales et coutumes universelles aux sources des règles juridiques en droit musulman hanéfite'. In *Contingency in a Sacred Law: Legal and Ethical Norms in the Muslim Fiqh*, 163–71. Leiden: Brill, 1999.

Johansen, Baber. *The Islamic Law on Land Tax and Rent: The Peasants' Loss of Property Rights as Interpreted in the Hanafite Legal Literature of the Mamluk and Ottoman Periods*. London: Croom Helm, 1988.

Johansen, Baber. 'A Perfect Law in an Imperfect Society: Ibn Taymiyya's Concept of "Governance in the Name of the Sacred Law"'. In *The Law Applied: Contextualizing the Islamic Shari'a: A Volume in Honor of Frank E. Vogel*, edited by Peri Bearman, Wolfhart Heinrichs and Bernard G. Weiss, 259–94. London: Tauris, 2008.

Johansen, Baber. 'Secular and Religious Elements in Hanafite Law: Function and Limits of the Absolute Character of Government Authority'. In *Contingency in a Sacred Law: Legal and Ethical Norms in the Muslim Fiqh*, 189–218. Leiden: Brill, 1999.

Joseph, Sabrina. 'An Analysis of Khayr al-Din al-Ramli's Fatawa on Peasant Land Tenure in Seventeenth-Century Palestine'. *Arab Studies Journal* 6–7, nos. 2–1 (1998–9): 112–27.
Joseph, Sabrina. *Islamic Law on Peasant Usufruct in Ottoman Syria: 17th to Early 19th Century*. Leiden: Brill, 2012.
Kafadar, Cemal. 'The Myth of the Golden Age: Ottoman Historical Consciousness in the Post- Süleymânic Era'. In *Süleymân the Second and His Time*, edited by Halil Inalcik and Cemal Kafadar, 37–48. Istanbul: Isis Press, 1993.
Kafadar, Cemal. 'On the Purity and Corruption of the Janissaries'. *Turkish Studies Association Bulletin* 15, no. 2 (1991): 273–80.
Kamali, Mohammad H. 'Fundamental Rights of the Individual: An Analysis of *Haqq* (Right) in Islamic Law'. *American Journal of Islamic Social Sciences* 10, no. 3 (1993): 340–65.
Kardari, Ibn al-Bazzaz al-. *Al-Fatawa al-Bazzaziyah aw al-Jami' Al-Wajiz fi Madhhab al-Imam al-A'zam Abi Hanifah al-Nu'man*. 2 vols. Beirut: Dar al-Kotob al-Ilmiyah, 2009.
Karpat, Kemal H. 'The Land Regime, Social Structure, and Modernization in the Ottoman Empire'. In *Beginnings of Modernization in the Middle East: The Nineteenth Century*, edited by William R. Polk and Richard L. Chambers, 69–90. Chicago: University of Chicago Press, 1968.
Kasaba, Reşat. 'Migrant Labor in Western Anatolia'. In *Landholding and Commercial Agriculture in the Middle East*, edited by Çağlar Keyder and Faruk Tabak, 113–21. Albany: State University of New York Press, 1991.
Katz, Marion H. 'Pragmatic Rule and Personal Sanctification in Islamic Legal Theory'. In *Law and the Sacred*, edited by Austin Sarat, Lawrence Douglas and Martha Merrill Umphrey, 91–108. Stanford, CA: Stanford University Press, 2007.
Kaya, Süleyman. *Osmanlı Hukukunda İcâreteyn*. Istanbul: Klasik, 2014.
Kaya, Süleyman, ed. *Osmanlı Hukukunda Fetva*. Istanbul: Klasik, 2018.
Kayaoğlu, Turan. *Legal Imperialism: Sovereignty and Extraterritoriality in Japan, the Ottoman Empire, and China*. New York: Cambridge University Press, 2010.
Kelley, Donald R., and Bonnie G. Smith. 'What Was Property? Legal Dimensions of the Social Question in France (1789–1848)'. *Proceedings of the American Philosophical Society* 128, no. 3 (1984): 200–30.
Kermeli, Eugenia. 'Caught in between Faith and Cash: The Ottoman Land System of Crete, 1645–1670'. In *The Eastern Mediterranean under Ottoman Rule: Crete, 1645–1840*, edited by Antonis Anastasopoulos, 17–48. Rethymno, Greece: Crete University Press, 2008.
Keyder, Çağlar. 'The Cycle of Sharecropping and the Consolidation of Small Peasant Ownership in Turkey'. *Journal of Peasant Studies* 10, nos 2–3 (2008): 130–45.
Keyder, Çağlar. 'Small Peasant Ownership in Turkey: Historical Formation and Present Structure'. *Review (Fernand Braudel Center)* 7, no. 1 (1983): 53–107.
Keyder, Cağlar, and Faruk Tabak, eds. *Landholding and Commercial Agriculture in the Middle East*. Albany: State University of New York Press, 1991.
Khoury, Dina Rizk. 'Administrative Practice between Religious Law (*Shari'a*) and State Law (*Kanun*) on the Eastern Frontiers of the Ottoman Empire'. *Journal of Early Modern History* 5, no. 4 (2001): 305–30.
Khoury, Dina Rizk. *State and Provincial Society in the Ottoman Empire: Mosul, 1540–1834*. Cambridge: Cambridge University Press, 1997.

Kiel, Machiel. 'The Smaller Aegean Islands in the 16th–18th Centuries according to Ottoman Administrative Documents'. In *Between Venice and Istanbul: Colonial Landscapes in Early Modern Greece*, edited by Siriol Davies and Jack L. Davis, 35–54. Princeton, NJ: American School of Classical Studies at Athens, 2007.

Koç, Yunus. 'Early Ottoman Customary Law: The Genesis and Development of Ottoman Codification'. In *Shattering Tradition: Custom, Law and the Individual in the Muslim Mediterranean*, edited by Walter Dostal and Wolfgang Kraus, 75–121. London: Tauris, 2005.

Kołodziejczyk, Dariusz. 'Between Universalistic Claims and Reality: Ottoman Frontiers in the Early Modern Period'. In *The Ottoman World*, edited by Christine Woodhead, 205–19. New York: Routledge, 2012.

Kolovos, Elias. 'Beyond "Classical" Ottoman *Defter*ology: A Preliminary Assessment of the *Tahrir* Registers of 1670/71 Concerning Crete and the Aegean Islands'. In *The Ottoman Empire, the Balkans, the Greek Lands: Towards a Social and Economic History*, edited by Elias Kolovos, Phokion Kotzageorgis and Sophia Laiou, 201–36. Istanbul: Gorgias Press, 2010.

Koyuncu, Nuran. 'Legal Basis, Development and Repeal of Craftsmen Gedik in the Ottoman Empire'. *Selçuk Universitesi Hukuk Fakültesi Dergisi* 26, no. 2 (2018): 47–76.

Krstić, Tijana. *Contested Conversions to Islam: Narratives of Religious Change in the Early Modern Ottoman Empire*. Stanford, CA: Stanford University Press, 2011.

Kuran, Timur. *The Long Divergence: How Islamic Law Held Back the Middle East*. Princeton, NJ: Princeton University Press, 2011.

Laçin, Bedirhan. 'New Inclinations Toward Land Usufruct in the 18th Century Anatolia'. Master's thesis, Bilkent University, 2017.

Layish, Aharon. 'The Transformation of the Sharīʿa from Jurists' Law to Statutory Law in the Contemporary Muslim World'. *Die Welt des Islams* 44, no. 1 (2004): 85–113.

Lee, Wayne E., ed. *Empires and Indigenes: Intercultural Alliance, Imperial Expansion, and Warfare in the Early Modern World*. New York: New York University Press, 2011.

Løkkegaard, Frede. *Islamic Taxation in the Classic Period, with Special Reference to Circumstances in Iraq*. Copenhagen: Branner & Korch, 1950.

Makdisi, John. 'The Kindred Concepts of Seisin and *Ḥawz* in English and Islamic Law'. In *The Law Applied: Contextualizing the Islamic Sharīʿa: A Volume in Honor of Frank E. Vogel*, edited by Peri Bearman, Wolfhart Heinrichs and Bernard G. Weiss, 22–41. London: Tauris, 2008.

Mardin, Ebul'ula. *Medenî Hukuk Cephesinden Ahmet Cevdet Paşa*. İstanbul: Turkiye Diyanet Vakfi Yayinlari, 2012.

Mardin, Şerif. *The Genesis of Young Ottoman Thought: A Study in the Modernization of Turkish Political Ideas*. Princeton, NJ: Princeton University Press, 1962.

Mardin, Şerif. *Religion and Social Change in Modern Turkey: The Case of Bediüzzaman Said Nursi*. Albany: State University of New York Press, 1989.

Masters, Bruce Alan. *Christians and Jews in the Ottoman Arab World: The Roots of Sectarianism*. Cambridge: Cambridge University Press, 2001.

McGowan, Bruce W. *Economic Life in Ottoman Europe: Taxation, Trade, and the Struggle for Land, 1600–1800*. Cambridge: Cambridge University Press, 1981.

Meshal, Reem A. 'Antagonistic Sharīʿas and the Construction of Orthodoxy in Sixteenth-Century Ottoman Cairo'. *Journal of Islamic Studies* 21, no. 2 (2010): 183–212.

Meshal, Reem A. *Sharia and the Making of the Modern Egyptian: Islamic Law and Custom in the Courts of Ottoman Cairo*. Cairo: American University in Cairo Press, 2014.

Messick, Brinkley. *The Calligraphic State: Textual Domination and History in a Muslim Society*. Berkeley: University of California Press, 1993.
Milkova, F. G. 'Sur la teneur et le caractère de la propriété d'état des terres *miriye* dans l'empire Ottoman du XVe au XIXe siècles'. *Etudes balkaniques* 5 (1966): 155–76.
Minkov, Anton. 'Ottoman *Tapu* Title Deeds in the Eighteenth and Nineteenth Centuries: Origin, Typology and Diplomatics'. *Islamic Law and Society* 7, no. 1 (2000): 65–101.
Moosa, Ebrahim. 'The Dilemma of Islamic Rights Schemes'. *Journal of Law and Religion* 15, nos. 1–2 (2000–1): 185–215.
Morgan, David O. 'The 'Great *Yāsā* of Chingiz Khān' and Mongol Law in the Īlkhānate'. *Bulletin of the School of Oriental and African Studies* 49, no. 1 (1986): 163–76.
Morgan, David O. 'The "Great *Yasa* of Chinggis Khan" Revisited'. In *Mongols, Turks, and Others: Eurasian Nomads and the Sedentary World*, edited by Reuven Amitai and Michal Biran, 291–308. Leiden: Brill, 2005.
Mundy, Martha. 'Islamic Law and the Order of the State: The Legal Status of the Cultivator'. In *Syria and Bilad al-Sham Under Ottoman Rule: Essays in Honour of Abdul Karim Rafeq*, edited by Peter Sluglett with Stefan Weber. 399–419. Leiden: Brill, 2010.
Mundy, Martha. 'Ownership or Office? A Debate in Islamic Hanafite Jurisprudence over the Nature of the Military "Fief", from the Mamluks to the Ottomans'. In *Law, Anthropology, and the Constitution of the Social: Making Persons and Things*, edited by Alain Pottage and Martha Mundy, 142–65. Cambridge: Cambridge University Press, 2004.
Mundy, Martha, and Richard Saumarez Smith. *Governing Property, Making the State: Law, Administration and Production in Ottoman Syria*. London: Tauris, 2007.
Murphey, Rhoads. *Exploring Ottoman Sovereignty: Tradition, Image and Practice in the Ottoman Imperial Household, 1400–1800*. London: Continuum, 2008.
Murphey, Rhoads. *Ottoman Warfare, 1500–1700*. New Brunswick, NJ: Rutgers University Press, 1999.
Naima, Mustafa. *Tarih-i Naima*. Istanbul: Darü't-tibaatı'l-Amire, 1834.
Nelson, Brian R. *The Making of the Modern State: A Theoretical Evolution*. New York: Palgrave Macmillan, 2006.
Owen, Roger. *The Middle East in the World Economy, 1800–1914*. New York: Methuen, 1981.
Özbek, Nadir. 'Tax Farming in the Nineteenth-Century Ottoman Empire: Institutional Backwardness or the Emergence of Modern Public Finance?', *Journal of Interdisciplinary History*, XLIX: 2 (Autumn, 2018): 219–45.
Ozel, Oktay. 'Limits of the Almighty: Mehmed Ii's "Land Reform" Revisited'. *Journal of the Economic and Social History of the Orient* 42, no. 2 (1999): 226–46.
Ozel, Oktay. *The Collapse of Rural Order in Ottoman Anatolia: Amasya, 1576–1643*. Leiden: Brill, 2016.
Özen, Şükrü. 'Osmanlı Dönemi Fetva Literatürü'. *Türkiye Araştırmaları Literatür Dergisi* 3, no. 5 (2005): 249–378.
Pamuk, Şevket. 'Institutional Change and the Longevity of the Ottoman Empire, 1500–1800'. *Journal of Interdisciplinary History* 35, no. 2 (2004): 225–47.
Pamuk, Şevket. *A Monetary History of the Ottoman Empire*. New York: Cambridge University Press, 2000.
Pamuk, Şevket. 'The Ottoman Empire in the Eighteenth Century'. *Itinerario* 24, nos 3–4 (2000): 104–16.

Pakalin, Mehmet Zeki. 'Tapu'. *Osmanli tarih deyimleri ver terimleri sözlügü*. Istanbul: Milli Eğitim Evi, 1972.

Papademetriou, Tom. *Render unto the Sultan: Power, Authority, and the Greek Orthodox Church in the Early Ottoman Centuries*. Oxford: Oxford University Press, 2015.

Parker, Geoffrey. *Global Crisis: War, Climate Change and Catastrophe in the Seventeenth Century*. New Haven, CT: Yale University Press, 2013.

Peters, Rudolph. 'What Does It Mean to Be an Official Madhhab? Hanafism and the Ottoman Empire'. In *The Islamic School of Law: Evolution, Devolution, and Progress*, edited by Peri Bearman, Rudolph Peters and Frank E. Vogel, 147–58. Cambridge, MA: Harvard University Press, 2005.

Punar, Bünyamin. 'Kanun and Sharia: Ottoman Land Law in Şeyhülislam Fatwas from Kanunname of Budin to Kanunname-i Cedid'. Master's thesis, Istanbul Şehir University, 2015.

Quataert, Donald. *The Ottoman Empire, 1700–1922*. Cambridge: Cambridge University Press, 2000.

Rafeq, Abdul-Karim. 'City and Countryside in a Traditional Setting: The Case of Damascus in the First Quarter of the Eighteenth Century'. In *The Syrian Land in the 18th and 19th Century: The Common and the Specific in the Historical Experience*, edited by Thomas Philipp, 295–332. Stuttgart: Steiner, 1992.

Rafeq, Abdul-Karim. 'Economic Relations between Damascus and the Dependent Countryside, 1743–71'. In *The Islamic Middle East, 700–1900: Studies in Economic and Social History*, edited by A. L. Udovitch, 653–85. Princeton, NJ: Darwin Press, 1981.

Rafeq, Abdul-Karim. 'The Syrian '*Ulama*. Ottoman Law and Islamic *Shari'a*'. *Turcica* 26 (1994): 9–32.

Raff, Thomas. *Remarks on an Anti-Mongol Fatwa by Ibn Taimiya*. Leiden: Brill, 1973.

Rapoport, Yossef. 'Royal Justice and Religious Law: *Siyāsah* and Shariʿah under the Mamluks'. *Mamlūk Studies Review* 16 (2012): 71–102.

Reilly, James A. 'Status Groups and Propertyholding in the Damascus Hinterland, 1828–1880'. *International Journal of Middle East Studies* 21, no. 4 (1989): 517–39.

Repp, Richard C. *The Müfti of Istanbul: A Study in the Development of the Ottoman Learned Hierarchy*. London: Ithaca Press, 1986.

Reynolds, Susan. *Before Eminent Domain: Toward a History of Expropriation of Land for the Common Good*. Chapel Hill: University of North Carolina Press, 2010.

Rubin, Avi. 'Modernity as a Code: The Ottoman Empire and the Global Movement of Codification'. *Journal of the Economic and Social History of the Orient* 59, no. 5 (2016): 828–56.

Salzmann, Ariel. 'An Ancien Régime Revisited: "Privatization" and Political Economy in the Eighteenth-Century Ottoman Empire'. *Politics and Society* 21, no. 4 (1993): 393–423.

Salzmann, Ariel. *Tocqueville in the Ottoman Empire: Rival Paths to the Modern State*. Boston: Brill, 2004.

Sariyannis, Marinos. *A History of Ottoman Political Thought up to the Early Nineteenth Century*. Leiden: Brill, 2019.

Sariyannis, Marinos. *Ottoman Political Thought up to the Tanzimat: A Concise History*. Rethymno, Greece: Foundation for Research and Technology-Hellas, Institute for Mediterranean Studies, 2015.

Schacht, Joseph. 'Law and Justice'. In *The Cambridge History of Islam*. Vol. 2B, *Islamic Society and Civilization*, edited by P. M. Holt, Ann K. S. Lambton and Bernard Lewis, 539–68. Cambridge: Cambridge University Press, 1977.

Schulze, Reinhard. 'The Birth of Tradition and Modernity in 18th and 19th Century Islamic Culture: The Case of Printing'. *Culture and History* 16 (1997): 29–72.

Seikaly, Samir M. 'Land Tenure in 17th Century Palestine: The Evidence from the al-Fatāwā al-Khairiyya'. In *Land Tenure and Social Transformation in the Middle East*, edited by Tarif Khalidi, 397–407. Beirut: American University of Beirut, 1984.

Shalakany, Amr A. 'Islamic Legal Histories'. *Berkeley Journal of Middle Eastern & Islamic Law* 1, no. 1 (2008): 1–82.

Shaw, Stanford J. *The Financial and Administrative Organization and Development of Ottoman Egypt, 1515–1798*. Princeton, NJ: Princeton University Press, 1962.

Shaw, Stanford J. 'The Land Law of Ottoman Egypt (960/1553): A Contribution to the Study of Landholding in the Early Years of Ottoman Rule in Egypt'. *Der Islam* 38, no. 1 (1963): 106–37.

Shaw, Stanford J. 'The Nineteenth-Century Ottoman Tax Reforms and Revenue System'. *International Journal of Middle East Studies* 6, no. 4 (1975): 421–59.

Shaw, Stanford J., and Ezel Kural Shaw. *History of the Ottoman Empire and Modern Turkey*. Vol. 2, *Reform, Revolution, and Republic: The Rise of Modern Turkey, 1808–1975*. Cambridge: Cambridge University Press, 1977.

Shemesh, A. Ben, ed. *Taxation in Islam. Volume III: Abū Yūsuf's Kitāb al-Kharāj*. Leiden: Brill, 1969.

Silverstein, Brian. 'Islam and Modernity in Turkey: Power, Tradition and Historicity in the European Provinces of the Muslim World'. *Anthropological Quarterly* 76, no. 3 (2003): 497–517.

Sluglett, Peter, and Marion Farouk-Sluglett, 'The Application of the 1858 Land Code in Greater Syria: Some Preliminary Observations'. In *Land Tenure and Social Transformation in the Middle East*, edited by Tarif Khalidi, 409–21. Beirut: American University of Beirut, 1984.

Sonbol, Amira El Azhary, ed. *Women, the Family, and Divorce Laws in Islamic History*. Syracuse. NY: Syracuse University Press, 1996.

Stoianovich, Traian. 'Land Tenure and Related Sectors of the Balkan Economy, 1600–1800'. *Journal of Economic History* 13, no. 4 (1953): 398–411.

Streusand, Douglas E. *Islamic Gunpowder Empires: Ottomans, Safavids, and Mughals*. Boulder, CO: Westview Press, 2010.

Taylor, Malissa. 'Forcing the Wealthy to Pay Their Fair Share? The Politics of Rural Taxes in 17th-Century Ottoman Damascus'. *Journal of the Economic and Social History of the Orient*, 62, no. 1 (2019): 35–66.

Taylor, Malissa. 'Keeping Usufruct in the Family: Popular and Juridical Interpretations of Ottoman Land Tenure Law in Damascus'. *Bulletin d'études orientales* 61 (2012): 429–43.

Tezcan, Baki. 'The "Kânûnnâme of Mehmed II": A Different Perspective'. In *The Great Ottoman-Turkish Civilisation*. Vol. 3, *Philosophy, Science and Institutions*, edited by Kemal Çiçek, 657–65. Ankara: Yeni Türkiye, 2000.

Tezcan, Baki. 'Law in China or Conquest in the Americas: Competing Constructions of Political Space in the Early Modern Ottoman Empire'. *Journal of World History* 24, no. 1 (2013): 107–34.

Tezcan, Baki. *The Second Ottoman Empire: Political and Social Transformation in the Early Modern World*. New York: Cambridge University Press, 2010.

Thieck, Jean-Pierre. 'Décentralisation ottoman et affirmation urbaine à Alep à la fin du XVIIIème siècle'. In *Mouvements communautaires et espaces urbains au Machreq*, edited by Mona Zakaria and Bachchâr Chbarou, 117–68. Beirut: CERMOC, 1985.

Thomas, Lewis V. *A Study of Naima*. Edited by Norman Itzkowitz. New York: New York University Press, 1972.
Tierney, Brian. *The Idea of Natural Rights: Studies on Natural Rights, Natural Law, and Church Law, 1150–1625*. Grand Rapids, MI: Eerdmans, 2001.
Tuğ, Başak. *Politics of Honor in Ottoman Anatolia: Sexual Violence and Socio-Legal Surveillance in the Eighteenth Century*. Leiden: Brill, 2017.
Turan, Osman. 'Türkiye Selçuklularında Toprak Hukuku. Miri Topraklar Ve Husûsî Mülkiyet Şekilleri'. *Belleten* 12 (1948): 549–74.
Turner, Bryan S. *Weber and Islam: A Critical Study*. London: Routledge & Kegan Paul, 1974.
Ursinus, Michael. 'The *Çiftlik Sahibleri* of Manastır as a Local Elite, Late Seventeenth to Early Nineteenth Century'. In *Provincial Elites in the Ottoman Empire*, edited by Antonis Anastasopoulos, 247–57. Rethymno, Greece: Crete University Press, 2005.
Veinstein, Gilles. 'Le législateur ottoman face à l'insularité: L'enseignement des *Kânûnnâme*'. In *Insularités ottomanes*, edited by Nicolas Vatin and Gilles Veinstein, 91–110. Paris: Maisonneuve & Larose, 2004.
Vogel, Frank E. *Islamic Law and Legal System: Studies of Saudi Arabia*. Leiden: Brill, 2000.
Wedgwood, C. V. *Richelieu and the French Monarchy*. London: Hodder & Stoughton, 1949.
White, Sam. *The Climate of Rebellion in the Early Modern Ottoman Empire*. New York: Cambridge University Press, 2011.
Winter, Michael. 'The Islamic Profile and the Religious Policy of the Ruling Class in Ottoman Egypt'. *Israel Oriental Studies* 10 (1980): 132–45.
Winter, Michael. *Society and Religion in Early Ottoman Egypt: Studies in the Writings of 'Abd al-Wahhab al-Sharani*. New Brunswick, NJ: Transaction, 1982.
Woodhead, Christine. 'After Celalzade: The Ottoman Nişancı c. 1560–1700'. In *Studies in Islamic Law: A Festschrift for Colin Imber*, edited by Andreas Christmann and Robert Gleave, 295–312. Oxford: Oxford University Press, 2007.
Yaycioglu, Ali. *Partners of the Empire: The Crisis of the Ottoman Order in the Age of Revolutions*. Stanford, CA: Stanford University Press, 2016.
Yazbak, Mahmoud. 'Muslim Orphans and the *Sharīʿa* in Ottoman Palestine According to *Sijill* Records'. *Journal of the Economic and Social History of the Orient* 44, no. 2 (2001): 123–40.
Yılmaz, Hüseyin. *Caliphate Redefined: The Mystical Turn in Ottoman Political Thought*. Princeton, NJ: Princeton University Press, 2018.
Yılmaz, Hüseyin. 'Containing Sultanic Authority: Constitutionalism in the Ottoman Empire before Modernity'. *Osmanli Arastirmalari/Journal of Ottoman Studies* 45 (2015): 231–64.
Yılmaz, Hüseyin. 'The Sultan and the Sultanate: Envisioning Rulership in the Age of Süleymān the Lawgiver (1520–1566)'. PhD Diss., Harvard University, 2005.
Zarinebaf-Shahr, Fariba. 'Tabriz under Ottoman Rule (1725–1730)'. PhD Diss., University of Chicago, 1991.
Ze'evi, Dror. *An Ottoman Century: The District of Jerusalem in the 1600s*. Albany: State University of New York Press, 1996.
Zilfi, Madeline C. 'The Kadızadelis: Discordant Revivalism in Seventeenth-Century Istanbul'. *Journal of Near Eastern Studies* 45, no. 4 (1986): 251–69.
Zilfi, Madeline C. *Politics of Piety: The Ottoman Ulema in the Postclassical Age (1600–1800)*. Minneapolis, MN: Bibliotheca Islamica, 1988.
Zürcher, Erik Jan. 'The Ottoman Conscription System, 1844–1914?' *International Review of Social History* 43, no. 3 (1998): 437–49.

INDEX

Note: Page numbers followed by "n" denote endnotes.

'Abd al-Rahim b. Abu'l-Lutf 95
'Abd al-Rahman al-'Imadi 91
'Abdürrahim Efendi, Menteşzade 59, 64, 65, 89, 90, 98, 99, 114, 115, 117
Abu Yusuf 35, 77
'advice literature' 34
Ağa, Ahmad 27
Ağa, Husayn 27
'Ala' al-Din al-Haskafi 78, 80, 84
al-Fatāwā al-Bazzāziyya 36, 39, 40, 80, 100
al-Ha'ik, Isma'il 96
al-'Imadi, Hamid 'Ali Ibrahim 81, 91–4, 117
al-Kardari, Ibn al-Bazzaz 35
al-Muradi, 'Ali 92, 94
al-Nābulusī, 'Abd al-Ghanī 81, 91, 99
al-Timurtashi, Muhammad 75
analogism 60–1, 63, 67, 88, 97–8, 100–2, 109, 115, 125; *see also* fatwas, analogist
Anatolia 4, 14–17, 29, 32, 36, 38, 41, 69, 72, 75, 80, 83, 89, 91–2, 95, 126
Anderson, Perry 33
Anṣārī, Farīd al-Dīn 'Ālim ibn 'Alā' al-Dīn al- 35
aradi al-mamlaka or *aradi al-hawz see* ownerless treasury lands
'Ata'i 18
Atiyas, Ekin Tuşalp 77
autonomism 50–1, 58–61, 65, 67, 93–4, 98–9, 115, 124–5; *see also* fatwas, autonomist
Ayoub, Samy 71, 72

Baha'i Mehmed Efendi 53, 54, 60–7, 77, 88, 97, 98, 116
Balizade, Mustafa 43, 83, 84, 96
Barkan, Ömer Lütfi 1, 8
baştina 16
Battle of Manzikert 14
Bayraktar, Mustafa 29
bayt al-mal (public treasury) 32, 34–7
Birgevi, Mehmet 20, 21, 24, 77, 80, 82–4, 125
Bodin, Jean 11–12, 12, 47
bundle of rights 9; *see also tasarruf* of *miri* land
  cultivator's 58, 91
  extension to non-cultivators as ijaratayn and malikane 26
  in the 1858 Land Code 106, 108
  peasantry's on the land 12, 13, 18, 19
Burak, Guy 8, 31, 72, 73, 75
Byzantine Empire 14

cadastral registers 7–8, 17, 55, 125
Çatalcalı Ali Efendi 23, 77
Cevdet Paşa, Ahmed 103, 105, 118
çiftliks 22, 89, 107, 112, 125, 165 n.7

Darling, Linda T. 22
Dayr al-Qanun 22
Debbāğzāde, Nu'mān Efendi 100
deputy (sahib al-ard); *see also* permission of the deputy
  in comparison with me'mur in the 1858 Land Code 108, 110
  powers over the cultivator's use of the land 20–1, 23, 44, 52, 57–61, 64, 91, 93, 99–100
  representative of the treasury 20, 91
  right to receive payment 20–1, 33, 51, 58, 64
Diogenes, Romanus 14
Duben, Alan 45

Ebu's-Su'ud Efendi 2, 5, 17, 18, 19, 21, 32, 37, 40, 43–5, 52, 72, 79, 86, 101, 113, 125–6, 142 n.83
on the bayt al-mal 32, 35, 37–8, 78, 90
legal rendering of cultivator tenure 16–21
on the sultan's legal stature 44
on the sultan's order-giving texts 52, 113
Egypt 14–15, 36, 42, 75, 80–1, 84, 90–1, 94–5
el-Erzurumī, ʿAbdurraḥmān Efendi 90, 96, 99, 100
el-Mostarī, Aḥmed Efendi 65, 89, 93, 98, 100
Es'ad Efendi, Hocasa'deddinzade 61, 62, 88

falahs see çiftliks
fatwas 8–9, 18, 19, 21, 25, 33, 46, 52–3, 71, 177 n.51
analogist 50, 52, 60, 65
Arabic-language 40
autonomist 51, 61
claim of *istihqaq* 57
difference between tithe and *kharaji* land 39
Esʿad Efendi's 62–3, 99–100, 157 n.75
Hanafism 2, 5, 79, 89, 94
by jurist (scholar of Islamic law) 6
Kanun-ı Cedid 60, 62, 64–6, 96, 153 n.21
for *Kanunname of Thessaloniki and Skopje* 37
kanun's practices 2, 46, 49, 52–3, 61, 66–7, 73, 89–90, 98, 102, 111, 115, 116, 118–19
library sources 6
manuals of jurisprudence 30
Mehmed Baha'i's 60, 62–4
Ottoman 50, 90
Pir Mehmed's 54–5, 60, 64, 67
property rights 39
of *şeyhülislams* 50, 54, 59, 80, 89, 93, 103, 113, 115
sultan's orders 7, 59
Turkish-language 40, 41
Vani Mehmed's 56, 76–7, 90
voyvoda or *mukataacıs* 23
on *waqf* 26, 66, 90
Yahya Efendi's 67
Feyzullah Efendi 77, 113
fiqh (Islamic jurisprudence) 2–3, 6, 20
firmans 7–8, 18, 25–7, 33, 41, 46–7, 49, 52, 55–6, 58, 61–2, 69, 71, 77, 85, 90, 116, 120; *see also* fatwas
'freehold' *(milk)* property 15
designating *kharaji* land 35
division *(qisma* or *taqsim)* of 100
Hanafi law of inheritance *(irth)* 19, 109
and *kharaji* 69–70, 79
land as 37–9, 43, 83
and *miri* land 56–7, 98

Gedizli Mehmed Efendi 113
Gelvin, James L. 103
Governing Property, Making the Modern State 3

Hanafism 4, 5, 7, 8, 16
according to the books of *fiqh* 74–8
Arab 36, 81
authorities 35, 40, 54, 73, 78, 80, 154 n.38, 175 n.34
bayt al-mal 38
Damascene 95
discourse 6
doctrine 5, 15, 35–7, 72, 74–5, 79, 82–4, 109, 124
Egyptian 36, 80
fatwas 5, 94–5
fiqh 17, 19, 39, 43, 45, 82, 92, 104, 113–14, 119–20, 141 n.79, 159 n.2
jurisprudence 9, 18, 24, 28, 32, 33, 36–40, 42–3, 48, 50, 55, 58, 63, 71, 73, 82, 95, 114, 124–5, 151 n.87
law of inheritance *(irth)* 19
loan 8
manuals 75, 80
muftis 4, 95
Ottoman 96, 146 n.19, 161 n.33
practice of law 7
rental law 40
scholarship 72, 81
in sixteenth century 17
teaching 9, 32, 35–8, 47, 82, 85, 154 n.38
transactions 20–1, 28
haqq al-qarar 40, 58, 91
harmonization 13, 88, 117
Burak's 8

consequences of 8
of cultivator's bundle 28
definition of rights 4
of *kanun* and sharia 49
or reconciliation 8–9, 13, 18, 125
of peasant's bundle 23
sharia 8
sixteenth-century 3
and sovereignty 7–9
harmony tradition of land law 50–1, 54, 59–60, 67, 70–3, 77–9, 87–92, 94, 97, 101, 113
has 20
Herzog, Tamar 47
Heyd, Uriel 8
Hobbes, Thomas 11
Hoca Eminefendizade, 'Ali Haydar 120
hüccets 6–8, 18–19, 46, 48, 65, 97, 123, 125

Ibn 'Abidin, Muhammad Amin 50, 81
Ibn al-Humam, al-Kamal 36, 37, 81, 84, 96
'death of the cultivators' 36
Ibn Nujaym, Zayn al-'Abidin Ibrahim 36, 42, 75, 95, 96
Ibn Taymiyya 31
İbrāhīm Edhem Efendi, Seyid 90
ijaratayn 4, 13, 28; *see also malikane;* property rights
advent of 24
bundle of rights 24
in eighteenth century 100
history of 26
mu'accele of 24
renter's 25
waqf by 25–6, 30, 65, 91, 100
ijtihad (jurisprudential reasoning) 18
ilmiye
of early nineteenth century 90
formation of 146 n.16
hierarchy of 8
huccets of 48
jurisdiction 52
learned branch of bureaucracy 5, 34
membership 53, 97, 157 n.74
personnel 60–1, 63
positions 29
seventeenth century 50
sixteenth century 126
iltizam 22, 26, 94, 140 n.71
Imber, Colin 8, 78
Inalcik, Halil 1, 7, 8, 16
institutionalization 7
intiqal see transmission
Islamization 7
Isma'il al-Ha'ik 96
istihqaq 57–8

jizya (poll tax) 35, 69
Johansen, Baber 36, 82

Kafr al-Zayt 22
kanun
and fatwas 2, 47, 49, 52–3, 61, 65–7, 73, 89–90, 98, 102, 111, 115, 116, 118–19
harmonization of 2, 17, 49
Islamized 34
judge's duty to apply 52
in *Kanunname of Bayezid II* 43–4
land laws 2, 6, 32, 49
'line of transmission' 119
marginalization of 3
miri land 46
'new law or new *kanun*' 7
Ottoman procedure 8, 18
'return to the *kanun*' reform movement 51, 77
and sharia 8, 10, 13, 50, 77, 118, 121, 127, 149 n.71, 162
sixteenth-century 2–3, 5
timars and land tenure 52
Kanun-ı Cedid-i Osmani
compiler of 51–4, 67
contents, *Kanun-ı Cedid* 7
contributors to 54, 60, 61, 65–6
Ebu's-Su'ud's theoretical mission 32
format of 153 n.21
impact on practice of land law 1, 49, 50, 90
kinds of omissions 65–6
land law text 1, 32, 47, 49–50, 71
laws enacted on sultan's authority 34
transformation of lawmaking 34
Kanunname of Candia 69–78, 82–3, 85–6, 125
kanunnames 5, 6, 7, 8, 10, 17, 18, 20, 21, 74–8; *see also* fatwas
Katz, Marion H. 38

kazasker (chief judge) 17, 78
Kemalpaşazade 18, 31, 36
kharaj (agricultural tax) 32, 35, 37–40, 42–3, 56, 69–70, 76, 79–80, 82–5, 96
kharaji land 35–43, 56, 69–70, 72, 75–6, 79, 83–5, 96, 111
kirdar 40, 91–2
'known' or 'customarily defined' *(ma'rufa)* period 43
Köprülü, Ahmed Pasha 56
Köprülü, M. Fuad 1
Köprülü, Mehmed Pasha 76

1858 Land Code 2, 5–6, 52, 90, 102, 103–12, 114, 118–21, 125–6
land's productivity 20, 100
land tenure system; *see also timar* system
  history of 12
  law 1–3, 5
  Ottoman 40, 80
  political and economic relations 2, 14–16, 21–3
  scholarship on 2
Leviathan (Hobbes) 11
Louis XIII 11

madhhab 2, 8, 48, 75, 85
Mahmud II 29, 30, 107
malikane 4, 12, 13; *see also ijaratayn;* property rights
  cultivators' *tasarruf* 24, 26–7
  lifelong tax farm 12–13, 26
  mutasarrif of 26–7, 29, 125
  resemblance to peasants' property-right bundle 4, 13, 24
  transmission of 27
malikane-divani 16
Ma'ruzat 45, 71, 80, 85, 150 n.78
me'mur (the official) 107–10, 117–18
Messick, Brinkley 6
Milli Tettebular Mecmuası 1
Minkarizade Yahya Efendi 70, 77
miri land
  agricultural land 26
  'building' fatwas for 50, 90, 158 n.86, 168 n.39
  cultivator of 19, 44, 58–9
  defined 42, 84, 85, 101
  institutionalization of 73
  kanunnames for 77, 159 n.1
  as *kharaji* 38–9, 85, 96
  land's exchange 17–18
  legal order of 16–21, 41–2, 54, 80, 85, 97, 120, 125–6
  and *milk* 55–7, 98, 102
  mutasarrif of 102, 109
  not subject to rules of *fiqh* 39, 41–2, 44
  Ottoman administration of 14–15
  permission of the deputy 23, 58, 60–1, 65, 92, 99, 101, 111
  rejection of *istihqaq* 57
  sultan's legislative authority 7–8, 42, 46, 50, 75
  taqsim on 100
  tasarruf of 27, 51, 58, 59, 88–9, 92, 97, 106–13, 112, 171 n.78
  tenure and transactions 39, 41, 44, 60, 67, 88, 97–9
  texts of *fiqh* 41–2
  as third category of land 39
  *timar*s designated as 14
  waqf in 54, 57, 65, 90, 93, 100, 103, 110, 138 n.48
  zeamet and *has* 20
mu'accele (advance payments) 13, 20, 24–8, 141 n.77
mü'eccele (regular payments) 24–5
muftis; *see also şeyhülislams*
  approach to *kanun*s 66–7, 90, 98
  of eighteenth century 50, 60, 66, 89, 94, 98–101, 105, 108–9, 116, 155 n.43
  and judges 47, 52–4
  Ottoman 6, 13, 24–6, 54, 171 n.78
  provincial 98, 154 n.25
    Damascene 90–2, 94, 150 n.75
    of Egypt and Jerusalem 94–5
    Rumi 96–7, 102
  scholarship on 53
  of seventeenth-century 25–6, 54, 97, 102
  views on harmonization 2, 8, 50, 66, 89
mukataacı's 23, 140 n.68
multezims 23, 140 n.71
Mundy, Martha 3, 9, 72, 73, 91, 92
mutasarrif (possessor); *see also tasarruf*
  'age of' 125
  death of 24, 107, 110
  definition 19–20, 24–7

foreign 112
of *ijaratayn* 24, 28, 88–9
of *malikane* 27–8
of *miri* land 19, 46, 57, 59, 73, 100, 102, 108–13, 125
of *miri* land who is military class or not a peasant cultivator 64, 89
who is a minor or orphan 119
mutawalli 15, 24–5, 62, 64–5, 93, 99–102, 156 n.65

Niceron, Jean-François 11

Ottoman military fiscal change 21–3
'Ottoman decline' 22
ownerless treasury lands 34

peasant's bundle 4, 13; *see also* property rights and *tasarruf*
legal harmonization of 23
legal institutionalization 7, 17
on *miri* land 25, 116
permission of the deputy *see miri* land
Pir Meḥmed Üsküpi 53–60, 62, 64, 67, 88, 96, 97
possession *see tasarruf*
property rights
bundles and layers 9–10, 13, 106, 141 n.75
cultivators' 9–10, 13, 17, 21, 26, 28, 33, 39, 41, 44, 58, 66, 91, 97, 111, 125, 148 n.55
evolution of 12
Hanafi teaching of 2, 4, 9, 19, 24, 38, 42, 91, 119
ijaratayn and *m alikane see ijaratayn; malikane*
lifelong tenure and heritability 17
on *miri* land 23, 38–9, 41–2, 73, 75, 92
for *mutasarrif*s 88–9, 105, 115
in Ottoman Empire 9, 10, 12–13
peasants' bundle 12–13, 23
proliferation of lifelong *tasarruf* 9
scholarship on Ottoman 2
and taxation 38, 42, 72–3
'trickle-up' 4

Qadikhan, Fakhr al-Din 35, 36, 40, 55, 58, 59, 80

reconciliation *see* harmonization
registers, sultan's cadastral 7–8, 17, 33, 38, 41–2, 49, 50, 55, 56, 59, 66, 75, 77, 90, 125
Repp, Richard 8

sahib al-ard (deputy) 20, 23, 25, 51, 107
Sakızi, Sadık Mehmed 58, 59, 89, 90, 92
salyane 15
Sasanian Empire 14
secular/religious dichotomy 8
şeyhülislams (chief mufti) 17, 48, 51–5, 59–62, 66, 70, 73, 77, 78, 89, 91, 93, 96–8, 100, 102, 113–15, 117, 120
sharia 8, 17
al-siyasa al-shar'iyya 31
as archive 6
books of 39
divine order of 18
fatwa 120
harmonization 8, 17, 49, 120
and *kanun* 8, 10, 13, 32, 50, 77, 118, 121, 127
law of Islam 2
as library 6
on *miri* land 42–3
Ottoman 48, 78
in texts of *fiqh* 46, 119, 120
violation of 95
sipahis 14, 16–17, 20, 23, 59, 93, 107, 124, 138 n.42, 154 n.40
Smith, Richard Saumarez 3, 9, 91–2
sovereignty 104, 121, 126–7
and harmonization 7–9
legislative 3, 5, 121, 126
and power 5
Süleyman I 2, 17, 21, 22, 25, 28, 32, 33, 36, 43–5, 47, 59, 80, 103, 124
sultan
change in doctrine regarding sultan's options for newly conquered land 81–5
coherent law 43–7
in defense of Islam 118–21
as early modern ruler 33–4
jurisdiction 31
entitlement to *kharaj* tax 32
as legislator 78–81

powers over land in the *bayt al-mal* (public treasury) 32, 34–7
Sultan Mehmed IV 55, 60, 75, 125
Sultan Selim II 45
Sultan Selim III 29, 100
Sun'ullah Efendi, Hacı Mustafa 59, 61, 63
Syria 3–4, 14–15, 31, 80–1, 84, 88–91, 94, 97

tafwid/tafarrugh transaction 41
Tanzimat 2, 103–4, 172 n.7, 173 n.10, 174 n.23
tapu/tapulu lands 19, 141 n.82, 142 n.85
certificates 40
dominant tenure for cultivators 19, 25, 55
fee 20–1, 25, 27–8, 41, 44–7, 51, 55, 57–8, 62, 76–7, 80, 89, 92, 100, 108, 112, 125, 138 n.55
tasarruf of land 19, 45, 91–2, 124
waqf and 25, 62
tasarruf (possession)
analogized to loan or rent 19, 70, 111, 125
cultivators' 19, 24, 26, 28, 43, 59, 61, 70, 105, 111, 126
definition 19–21, 102, 115, 121, 126
ijaratayn's 24, 27, 30
in the 1858 Land Code 105, 107–11, 115
lifelong forms of 21, 24–5, 28–30, 105, 121, 123–5
malikane's 27
of *miri* land 27, 51, 57–8, 88–9, 92, 97, 106–9, 111–13
question of its liberalization 102, 108, 111
transacting of 20, 94
taxation
administrative authority 18
fiqh's rules governing 31, 42, 56, 71, 75–6, 86
jizya tax 34
kharaj tax 32, 35–43, 56, 69–70, 72, 76, 79–80, 82–5
Ottoman taxation on cultivators 76–7, 89, 105, 112–13
rates 19, 41–2
regulation by imperial register 41, 51, 73, 105
tithe (*'ashar/öşr*) 35, 38–42, 79
tax farming
ayan 125
expansion of 22, 24, 87
iltizam 94, 140 n.71
malikane 12–13, 26–7, 29
with political office 29
temlik 15–16
Tezcan, Baki 63
timar system
classical Ottoman land order 14
corruption of 51
decline of 22
growth of 15
heritablility in 16
kanun governing 52, 87
military-fiscal administration 20, 22
rights of peasantry residing in 19, 96
sipahis role in 14, 16, 23, 93, 107
and tax farms 29, 113, 139 n.65
transmission *(intiqal)* 19, 41, 45–7, 51

ulema
Arab 84, 96, 169 n.49
bureaucratization of 48
Egyptian 90, 95, 169 n.49
Hanafi 125
Islamic scholars 2, 5, 31
Ottoman 31, 58, 89
Rumi 95, 96, 147 n.33
selefi-oriented 83
sixteenth-century 95
Syrian 94
Turkish-speaking 52

Vani Mehmed Efendi 55, 56, 66, 74, 76–8, 88, 90
voyvoda 23

waqf
analogies with *miri* land 50, 90–1, 93, 99–100, 102
of agricultural land 26, 62
Egyptian 42, 149 n.60
emergence of 123
differentiation from *miri* land 54, 57, 65, 110, 138 n.48

as family charters 151 n.86
fatwas on 90, 142 n.83
founder of 15
Hanafi jurisprudence of 63
kharaji land as 35, 69, 79
lifelong *tasarruf* and *ijaratayn* contracts 25, 30, 91, 93, 100
maximizing tax receipts 16
mutawalli (superintendent) 15, 25, 62, 64, 99, 156 n.65, 167 n.37
owned properties of Istanbul 24–6
rahn and *qisma* 100
rental property 24, 142 n.91
residential renters on 125
sultan's 25
tapu and 141 n.82
taxation rates 19
Western law 5, 47

Yahya Efendi, Zekeriyazade 25, 53, 54, 60, 61, 63, 65, 67
Yilmaz, Hüseyin 34, 53

zeamet 20, 22, 138 n.50, 159 n.10

www.ingramcontent.com/pod-product-compliance
Lightning Source LLC
Chambersburg PA
CBHW052114300426
44116CB00010B/1662
* 9 7 8 0 7 5 5 6 4 7 7 2 9 *